T0337454

MIGRATION, FOOD SECURITY AND DEVELOPMENT

Migration, Food Security and Development examines the role of migration as a livelihood strategy in influencing food access among rural households. Migration forms a key component of livelihoods for an increasing number of rural households in many developing countries. Importantly, there is now a growing consensus among academics and policymakers on the potential positive effects of migration in promoting human development. Concurrently, the significance of food security as an important development objective has grown tremendously, and the Sustainable Development Goals agenda envisages elimination of all forms of malnutrition. However, academic and policy discussions on these two issues have largely proceeded in silos, with little attention devoted to the relationship they bear with each other. Using the conceptual frameworks of 'entitlements' and 'sustainable livelihoods', this book seeks to fill this gap in the context of India – a country with the most food-insecure people in the world and where migration is integral to rural livelihoods.

Chetan Choithani is Assistant Professor in the Inequality and Human Development Programme at the School of Social Sciences, National Institute of Advanced Studies, Bengaluru. The broad disciplinary domain of his work is development studies. Within this area, his research and teaching interests include migration and urbanisation, food and nutrition, livelihoods, gender and social policy, and how they relate to development, particularly in the Indian context.

MIGRATION, FOOD SECURITY AND DEVELOPMENT

INSIGHTS FROM RURAL INDIA

CHETAN CHOITHANI

CAMBRIDGE
UNIVERSITY PRESS

University Printing House, Cambridge CB2 8BS, United Kingdom

One Liberty Plaza, 20th Floor, New York, NY 10006, USA

477 Williamstown Road, Port Melbourne, vic 3207, Australia

314 to 321, 3rd Floor, Plot No.3, Splendor Forum, Jasola District Centre, New Delhi 110025, India

103 Penang Road, #05–06/07, Visioncrest Commercial, Singapore 238467

Cambridge University Press is part of the University of Cambridge.

It furthers the University's mission by disseminating knowledge in the pursuit of education, learning and research at the highest international levels of excellence.

www.cambridge.org
Information on this title: www.cambridge.org/9781108840378

© Chetan Choithani 2022

First published 2022

Printed in India by Avantika Printers Pvt. Ltd.

A catalogue record for this publication is available from the British Library

ISBN 978-1-108-84037-8 Hardback

CONTENTS

FIGURES, TABLES AND BOXES

FIGURES

TABLES

BOXES

PHOTOS

PREFACE

I write this preface at a time when the world has experienced the horrors of the Covid-19 pandemic for almost two years now. The devastating impacts of this pandemic on economic and social systems have affected communities across the world. In many countries, one particular group has arguably shared the disproportionate burden of the pandemic: migrant workers. The fear of the spread of the virus, abrupt halting of economic activities and the resultant loss of employment, lockdowns and travels restrictions left them stranded without adequate support from host communities and governments.

In India, the broad geographic focus of this book, the Covid-19-induced lockdown caused a full-blown migrant-workers crisis. To contain the spread of the virus, on 24 March 2020, the Government of India announced, on a mere four-hour notice, a complete shutdown of the country for 21 days (which was subsequently extended a few times, with phased reopenings beginning in June). All transport operations were grounded, and non-essential services were shut overnight. This sudden countrywide lockdown saw millions of India's rural migrant workers stranded in cities without income, shelter and food. Employers abandoned them and landlords evicted them. The cities they had helped build and fuel had overnight turned their backs on them. The health crisis soon turned into a humanitarian crisis of an enormous scale. In a scene reminiscent of India's Partition, chaos and confusion sent millions of poor migrants on the country's highways, bus stands and train stations. Unsure of support from the state that did not consider their existence in the abrupt lockdown decision, migrants started to head home on foot, arduously walking hundreds of kilometres to their native places, without adequate food and water along the way. On their treacherous journeys, some were killed by police brutalities, others died of exhaustion and road accidents, and many lost their lives to starvation. In an incident that shook the nation, a freight train ran over and killed 16 exhausted migrants who had fallen asleep on the rail tracks on their walk back home.

The irony of the situation was that the lockdown which had the objective of saving lives, claimed lives. Media coverage and public sympathy on the plight of stranded migrants swung the government into action to provide them with relief. Civil society and citizen groups led relief efforts from the front. The concerns of hunger and starvation among migrants figured prominently in relief measures. The Government of India announced free food rations and meals for poor workers. Some Indian states relaxed document requirements, such as ration cards, for migrants to avail free food grains; and work began to strengthen the One Nation One Ration Card scheme under which migrants could access subsidised food rations outside their domicile. These efforts were far from adequate, and independent assessments of these relief measures by civil society working on the ground with migrants showed that a sizeable proportion of them had difficulties accessing food rations and faced food insecurity. But there was a widespread recognition that migrants needed food support in these distressing times. In fact, food was considered synonymous with relief, and the issue itself was framed in those terms. In response to a public interest litigation that sought financial support for migrants, the Supreme Court of India reportedly refused to supplant the Government of India's wisdom on relief assistance and remarked: 'If they are being provided meals, then why do they need money for meals?'

Relief efforts in distress situations often include food provisioning as a logical first response. But this *distress lens* has also been the most dominant way of viewing the migration–food-security relationship. Indeed, migration itself is largely seen as driven by food shortages by academics, policymakers and civil society, and the solution therefore has focused on strengthening the food-based safety nets to prevent migration. This thinking has further solidified in the past few years as the disrupting effects of conflict, climate change and economic downturns heighten global hunger and prompt migration in many parts of the developing world. Aside from this distress-centred framing, there appears to be a dearth of understanding of the mutual connections between migration and food security despite the growing significance of these two issues in global development research and policy agendas in recent years. While food insecurity can act as a key catalyst for migration, this account provides a less than complete understanding of migration–food-security linkages. This book seeks to bridge this gap.

Drawing on primary fieldwork with rural households and their urban migrant members in India, this book develops a conceptualisation that considers different aspects of the migration–food-security relationship. It views migration as forming an integral part of dynamic rural livelihoods and examines the role migration as a livelihood strategy plays in influencing household food security outcomes. Contrary to conventional wisdom that posits migration as a household food security strategy only in times of food shortages, this book argues that the relationship between them is bidirectional. Food insecurity can be a critical driver of households' migration decisions, and subsequent remittances can ease the households' food insecurity. The empirical evidence in this book asserts an appreciation of three key pathways that shape these forward–backward linkages: (*a*) the role of food and livelihood safety nets in influencing the food security situation of households and their migration decisions, (*b*) the extent to which migrants' remittances are received by households and the manner in which they are used, and (*c*) the ways in which migration affects gender dynamics within the household.

Bengaluru
7 December 2021

Chetan Choithani

ACKNOWLEDGEMENTS

This book on migration–food-security nexus has its origins in my doctorate in Human Geography from the School of Geosciences, University of Sydney, Australia. I researched and wrote my PhD thesis over the period of four years, between 2011 and 2015. In writing the doctoral dissertation, I departed from the typical thesis layout and followed a book-style format instead, wherein each individual, self-contained chapter engaged with different issue(s) of relevance but in ways that appreciated interdependence between different themes and chapters, with the overall narrative linking the seemingly disparate parts together to form a whole. I also avoided jargons for I had learned early on in my PhD studies that academic writing need not be convoluted, and that the most complex ideas can be conveyed in the simplest of words. In that sense, much of the content that would go in this book was already there. But it still took me a few more years to complete the task of finalizing the manuscript for the book.

My preference for the book-style form of narrative notwithstanding, the idea of writing a book by myself felt a bit overwhelming to the freshly minted PhD that I was then. Like many of my peers, I had initially only wanted to publish parts of this work as journal articles. But over the course of writing shorter journal articles based on this work, I also realised that a book-length analysis of the migration–food-security relationship was wanting and gained the courage to attempt it. I began working on this book in 2019 when I was a postdoctoral researcher at the Urban Studies Institute of Andrew Young School of Policy Studies, Georgia State University, Atlanta, and I submitted the manuscript in 2021 during my current occupation as Assistant Professor at the National Institute of Advanced Studies (NIAS), Bengaluru. So this work has traversed with me through three career points, countries and continents. I am thankful to several individuals and institutions for their help and support along the way, without implicating them for errors and omissions, if any, of my own making.

This monograph is based on primary, field-based research I carried out in 2012 and 2013 with rural households in Siwan district in Bihar and their migrant members working at that time in cities in the National Capital Region's constituent states of Delhi, Haryana and Uttar Pradesh. My gratitude and appreciation, first and foremost, go to all the study participants for unconditionally welcoming me into their lives and letting me learn more about them. Conducting field research on the issue of food (in)security inevitably meant that several of the rural households I spoke to did not have the material conditions to be food secure all-year round. This did not, however, deter them from offering me food. The urban-based migrant members of these Siwani rural households took time out of their busy working schedules to talk to me; some of them did not even mind losing their daily wages. There is perhaps no way I can pay back for the warmth and hospitality I received from my research participants. But it is my sincere hope that I have done some justice to their voice. My sincere thanks also go to my local research assistants, Shree Bhagwan Sah, Jitendra Yadav and Shiv Shankar, for their help with fieldwork in Siwan, and for teaching me a few Bhojpuri greetings which smoothened the field research. Financial support for this work was provided through the Australian government's competitive Prime Minister Australia Asia Postgraduate Award, and the fieldwork for this research was partially funded by the Australian Research Council-funded Project 1094112 titled 'Institutions for Food Security: Global Insights from Rural India'.

I thank Cambridge University Press for carving a space for this book. In particular, I wish to record my heartfelt appreciation for my commissioning editor, Anwesha Rana, for seeing value in this project. Over the course of more than two years that I spent finalising this monograph, I got only a few weeks' time at a stretch to work on it. I spent a good part of 2019 doing fieldwork for another project, and 2020 saw me changing jobs and countries in the middle of the Covid-19 pandemic. Anwesha has been extraordinarily patient with me and outstandingly understanding of my other commitments. Two anonymous reviewers for the Press provided wide-ranging and critical comments from which this book has benefitted a good deal. I also acknowledge the help of Priyanka Das, the production editor for this monograph, who diligently oversaw the entire pre-press process, including performing thorough quality-checks on the proofs.

At the University of Sydney, I am grateful to Bill Pritchard who supervised my doctorate. Bill saw me grow with this work, lent his expertise that enabled me to look at this research in a holistic manner, commented on individual chapters and encouraged me to be bold in asking questions. It was from Bill that I learned that research is not necessarily about answering the question but is more about engaging with it. That approach guides this work. My sincere thanks are also due to John Connell who took a good deal of interest in this research, raised stimulating questions and provided several useful comments on the drafts of two chapters, which aided me in refining some of the arguments. My friend Alex Thomas also read the drafts of a couple of chapters and provided critical inputs on arguments and style. This work has also benefitted from my discussions with Bob Fisher, Yayoi Fujita, Jo Gillespie, Phil Hirsch, Kurt Iveson, Phil McManus and Jeffery Neilson. Three external PhD thesis examiners that included Priya Deshingkar, Douglas Hill and T. V. Sekher provided detailed, incisive comments on the earlier incarnation of this book, and many of those inputs have immensely strengthened its present avatar. Two other external mentors during my time at the University of Sydney include Madhushree Sekher of the Tata Institute of Social Sciences, Mumbai, and Anu Rammohan of the University of Western Australia, Perth.

At Georgia State University, I thank Jan Nijman for his encouragement and support. The discussions with Jan strengthened my belief on the importance of primary, field-based insights to engage with large, often abstract, theoretical ideas and debates. Jan also read and commented on versions of this work. Other friends and colleagues who deserve mention for their support during my time at the Urban Studies Institute include Jean-Paul Addie, Dan Immergluck, David Iwaniec, Fei Li, Risa Palm and Sam Williams. Thanks to my fellow postdocs – Lelani Mannetti, Xinyu Fu and Chris Wyczalkowski – for being my sounding boards and for making work fun. Laura Viilo provided excellent administrative support during my postdoc.

At NIAS, I greatly acknowledge and appreciate the support of Shailesh Nayak. At a time when work demands of academia are making folks in my tribe more insular, I have found Narendar Pani's insistence on the importance of open discussions for academic work useful. Through informal conversations and casual modes, I bounced my ideas off many other colleagues. My thanks go to Anant Kamath, Debosree Banerjee, Kshipra Jain and Soundarya Iyer for lending their ears and expertise.

Outside the three aforementioned institutions and the people affiliated with them, several other good souls helped me with different aspects of this work, and I thank them wholeheartedly: Soumi Mukherjee, Bidhyadhar Dehury and Sujata Ganguly for their assistance in the analysis of the Indian census data on migration; Srinivas Goli for providing some relevant secondary data as well as for answering my queries on some of the statistical analysis; and Laishram Ladusingh and Chander Shekhar for clarifying my doubts on the sampling design for household surveys. Laishram Ladusingh is also my first research mentor, and I learned the importance of statistics in research from him. Other mentors who inspired and motivated me and from whom I have had some of my early research lessons include R. B. Bhagat and Bino Paul G. D. I thank Nalin Singh Negi for valuable discussions on the effects of male migration on the women left behind; in fact, discussions with Nalin encouraged me to explore the migration–gender–food-security relationship, which is one of the key themes of this work. My conversations with Robbin Jan van Duijne during our joint fieldwork in remote parts of India further enriched my understanding of this issue; Robbin Jan also read and commented on a version of the chapter on gendered impacts of male migration on household food security.

I have presented versions of this work in various forums, including the 'Thinking Space Seminar Series' of University of Sydney's Human Geography Department in 2012, 2013 and 2014; the International Sociological Association's World Congress of Sociology in Yokohama in 2014; Agri-Food Network's annual conferences in Sydney and Brisbane in 2014 and 2018; the international conference of Asian Dynamics Initiative of Copenhagen University in Copenhagen in 2015; the Monash Business School's conference on sustainable development in Prato in 2017; Georgia State University's 'Urban Studies Institute Speaker Series' in Atlanta in 2018; and the NIAS' 'Wednesday Talk Series' in Bengaluru in 2021. I thank the participants at all these places for their comments, which helped me add nuance to my arguments and improve the final product. Parts of this book have been published in peer-reviewed journals that include *Gender, Place and Culture: A Journal of Feminist Geography*, *Geographical Research* and *Economic and Political Weekly*. I thank these publishing outlets for the permission to reuse the content in this book.

For warm friendships in this journey, my gratitude, in the alphabetical order of their last names, is due to Sahar Bajis, Syed Atif Bukhari, Jipin Das, Olivia Dun, Parth Gathani, Kate Griffiths, Reshma Gupta, Tegan Hall, Michele Hopkins, Anders Thengs Horntvedt, Apollo Pou, Sophia Maalsen, Sarthak Ray, Triveni Sati, Ian Sinclair, Erin Smith, Mattijs Smits, Nobin Thomas, Laurence Troy, Mark Vicol and Nathan Wales.

Last but not least, I am grateful to my family for their unwavering support for my academic activities. The pursuit of higher education and work has required me to be increasingly away from my parents and siblings, but I have felt much loved and cheered on from afar. Pratishtha, my wife, has been my rock and has nudged me to submit this manuscript more than my publisher; she has also read parts of this work and efficiently navigated through her roles as a fair critic and a supportive partner. I grew up in a joint family with my grandparents who had migrated to India during the Partition. From them I heard the first-hand accounts of food insecurity experienced by them and other Partition migrants at the time, and the resilience with which they built new lives and livelihoods to deal with that challenge. It is to the memory of my migrant grandparents that I dedicate this book.

Chetan Choithani

ABBREVIATIONS

AAY	Antyodaya Anna Yojana
ABC	Achievement of Babies and Children
APL	above poverty line
BIMARU	Bihar–Madhya Pradesh–Rajasthan–Uttar Pradesh
BIMARUO	Bihar–Madhya Pradesh–Rajasthan–Uttar Pradesh–Odisha
BMI	body mass index
BPL	below poverty line
CDPO	Child Development Programme officer
DFID	Department for International Development
FAO	Food and Agriculture Organization
FIES	Food Insecurity Experience Scale
FPS	fair price shop
FSOI	Food Security Outcome Index
GDP	gross domestic product
GDDP	gross district domestic product
GHI	Global Hunger Index
GP	*gram panchayat*
HDI	Human Development Index
HLPE	High Level Panel of Experts (of World Committee on Food Security)

ICDS	Integrated Child Development Scheme
IFPRI	International Food Policy Research Institute
IHD	Institute for Human Development
IIPS	International Institute for Population Sciences
INR	Indian rupee
IOM	International Organization for Migration
KBK	Kalahandi–Balangir–Korutput
MDERs	minimum dietary energy requirements
MDGs	Millennium Development Goals
MPCE	monthly per capita expenditure
MPCI	monthly per capita income
MSP	minimum support price
NELM	New Economics of Labour Migration
NFHS	National Family Health Survey
NFSA	National Food Security Act
NREGS	National Rural Employment Guarantee Scheme
NSS	National Sample Survey
PDS	public distribution system
PER	purchase–entitlement ratio
PHH	priority households
PLFS	Periodic Labour Force Survey
PoU	prevalence of undernourishment
PUCL	People Union for Civil Liberties
RPDS	revamped public distribution system
SDGs	Sustainable Development Goals
SHI	State Hunger Index
SLA	sustainable livelihood approach
SoFI	*State of Food Insecurity in the World*
SC	Supreme Court
SR	sex ratio
TPDS	targeted public distribution system

UNDP	United Nations Development Programme
UNFPA	United Nations Population Fund
UNICEF	United Nations Children's Fund
USD	United States dollar
WFP	World Food Programme
WHO	World Health Organization

1

INTRODUCTION

This book examines the linkages between migration and food security in India. More specifically, it investigates the role of internal migration as a livelihood strategy in influencing food access among rural households in India. The need for this undertaking stems from a dearth of understanding of the role work-related migration plays in shaping food access among rural communities. Indeed, the relationship between migration and food security is arguably one of the most under-investigated aspects of development in contemporary India.

The larger motivation that guides this work is provided by the pressing policy need to seek insights into the mechanisms governing access to food among rural populations of India. The persistence of staggering levels of food insecurity is a major development challenge in India, and nearly 190 million people in the country suffer from chronic levels of hunger (FAO et al., 2020). The burden of chronic food insecurity is disproportionately shared by the country's rural dwellers who account for a large majority of the undernourished people. While this is the case, rural dwellers are not passive actors, and they devise multiple livelihood strategies to mitigate threats to their food security. Migration constitutes an important component of rural livelihood strategies. While migration has traditionally been an integral part of rural livelihoods in India (Tumbe, 2018), recent years have witnessed an unprecedented surge in mobility levels among the rural poor (Choithani, Van Duijne and Nijman, 2021). Thus, the question as to how rural outmigration impacts the well-being outcomes of poor households assumes greater significance. Various forms of population mobility and their impacts on source and destination communities have been extensively studied. However, despite food security being an important public policy concern, systematic knowledge on how migration can influence household food security outcomes. Most of the research thus far has invariably focused on the unidirectional relationship between the two – that is, food insecurity as a driver of distressed household migration (Mosse et al., 2002; Maharatna, 2014). Insufficient attention has been paid on the reverse causalities – that is, how migration can affect the patterns of food consumption and nutritional well-being in source regions. In large parts of India, rural outmigration commonly involves migration by relatively younger males while the other household members stay behind. This pattern of migration implies that there are several channels through which migration can have a potential bearing on household food and nutritional security. The flow of migrants' remittances, alteration in the composition of household labour and resultant changes in time allocation for childcare and household work, and changes in gender roles are some of the important factors that can have a significant impact on the food security outcomes of household members (Zezza et al., 2011). However, there is a paucity of systematic research that provides insights into how different migration mechanisms unravel to affect the household food security outcomes. Rising rural outmigration in India warrants a need for a holistic understanding of the role of migrant members in contributing to food and nutritional security of the resident group that can provide insights to foster the development objectives of promoting livelihood and food security among vulnerable rural populations.

Against this background, the book investigates whether and how migration as a rural livelihood strategy plays a role in influencing rural households' food security. The focus of this work is specifically on the issue of *food access*, and accordingly food security is defined as the ability of households to command access to food by fair means (see Chapter 2). In a broader sense, this book seeks to engage with three key questions that include: (*a*) whether, and to what extent, food needs act as a driver of household migration decisions, (*b*) and if so, how the act of migration by individual household member(s) affects the food security of the households, particularly of the left-behind populations in origin villages, (*c*) given that male migration often triggers fundamental changes in the intra-household gender power relations, whether and how alternations in gender relations as a result of migration weigh on household food security.

The book approaches these questions using the theoretical frameworks of *entitlements* and *sustainable livelihoods approach* (SLA). With the focus of this study being on food access, it conceptualises the issue of food security through the lens of entitlements, and then uses SLA to understand the role of migration as one of the livelihood strategies in allowing rural households to gain access to food. Migration is a complex phenomenon and thus requires a deep investigation of the context-specific factors that explain household decision-making. The SLA framework provides an important means to understand the non-economic attributes embedded in rural livelihood strategies, including socio-economic and policy contexts in their co-produced institutional environments. Through SLA, this research attempts to understand and disentangle the under-researched relationship between migration and food security.

Methodologically, this book relies on extensive primary data collected from an equally proportional sample of 392 migrant and non-migrant households in one district of rural India (Siwan district, Bihar) in order to undertake a comparative assessment of dynamics and contextual correlates of migration and household food security. In doing so, the book focuses specifically on internal migration. This is aimed to correct a bias in the dominant discourse on migration. Because of the high volume of international remittances flows to India – over USD 75 billion in 2018 alone (World Bank, 2019) – much of the academic and policy attention on the development and livelihood impacts of migration tends to focus on international migration. However, it is rather unambiguous that a far greater number of rural households resort to internal rather than international migration for employment reasons, given the importance of distance and relatively higher barriers to international mobility. Indeed, the number of people moving from one area to another within India is estimated to be 100 million, which is more than seven times the number of people migrating across national borders (Government of India, 2017, 2021). The sheer volume of people moving within national boundaries suggests the greater significance of internal migration for rural dwellers, with potentially huge human development impacts (Deshingkar and Akhter, 2009; United Nations Development Programme [UNDP], 2009). The analysis presented in this book shows that internal migration has much more direct relevance for household food security which remains largely ignored.

While the geographic focus of this work is on India, the book also contextualises this relationship in the wider global context. Indeed, as the discussion in Chapter 2 will reveal, the relationship between migration and food security remains a hugely understudied subject in development studies in general despite the fact that these two issues have come to occupy a prominent place in global development policy and research agendas over the past couple of decades. Viewed this way, the book draws on Indian experience to bridge this larger disconnect between migration and food security (Crush, 2013). India has global significance and provides an appropriate setting to study these linkages. The country houses the largest pool of chronically undernourished population in the world and figures prominently in global debates on food and nutritional deprivation. Moreover, the existing development paradox of rising affluence among the urban, middle-class populations but livelihood stagnation, and even deterioration by some measures, among a large proportion of rural population makes for an important study. Also, while recent evidence points to significant increase in labour outmigration, the pre-existing research on rural livelihoods does not provide answers to whether and how migration relates to rural households' food security. The following discussion contextualises the importance of understanding the connections between migration and food security in India, which also serves to highlight the wider significance of the Indian case.

OVERVIEW OF FOOD (IN)SECURITY IN INDIA

In India, despite the considerable increases in agricultural production following the Green Revolution in the 1970s, a bleak state of food security among a significantly huge proportion of its population still remains a challenge to be addressed. The adoption of Green Revolution technologies and resultant gains in the levels of food production has improved India's abilities to avert the large-scale recurring famines of the past, and in the post-independence era India has emerged as a major net exporter of food. Nevertheless, it is still home to the largest number of chronically undernourished people in the world. According to the most recent statistics by the United Nation's Food and Agriculture Organisation (FAO), during 2017–19, the number of undernourished people in India was estimated to be 189.2 million, representing over a quarter of the total undernourished people in the world and nearly 75 per cent of the undernourishment burden of the South Asian region (FAO et al., 2020, pp. 177–82). To put these numbers in perspective, if undernourished people in India were to constitute a single country, it would be the eighth most populated country in the world.[1] In relative terms, the prevalence of food insecurity in India is worse than in many countries in Sub-Saharan Africa. In 2020, India ranked 94 in the Global Hunger Index (GHI) that covered 107 countries – a rank which placed the country lower than even the extremely poor and politically highly unstable nations of Cameroon, Republic of Congo and Tanzania (von Grebmer et al., 2020, p. 9).

Chronic food insecurity, which ultimately manifests into poor nutritional and health outcomes with wider implications for the nation's health and wealth, remains a major public policy challenge in India.[2] Indeed, with such a large proportion of India's population being food insecure, the country faces what is generally viewed as a nutritional emergency (Drèze, 2004; Care India, 2012). The prevalence of undernutrition remains stubbornly high across the different population groups in India, in particular women and children. The anthropometric data from India's National Family Health Survey (NFHS) showed that in 2015–16, 35.7 per cent of all children below the age of five years were underweight (a composite indicator of child malnutrition, reflecting both acute and chronic forms of nutritional deprivation) and 58.5 per cent of them suffered from anaemia.[3] More than one-fifth (22.9 per cent) of women in the reproductive age group of 15–49 years had the below normal body mass index (BMI) of 18.5.[4] Additionally, more than half of the women in the same age group were reported to be anaemic (all data, IIPS and ICF International, 2017b).

Food insecurity and undernourishment of such a magnitude in contemporary India persists despite the fact that the nation's granaries bulge with enough food stocks to adequately meet the food needs of the country's population. Furthermore, in the past three decades the Indian economy has grown at remarkable rates. And yet, contrary to the international experience, the role of high economic growth in improving the nutritional well-being of a large majority of India's population has been rather minimal, leading the country to be described as an enigma (see the following discussion). Although the answers to this enigma lie in a complex set of social, economic and political reasons (some of which will be discussed in subsequent chapters), it is clearly the case that the issue of food insecurity in India is not about food production per se but is rooted in food access – that is, the ways in which the country's populations, particularly the rural poor with limited means, gain access to food. In turn, it relates to the broader issue of livelihood security. Indeed, one of the key arguments of this book is that the issue of food insecurity in India is fundamentally situated within the larger set of livelihood circumstances of people, and thus public policy to redress this challenge requires a better understanding of those livelihood contexts.

ECONOMIC GROWTH AND NUTRITION DISCONNECT

Following the systematic economic reforms initiated since the early 1990s, the Indian economy has witnessed gargantuan leaps in terms of growth and has moved on to become one of the fastest growing economies in the world. However, the rapid economic growth in India has contributed only marginally to improving the food and nutritional security outcomes of a large majority of the country's populace. Although nutritional outcomes are affected by a range of factors other than a country's level of income, the cross-country evidence suggests that economic growth and consequent rise in average incomes are negatively correlated with the rates of undernutrition. In quantitative terms, it has been observed that for many countries, the decline in the prevalence of child-underweight (a good measure of undernutrition) tends to be nearly half the rate of growth of the per capita gross domestic product (GDP) (Haddad et al., 2003). Thus, for example, an annual per capita GDP growth rate of 5 per cent would be expected to be associated with a corresponding decline in the prevalence of child undernutrition by 2.5 per cent annually. However, this relationship is virtually absent in India. Between 1990 and 2015, the average per capita GDP in India grew at an average annual rate of 4.5 per cent (World Bank, 2021b). This income growth should have provided a potent force to address the problem of childhood undernutrition; and if the observed relationship between GDP per capita and undernutrition held perfectly in India, this would have eliminated childhood undernutrition during this 25-year period (also see Gillespie and Kadiyala, 2012, p. 173). Yet the progress on this front has been sluggish, and the expected negative relationship between GDP per capita and child undernutrition is weak across most Indian states (Figure 1.1).

Four rounds of the NFHS conducted during this period show that over a half of all children below the age of five years were underweight in 1992–93, which declined to 35.7 per cent in 2015–16 – a reduction of merely 15 per cent over this quarter century (IIPS, 1995; IIPS and ICF International, 2017b).[5] Similarly, a recent multi-country study that analysed progress towards child stunting (another indicator of child undernutrition that indicates low height in relation to age) in 174 countries between 1990 and 2015 found that India is one of the countries which saw stalling of progress on childhood nutrition in the period from 2000–05 to 2010–15 (Balla et al., 2021). Worryingly, moreover, preliminary data from the most recent (fifth) round of the NFHS available at the time of writing this book revealed a worsening of the child undernutrition

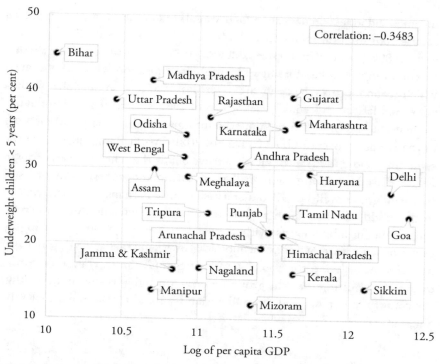

Figure 1.1 Association between gross domestic product (GDP) per capita and child nutritional status, 2015–16

Source: Reserve Bank of India (2020); IIPS and ICF International (2017b).

situation: between 2015–16 and 2019–20, the proportion of under-five children who were underweight increased in seven of 10 major states for which the data were released (IIPS and ICF International, 2020).[6] This reversal is historic. There is no country in the world – certainly not a democratic nation that has experienced rapid economic growth – where a reversal in progress on child nutrition has been observed. This rather weak negative correlation between economic growth and food security in India has led the country be described as an 'enigma' (Ramalingaswami, Jonsson and Rohde, 1996; Pritchard et al., 2014).

Furthermore, there is evidence that in the post-reform period, disparities in child nutritional outcomes have widened between the rich and the poor and across the geographical regions and states of India (Pathak and Singh, 2011). It is also important to note that in spite of a rise in average per capita incomes and indeed in per capita food availability in the country, the average calorie consumption intake in India has also witnessed a decline since the early 1980s (Deaton and Drèze, 2009). This deterioration of nutritional outcomes in the wake of rising affluence raises questions about the ways in which economic growth has apparently bypassed a large proportion of India's poor population. Indeed, the net worth of India's 10 richest billionaires is estimated to be USD 253 billion, accounting for approximately 10 per cent of the country's overall GDP (Karmali, 2021; World Bank, 2021c). At the same time, close to 270 million people live below the official poverty line in India (Planning Commission, 2013a), a benchmark with such low cut-off that it might as well be called a starvation line. Perhaps no other country in the world offers as much a contrast as India, where the dire poverty of such a magnitude coexists with tremendous wealth. Noting the highly exclusionary nature of India's economic growth, further widening the gap between the rich and the poor, Drèze and Sen (2013, p. ix) even go to the extent of suggesting that 'the growth process [in India] is so biased, making the country look more and more like islands of California in a sea of sub-Saharan Africa'.

RURAL–URBAN DISPARITIES IN THE NUTRITIONAL OUTCOMES

Nearly 70 per cent of India's population resides in rural areas, which are characterised by low levels of income, poor quality of life and inadequate health and educational infrastructure. The relative neglect of rural areas in India's economic development planning is manifested in wide rural–urban disparities in the human development indicators of income, education, health and nutrition. Moreover, the disregard for the country's rural areas, and by implication the needs of rural populations, seems to have accentuated following the economic reforms since the early 1990s, which have been highly urban-centric in their distribution of benefits. It is therefore no surprise that the character and incidence of food insecurity and deprivation in India are predominantly rural. Indeed, the largest number of underweight children in the developing world are from the rural areas of India (Paciorek et al., 2013), and rural children suffer from greater marginalisation due to geography. At the global level, South Asia remains the hotspot of chronic hunger, where malnutrition begins early in childhood. The United Nations Children's Fund's

(UNICEF) *State of the World's Children 2019* report shows that nearly half of the children aged under five years in South Asia are not growing well, and India has the highest prevalence of such children in the region (UNICEF, 2020). Children born in rural areas are more prone to malnutrition, and progress in improving childhood nutritional well-being has largely bypassed rural children in India.

The NFHS 2015–16 data on the nutritional status of children by the place of residence suggest that the prevalence of stunting, wasting and underweight among children under five years of age in rural areas were 41.2 per cent, 21.4 per cent and 38.3 per cent, respectively, while the corresponding figures for children living in cities and towns were 31.1 per cent, 20 per cent and 29.1 per cent (Figure 1.2). Differences in several socio-economic factors such as better maternal education, greater involvement of women in household decision-making and improved water and sanitation services in urban areas tend to favour urban children's nutritional status over that of children living in rural areas (Smith, Ruel and Ndiaye, 2005). Indeed, the severity of rural disadvantage is such that children living in urban slums fare better on some key nutritional indicators than their rural counterparts (Nguyen et al., 2021).

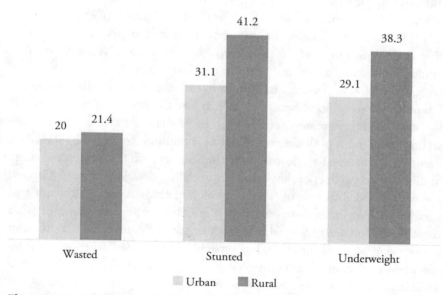

Figure 1.2 Prevalence of undernutrition among children aged under five years in India by place of residence, 2015–16

Source: IIPS and ICF International (2017b, p. 309).

Similarly, there is also a rural–urban divide in terms of the prevalence of undernutrition among adults, as measured by the BMI status. Guha-Khasnobis and James (2010) found that adult undernutrition among the slum populations of eight Indian cities was 23 per cent, and the corresponding proportion for the rural areas of the same Indian states was nearly 40 per cent. Additionally, even though large-scale famines have become history in India, deaths due to starvation and malnutrition continue to be reported even today, particularly among the socially and economically disadvantaged rural populations (Jha, 2002; Mander, 2012; Parulkar, 2012; Patel, 2018). This apparent disconnect between buffer food stocks and surging economic growth on one hand and widespread incidence of nutritional deprivation on the other has created the situation where the *right to food* has emerged as a new set of foundations to India's approach to undernutrition, which is the focus of the next section.

RIGHT TO FOOD REVOLUTION IN INDIA: IMPORTANCE AND CHALLENGES

The right to sufficient food has long been recognised in various international treaties and instruments, such as the Universal Declaration of Human Rights in 1948 and the International Covenant on Economic, Social and Cultural Rights in 1976. However, in principle, the right to food as a fundamental human right gained political significance only since the mid-1990s. The second World Food Summit in 1996 in Rome, alternatively called the Rome Summit on World Food Security – which saw the participation of heads of the states and their representatives from more than 180 countries – marked an important event in this regard. The Rome Summit, convened by the FAO, occurred against the backdrop of persisting hunger despite an enormous surge in global food-production levels in the preceding decades achieved through the widespread diffusion of Green Revolution technologies. Although this paradox of hunger amidst plenty led to a considerable rethinking of what constitutes food security – which, most importantly, involved a shift from a narrow production-orientated approach of *food availability* to a wider conception of food security involving issues such as *food access* and *food utilization* (more on this later) – one of the most important aspects of the Rome Summit was the framing of food security through the paradigm of human rights. This conceptualisation of food security through a rights-based approach was in line with the growing importance of human-centred thinking since the early 1990s. By placing people at the centre of development, rights and entitlements were placed at the core of new discourses and metrics (this is reflected in the UNDP's annual *Human Development Reports*, the first of which was published in 1990). The Rome Summit thus recognized not only 'the right of everyone to be free from hunger' but also the 'right to have access to safe and nutritious food' (FAO, 1996).

The Rome Summit marked a significant event in terms of generating a global consensus on the right to adequate food. In order to monitor the compliance of the member countries on the Summit's plan of action, in 2000 a Special Rapporteur on the Right to Food was appointed. Later, in 2004, the FAO's council adopted a set of 'Voluntary Guidelines' to help member countries towards their efforts on the progressive realisation of the right to food (FAO, 2005). Although the right to food still remains a distant reality for close to 700 million people in the world who go to bed hungry every night (FAO et al., 2020), the framing of food security through the prism of a rights-based approach has provided considerable impetus for public action, particularly in democratic settings with a strong, and widening, presence of civil society. This has resulted in many countries amending their constitutions or legislative frameworks to incorporate the right to food as a legal right accorded to their citizens (De Schutter, 2012), including India which, following almost a decade-long debate on the issue, passed a legislation in August 2013 that provided a constitutional stamp to the right to food.

The origin of this right to food legislation in India lies in a writ petition filed in the Supreme Court (SC) in April 2001 by the Rajasthan state arm of India's People Union for Civil Liberties (PUCL), an umbrella civil society organisation working on a wide range of human rights issues in the country. The petition, officially known as *PUCL v. Union of India and Others, Writ Petition [Civil] 196 of 2001*, argued that because Article 21 in the Directive Principles of the Indian Constitution enshrined the right to life to the citizens, it was incumbent on the state to protect the citizens' right to food, which was fundamental to right to life. The trigger for this petition by the PUCL was a series of hunger and starvation deaths around the country, particularly in southern Rajasthan, which suffered from a severe drought for three consecutive years from 1999 to 2001. The main victims of starvation were the socially and economically marginalised Scheduled Tribe populations living in remote villages in southern Rajasthan. These starvation deaths occurred even when India had a reserve food-grain stock of 50 million tonnes – far in excess of the buffer-stock norms of 20 million tonnes – which in any case had the broader aim of dealing with crisis situations such as this one. Thus, invoking Article 21, the PUCL sought the intervention of the SC to check this situation when 'food stocks reached unprecedented levels while hunger in drought-affected areas intensified' (Patnaik, Reddy and Singh, 2008, p. 6). Although this case has not yet been formally concluded, the SC has passed several interim orders directing the federal and state governments in India to release food grains to the hungry and starving in order to protect their right to life. In one such interim order passed on 2 May 2003, the SC observed:

> ... of utmost importance is to see that food is provided to the aged, infirm, disabled, destitute women, destitute men who are in danger of starvation, pregnant and lactating women and destitute children, especially in cases where they or members of their family do not have sufficient funds to provide food for them ... In case of famine, there may be shortage of food, but here the situation is that amongst plenty there is scarcity ... The anxiety of the Court is to see that poor and the destitute and the weaker sections of the society do not suffer from hunger and starvation. The prevention of the same is one of the prime responsibilities of the Government – whether Central or the State. (Supreme Court of India, 2003, p. 2)

Over the years, the scope of the petition filed by the PUCL, which initially sought mainly drought relief to prevent starvation deaths among the poor communities, has expanded significantly. It has expanded to include a range of other issues – the most important of which has been the state provisioning of free and/or subsidised food for poor households on a continuous basis in order to deal with the problem of chronic malnutrition. Subsequent interim orders of the SC have correspondingly reflected the PUCL's concerns and directed the Government of India (GoI) to take appropriate actions in this regard, including providing free cooked meals to school-going children, food rations for pregnant and lactating mothers, and so on (for a lucid account of the SC's interim orders on the right to food case, see Patnaik et al., 2008).

The sustained litigation by the PUCL and the SC's interventions put considerable pressure on the GoI. And in 2010, the incumbent ruling coalition led by the Indian National Congress party, carrying on its 2009 election manifesto promise, announced the implementation of the right-to-food legislation. Intense debates then ensued for approximately two-and-a-half years between 2010 and 2013 over the provisions it ought to contain.

The debates revolved mainly around two core issues pertaining to (*a*) coverage of the legislation, that is, what proportion of population should be provided subsidised food grains and (*b*) delivery mechanisms, that is, whether this right should be ensured through the existing in-kind provisioning of food rations or be replaced with supposedly the more efficient system of food coupons or cash transfers that enable eligible beneficiaries to source food from the market. In 2013, the Bill was passed by the Parliament and turned into the National Food Security Act (NFSA). The Act provides legal protection against hunger and takes a gender-sensitive life-cycle approach to tackling the issue of food insecurity in India. The major provisions in the NFSA include providing food and cash benefits to pregnant and lactating mothers so that they and their newborns are well-cared for, nutrition benefits for children aged between 6 and 59 months, free school meals for children attending schools and, importantly (something which has been the source of much debate), 5 kilograms of subsidised food ration per person each month to 67 per cent of the country's population through the existing public distribution system (PDS) (Government of India, 2013a).

With such a huge proportion of India's population lacking access to adequate food, the right-to-food law, no doubt, holds utmost importance. Indeed, as Drèze (2004) argued, pervasive undernutrition in India seems to have been accepted as natural with virtually no policy discussion on this aspect of human crisis. Seen in this light, the food security law certainly represents a major step forward. Yet, given the scale and multiple dimensions of food and nutrition insecurity in India (which will become clearer as the discussion proceeds), the NFSA is only a fraction of what is really needed to tame the problem. Moreover, most of the food security provisions, as mentioned earlier, which the NFSA covers have already been in place in India, with some of them, such as the PDS, existing since as early as the late 1960s. Thus, in many ways the NFSA is a consolidation of the existing food safety nets which, although significantly important, remain beset with difficulties. For example, there is a wide body of evidence suggesting that vast amounts of food grains meant to reach the poor under the PDS get illegally diverted along the way (Planning Commission, 2005; Jha and Ramaswamy, 2010; Gulati and Saini, 2015). And media reports abound on the large-scale corruption and leakages in the National Rural Employment Guarantee Scheme (NREGS), a scheme implemented in 2006, which promises 100 days of guaranteed manual-labour employment to rural households at the legally stipulated wage rate.[7] Some evidence points to signs of improvements in the functioning of these schemes in recent years, seemingly in part because poor households are now becoming more assertive in claiming their entitlements (Khera, 2011b; Drèze and Khera, 2014). However, by and large, the state of social provisioning in India continues to remain dismal. And it is a peculiar irony of social welfare systems in India that the safety nets remain more dysfunctional in the poor regions or states where they are needed the most.

In such a situation whereby a large majority of the rural poor is left to fend for themselves, insights on the livelihood strategies devised by rural households to gain access to adequate food are of significant policy relevance. In particular, this book focuses on migration as a rural livelihood strategy for the reasons stated as follows.

RURAL OUTMIGRATION AND FOOD SECURITY: A PRESSING NEED FOR POLICY INPUTS

In India, the agriculture sector has traditionally been the most important source of food and livelihood security for a large majority of the rural population. Through own-account farming or wages obtained from farm work, and often through the combination of both, agriculture has provided an important means to meet the income and food needs of rural dwellers. Although agriculture still remains the mainstay of a large majority of the rural population, employing over 40 per cent of India's total labour force, the changes in the pattern of economic growth are rapidly altering rural livelihood trajectories in India. There is a continuing decline in the share of agriculture sector in the national income and, with it, the fortunes of agriculture-based livelihoods. Between 1990 and 2019, the share of agriculture sector in national income more than halved – from 33 per cent to 16 per cent (Mehrotra et al., 2013; World Bank, 2021a). This decline is accompanied by a significant shift of employment out of agriculture. Statistics from successive national censuses and surveys highlight a gradual shift away from farm-based livelihoods although there are wide regional-level variations. At the national level, over seven million people whose main occupation was cultivation quit farming during the inter-censal period of 1991–2001. This trend accelerated in the following decade, with 2011 census recording 8.6 million fewer main cultivators compared to the 2001 census (Census of India, 1991b, 2001c, 2011c). More recent estimates based on the National Sample Survey's (NSS) and the Periodic Labour Force Survey's (PLFS) data show that between

2004 and 2016, there has been a net loss of 40 million jobs in agriculture (Himanshu, 2011; Thomas, 2012; Mehrotra et al., 2014; Abraham, 2017; Van Duijne and Nijman, 2019), and for the first time in the history of independent India, the share of agricultural employment has fallen to less than 50 per cent (Mehrotra et al., 2013). Given that livelihoods in rural India are constructed in the context of the family, the real impact of these livelihood shifts away from farming is perhaps much higher. Assuming an average household size of five members, 40 million jobs losses in agriculture means that 200 million people are affected in their daily lives in this transformation (Choithani, Van Duijne and Nijman, 2021). This transition has not been smooth, and it has produced significant distress, which is manifested in the spate of farmers' suicides across the country (Sainath, 2011; Banerjee, 2022; Pani, 2022).

Although the role of the agriculture sector in economic and human development remains highly contested, cross-country evidence across a range of low-income countries suggests that compared to the secondary and tertiary sectors of the economy, growth in agriculture has a highly significant impact on reducing the levels of rural poverty and food insecurity and raising consumption levels among the poorest segments of the population (inter alia, World Bank, 2007; Ligon and Sadoulet, 2008; Christiaensen, Demery and Kuhl, 2010). In India, the remarkable gains in agricultural productivity following the Green Revolution in the 1970s not only helped the country achieve self-reliance in food production and thwarted the looming possibility of mass hunger but also increased farmers' incomes, improved wages for agricultural labourers and reduced prices of food, leading to overall decline in poverty (Ahluwalia, 1978; Bell and Rich, 1994; Ravallion and Datt, 1996). Subsequently, however, agriculture growth had made a far less impressive dent on the outcomes of food insecurity in India (Headey, 2011; FAO, 2013). Furthermore, the rapidly changing sectoral composition of economic growth in India following the economic reforms of the early 1990s – with much of the addition to the national income now emanating from the urban-based service sector to the disadvantage of the agricultural activities – has led to a further weakening of the role of agriculture in improving the food and nutritional well-being of the Indian population, and there exists an *agriculture–nutrition disconnect* in India (Headey, Chiu and Kadiyala, 2011; Gillespie and Kadiyala, 2012). On the other hand, recent evidence suggests that in the post–economic reform period, urban economic growth has become a more important driver of rural poverty reduction compared to the pre-reform period when the growth in the urban sector had no discernable impact on rural poverty reduction; it was the economic growth in the rural sector from which both the rural and urban poor benefitted. This is not to suggest that growth of the rural economy is not important. Indeed, with nearly 70 per cent of India's population still residing in the countryside, rural economic growth holds an important key to improving the living standards of rural dwellers. At the same time, the spillover effects of urban growth on rural incomes and employment seem to have become increasingly more crucial insofar as rural poverty reduction in the post-1990s period is concerned (Ravallion and Datt, 1996; Datt and Ravallion, 2011; Datt, Ravallion and Murgai, 2020).

It is important to note that the highly fragmented pattern of agricultural landholdings in India implies that most rural households constitute smallholder farmers: over 85 per cent of landholdings in India are less than 2 hectares (Ministry of Agriculture, 2019), and nearly 42 per cent of households in rural India do not own any agricultural land (Rawal, 2008). These patterns get compounded further by the fact that most Indian states officially prevent the renting or leasing of farmland. Thus, for landless and land-poor households of India, wage income has been traditionally a central component of household income. However, the low level of economic activity with imperfectly operating rural-labour markets means that, more often than not, wage options are pursued in the distant labour markets. Thus, migration has long been an essential component of rural livelihood systems in India.

The predominant stream of migration in India has involved rural-to-rural migration of labour. The systematic insertion of Green Revolution reforms in the Indo-Gangetic plains of Punjab and Haryana in north-western India led agricultural labourers from the economically backward regions of eastern Uttar Pradesh and Bihar to migrate to these states in large numbers. In fact, the success of the Green Revolution in India is largely attributed to this migration. Writing of poor labourers from Bihar who migrated to Punjab for agricultural work during this period of farm intensification, Singh (1997, p. 518) suggests: 'Punjab farmers know that green revolution would not have been as green right from the beginning in the late 1960s, as it is found today, had there been no use of migrant labour from Bihar.' However, the rising stress on the agriculture-based income and livelihoods and the urban-centric nature of economic growth is changing the patterns of migration, with rural-to-urban migration rising in significance.[8] Rural-to-urban migration is now the most dominant stream of mobility for male migrants who account for a bulk of economic migrants in India (National Sample Survey, 2010, p. 30).

An important characteristic of rural–urban migration in India is its seasonal and circular nature, which constitutes a significant bulk of migratory movements. It is for this reason that rural migrants in India are often described as 'nowhere people' (Breman, 2010, p. 17). In fact, the embedded circularity in migration is the reason which has kept the official levels of urbanisation low in India (Kundu, 2003, 2014). Although labour mobility in India is predominantly of a non-permanent nature, migrants now increasingly spend a longer duration away from their places of origin (Choithani, Van Duijne and Nijman, 2021), suggesting the rising significance of non-local incomes in households' lives and livelihoods. Indeed, rural India is witnessing what Rigg, Salamanca and Parnwell (2012, p. 1470) call 'a delocalization of life and living'. The official data agencies, however, barely capture the true extent of temporary migrants in India. The estimates derived by Keshri and Bhagat (2012) using the NSS data suggest that temporary migrants in India account for nearly 13 million people. The 2011 census yielded the number of work migrants in India to be 41.4 million (Census of India, 2011b).[9] Alternative estimates, however, show that over 100 million people remain on the move for their livelihoods in any given year and that migrants constitute 20 per cent of the total workforce of 500 million people (Deshingkar and Akhter, 2009; Government of India, 2017). Moreover, recent evidence points to a substantial rise in labour mobility in India (Nayyar and Kim, 2018; Choithani, Van Duijne and Nijman, 2021).

Despite the crucial role played by migration in the lives and livelihoods of rural dwellers in India, rarely is its significance acknowledged among the policy-making communities. The policy neglect partly emanates from the fact that much of the rural outmigration characteristically takes the form of seasonal and circular mobility and does not fit into the officially structured contexts. Contrarily, rural outmigration is often viewed by the policymakers as a sign of distress and often evokes misguided images of disruption in the idealised conceptions of sedentary rural life. Not surprisingly, as is the case in many developing countries, development policy in India has sought to control the flow of rural migrants. A close examination of rural development policies makes this stand clear. For example, one of the objectives of the NREGS is to prevent migration from rural areas. To cite another example, a key stated goal of the Rajasthan State Agricultural Policy is 'to discourage migration, both seasonal and permanent migration, of rural people to urban areas through various means of improved rural livelihood and income generation through on-farm and off-farm opportunities' (Government of Rajasthan, 2013, p. 4). Given the substantial decline in the capacity of agriculture to support livelihoods over the past few decades, policy interventions to promote rural non-farm jobs are much needed. But these measures need not, and often cannot, control rural outmigration as it is rather unambiguous that 'migration and rural livelihoods are falsely opposed' (Mosse et al., 2002, p. 60).

A related concern often expressed by scholars in the case of rural–urban migration is that most migrant workers get absorbed in the urban informal sector where average wages are low, working conditions deplorable and exploitation high, which means labour mobility does not help improve migrants' (and their households') social and economic position (Breman, 1996, 2010). Indeed, this is a valid concern, particularly in the wake of signs of relocation of poverty from rural to urban areas. But another pertinent question, which ought to beg equal attention but is rarely asked, is 'what these households and individuals would have done in the absence of the opportunity to migrate' (Deshingkar and Grimm, 2005, p. 40).

The growing importance of migration in the rural livelihood systems of India warrants a greater policy attention than it currently receives. Despite the concern around migrants' vulnerabilities associated with urban informal jobs, migration can also provide a route out of poverty and potentially contribute to enhanced human development outcomes (UNDP, 2009). Surprisingly, however, there is very little conceptualisation and direct evidence on how migration as a rural livelihood strategy impacts food and nutritional security outcomes at the household level. The lack of research is surprising because the connections between migration and food security are obvious. The prevailing agriculture–nutrition disconnect in India warrants a need for a greater understanding of alternative mechanisms that may explain the food security outcomes among rural households. Drawing from primary field research, this book aims to highlight the often overlooked connections between migration and food security.

A NOTE ON FIELD SITE, RESEARCH METHODS AND ANALYTICAL APPROACH

As noted earlier, this study contextualises the link between migration and food security using a case-study-based approach involving the collection of primary, field-based data from a sample of households. Given the lack of prior knowledge on the subject matter, field research provided the most suitable way to generate insights into this inadequately explored relationship between migration and household food security. But logistical and time constraints associated with field research inevitably required selecting a field site that not only enabled studying this relationship in a grounded, empirical context but also provided insights that had wider significance beyond the case-study site. It is for these reasons that this study chose Siwan district in western Bihar for fieldwork (Figure 1.3). Within Siwan, fieldwork focused on a set of villages which had a high incidence of rural outmigration. The selection of field-research site(s) followed several strategic and statistical considerations, and the following discussion provides a brief note on site selection and methodology followed in this research.

First, Bihar was selected as a broader study site because it provided an appropriate setting to study the connections between migration and food security. Bihar is largely a rural state and nearly 90 per cent of the state's population resides in the countryside (Census of India, 2011c). It is also among the poorest Indian states with over one-third of its population living below the official poverty line (Planning Commission, 2013a). It is not just poverty; on all the other measures related to education, health and mortality, most of the individual districts (and villages within them) in Bihar constitute pockets of deprivation. The incidence of food insecurity and hunger is rampant in Bihar, and it ranked 15 in the State Hunger Index (SHI) of 17 Indian states (Menon, Deolalikar and Bhaskar, 2009). Lack of gainful employment opportunities coupled with high poverty force a large majority of households to migrate to other states in search of livelihood. Migration has been traditionally a central component of livelihood strategies among rural dwellers of Bihar, and some scholars have termed migrants from Bihar as 'unsettled settlers' (De Haan, 1997b, p. 919), an apparent reference also to the circular or temporary nature of migration from Bihar. Remittances provide a crucial source of incomes for a sizeable majority of Bihar's rural populations.

Within Bihar, the western district of Siwan was selected for field research because it had high incidence of interstate outmigration. The district-wise interstate outmigration, calculated using the population census data, shows that Siwan had an outmigration rate of 4.9 per cent between 1991 and 2001 – the second highest among all the districts of Bihar (Census of India, 2001b).[10] In 2011, Siwan's total population was 3.14 million, with a population density of 1,495 persons, which was more than three times than that of India. The district is also among the least urbanised in the country, with nearly 95 per cent of the population living in the rural hinterlands (Census of India, 2011c, 2011d). The district is among the most backward districts of India, facing acute deficits in

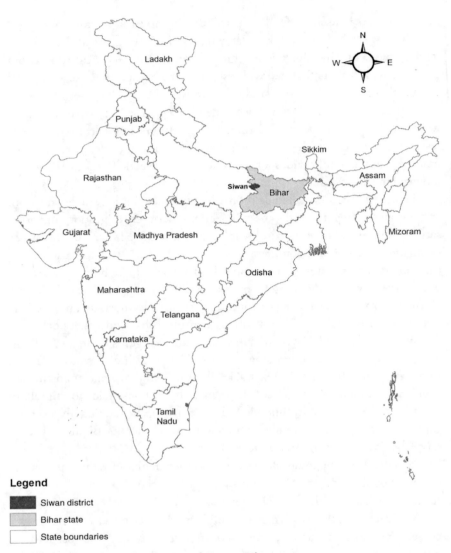

Figure 1.3 Case-study district of Siwan, Bihar

Source: Map by the author.

Note: Map not to scale and does not represent authentic international boundaries.

living standards, food security, education and healthcare outcomes (Debroy and Bhandari, 2003; Bakshi, Chawla and Shah, 2015). Deprived of any major industrial activity, local livelihoods in Siwan are heavily reliant on agriculture. However, high population pressures on land mean that landholdings are small and farming is largely subsistence-based. Consequently, a large majority of the district's population depends on wage income options pursued in distant labour markets, usually to urban centres in other Indian states. Migration from the district is largely of a circular nature and undertaken predominantly by men (see Chapter 4 for detailed profiles of Bihar and Siwan).

This criterion of male-dominated migration was used to select villages for fieldwork. The district of Siwan had 1,438 villages (Census of India, 2001c). Out of this gigantic number, a total number of 10 villages spread across nine administrative blocks were randomly chosen based on the sex ratio (SR) of the population aged six years and above (SR6+). All the case-study villages had an SR of at least 1,000 females per 1,000 males. This was guided by the fact that villages having a high SR in favour of females will likely have high outmigration rates. The SR6+ was used considering the fact that population under the age of six years is not exposed to labour migration. (Taking the SR of the population aged 10 years and above would have been ideal; however, the village-level Indian census data did not permit the same.) Even though the number of case-study villages was rather arbitrary, these 10 villages nonetheless provided large within-district geographic heterogeneity.

From these 10 villages, the data were collected using both quantitative and qualitative methods, including surveys, observations and interviews. The principal method was *household surveys* with a representative sample of 392 rural households, including 197 migrant households and 195 non-migrant households. Migrant households were defined as those that had one or more members who undertook work migration for at least two months in the past year, while those without such members were considered non-migrant households. A representative sample of 20 migrant households and 20 non-migrant households was chosen from each village (eight households chose not to participate). Prior to the survey, household migration particulars were obtained through a house-listing exercise, which served as a basis for drawing the sample. Among migrant households, 144 wives of male migrants were also surveyed with the purpose of understanding the migration–gender–food-security nexus. These rural surveys collected data on households' socio-demographic characteristics, engagement in farm and non-farm livelihoods, income and expenditure, land and livestock ownership, saving and investments, food security, and gender relations. The rural fieldwork also involved *key informant interviews* with members of *gram panchayats* (local village councils) (GPs) to understand the broader village-level dynamics, *freewheeling or unstructured interviews* with government officials in charge of local administrative affairs to get a sense of development issues and *semi-structured interviews* with members of some of the surveyed households to gain deeper qualitative insights.

Although the focus of this study was the rural communities at the place of origin, an attempt was also made to understand the perspectives of migrants at the destination. For this purpose, *semi-structured interviews* with 10 migrants belonging to the sample rural households in Siwan working in urban destinations in the National Capital Region (Delhi, Haryana and Uttar Pradesh) were also carried out. These interviews with urban migrants were conducted to complement the rural fieldwork, and they generated information on the factors and events that shaped their decisions to migrate, on the dichotomy of choice versus compulsion migration, on their living and working conditions, on their food consumption patterns, on their access to welfare entitlements at the place of destination, and so on.

The fieldwork was accomplished in three phases. In the first phase during January–February 2012, a mapping and house-listing exercise was performed in the case-study villages that created a sample frame from which eligible households were chosen using probability sampling. In the second phase, household surveys were conducted during April–May 2012, and interviews with migrants in urban areas were carried out in June 2012. The reference period used in rural household surveys for annual data pertaining to indicators such as household income and food security is April 2011 to March 2012. Interviews with key informants and government officials in Siwan were simultaneously carried out during the rural fieldwork spanning these two phases between January and May 2012. Lastly, following a little more than a year of analysis of the primary survey data, some case-study villages were visited again during September–October 2013 to obtain more qualitative information.

A brief comment on the approach of this book is now in order. First, while this book is based on fieldwork with rural households and their urban-based migrant members from a single district in western Bihar in India, it adopts an analytical strategy that situates this case-based research in the larger context and tries to highlight the wider significance of fieldwork findings beyond the immediate research setting. Second, and relatedly, the fieldwork reported in this book was done in 2012 and 2013, which predates some key developments pertinent to the analysis. For example, the implementation of the NFSA, 2013, has brought about major changes in several operational aspects of food-based safety nets in India, which is one of the key analytical themes of this book. To account for such changes, the discussion includes recent studies to contextualise the relevance of fieldwork findings. There has also been an endeavour to use the most recent secondary data available, except for census migration statistics where this work had to rely on the 2001 census. This is because these data are often released much later, and detailed migration tables from the 2011 census were released only in 2019. In any case, the primary aim of this book is to highlight the processes and pathways of the migration–food-security relationship and identify larger, pertinent issues.

THE BOOK'S OUTLINE

The remainder of the book is organised as follows: Chapter 2 seeks to contextualise the links between migration and food security in the wider global context. The discussion in this chapter suggests that while the recent years have witnessed heightened importance of these two issues in the global-, regional- and national-level development policy deliberations, there currently exists a huge disconnect between the two, and it also dwells on the possible reason for this disconnect. Further, the chapter lays out the key conceptual frameworks of *entitlements* and *livelihoods* employed in the present study to understand the connections between migration and food security. These frameworks provide the theoretical and analytical foundations to this research. Finally, the chapter reviews the existing evidence on the type and nature of migration and the role of migration in rural livelihoods, and suggests the possible pathways of linkages between migration and food security. These pathways of linkages inform the empirical analysis carried out in the later chapters (Chapters 5, 6 and 7).

Chapter 3 discusses the broad dynamics of food insecurity, migration and urbanisation in India. Beginning with an overview of the magnitude of the problem of food insecurity and undernourishment, the chapter assesses India's progress on hunger reduction. It then assesses the regional, social and cultural dimensions of food insecurity in India. Finally, it evaluates the recent trends in the country's rural employment landscape, and the linkages they bear with the patterns of migration and urbanisation. This evaluation attempts to understand the shift in the rural livelihood patterns in recent years, with particular attention paid to rural–urban migration, and the implications it may have on household food security in rural India. The overarching purpose of this chapter is to set the scene for the empirical analysis that follows of the migration–food-security nexus, based on the field research findings in the case-study site of Siwan.

Chapter 4 sets out to provide the context of migration from Bihar and Siwan. It first places contemporary Bihar on the Indian map of development and discusses the reasons for its backwardness. This discussion contextualises the political economy of underdevelopment in Bihar and also traces the historical origins of the state's contemporary problems. Then it discusses the dynamics of food insecurity and migration in Bihar and the possible linkages they bear with each other. Following on from this broad state-level discussion, the final major section of the chapter, in a reverse step-migration (pun intended!), turns attention to the region of western Bihar in general and to the case-study district of Siwan in particular. Drawing on historical and contemporary evidence, it provides an overview of the place, people and livelihoods in western Bihar, seeks to understand the importance of migration in the livelihoods of rural dwellers of the region and discusses how the lives and livelihoods in the region compare and contrast with the *immobile-peasant* characterisation of rural populations of the underdeveloped world that has dominated academic and policy discussions. Finally, the chapter highlights the two key features of migration from Siwan, namely (*a*) circular mobility and (*b*) male-dominated pattern of migration. The chapter concludes by pointing out how they potentially interact with household food security outcomes, and the detailed empirical analysis of these linkages is carried out in Chapters 6 and 7.

Chapter 5 assesses the connections between food-based safety nets and migration. India operates an extensive set of food-based safety nets to provide food security to its most vulnerable citizens, and it would perhaps not be absolutely incorrect to state that no discussion on food security is complete without their detailed consideration. Moreover, the right-to-food legislation passed in 2013 has only increased their significance. Drawing on the field-based evidence from Siwan, this chapter scrutinises, in particular, the three major food-based safety net programmes – namely (*a*) the PDS, (*b*) the NREGS and (*c*) the Integrated Child Development Scheme (ICDS) – in their grounded contexts, and attempts to understand their linkages with rural households' food security situations and migration decisions, the two key themes that are at the heart of this book.

Chapter 6 asks whether and how migration by individual members of a household influences the food security outcomes of members in the origin villages in Siwan. Using a livelihood approach that brings together insights from the macro-level changes in India's economic and employment landscape in the post-reform period and decision-making matrices of rural households at the micro level, the chapter appraises the changes in rural livelihoods' trajectories and the importance of non-local migration incomes for food security of rural households in the case-study district. In particular, the chapter discusses the rural–urban and farm–non-farm linkages that circular migration creates through remittances, and how these linkages, in turn, play out to influence food security outcomes among rural households. The chapter also throws light on the role of migration in altering the local land and agrarian relations, and how they relate to the food security of the landless and land-poor households and those without any migrant members.

Following on from this inter-household comparison, Chapter 7 seeks to look within the household in order to understand the impacts of migration on intra-household power dynamics and relations, and the bearing of these impacts on food security outcomes in Siwan. As noted earlier, an important feature of labour mobility in large parts of the developing world is the male-dominated pattern of migration. Labour migration from Siwan (and Bihar more generally) is almost exclusively a male pursuit, while women stay behind. Thus, the chapter first sheds light on the gendered nature of migration and the factors underlying this pattern. Then it assesses migration's impacts on left-behind women's roles and responsibilities in household affairs and explores the female-autonomy–responsibility aspects of male migration. Thereafter, the chapter looks at the effects of migration in changing traditional familial arrangements. In the end, through the wider lens of gender, the interactions of each of these effects with household food security are analysed.

Finally, Chapter 8 brings together the key insights from each of these chapters, extrapolates the findings of case-study-based research for their wider policy significance and comments on the future direction of research on the links between migration and food security.

NOTES

1. This is arrived at based on the *2019 Revision of World Population Prospects* (United Nations, 2019).
2. Poor nutritional and health outcomes may also be a result of several non-food factors such as unfavourable hygiene and sanitation practices and resultant disease environment. However, lack of food often amplifies the effect of disease.

3. Anaemia figures quoted from the NFHS are for children aged 6 to 59 months.

4. BMI is measured as weight (in kilograms) divided by height (in metres square). In other words, BMI = kg/m2.

5. The first round of the NFHS (1992–93) measured undernutrition among children under four years of age. In five states of Andhra Pradesh, Himachal Pradesh, Madhya Pradesh, Tamil Nadu and West Bengal, only the weight of children was measured due to the unavailability of height measuring boards (IIPS, 1995, p. 281).

6. These states include Assam, Gujarat, Himachal Pradesh, Kerala, Maharashtra, Telangana and West Bengal.

7. The NREGS emanated from the constitutional act of the same name – the National Rural Employment Guarantee Act. In 2009, it was renamed as the Mahatma Gandhi National Rural Employment Guarantee Scheme. This book, however, uses the old name.

8. Between 1995 and 2010, a quarter million farmers have committed suicides in India owing to debt and distress (Sainath, 2011). And according to the nationwide survey of 51,770 farm households conducted in 2003, 40 per cent of the households indicated that provided the choice, they would take up some other profession, with 27 per cent out of the 40 per cent citing lack of profitability as the main reason for this decision (National Sample Survey, 2005).

9. This number excludes those who cited 'business' as the reason of migration.

10. This study was conceptualised in 2011 when another decadal population census was underway. Hence, much of the census data used in devising the methodology for this study pertains to the 2001 census. In any case, migration data are often released years after the census is conducted, and detailed migration tables from the 2011 census were released in 2019.

2

BRIDGING THE DISCONNECT BETWEEN MIGRATION AND FOOD SECURITY

INTRODUCTION

Migration, both internal and international, has become a key component of the livelihood strategies of an increasing number of households in developing countries. The flow of migrants' remittances has expanded significantly and is now a major contributor to the national income of several countries (World Bank, 2011a, 2019). This has promoted a spike in researchers' and policymakers' attention on the migration–development nexus. Importantly, unlike earlier periods when migration was often viewed as a problem with negative implications for development, there is now growing global consensus on its potential positive effects, including both financial as well as social benefits such as transfer of migrants' skills and knowledge. Leading international organisations have therefore lent unequivocal institutional backing to encourage migration in the past few years (Department of International Development [DFID], 2007; UNDP, 2009; World Bank, 2009; International Organization for Migration [IOM], 2013, 2020). Consequently, after having been sidelined in the Millennium Development Goals (MDGs), its successor, the Sustainable Development Goals (SDGs), acknowledge the positive contributions migrants make in their source and destination communities, and migration and mobility have been included in 4 of the 17 SDGs (IOM, 2015).

Concurrently, the significance of *food security for all* as an important development objective has been growing, particularly since the 2007–08 global food crisis. The spikes in global food prices since 2006 stalled the global progress on hunger reduction, and in 2009, for the first time in human history, the number of undernourished people crossed a billion people (FAO, 2009). While hunger prevalence has fallen from its billion-plus peak, recent estimates suggest that even a decade later, in 2019, a staggering 690 million people remained chronically underfed. Moreover, hunger has been on the rise since 2014, even before the Covid-19 pandemic intensified global food insecurity, adding an estimated 83–132 million additional people to the ranks of the undernourished. Additionally, nearly two billion people in the world experience moderate to severe food insecurity. A large majority of the world's hungry and food-insecure populations reside in the rural areas of the developing world (FAO et al., 2020). The sheer magnitude of hunger has warranted calls for effective action on hunger reduction. At the United Nations Conference on Sustainable Development in Rio de Janeiro in 2012, the then UN Secretary General, Ban Ki-moon, launched the 'Zero Hunger Challenge', calling the member countries to work for a future where no one in the world goes to bed hungry. This was later formally included in the SDG agenda adopted in September 2015, and SDG-2 envisages eliminating all forms of malnourishment from the face of the planet by 2030. Then, in April 2016, to encourage action on this goal, the United Nations General Assembly declared the next 10 years (2016–25) as the 'UN Decade of Action on Nutrition' (United Nations, 2012, 2015, 2016).

However, barring a few notable exceptions (Zezza et al., 2011; Crush, 2013; Craven and Gartuala, 2015; Crush and Caesar, 2017), discussions on these two issues have largely tended to proceed in separate silos, with little attention devoted to the relationship they bear with each other. This is despite the fact that linkages between migration and food security are rather obvious. As Crush (2013, p. 62) observed, there appears to exist 'a massive institutional and substantive disconnect between these two'. Leading global bodies working on these issues, such as the United Nations' FAO and the IOM, routinely treat these two issues as if they bear no mutual connections. In recent years, there appears to be some recognition of the importance of this relationship, and the FAO's *State of Food and Agriculture 2018* report highlights the linkages between migration and food security (FAO, 2018). But there still persists a huge disconnect, and by and large these two issues are discussed as independent of each other.

The aim of this chapter is to bridge this divide between migration and food security. It is important to address this issue, as the disconnect seems to arise, in large part, because of lack of clear understanding of conceptual linkages that migration and food security share. The chapter teases out the ways in which migration and food security intersect and develops a conceptual framework that links these two themes. To this end, it draws on Amartya Sen's 'entitlements' and Robert Chambers and Gordon Conway's 'sustainable livelihoods' approaches. It also lays out the possible pathways of linkages that exist between migration and food security, and these pathways then guide the empirical strategy this book follows. In other words, the conceptual framework developed here informs the analytical approach of the book. In elucidating these linkages, the discussion joins Crush (2013, p. 63) to call for the need to understand the 'reciprocal relationship between migration and food security'. However, unlike Crush whose focus is more on urbanisation and urban food security, this chapter conceptualises this relationship through the rural lens, and the conceptual framework presented here centres on understanding the role of internal labour migration as a livelihood strategy in influencing food security outcomes among rural households at the origin of migration.

The layout of this chapter is as follows: The next section dwells on the possible reasons for the disconnect between migration and food security in research and policy discussions. The chapter then spells out the key conceptual frameworks of 'entitlements' and 'livelihoods', which provide theoretical foundations to link migration and household food security. Following this, it provides an overview of different theoretical perspectives on migration and asserts the merit of livelihood approach to migration for understanding migration decisions and outcomes (food security in this context). The final section develops three pathways of linkages between migration and food security which have much significance in understanding the connections between the two more holistically. These three pathways take into account, in a scalar fashion, (*a*) wider institutional and policy environment, (*b*) inter-household comparisons of income, remittances and food security and (*c*) within-household dynamics of migration and food security. The three analytical chapters (Chapters 5, 6 and 7) are developed around these themes.

POSSIBLE REASONS FOR DISCONNECT BETWEEN MIGRATION AND FOOD SECURITY

The vast, albeit largely separate, literatures on migration and food security reveal four key possible reasons for the disconnect between the two.

First, discussions on the impacts of migration and remittances on poverty alleviation and economic development have tended to focus invariably more on international migration than internal migration. This bias towards international migration is further augmented in recent years by efforts at systematic compilation of data on international remittances by the World Bank, which show the continually rising flow of the international remittances to developing countries. International remittances to low- and middle-income countries increased from USD 55 billion in 1995 to USD 529 billion in 2018, and the current levels of remittances received by developing countries are more than three times as much as their receipts of official development assistance (World Bank, 2011a, 2019). The discussion on international migration and remittances tend to centre on larger issues of economic growth and financial development in developing countries (Giuliano and Ruiz-Arranz, 2009; Nyamongo et al., 2012; Olayungbo and Quadri, 2019), whereas basic issues, such as how remittances enable households to meet their food security needs, tend to be sidelined. Studies show international remittances play a crucial role in household food security. For instance, in El Salvador, de Brauw (2011) found that during the food-price shocks of 2007–08, young children in households with access to international remittances witnessed lower declines in their nutritional status as compared to children residing in households without international migrants. Similarly, a recent study based on a primary survey in two districts in south-eastern Bangladesh found international remittances increased households' food-consumption expenditure and reduced food-related anxieties and uncertainties (Moniruzzaman, 2020). Household food security outcomes are certainly influenced by international remittances. However, from the perspective of the migration–food-security relationship, internal migration is far more significant than international migration. Higher economic (and social) costs, and the increasingly selective immigration policies that favour financially and educationally endowed individuals, mean that international migration remains beyond the reach of a large majority of rural populations of the developing world. The number of people moving from one area to another within national boundaries is estimated at 763 million, which is far more than 281 million international migrants (United Nations Department of Economic and Social Affairs [UN-DESA], 2013, 2020). The sheer number of people moving within the national borders suggests that the poverty-reducing and development-enhancing potential of remittances from internal migration is more significant than international migration. Available evidence on the significance of domestic remittances suggests the same. For instance, a study by Castaldo, Deshingkar and McKay (2012) found that in India and Ghana, internal migrants and domestic remittances outnumbered international migrants and their total receipts, with potentially significant human development impacts. For India alone, in 2007–08, internal remittances amounted to USD 10 billion, and 30 per cent of all household expenditure was financed by these transfers among remittance-receiving households, estimated at 10 per cent of all rural households in India (Tumbe, 2011). But systematic research on the direct role of domestic remittances in influencing rural households' food security is scarce, and greater attention to international remittances has barred this enquiry.

Second, in migration research, there has recently been a tendency to treat migrants as separate entities at destinations (Hewage, Kumara and Rigg, 2011), which ignores the origin–destination linkages that migration creates. Indeed, in many countries of Asia and Africa, which account for much of the global burden of food and nutritional insecurity (FAO et al., 2020), migration is not always a one-time, permanent move – far from it. Circular mobility dominates migration patterns (Deshingkar and Farrington, 2009; Breman, 2010; Potts, 2010; Tumbe, 2018), with migrants making periodic visits to places of origin, maintaining close relations with family and sending home remittances that are crucial for the food security of members at their places of origin. Remittances do not always flow from migrants to origin households but are bi-directional. In Harare, Zimbabwe, for instance, the predominant flow of resources is now from rural households to their urban members, which helps the latter to cope with income shocks in uncertain urban labour markets (Tawodzera, 2010). Migration thus represents a joint household strategy, and the dispersion of members across different activities and locations helps households attain a diversified livelihood portfolio (Stark, 1991) and avoid risks to their income and food security. This means that conceptualisations of households need to move away from viewing them as homo-spatial units to viewing them as multi-local or locational ones (Deshingkar and Farrington, 2009; Schmidt-Kallert, 2009; Greiner, 2012).

Third, the studies that give attention to migration and food security are often guided by concerns around urbanisation. In 2008, for the first time in history, more than half of humanity lived in urban areas, and urban population growth is expected to rise further in the coming years (United Nations Population Fund [UNFPA], 2007). This seems to have reinforced what Lipton (1977) called 'urban bias'. Indeed, proclamations that we now live in an urban age abound in academic and policy discourses; and even critical scrutiny of this notion by leading urban theorists arguing that urban age represents a 'statistical artifact' (Brenner and Schmid, 2014, p. 740) propagates a view of greater, not lesser, urbanisation, occurring at a planetary scale (also see Brenner and Schmid, 2015). Moreover, as populations move from the countryside to towns in search of livelihoods, there is evidence of relocation of poverty and undernourishment from rural to urban areas, which has called for the need to provide urban populations with adequate food and nutrition (Ruel, Garrett and Haddad, 2000; Crush, 2013; International Food Policy Research Institute [IFPRI], 2017). Additionally, the increasing levels of urbanisation and peri-urbanisation and the growing land demands for commercial and residential purpose are placing heavy pressures on rural land, with analysts arguing for fresh thinking on the links between livelihoods and food security; urban agriculture has emerged as one of the important topics within this discourse (Losada et al., 1998; Mougeot, 2000; Lerner and Eakin, 2011; FAO, 2019). These are certainly important themes, and they need to be mainstreamed in future migration and food-policy agendas. The growing attention to urban aspects of migration–food-security linkages, however, has obscured the rural dimension of this relationship. The arguments around urban food security often narrowly focus on migrants in cities, whereas the fact remains that in many parts of the developing world, migration usually takes place within the context of a family, whereby rural members depend on urban migrants' remittances for their food security, as noted earlier. And rise in urban food insecurity in developing countries notwithstanding, hunger and undernourishment are still primarily concentrated in rural areas. Second, the discourse on urban agriculture implicitly assumes that the problem of food insecurity is caused by lack of food production. While food availability is certainly an important part of the equation, this *productivist* view ignores that the problem of food insecurity as it currently exists lies in unequal *access* to food.

The final reason is the land- and agriculture-focused notions of rural households at the level of food policy. This means that prescriptions to improve the rural poor's access to food have invariably tended to focus more on improving local, land-based livelihoods. The view that rural households comprise members who solely depend on farming, although fading, still remains widely prevalent in rural development thinking. By extension, the problem of rural food insecurity is often viewed as a problem of land and agriculture, and the solution therefore to strengthen food security of rural populace, it is held, lies in improving the gains of farm-dependent livelihoods. However, research across a range of countries suggests growing diversity of rural livelihoods, with non-farm, non-local, migration incomes becoming increasingly central to rural livelihoods in the past couple of decades (Bryceson, 1997, 2002; Ellis, 1998, 2000b; Barrett, Reardon and Webb, 2001; Reardon, Berdegué and Escobar, 2001; Foster and Rosenzweig, 2004; Shariff and Lanjouw, 2004; Rigg, 2006; Rigg, Salamanca and Parnwell, 2012; Pritchard et al., 2014; Cole and Rigg, 2019; Choithani, Van Duijne and Nijman, 2021).

Moreover, the evidence suggests that although agriculture plays an important role in reducing poverty and improving food security (by increasing farm productivity and incomes), it alone may be insufficient (FAO, 2013). Indeed, given the complementariness between rural–farm and urban–non-farm livelihoods, the extent to which farm incomes allow the rural households to meet their food and nutrition needs may itself be contingent upon the income from non-agricultural sources.

CONCEPTUALISING FOOD SECURITY THROUGH THE FRAMEWORKS OF 'ENTITLEMENTS' AND 'LIVELIHOODS'

The past few decades have witnessed a significant shift in the way the issue of food security has been conceptualised and problematised. Up until 1980, the global food security discourse predominantly stressed on the volume and stability of food supplies as the only measure to ensuring food security for all. This was largely due to the dominance of the Malthusian perspective in food security research. In his *Essay on the Principles of Population*, first published anonymously towards the end of the eighteen century, Malthus (1798) postulated that population growth always outpaces increases in food production (which he termed as 'means of subsistence'), and when this situation is left unchecked, this will potentially lead to acute food shortages. Thus,

> … the power of population is indefinitely greater than the power in the earth to produce subsistence for man. Population, when unchecked, increases in a geometrical ratio. Subsistence increases only in an arithmetical ratio. A slight acquaintance with numbers will shew the immensity of the first power in comparison of the second. (Malthus, 1798, p. 4)

Although research by Boserup (1965, 1981), based on extensive fieldwork in Africa and Asia, showed that high population growth rates can stimulate innovative agricultural practices through factors such as use of improved agro-technologies and transition from long-fallow to short-fallow periods, thereby boosting overall food production, this did not change global preoccupation with the issue of food availability. Malthusian concerns continued to be frequently echoed by international development agencies through the 1960s and 1970s. The food crisis of 1972–74 only served to accentuate these fears. In the aftermath of food crisis, the first-ever World Food Summit that took place in Rome in 1974 thus conceptualised the problem from the production-oriented perspective, reflected in the definition of food security adopted at the Summit. Food security was defined as the 'availability at all times of adequate world food supplies of basic foodstuffs to sustain a steady expansion of food consumption and to offset fluctuations in production and prices' (FAO, 2003b, p. 27).

The official policy thinking on food security, however, witnessed a paradigm shift, following the pioneering work by Amartya Sen in 1981 on the causes of starvation and famines. In a marked departure from the dominant, albeit reductionist, thinking based around food production, Sen argued that hunger and starvation are not always caused by food-supply shortages and that they may persist even in the wake of abundant food supplies. Sen (1981b, p. 1) reasoned:

> Starvation is a characteristic of some people not having enough food to eat. It is not a characteristic of there being not enough food to eat. While the latter can be a cause of the former, it is but one of many possible causes. Whether and how starvation relates to food supply is a matter of factual investigation.

The crux of his argument was that the availability of food does not necessarily translate to adequate access of food for all individuals, and one's ability to command food is contingent upon his or her position within societal and economic structures. He contended that the ways in which people are connected with society, patterns of ownership, modes of production, and formal and informal institutional and legal structures determine their ability to gain access to food. He expressed these relationships in a wider framework of entitlements which 'refers to the set of alternative commodity bundles that a person can command in a society using the totality of rights and opportunities that he or she faces' (Sen, 1983, p. 754). He argued that the patterns of ownership of goods and assets form a chain relationship of legitimacy, with possession of a particular asset or good linked with, and legitimising, one's authority over another (Sen, 1981b, pp. 1–2).

Applied to the analysis of hunger and starvation, it is this chain of relations that determines one's entitlements to food. In order to simplify, Sen (1981b, p. 2) listed these entitlements as mainly including (*a*) trade entitlement, (*b*) production-based entitlement, (*c*) own-labour entitlement and (*d*) inheritance and transfer entitlement. The ownership and possession of assets, or endowments (for example, land, labour power and financial resources), determine how these entitlement relations are structured. And it is the interactions of these entitlements, which he termed as 'exchange entitlement' (Sen 1981b, p. 3), that determine one's ability to command food and avoid hunger. In other words, the combination of endowments and exchange possibilities together determine a person's overall entitlement (Sen, 1983, p. 754). Hence, given a fixed ownership bundle, a person's exchange entitlement is influenced by several factors. For example, for a wage labourer with no land, his ability to command food depends on 'whether or not he can find employment, and if so for how long and at what wage rate' (Sen, 1981b, pp. 3–4). If he is unable to sell his labour power for the time, and at the wage rate needed to buy adequate quantities of food (as often happens in distress situations), he may suffer from food insecurity and hunger, even though the actual food supplies may be steady.

Put simply, Sen's work warranted attention to the fact that entitlement failures – and not food availability, although important – causes hunger. This follows that people may be subjected to hunger and starvation even during normal times. Indeed, he theorised the entitlement framework based on empirical case studies of four major famines in Bengal (in pre-partition India), Ethiopia, Sahel and Bangladesh. The empirics revealed that factors leading to widespread famine conditions in these countries extended beyond the lack of food availability and represented entitlement failures, particularly among the vulnerable sub-populations who were least able to acquire food through any means and were hence hit the hardest. In fact, Sen described the Great Bengal Famine of 1943 as a 'boom famine' (Sen, 1977, 1981a, 1981b).

At a more immediate level, the empirical merit for viewing food insecurity through the prism of entitlement relations was provided by the concurrent evaluations of the Green Revolution. The widespread diffusion of the GR since the late 1960s had boosted global food production levels. Yet its gains were unevenly distributed among different population segments across landholding and income categories (Lipton and Longhurst, 1989), which, in Sen's nomenclature, varyingly affected their exchange entitlements. A key policy prescription emanating from Sen's approach thus involved expanding people's entitlements, particularly for the economically disadvantaged populations who had greater vulnerability to, and indeed faced on a routine basis, entitlement failures (Sen, 1983, pp. 755–60; also see Drèze and Sen, 1989).

Founded on the principles of social and economic justice, Sen's subsequent writings extended the entitlement analysis in his now widely known *capability approach* (inter alia, Sen, 1984a, 1984b, 1985, 1993, 1999, 2009). This approach provided a framework for understanding how the entitlements translated into enhancing the capabilities of people. With reference to the example of own-labour entitlement mentioned earlier, this meant, for instance, whether or not the (quality of) employment (regularity, wages, working conditions, and so on) that the person is engaged in allows for his or her capability to avoid hunger and to be well-nourished. The wider significance of the capability approach was that it distinguished between the means (economic growth and prosperity) and ends (welfare of people) of development, and placed people at the centre of the development. Contrary to the conventional approaches, Sen (1999, p. 3) contended that development must ultimately be viewed 'as a process of expanding the real freedoms that people enjoy', and 'it requires removal of major source of unfreedoms: poverty as well as tyranny, poor economic opportunities as well as systematic social deprivation'. Without dwelling much on the specificities of the capability approach here (for which you may refer to Sen's original writings cited earlier; also see Alkire, 2002; Robeyns, 2005; Nussbaum, 2011), it is important to note that Sen's line of analysis placed the rights and entitlements of people at the core of the development discourse and redirected the development policy and practice. This shift in thinking is reflected in the adoption of the wider concept of *human development*, promoted and advanced by the UNDP in its annual *Human Development Reports* since 1990. The UNDP defined development as a process of 'enlarging people's choices' (UNDP, 1990, p. 1).

At the level of food policy research and practice, Sen's line of analysis led to a reappraisal of the concept of food security. In 1983, FAO, in its report entitled *World Food Security: A Reappraisal of the Concepts and Approaches*, expanded its earlier definition of food security as 'ensuring that all people at all times have both physical and economic access to the basic food that they need' (FAO, 1983, cited in FAO, 2006, p. 1). Then, in 1986, the World Bank's report titled *Poverty and Hunger*, which was highly influenced by Sen's work, categorised food insecurity in 'chronic' and 'transitory' terms and acknowledged that food insecurity (primarily) resulted from the lack of access to food. Thus, the report defined food security as 'access by all people at all times to enough food for an active, healthy life' (World Bank, 1986, p. 1). The report explicitly mentioned that the essential elements of food security are availability of food and the ability to acquire it. The discourse thus shifted from the mere availability of food supply at the national and international levels to access to food.

Accompanying this shift was the focus on the importance of food security at the individual and household levels. As more research evidence has become available on what causes food insecurity, and its wider relationship with individual health and well-being, there have been more reappraisals of the concept over subsequent years. In particular, persistently high levels of undernourishment have also led to a widespread recognition that meeting calorific needs does not necessarily result in the adequate nutrition required for leading a healthy life. The concept of food security thus widened into a more expansive notion of nutritional security. The nutritional status of individuals, however, is also contingent upon several public health parameters, including safe drinking water, access to healthcare and environmental hygiene. Also, dietary preferences are based on social and cultural norms about food. For instance, consumption of meat in many societies and cultures is common, whereas many Hindu Brahmins in India do not generally eat meat due to religious reasons. Thus, food security is a complex and dynamic concept and has widely diverse interpretations and framings. Nonetheless, the most acceptable and comprehensive definition of food security, first adopted in the World Food Summit in 1996, puts it as

> … a situation that exists when all people, at all times, have physical, social and economic access to sufficient, safe and nutritious food that meets their dietary needs and food preferences for an active and healthy life. (FAO, 2010, p. 8)

This definition highlights that the four key components of food security involve (*a*) adequate availability of food, (*b*) physical and economic access to socially and culturally acceptable food, (*c*) effective utilisation of food in the body for it to perform normal bodily functions and (*d*) stability of food supplies in the long run (the latter assumes greater relevance in the context of climatic shocks to agricultural production). The continued relevance of this 1996 definition is because of its all-encompassing and people-centric character. The focus is not just on food production or consumption but on its nutritive value, and how it, in turn, connects to human health and well-being. It is because of these food–nutrition–health linkages that the concept of food security has been broadened to *food and nutrition security* in the recent food-and-development policy lexicon (Pritchard, 2016).

Using the notion of entitlements, the focus of this study is on the *accessibility* aspect of food security, for despite the fact that the world produces enough food to meet the food and nutritional needs of everyone, inadequate access to food remains stubbornly high. As noted at the beginning of this chapter, there are nearly 700 million people globally whose dietary energy consumption levels fall below the threshold required for normal bodily functions. This number does not include populations afflicted by essential micro-nutrient deficiencies and those suffering from moderate and severe food insecurity, which amount to about two billion people each (Box 2.1).

The second key conceptual framework employed in this book is the broadly defined SLA. Complementing the notion of entitlements, the SLA provides a useful framework to assess the different livelihood strategies devised by people that either enable or restrict them to meet their livelihood goals and aspirations. From the specific perspective of themes germane to this book, the question of how different livelihood strategies pursued by rural households impact their food security outcomes is an important one.

The concept of SLA officially emerged in rural development thinking in the early 1990s. It was formally laid out by Robert Chambers and Gordon Conway in a discussion paper in 1991. Their working definition specified:

> A livelihood comprises the capabilities, assets (stores, resources, claims and access) and activities required for a means of living: a livelihood is sustainable which can cope with and recover from stress and shocks, maintain or enhance its capabilities and assets, and provide sustainable livelihood opportunities for the next generation; and which contributes net benefits to other livelihoods at the local and global levels and in the short and long term. (Chambers and Conway, 1991, p. 6)

Influenced in many ways by, and building on, Sen's notions of entitlements and capabilities, the SLA sought to place the notions of 'capability', 'equity'

Box 2.1   Indicators to measure food insecurity

The multi-dimensional nature of the concept of food security means that different concepts and criteria exist in terms of how food and nutritional security outcomes are assessed. These indicators could be clustered in three broad categories.

A. Anthropometric indicators

Food and nutritional insecurity signifies intake deficiencies in essential calorie, protein and micronutrients, and/or inadequate absorption of food consumed, resulting in weak physical and health status. Food and nutritional needs are contingent on a person's age, weight, height and physical-activity levels. Additionally, environmental and health factors, such as prevalence of infection and disease, are important determinants of food-energy needs, as they affect the conversion efficiency of food in the body. For instance, an individual suffering from diarrhea will likely excrete the food consumed more rapidly than those without this condition. And if the energy lost to diarrhea is not replaced, this would negatively affect his or her nutritional status. Food and nutritional deficiencies are manifested in poor physical-growth outcomes, the degree of which depends on the extent of deficiencies. These outcomes are measured through different anthropometric indicators, which commonly include stunting (short height in relation to age), wasting (weakening of the body or a part of the body) and underweight (low weight in relation to age) for children, and the body mass index (BMI) for adults (World Health Organization [WHO], 2010).

B. Dietary energy-based indicator

Based on a person's age, gender, BMI and activity level, the FAO calculates the minimum dietary energy requirements (MDERs). And using national-level data on food availability and consumption, it provides cross-country estimate of the proportion of people whose energy intake is lower than their MDER threshold, expressed in terms of the outcome indicator of 'prevalence of undernourishment' (PoU) (FAO et al., 2020, pp. 190–91).

However, PoU only measures the energy deficiencies (of macronutrients), whereas nutritional outcomes are also crucially influenced by the consumption of essential micronutrients (dietary substances that the body needs in small

(Contd)

(Contd)

amounts to produce several enzymes and hormones for physical and cognitive growth and development). It is estimated that 40 per cent of women of reproductive age and 40 per cent of children under the age of five years, mainly in the developing world, suffer from iron deficiency and are anemic (WHO, 2021). Seen this way, the PoU measure of the FAO underestimates the actual magnitude of undernourishment in the world. At the same time, the sheer number of people unable to meet their basic food-energy needs remains staggering.

C. Food insecurity experience indicator

In 2019, the FAO included 'prevalence of moderate or severe food insecurity' (FImod+sev) as another indicator in its annual *The State of Food Security and Nutrition in the World* report. Along with PoU, the FImod+sev indicator is part of the Sustainable Development Goals (SDG) target 2.1, endorsed and adopted by the United Nations General Assembly in July 2017. This indicator is derived from the Food Insecurity Experience Scale (FIES). The FIES includes eight questions on self-reported food behaviours through which it captures incidences of food insecurity among individuals or households due to a lack of resources. The aim is to understand people's experiences with difficulties associated with accessing adequate, safe and nutritious food. According to this indicator, during 2017–19, there were 1.95 billion people who suffered from moderate to severe levels of food insecurity.

An earlier incarnation of this indicator was 'prevalence of severe food insecurity' that first appeared in the 2017 edition of *The State of Food Security and Nutrition in the World* report and continued in the 2018, 2019 and 2020 annual reports. While severe food insecurity is closely associated with hunger, moderate food insecurity signifies uncertainties that individuals and households face about their ability to access food and people being forced to compromise on the quantity and quality of their diets (FAO et al., 2017, 2018, 2019, 2020).

and 'sustainability' as the core principles of rural development practice (Chambers and Conway, 1991, pp. 3–4). In a marked departure from the earlier economic-centric approaches that revolved around 'production thinking', 'employment thinking' and 'poverty-line thinking' (Chambers and Conway, 1991, pp. 2–3), the SLA argued for understanding the complex rural realities from the perspective of those involved. In terms of research practice, the SLA challenged the dominant paradigm of 'rural development tourism' (the tendency of development researchers and policymakers to understand problems and causes of rural poverty and deprivation through brief visits to problem areas and through filling pre-structured quantitative questionnaires [Chambers, 1983, pp. 10–12]), and stressed that insights on rural problems could (only) be gained by understanding the life and livelihood realities of the rural poor. It stressed, in particular, the need for grounded research approaches in order to understand the dense social, cultural and institutional contexts within which peoples' lives and livelihoods were situated.

Within a few years, it was adopted as a key framework by leading international development agencies (Solesbury, 2003, p. 6). The wider backdrop for its quick adoption was provided by the disappointing results of the *top–down* approach to rural development practice that held sway in the 1970s and 1980s. The idea that dominated rural development thinking at that time was that virtues of a market-based economy were powerful enough to cure all the ills, and thus the prescriptions to tackling rural poverty inevitably involved achieving faster economic growth. By the early 1980s, the shortcomings of this *trickle-down* logic of the market-driven policies became increasingly apparent. As Sen (1983, p. 754) suggested: 'Not merely is it the case that economic growth is a means rather than an end, it is also the case that for some important ends it is not a very efficient means either.' The extremes of poverty, hunger and deprivation persisted at unacceptable levels in too many rural regions.[1] Indeed, the field of economics, which ruled the roost, began to be increasingly seen as narrow and insufficient to provide an explanation to rural poverty and deprivation. In its annual report in 1979, Sage Foundation, the leading publisher and supporter of social science research, lamented: '… The discipline [of economics] became progressively more narrow at precisely the moment when the problem demanded broader, more political, and social insights' (cited in Hirschman, 1981, p. v). It was in this context that the growth-centered mode of thinking and doing development began to be challenged beginning from the early 1980s. Important changes occurred in the field of economic theory, and development economics in particular, with Sen, among others, leading the charge.[2]

The SLA's stress on grounded approaches to understand the contextual and institutional correlates of the problems of rural poverty and underdevelopment meant that although the approach was flexible, the emanating framework of doing rural livelihood analysis rested on a four-fold strategy. This included (*a*) charting the socio-economic and institutional context and policy setting, (*b*) assessing the resource endowments of people or livelihood assets or capitals (human, natural, social, physical and financial) that shape their livelihood space and possibilities, (*c*) analyzing how the livelihood space as shaped by the (five) capitals or assets translated into different livelihood strategies (farm–non-farm, local–extra-local) and, finally, (*d*) evaluating the impact of the livelihood strategies on the livelihood goals and aspirations in well-being outcomes, such as income, food security, health and education (Scoones, 1998, pp. 3–5; Pritchard et al., 2014, pp. 9–10). A crucial aspect of the SLA was that it sought to emphasise the importance of non-economic attributes of livelihoods, such as social relations (caste, kinship, gender) and institutions, in mediating people's access to livelihood assets and strategies that were missing in the earlier economic-centric livelihood analysis. The idea of social capital exemplifies this, and it is a concept that is crucial to the two central themes of migration and food security this book pursues. Migration requires not just financial resources; individual and household actors often rely on their caste and community networks to make migration decisions. For the resource-poor households, social networks can provide the capital to finance the initial costs of migration. Contrarily, individuals and households disadvantageously positioned in social relations (for example, members of lower castes) can have their migration chances curtailed by a lack of social capital. Similarly, social ties can enable or constrain one's ability to access food. Indeed, as will be discussed in the later chapters, a household's social position is a crucial determinant of well-being outcomes.

From the perspective of the discussion in this book, a particular significance of the SLA approach was increased recognition of diversity of rural livelihood strategies. The DFID's sustainable livelihoods glossary defined 'livelihood strategies' as

> … the range and combination of activities and choices that people make in order to achieve their livelihood goals. Livelihood strategies include: how people combine their income generating activities; the way in which they use their assets; which assets they chose to invest in; and how they manage to preserve existing assets and income. Livelihoods are diverse at every level, for example, members of a household may live and work in different places engaging in various activities, either temporarily or permanently. Individuals themselves may rely on a range of different income-generating activities at the same time. (DFID, 2001, p. 5)

While the diversity of rural livelihood and income streams is not a novel phenomenon, the explicit recognition of livelihood diversity in the SLA was crucial in reorienting rural development thinking and research. This was because up until the early 1990s, rural development policies tended to treat rural households as homogeneous units, focusing exclusively on farm-related activities for their income and livelihoods (this view, as noted earlier, has not completely disappeared from rural development thinking). This inevitably meant that the solutions offered to reduce rural poverty revolved around land and agriculture through measures such as facilitating land access, improving farm productivity and output through irrigation and improved seeds, providing farm credit, and so on. Significant as these measures may be, livelihoods based on land and farming represent one of the many avenues for income generation. Crucially, moreover, for the land- and asset-poor households (main focus of development interventions), diversification of livelihoods provides a means to cope with seasonality and income shocks, and/or improve their well-being. As Ellis (2000a, p. 299) suggests: 'Diverse livelihood systems are less vulnerable than undiversified ones.' The participatory nature of the SLA meant that it stressed on involving the actors (rural populations) in setting and addressing their own livelihood priorities instead of imposing livelihood choices upon them.

The SLA categorises livelihood strategies pursued by rural households in three important clusters. These include (*a*) agricultural intensification and extensification, (*b*) livelihood diversification and (*c*) migration. Thus,

> ... either you gain more of your livelihood from agriculture (including livestock rearing, aquaculture, forestry etc.) through processes of intensification (more output per unit area through capital investment or increases in labour inputs) or extensification (more land under cultivation), or you diversify to a range of off-farm income earning activities, or you move away and seek a livelihood, either temporarily or permanently, elsewhere. Or, more commonly, you pursue a combination of strategies together or in sequence. (Scoones, 1998, p. 11)

Though distinct as they may sound, these livelihood strategies are not mutually exclusive, and in fact they are highly interrelated. Many rural households combine the elements of all three strategies to attain an optimal balance of income that helps meet their livelihood outcomes. Also, not only does there exist significant overlaps between these livelihood strategies, but their highly complementary nature also means that gains derived from one activity could be utilised to maximise returns from the other(s). For instance, agricultural intensification in the form of on-farm diversification, with households growing cash crops instead of, or in addition to, subsistence agriculture could also fall under the broad domain of livelihood diversification, as the latter includes income from both on-farm and non-farm sources. Also, local non-farm and migration incomes could boost investment capabilities of households for agricultural intensification. Indeed, this book argues that appreciating this complementariness of different livelihood strategies provides a crucial foundation for a holistic understanding of the food security outcomes of rural households.

That said, this book focuses, in particular, on the role of migration as a livelihood strategy in influencing food access among rural households. This is because migration forms an important component of livelihood strategies of a large majority of resource-poor rural households in developing countries. Entitlement and SLA frameworks hold that livelihood strategies and outcomes are shaped by endowment or assets at a person's disposal. This means that for landless and land-poor households, entitlement and access to food crucially depends on their ability to find wage income. As Sen (1983, p. 755) suggests: 'For most of humanity, about the only commodity a person has to sell is labour power, so that the person's [food] entitlements depend crucially on his or her ability to find a job, the wage rate for that job.' However, as noted in Chapter 1, the imperfect nature of rural labour markets compels a large majority of these rural households to seek alternative employment in distant places. Migration, however, is not always a response to distress or lack of employment; it may represent a calculated strategy of rural households to allocate household labour more efficiently in order to attain a diversified livelihood portfolio and reduce income risks (Stark, 1991; Bigsten, 1996). More recent evidence points to a growing importance of migration in the lives and livelihoods of rural poor households across a range of developing countries due to a complex set of distress-push and income-pull factors (Deshingkar and Farrington, 2009; UNDP, 2009; Rigg, Salamanca and Parnwell, 2012; Choithani, Van Duijne and Nijman, 2021). In turn, this implies that migration is also becoming increasingly crucial for rural income and food security. However, as the discussion later in this chapter will reveal, although a range of studies across different countries and contextual settings have highlighted the role of migration in rural livelihood security, research on whether and how migration helps rural households to attain food security remains scanty.

The following section discusses the different theoretical perspectives on migration. A close scrutiny suggests that migration has been often perceived as problematic by academics and policymakers and rarely is its importance acknowledged from the perspective of rural livelihoods.

MOVING BEYOND THE BINARIES: A LIVELIHOOD APPROACH TO MIGRATION

There is no dearth of literature on migration. Broadly, migration refers to change in the usual place of residence on a permanent or semi-permanent basis from one geographically or administratively defined boundary to another. Migration can be a response to several push and pull factors relating to social, economic, environmental, political and cultural conditions, and it can take several forms – from international to internal migration, from voluntary to forced migration, from permanent to temporary migration, and so on.

Given this multitude of types, motives and reasons, it is no surprise that perspectives on migration abound. This book focuses on domestic labour outmigration among rural households, which characteristically takes the form of seasonal and circular mobility in which one or more household members, usually young men, migrate out of their origin villages for a part of the year. And although this also involves migration from one rural area to another, more recent streams of migration involve heighted importance of rural-to-urban migration in households' livelihoods across the developing world, in part because returns from migration to urban areas have increased (Selod and Shilpi, 2021). The centrality of economic motives in rural households' migration decisions notwithstanding, migration is a complex phenomenon, and thus requires attention to the various social, cultural and institutional factors that drive both mobility and shape migration outcomes.

The dominant economic explanations of rural outmigration have often tended to take a single-sided view of what drives migratory decisions. On the one hand, the neo-classical economic models have tended to emphasise the rationality of individual actors. The much-cited dual economy model of wage differentials held that labour migration from rural to urban areas is a response to expected rural–urban wage differentials, with individual migrants responding rationally to higher urban wages (Todaro, 1969; Harris and Todaro, 1970). On the other hand, scholars rooted in structuralist and Marxist strands of thought have tended to view migration with respect to a wider set of political–economic arrangements and modes of production. They argue that far from being a rational response to better wages, migration at best is the survival strategy forced upon the rural poor by the capitalist forces and structures which does not improve their lot in the long run (Breman, 1985, 1996, 2010).

This binary of choice versus compulsion is alternatively expressed in literature in terms of structure–agency and push–pull approaches, the latter most notably in geography following Ravenstein's (1885, 1889) laws of migration. In rural economies, the common push factors of migration include poverty, population pressures on land, the seasonal nature of agricultural income, and environment vagaries such as drought and floods resulting in crop failures. On the other hand, the pull of migration often comprises factors such as better income and employment opportunities in destinations, reduced barriers on mobility (as in the case of the relaxing of the *hukou* system in China that earlier controlled rural–urban migration) and the latest advancements in infrastructure and communication networks. However, there is a very narrow line between these push and pull factors, making a clear demarcation between them virtually impossible. For instance, labour migration from rural to urban areas may be a response to both crop failure at origin and better income opportunities at destination. Indeed, the field research reported in this book suggests the coexistence of these factors (see Chapter 6). Moreover, the rural–urban dichotomy has become obsolete with the increasing expansion of peri-urban regions worldwide which 'encompass a fragmented mixing of rural and urban worlds' (Lerner and Eakin, 2011, p. 311). In turn, this has led to a narrowing of the gap between push and pull factors even further.

Another key theoretical framework in migration research includes the New Economics of Labour Migration (NELM). Influentially propounded and advanced by Oded Stark (1978, 1981, 1983, 1991), the NELM is rooted principally in neo-classical economics. Thus, it views migration decisions as being driven by imperfect rural financial, labour and credit markets, information asymmetries and participants' desires to maximise incomes in the wake of these conditions and constraints. Nonetheless, a useful starting point of the NELM is the recognition that 'there is more to labour migration than a response to wage differentials. Thus migration in the absence of (meaningful) wage differentials, or the absence of migration in the presence of significant wage differentials, does not imply irrationality' (Stark, 1991, p. 3). Of particular relevance to the subject matter of this book is that, unlike the earlier individual-centric economistic approaches to migration (for example, Todaro, 1969; Harris and Todaro, 1970), the NELM places the household at the heart of analysis. It views migration as a combined household strategy aimed at risk aversion and livelihood portfolio diversification. Stark (1991, p. 3) suggests that

> … even though the entities that engage in migration are often individual agents, there is more to labour migration than an individualistic optimizing behavior. Migration by one person can be due to, fully consistent with, or undertaken in pursuit of rational optimizing behavior by another person or by a group of persons, such as family.

Stark (1991, p. 5) continues:

> The family can be considered as a "coalition", a group of players committed by choice to act as one unit vis-à-vis the rest of the world and migration by family members can be interpreted as a manifestation of the viability of the family.

According to the NELM, the geographic dispersion of family members in different income activities provides one of the ways through which smallholder households in rural areas attain a diverse portfolio of livelihoods that enable them to minimise income risks from a single source and maximise insurance against shocks. Thus, Stark (1991, p. 25) notes:

> Migrants and their families enter into an inter-temporal contractual arrangement, in which the costs and returns are shared by all family members with the rule governing the distribution of both spelled out in this implicit contractual arrangement.

The household bears the initial costs of migration in the expectation of remittances, and on their part, migrants, in turn, continue to maintain close association with the households with the expectation of returns, such as inheritance of land or property at the origin. The end result is that of 'both parties being better-off as a result of migration since, in this case, an exchange of commitment to share income provides co-insurance' (Stark, 1991, p. 26).

The NELM provides an important lens to understand the economics of migration more holistically, and this book makes use of the theoretical foundations of this approach. At the same time, an obvious limitation of the NELM is that it does not necessarily address the social, cultural and institutional factors that drive both migratory decisions and, in turn, get shaped by it. In arguing that migration represents more than just a response to income differentials, it falls short of addressing the non-economic aspects of migration. For example, how do households decide on who migrates out and who stays put? Do male and female members of the households have the same chance to be chosen as migrants? These are particularly pertinent questions. As the discussion later will reveal, in many developing countries, a common pattern of rural labour migration involves male outflows while women stay behind. In turn, this pattern of migration restructures household gender relations, which carry implications for food security (see Chapter 7).

Indeed, none of the approaches described thus far elucidates the dynamics of migration from the perspective of rural livelihoods. As Mosse et al. (2002, pp. 60–61) suggest: 'A perspective on migration is needed which goes beyond dichotomous models of push or pull, structure or agency, urban or rural, and allows labour migration to be seen as part of local and diverse livelihood strategies.' It is for this reason that this study uses livelihood approach to migration (see Table 2.1 for a summary of key theoretical approaches to migration).

The advantage of the livelihood approach is that, while weaving together the threads of different perspectives, it also stresses on the institutional processes and vulnerability contexts within which migration occurs. It draws from the NELM in terms of placing the household as the prime unit of analysis. Livelihood perspectives to migration state that migration has traditionally formed an integral part of rural livelihood strategies and is not necessarily a response to shocks. Furthermore, alongside economic motives, it also views migration as a social process structured by the institutional and contextual factors such as gender, caste, class, social networks and relations, which, in turn, affects these social structures (Mcdowell and de Haan, 1997; de Haan, 1999; de Haan, Brock and Coulibaly, 2002; Mosse et al., 2002).

Table 2.1 Different theoretical perspectives on migration: a summary

Perspective	Policy prescription
Dual economy model: Developed around the 1970s to highlight the contradiction of high rural to urban migration in less developed countries in spite of positive agriculture marginal products and high urban unemployment, this model recognised 'the existence of a politically determined minimum urban wage at levels substantially higher than agriculture earning' (Harris and Todaro, 1970, p. 126) as the reason for rural–urban mobility. According to the model, migration thus represents a response to not real but *expected* rural–urban wage differentials.	This model views that the impact of higher urban wages is offset by a slower growth of urban employment which exacerbates the problem of unemployment in the cities, with larger consequences for the social and political order of the less developed nations. The emanating policy prescription thus was to control migration by making rural areas attractive to stay and work.
Marxist perspective: According to the Marxist perspective, transition from a 'rural-agrarian to urban-industrial mode of life and work' (Breman, 2010, p. 1) is a result of capitalist forces pushing people out of agriculture. Marxist scholars contend that migration is not a rational response to wage differentials but a survival strategy. It is forced upon the labouring poor to serve the interests of the capital, with little to no benefits and/or prospects for their upward mobility.	This line of argument sheds important insights on the deplorable work and living conditions of the unskilled rural out-migrants in the developing world. Although it calls for policy attention on addressing the structural causes of their deprivation, such as regulations related to minimum wages and working hours, it remains highly sceptical about policy action because of the *lack* of agency of the poor migrants and, in the process, evokes a cautionary note on the gains of migration.
New Economics of Labour Migration (NELM): The distinguishing feature of the NELM is that it places the household at the centre of migration analysis, as opposed to earlier individual-centric economic approaches. According to this model, migration represents a combined household strategy aimed at livelihood portfolio diversification and risk aversion (Stark, 1991).	Unlike the earlier economistic approaches, the NELM views migration as a positive process which allows households to allocate its labour across activities and locations. This act of livelihood diversification by means of sending members to other places provides an insurance against income shocks from local sources. It argues that the overall aim of the policy should be to encourage migration.

(Contd)

Table 2.1   (Contd)

Perspective	Policy prescription
Livelihood approach: The livelihood approach to migration stresses on understanding the importance of social, economic, political and cultural contexts within which migration occurs. While acknowledging the importance of, and weaving the threads from, dichotomous migration perspectives such as push–pull and structure–agency, it argues for moving beyond these binaries to be able to objectively analyse varied migration outcomes across contexts (Mcdowell and de Haan, 1997; Mosse et al., 2002).	The livelihood perspective recognises the traditional importance of migration in the lives and livelihoods of the rural dwellers. It argues that there is nothing novel about rural outmigration, and it has been a central feature of rural livelihood strategies since time immemorial, which has allowed rural populations to meet their income and food needs during the agriculturally lean cycles. The overall policy message is to facilitate migration.

ROLE OF MIGRATION IN RURAL LIVELIHOODS: POSSIBLE PATHWAYS OF LINKAGES BETWEEN MIGRATION AND FOOD SECURITY

In many countries of Asia and Africa, migration has been an integral part of livelihood strategies of the rural poor. Rural livelihoods in Indonesia involve a frequent engagement of farm families in urban labour markets (Elmhirst, 2002). In India, regions comprising 20 per cent of the country's population have witnessed persistent remittance-based migrations for over 100 years (Tumbe, 2012, 2018), and in some parts of India, three out of four households include a migrant (Srivastava and Sasikumar, 2003, p. 1). In a study of two villages in Mali, de Haan, Brock and Coulibaly (2002) noted contrasting patterns of migration, with migration in both villages nonetheless being a central feature not only of their local economies but also of social relations. While migration has traditionally formed a key component of rural livelihood systems, in recent years mobility levels among rural populations have increased significantly (Deshingkar and Grimm, 2005; Rigg 2006; UNDP, 2009; Choithani, Van Duijne and Nijman, 2021).

Given the centrality of migration in rural livelihoods, it is not surprising that the relationship between migration and rural development has been of long-standing interest to academic and policy-making communities. However, in the wake of rising rural outmigration levels, the question of the potential role of migration in enhancing the rural income and livelihood security and promoting rural development assumes greater significance. That said, this relationship is very complicated. Thus, while research findings of some studies suggest that the selective nature of rural outmigration, often involving young and able-bodied workers, deprives the rural economies of the already scarce productive human resources (Lipton, 1980), others find that migration helps households to efficiently allocate their labour among activities so as to maximise welfare (Bigsten, 1996). Also, while absence of quality educational facilities in rural areas of many developing countries often motivates families to migrate to urban centres to seek good education for their children (UNDP, 2009, p. 57), which potentially improves household earning prospects, household migration by the poor can also deprive the children of their basic education.[3]

For long, sceptical views that rural migration to urban towns and cities would create stress on urban resources, push urban wages down leading to conflict between native and migrant communities, saturate urban labour markets, and raise unemployment rates, and so on, dominated the discourses on migration. In the academic literature, rural outmigration has often been portrayed as problematic. For instance, the dual economy model of rural–urban wage differentials, cited earlier, while acknowledging the agency of individual migrants, argued against rural-to-urban migration. The main policy prescription thus included:

> ... instead of allocating scarce capital funds to urban low cost housing projects which would effectively raise urban real incomes and might therefore lead to a worsening of the housing problem, governments in less developed countries might do better if they devoted these funds to the improvement of rural amenities. In effect, the net benefit of bringing 'city lights' to the countryside might greatly exceed whatever net benefit might be derived from luring more peasants to the city by increasing the attractiveness of urban living conditions. (Todaro, 1969, p. 147)

On the other hand, the dominant view among structuralists has tended to be that rural outmigration is largely a response to distressing conditions at home, with little or no prospects for the upward economic mobility of the migrants and their households (Breman, 2010, pp. 10–11).

Not surprisingly, development policies in many countries have often tended to control the flow of rural–urban migrants (de Haan, 1999). However, given the precarious nature of rural economies in many low-income countries, an important question which is often not asked is 'what these individuals or households would have done in the absence of the opportunity to migrate' (Deshingkar and Grimm, 2005, p. 40). As Stark (1991, p. 19) suggests: 'Good policies should employ effective means to minimize or eliminate the few (if any) undesirable consequences, but not eliminate migration itself.'

These considerations have been crucial in reorienting the global development policy thinking on migration in recent years. For instance, the *World Development Report 2009* noted: 'The policy challenge is not how to keep households from moving, but how to keep them from moving for the wrong reasons' (World Bank, 2009, p. 147). Moreover, there is compelling evidence that despite the distress-induced nature of migration, not only can it provide a safety valve for poor populations, but it can also contribute to sustainable human development for both origin and destination communities. And international policy-making bodies have increasingly argued that migration has several positive attributes and that the gains of migration far outweigh the losses, albeit varying by the skills, resources and social networks of the migrants (DFID, 2007; UNDP, 2009; World Bank, 2009; IOM, 2020). Empirical evidence across a range of countries highlights the positive impacts of migration on household welfare – income, health status, educational attainments, female autonomy, and so on (see the *Human Development Report 2009* for an extensive review of literature).

However, while various impacts of migration have been extensively researched and documented, very little attention has been paid to the relationship between migration and food security, and the *direct* evidence on the impact of migration on household food security is scarce.[4] This disregard for the relationship between food security and migration is surprising because the connections between the two are rather obvious. Nonetheless, the available evidence provides several possible pathways of interactions between migration and food security, and it points to a two-way relationship between these two phenomena. Thus, while risks to food security and local food entitlement failures (for example, poverty, lack of decent employment and wages, and absence of social protection) often drive household migration decisions, the act of migration can, in turn, lead to improved household ability to access food. In many developing countries, a common pattern of rural outmigration involves circular moves, usually undertaken by the male members of the household, as noted earlier. This means that through factors such as remittances and changes in gender roles, migration has the potential to influence household food security. As noted before, the focus of this work is on the rural end of the household. The following discussion identifies three direct pathways of the linkages between migration and food security which have immediate significance, and the three analytical chapters presented in this book (Chapters 5, 6 and 7), based on the field evidence from the case-study site (Siwan, Bihar), also develop around these themes.

ENTITLEMENT AND INSTITUTIONAL FAILURES AND MIGRATION AS A FOOD SECURITY STRATEGY

Rural households that face risks to their food security often plan strategically to minimise negative impacts of food shocks and employ migration of one of more members as one of the crucial strategies to prevent food entitlement failures. For instance, studies of household strategies during famines in Africa show that labour migration is one of the key coping mechanisms that households adopt to deal with food shortages (Corbett, 1988). Famines represent an extreme of distress and are caused by, and also cause, a collapse of wider set of institutions. Although large-scale famines have been largely eradicated in most countries (Devereux, 2009; de Waal, 2015), some countries in Sub-Saharan Africa have not fully come out of the grip of famines, with the two recent famines reported in Somalia in 2011 and South Sudan in 2017. Moreover, recent assessments show that many other countries in Africa and Western Asia have a crisis-level food security situation. Indeed, after decades of steady decline, the progress on global hunger has largely reversed since 2014, and an additional 60 million people have been afflicted by hunger between 2014 and 2020. This is largely because of new risks posed by a rise in conflicts, climate change and economic slowdowns that have hindered people's ability to access food. Rise in violent conflicts has had the effect of displacing people; climate variability-induced events, such as droughts, have impacted natural resources and food production systems with severe impacts on rural livelihoods; and economic decline has prevented people from escaping hunger and improving their lot. Furthermore, the Covid-19 pandemic has added to the hunger woes created by these drivers, and estimates show that the impact of the pandemic alone will be to add another 83–132 million chronically undernourished people in the world (FAO et al., 2017, 2018, 2019, 2020). A likely outcome of these processes is heightened importance of migration as a food security strategy among rural households, even as Covid-19 temporarily disrupts mobility. For instance, to highlight the significance of environmental migration, a recent report by the World Bank (2018) projects that by 2050, climate change alone could potentially cause an additional 143 million people in Sub-Saharan Africa, South Asia and Latin America to migrate internally.

Crucially, moreover, persistence of chronic hunger afflicts a sizable chunk of rural populations in the developing world, and many more face risks to food entitlement failures on a routine basis even during normal times. In many countries in Asia and Africa where the local rural institutions (land, labour, financial markets) to manage risks to income and food security are absent, rural households, particularly the landless and land-poor, often employ migration as a critical food security strategy. For example, research by Mosse et al. (2002) among the Bhil tribal villages in three western Indian districts in the states of Madhya Pradesh, Gujarat and Rajasthan found that food insecurity was among the important drivers of household migration decisions.

These old and new food security hazards have led to widespread international consensus on the importance of social protection to achieve food and nutrition security for all. Indeed, as the report by the High Level Panel of Experts (HLPE) of World Committee on Food Security shows, the current debate seems no longer about whether or not to provide social protection but is about design and implementation choices (for example, food or cash transfers) so as to provide safety nets to the needy more effectively. Moreover, there is also a paradigm shift of making social protection for food security right-based rather than discretionary (HLPE, 2012). Growing political significance of the right to food has led to many countries pledging to guarantee food security to their vulnerable rural populations through in-kind or income support to their most vulnerable populations (De Schutter, 2012). The importance of social protection is further affirmed in the SDG agenda's key slogan of 'leaving no one behind' (United Nations, 2015); and in the last four annual reports tracking global progress on the SDG goal 2 of a malnutrition-free world, FAO et al. (2017, 2018, 2019, 2020) have repeatedly stressed on the importance of social protection to achieve this goal.

The issue of social protection is particularly important to understand the relationship between migration and food security in India, which has recently passed a right-to-food legislation (Government of India, 2013a). If the institutional arrangements pertaining to income, livelihood and safety nets are robust and insure the vulnerable rural populations against food entitlement failures and enable them to meet their basic food needs, this will have a positive impact of the food security of those covered under these nets and may also reduce the need for individuals and households to employ migration as an alternative risk-reducing strategy. Conversely, the failure of these institutions may force the populations to employ migration (often distress-induced) as a critical food strategy. Whether and to what extent social safety nets help the rural poor avert the perennial risks to their income and food security and provide an alternative means to migration as a livelihood strategy are important questions that need investigation.

Chapter 5 engages with these questions. Consistent with the SLA analytical framework of charting out the policy and institutional setting, the chapter expresses these themes within the broader frame of the role of institutional arrangements pertaining to food and livelihood security in influencing household migration decisions and food security outcomes.

REMITTANCES, LAND AND AGRICULTURE AND FOOD SECURITY

Migration can also positively influence household food security. The most direct impact of migration on household food security outcomes may be felt through the remittances sent by migrant members. Income from migration can equip households at the origin with the cash that can not only help them prevent food entitlement failures but also enhance access to food among household members.

In addition to providing money to maintain and enhance food consumption levels, remittances often have significant interactions with household food security through their impacts on supporting local livelihoods. In Mexico, remittances sent by migrants were found to relieve credit and risk constraints on farm production, and thus had stimulating effects on farm production and income (Taylor and Wyatt, 1996). Similarly, a study by Oberai and Singh (1983) in Ludhiana district of the Indian state of Punjab, one of the Green Revolution frontiers in northern India, found that outmigration of members from farm households led to improved land productivity, particularly in the long run. In contrast to the earlier research by Lipton (1980) that suggested that investment in productive resources was of least priority to rural migrants as paying off debts, meeting daily needs and conspicuous consumption absorbed most of the village remittances, a study of migrant households in rural Egypt found that migrants spent a substantial proportion of remittances in productive resources such as housing and agricultural land (Adams, 1991). Similarly, de Haan's (2002) study of migration from Saran district of western

Bihar also found that migrants invested their savings and remittances in the land and agriculture at the origin. In crisis situations when local lives and livelihoods are disrupted, remittances often come to the rescue of households with migrants. For instance, a recent study in Nigeria found that remittances guarded households against food crisis: they increased their overall purchasing power, enabling them to invest in domestic food production as well as purchase food for consumption. Moreover, remittance-receiving households were found to be less likely to resort to unhealthy dietary practices and also less likely to be worried about meeting their food consumption needs due to a lack of resources, compared to households not receiving remittances (Obi, Bartolini and D'Haes, 2020). Similarly, another study on the linkages between remittances and natural disasters in Bangladesh, Ethiopia, Burkina Faso and Ghana found that remittances equipped households to respond to natural disasters better than those households without access to remittance incomes. In Bangladesh, remittances allowed households to maintain their household consumption level in the aftermath of the 1998 floods; in Ethiopia, households relied more on cash reserves to deal with food security shocks and less on selling productive agricultural and livelihood assets; and in Burkina Faso and Ghana, remittance-receiving households had better quality housing that enhanced the households' ability to cope with natural disasters (Mohapatra, Joseph and Ratha, 2012). If remittances are significant, they can also provide money for modern farm inputs and agriculture equipment (pesticides, fertilisers, tractors) (Mendola, 2008), which likely improves income gains from household-owned agricultural lands. These findings suggest that apart from the increased farm incomes, the rise in production also implies that food availability for a household's own consumption improves as well which can enhance household food security.

For rural households with small and marginal landholdings who constitute a bulk of farm households in the developing countries (World Bank, 2007; Lowder, Skoet and Raney, 2016), migration of one or more members may provide a way to reduce the pressure on the land. The problem of underemployment in agriculture, also referred to as disguised unemployment, characterises the agricultural landscape of most low-income countries. In places where the rural non-farm sector does not offer adequate employment, which is often the case in many countries in Asia and Africa, migration of one or more members can provide a means to allocate the family labour across activities to maximise returns (Stark, 1991). From the perspective of food security, this means that on the one hand the remittances add up to the total household earnings, providing money to raise household food consumption levels. On the other hand, reduced household size as a result of migration by family member(s) may increase the per-capita availability of food from the land owned. However, this also means loss of labour for family agriculture, which could either have a countervailing effect on food production or change the dynamics of household labour with women having to work more on farms.

Moreover, dependence on migration and remittances can also make agriculture at origin vulnerable and unsustainable, posing long-term threat to food security. Craven and Gartuala's (2015) field research in Nepal and Vanuatu documented that migration led to changes in sociocultural values associated with food production and consumption in origin villages, with households moving away from direct farming as well as shifting their preference for imported food over home-grown produce. These value changes can have the effect of threatening food security in the long run, especially in contexts where the opportunity to migrate is precarious. Withdrawal from direct farming, however, can also instigate changes in agrarian relations. It is often the case that rural land is owned and controlled by households that are socio-economically better off. These households also have the advantage of resources and networks to partake in migration. Their detachment from direct farming can create space for landless and land-poor households from disadvantageous social groups to access land, which can improve their food security.

Chapter 6 explores the migration–remittance–land–food-security nexus, compares and contrasts the food security outcomes of households with or without migrant members and assesses the food security implications of changes in agrarian relations.

MALE MIGRATION, CHANGES IN INTRA-HOUSEHOLD GENDER POWER RELATIONS AND FOOD SECURITY

Mobility among women for employment reasons, both within and across the national borders, is on the rise, owing to reasons varying from local livelihood failures leading to attitudinal shifts towards female migration to more demand-driven responses and better-paying employment opportunities outside the places of origin. Furthermore, an increasing number of women is now also migrating independently and, indeed, as the 'principal breadwinners' (Martin, 2004; Neetha, 2004; Fleury, 2016). Notwithstanding this increasing 'feminisation of migration', as recent articulations of the phenomenon put it

(United Nations, 2007, 2017), in many societies, social and cultural norms about the role and responsibilities of women still restrict their participation in distant labour markets. Women are confined to agriculture-related activities and household chores, while men assume obligations to ensure financial security of family members. This clear demarcation of the gender-based societal roles means labour migration is usually undertaken by men, leading to a phenomenon of left-behind women heading their households.[5] In the world's two most populous countries of China and India, for example, male migration dominates labour mobility. In China, the number of women left behind is estimated at 47 million (Zhang and Zhang, 2006, cited in Ye et al., 2016, p. 2). Nationwide data from India show that work-related male migration is prevalent in regions covering over 200 million people (Tumbe, 2015a). While there are no global estimates of left-behind women, the rising significance of migration in rural lives indicates that the number of women left behind may be on the rise and so may be the households headed by women.

Thus far the research findings on how women cope with male migration and its impact on women's lives have been mixed. In her research on the Sylhet region in north-eastern Bangladesh, Gardner (1993, p. 1) notes a popular song sung by women, which translates as:

> How can I accept that my husband has gone to London? I will fill up a suitcase with dried fish / All the mullahs – everyone – have gone to London / The land will be empty – what will I do? When my brother goes to London, he will give orders at tailor's / He will make a blouse for me / How can I accept that my husband has gone to London?

Though Gardner's work focused on the ethnographic constructs of localities in terms of images of homeland and abroad, and thus goes beyond the subject under discussion here, the beginning phrase of the song highlights the unwillingness of women to accept migration by their men. On the other hand, in the case of male migration from the southern Indian state of Kerala to countries in the Persian Gulf, women are found to aid their sons and husbands in migration (Gulati, 1987). However, male migration raises a range of issues for the women left behind in terms of role of women in the family, their need for support, dependence and protection, their autonomy in social and financial affairs, work burden – all of which have implications for the household food security.

The persistence of widespread gender inequalities and discrimination is a key feature of most of the rural societies in developing nations. Not only is women's say in everyday household affairs minimal, but decisions about their own reproductive and sexual health, education, consumption, and so on, are also made by the male members of the households. However, findings of several studies reveal that male migration improves the autonomy of women who stay behind, with women having a greater say in the day-to-day household decisions in the absence of their men (Gulati, 1987, 1993; Hadi, 2001; Paris et al., 2005), and the effects of this autonomy prevail even after men return (Yabiku, Agadjanian and Sevoyan, 2010). The structure of family plays a critical role with women in nuclear households enjoying more independence than their counterparts in the extended families where elder household members (father-in-law or mother-in-law) step in for absentee migrants to take charge of household affairs and maintain established patriarchal norms (Desai and Banerji, 2008; Ahmed, 2020). The remittances sent by the male migrants often enhance women's standing in the household, improve child education and boost investment for quality health services. A study on male migration from Kerala to the Middle East observed that remittances received by left-behind women also broadened their vision of managing the household finance matters efficiently, aside from its positive impact on child education and women and child health (Gulati, 1987). In Nepal, male migration was found to deepen women's engagement in rural society, though the autonomy outcomes were not the same for all women and they were crucially contingent on remittance flows (Maharjan, Bauer and Knerr, 2012). Furthermore, Gartaula, Niehof and Visser (2010, p. 573) found that in some households headed by women left behind, land titles were purchased in the wives' name when husbands were absent, providing some women legal ownership of land, an important determinant of well-being, social status and autonomy in South Asia (Agarwal, 1994). Rise in women's autonomy as a result of male migration can produce several household welfare impacts. The available research suggests that 'as compared to men, women are more likely to utilize the resources they control to promote the needs of the children in particular and of the family in general' (UNICEF, 2006, p. 23). When seen from the perspective of household food security, this efficient allocation and utilisation of household food resources may enhance access to food of household members, particularly women and children. It may also produce more gender-balanced food security outcomes.

On the other hand, male-only pattern of migration can lead to added burden of production and reproduction responsibilities on women. Village-level case studies on labour migration reveal that absence of men meant that women had to take over tasks that were traditionally performed by men in household agriculture (Jetley, 1987; Paris et al., 2005; Gartaula, Niehof and Visser, 2010; Maharjan, Bauer and Knerr, 2012; Ye et al., 2016). Women's increased involvement in productive functions, however, does not usually relieve them of responsibilities of housework and childcare. Rigid social and cultural norms often result in what Hochschild and Machung (2012) refer to as a *second shift* where women continue to be responsible for most of housework and child-caring duties even though they increasingly work outside home. In many developing countries, male out-migration from rural areas is one of the key drivers of feminisation of agriculture, with women performing increasingly enhanced responsibilities in agriculture for household survival alongside managing the traditional gender roles at home (Lastarria-Cornhiel, 2006). While women's greater involvement in the productive sphere is often viewed as positive for their autonomy, this may not always be the case. Based on research in India, Pattnaik et al. (2018) caution that a greater role of women in agriculture should not be confused with a rise in women empowerment. They argue that women's increasing engagement in farming is occurring in the context of diminishing viability of agriculture as an effective source of livelihood, leading instead to 'feminization of agrarian distress' (Pattnaik et al., 2018, p. 151). Indeed, there is a growing stress on agrarian livelihoods across the developing world (Hebinck, 2018), and feminisation of farm distress is perhaps occurring on a wider scale. In many ways, this is representative of the deeper marginalisation of women as their mobility is contained through patriarchal norms and practices. The added burden of the household's responsibilities can also negatively affect women's health and well-being (Lei and Desai, 2021). Furthermore, as climate change pushes rural households to migrate to meet their income and food needs, gender power relations can confer more disadvantages to women (Alston and Akhter, 2016; World Bank, 2018). In terms of food security impacts, in cases where remittances are low, positive impacts of women autonomy may be offset by increasing work burden, which negatively influences food security. This can also result in less gendered labour time for home spaces and activities, including cooking, which, in turn, can lead to poor dietary practices (Nichols, 2016). Moreover, and this is important, the pervasiveness of gender-based discrimination – particularly in societies with rigid patriarchal norms, in accessing various services, including social protection benefits like food rations – may mean that the sheer fact of being a woman may undermine the total gains of the rise in women's autonomy, which may adversely affect the food security.

Through the lens of gender, Chapter 7 looks within the household to understand the impacts of male migration on family power dynamics and gender relations, and how they relate and interact with household food security.

CONCLUSION

The chapter has attempted to contextualise the linkages between migration and food security. Beginning with the discussion on the importance of these themes in the global development agenda, the chapter has argued that there currently exists a huge disconnect between the two despite the obvious and two-way relationship between them, discussed the possible reasons for this divide and suggested the need to bridge this gulf. The discussion has also attempted to set forth the key conceptual and theoretical ideas that underpin the analysis in this book. With the main focus of the analysis being on food access among rural households, the book conceptualises the issue of food security through the prism of entitlements. Then, building on the SLA, it argues that a livelihood approach to migration provides an important framework to understand the linkage between migration and food security. The discussion earlier makes it clear that these frameworks are highly complementary. In the final section, drawing on existing evidence from a range of countries across the world, the chapter has pointed out the lack of direct empirical evidence on the relationship between migration and food security and attempted to develop an analytical framework that includes three conceptual pathways of linkages between the two. These include (*a*) the role of institutional arrangements, pertaining to food and livelihood safety nets, in influencing household food security outcomes and migration decisions, (*b*) the effect of migrants' remittances on the food security of household members at the place of origin and (*c*) the interaction of gender with household food security outcomes. Using primary data collected from the case-study district of Siwan in western Bihar, these linkages are empirically tested in later chapters. The next chapter examines in detail the broad dynamics of migration, urbanisation and food (in)security in India in order to provide a wider perspective on the patterns of rural livelihoods and their significance for food security in the country.

NOTES

1. This was also because of the urban bias in resource allocation and investment (Lipton, 1975, 1977).

2. The importance of development economics declined as well. Albert Hirschman, an influential economist, even went on to read an obituary of development economics (Hirschman, 1981, pp. 1–24). While recognising the increasing reductionist nature of development economics in the 1970s and 1980s, Amartya Sen, however, regarded this obituary as rather premature (Sen, 1983).

3. For instance, a study on the migrant workers in the sugarcane industries in Maharashtra found that about 200,000 children of migrant sugarcane workers are bypassed by the education system, as many of them worked alongside their parents in the fields (see Minwalla, 2003).

4. The exceptions include some recent studies that attempt to link and provide some evidence on the interface of migration and food security (see Azzarri and Zezza, 2011; de Brauw, 2011; de Brauw and Mu, 2011; Zezza et al., 2011; Crush, 2013; Craven and Gartuala, 2015). A recent notable initiative on the issue is the multi-country research project entitled *Hungry Cities Partnership: Informality, Inclusive Growth and Food Security in Cities of the Global South.* It aims to generate evidence on migration–urbanisation–food-insecurity linkages in Asia, Africa and Latin America. Led by Jonathan Crush of Balsillie School of International Affairs, Waterloo, this research initiative has started a useful conversation on migration–food-security connections though the focus of the enquiry is on cities (The Hungry Cities Partnership, 2020). However, the research on the relationship between migration and food security is still at an infant stage and in need of studies that could provide insights into the interactions between rural livelihood patterns and food security.

5. The term 'left-behind women' is used in this book to refer to women whose husbands migrate for work without them while they stay behind in origin places.

3

DYNAMICS OF FOOD INSECURITY, MIGRATION AND URBANISATION IN INDIA

INTRODUCTION

At the global level, India has more undernourished people than any other country in the world. During 2017–19, the most recent period for which comparable cross-country data are available, the number of chronically undernourished people in India was estimated to be 189 million. To put this figure in perspective, the absolute number of people suffering from undernourishment in India is only slightly lower than the number of undernourished people in 48 countries of Sub-Saharan Africa combined. Seen in percentage terms, this figure is equivalent to over a quarter of the world's undernourished people, and it represents almost half of the total burden of undernourishment of the whole of Asia and nearly 75 per cent of the South Asian region (FAO et al., 2020). Furthermore, a trend analysis of undernourishment reveals that during 1990–92 – the baseline period used by the FAO in order to track the progress of the countries on the World Food Summit, 1996, and the MDG target on hunger and undernourishment[1] – India's neighbouring countries in South and Southeast Asia, including Bangladesh, Cambodia, Laos, Myanmar, Thailand and Vietnam, had a higher percentage of their population who suffered from hunger. Yet these countries achieved the MDG target of halving the proportion of undernourished people by 2015, while India slid off the track (FAO, IFAD and WFP, 2015, p. 46). This is despite the fact that the Indian economy performed much better than most of these countries in this period. The post-2015 SDGs agenda envisages eliminating undernourishment completely from the planet (United Nations, 2015). The sheer magnitude of the number of undernourished people in India suggests the wider significance of the country from the perspective of global progress on hunger reduction.

The aggregate figure on the number of undernourished people, however, conceals several regional and social aspects of the problem. In India, the prevalence of undernourishment varies significantly across different states and rural–urban areas within the states. Furthermore, there are marked asymmetries in the levels of undernourishment among different social groups, with Scheduled Castes and Scheduled Tribes faring the worst on this front. Indeed, although India has been fairly successful in averting the large-scale recurring famines of the past in the post-independence era, incidences of deaths due to starvation and child malnutrition among the lower caste and tribal communities continue to be reported (Jha, 2002; Mander, 2012; Parulkar, 2012; Patel, 2018) even in the more developed states such as Kerala (Manikandan, 2014). Additionally, and this is an important point to emphasise, the persistence of widespread gender inequalities in many parts of India means that women and girls are more prone to hunger and undernourishment as compared to their male counterparts. This has severe implications from the perspective of intergenerational transfers of health and nutrition outcomes, as children born to ill-nourished mothers are more likely to be malnourished.

Cutting across these inequalities is the problem of rural–urban disparities in food and nutrition security in India. As noted in Chapter 1, the prevalence of food insecurity and undernourishment is much higher in rural than urban areas. Moreover, the urban-centric nature of economic growth since the early 1990s is throwing down a new set of challenges for rural food security. One outcome of urban-led economic growth is the growing significance of rural–urban migration for work. However, much of the urban employment growth has occurred in the informal economy. This means labour mobility is predominated by circular migration flows, keeping the overall levels of urbanisation relatively lower than other countries (Kundu, 2003, 2009, 2014). Not all moves, however, are characterised by the push of rural distress, and the pulls of better urban incomes and improved transportation system are also propelling mobility (Deshingkar and Anderson, 2004; Tumbe, 2018). From the perspective of food security, these processes imply that the sources of rural food security are changing, which necessitates an understanding of these changes.

Against this general background, this chapter discusses the various facets of undernourishment in India. It first establishes India in the global debates on hunger, with particular reference to the country's progress on the MDG on hunger, followed by a brief reflection on what this means for the post-2015 development agenda of a hunger-free world. Then, it highlights the regional and socio-economic disparities in hunger and undernourishment. In the third major section, the discussion focuses on the changing character of rural livelihoods and broad dynamics of migration and urbanisation in India. This section also attempts to highlight the rising significance of migration within rural livelihood systems in India and what this would seem to imply for rural food security. This discussion on broader trends of rural livelihoods, migration and urbanisation aims to set the scene for the empirical household-level analysis of linkages between migration and food security that is presented in later chapters. The last section sums up the observations and inferences drawn from the discussion thus far.

ASSESSING INDIA'S PROGRESS ON THE MDG ON HUNGER REDUCTION

The MDGs represented a blueprint consisting of a set of time-bound development goals, agreed to by the world's nations in September 2000 at the Millennium Summit held at the United Nations' headquarters in New York. MDGs consisted of a total of 8 goals and 21 targets, country-wise progress on which was to be measured through 60 quantitative indicators with the baseline year of 1990 and the end-line year of 2015 (United Nations, 2013, p. 58).[2] MDG 1 was to *eradicate extreme poverty and hunger*, and target 2 within this goal was to halve, between 1990 and 2015, the proportion of people who suffered from hunger.[3] India, among other countries, was a signatory to these goals which, while not binding, reflected the country's commitment to broad-based inclusive development alongside the economic reforms initiated since the early 1990s.

Poverty is the significant cause of hunger and undernourishment around the world. In fact, it is this connection that guided the official policy thinking to tie up the MDG goal on halving hunger with that of reducing poverty. In other words, the grouping of these goals was based on the logic that decline in poverty would automatically make a dent on hunger prevalence. In the case of India, the macroeconomic reforms since the early 1990s and ensuing economic growth were believed to set the preconditions for reducing poverty and food insecurity in the country. In particular, parallels began to be drawn between

China and India. Rapid economic growth in China since the mid-1980s witnessed concomitant improvements in food security. India was expected to follow the same path (FAO, 2000). The progress in these two countries was considered crucial because by the sheer size of their populations, the fate of global progress on hunger hinged upon them. Whereas China continued to make progress, the narrative about India changed quite dramatically within a few years. As early as 2003, India began to be seen as a worrying case. Thus, in its 2003 edition of *State of Food Insecurity in the World* (*SoFI*), the FAO observed:

> These numbers and trends are dominated by progress and setbacks in a few large countries. China alone has reduced the number of hungry people by 58 million since [1990–1992] ... At the same time, India has shifted into reverse. After seeing a decline of 20 million in the number of undernourished between 1990–1992 and 1995–1997, the number of hungry people in India increased by 19 million over the following four years. (FAO, 2003a, p. 6)

By 2005, India began to be characterised as a paradox where economic growth did little to nothing in the way of improving the outcomes of food and nutrition security for a large majority of the country's population. The international scepticism that India would falter on its MDG goal of hunger reduction grew further with the visit to the country in 2005 by Jean Ziegler, the United Nations Special Rapporteur on the Right to Food. Using the catchphrase 'hunger amidst plenty', Ziegler (2006, p. 5), raised apprehensions about the country's ability to honour its MDG commitments:

> Despite the progress made in the progressive realisation of the right to food in India since independence, the Special Rapporteur is concerned that there are signs of regression, particularly amongst the poorest. In monitoring progress towards the Millennium Development Goals (MDGs), the Planning Commission has noted that India was not currently on track to achieve the goals set in relation to malnutrition and undernourishment. (Ziegler, 2006, p. 15)

This paradoxical narrative of disjuncture between economic growth and food security about India continued to be echoed in the global discourse on food security. Over the years, India slipped behind the reach of the MDG on hunger. In order to quantitatively assess how India fared on its MDG commitments, it is necessary to understand the benchmark indicators used to evaluate the country-wise progress on the MDG of hunger. Although undernourishment has various facets and thus methodological debates continue on how it should be defined and measured, two commonly used measures include:

1. proportion of underweight children aged 0–59 months, expressed in terms of under-five children whose *weight-for-age* is minus two standard deviations from the median of international reference population, and
2. proportion of population who suffer from dietary energy deficits.

Before assessing the MDG progress of India on reducing the proportion of underweight children, it is important to note that there are two other anthropometric indicators for assessing child-nutrition outcomes. These include (*a*) stunting (expressed as *height-for-age*) which captures height or growth retardation among children with respect to age and is an indicator of chronic undernourishment and (*b*) wasting (expressed as *weight-for-height)* which measures body mass in relation to height and represents acute undernourishment. While these two indicators are important, the United Nations' annual MDG reports used child underweight as the preferred indicator, as it is a composite measure of stunting and wasting and reflects both chronic and acute forms of childhood malnourishment. Since the Government of India also used this measure in its India-MDG reports, the same is used here to ensure consistency.[4]

It must be added that although the MDG target indicator refers to the proportion of underweight children in the age group of 0–59 months (or children aged under five years), the MDG indicator in India includes children under three years of age. This is because in the four successive rounds of the NFHS (conducted in 1992–93, 1998–99, 2005–06 and 2015–16), which is the main source of data on child-nutrition outcomes, the age groups of children whose height and weight were measured varied. The height and weight were measured for children below the age of four years in the NFHS-1 (1992–93), for children below the age of three years in the NFHS-2 (1998–99) and for children below the age of five years in the NFHS-3 (2005–06) and the NFHS-4 (2015–16). Thus, to ensure consistency over the period, children below the age of three years were considered in annual assessments (Ministry of Statistics and Programme Implementation, 2017, p. 29).

Using this measure, the final country report of India on MDGs estimated that the proportion of under-three underweight children in the country was 52 per cent in the 1990. Thus, in order to achieve the MDG target, this should have declined to 26 per cent by 2015. This translates to an average annual reduction of 1.04 per cent over a 25-year period – from 1990 to 2015. Although the progress on this indicator closely followed the MDG target value up until 1998–99, subsequent years saw inadequate advances. According to the NFHS data, in the six-year period between 1992–93 and 1998–99, the proportion of underweight children below the age of three years declined by close to 9 per cent at an average annual rate of 1.5 per cent – from 51.5 per cent to 42.7 per cent. In fact, this rate of decline was higher than the average annual expected decline of 1.04 per cent. However, the pace of improvement in child underweight prevalence witnessed a sharp deceleration afterwards: between 1998–99 and 2005–06 it decreased by merely 2.3 per cent, and between 2005–06 and 2015–16 the decline was of 6.7 per cent. This put India off the track of its MDG target. In 2015–16 the proportion of underweight children in India was 33.7 per cent, missing the MDG target by 7.7 per cent (Figure 3.1). According to the 2011 census, India had approximately 89.01 million children below the age of three years (Census of India, 2011h). Thus, in absolute terms, the MDG shortfall of 7.7 per cent translates into nearly seven million more children remaining underweight than what would have been the case had this MDG target been achieved.

There is substantial international evidence on the huge social and economic costs of child undernutrition. The lack of adequate nutrition at the early stages of life leads to poor cognitive development, which has wider implications on productivity in the adult ages and economic growth as a whole (Strauss and Thomas, 1998; Thomas and Frankenberg, 2002; World Bank, 2006; UNICEF, 2012). It is estimated that more than 200 million children around the world fail to reach their full cognitive potential due to inadequate nutrition and health care (Grantham-McGregor et al., 2007). The economic costs of malnutrition amount to nearly 10 per cent of the lifetime earnings of malnourished individuals, and the overall losses to the national income hover around 2–3 per cent of the country's GDP; for India, productivity losses due to malnutrition and micronutrient deficiencies were estimated to cost the country around USD 114 billion between 2003 and 2012 (World Bank, 2006, p. 26). Not only does child undernutrition affect cognitive development, but

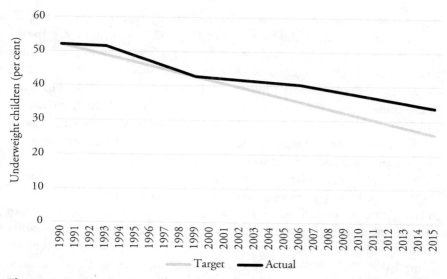

Figure 3.1   India's progress on the Millennium Development Goals (MDGs) indicator of underweight children below the age of three years, 1990–2015

Source: Author's work based on data provided by the Ministry of Statistics and Programme Implementation (2017).

Note: Using the baseline and endline values of 52 and 26 per cent in 1990 and 2015, respectively, the target curve has been obtained assuming an average annual reduction of 1.04 per cent over a 25-year period. For the actual curve, the average annual rate of progress has been applied from the National Family Health Survey (NFHS) estimates of the respective periods. For instance, a 0.5 per cent decline between 1990 and 1992–93 translated into an average annual decline of 0.17, which has been applied to years from 1991 to 1993; an 8.8 per cent decline between 1992–93 and 1998–99 led to an annual decline of 1.47 per cent, which has been applied to all years from 1994 to 1999, and so on.

it is also a significant predictor of infant and child mortality. Poor nutrition weakens the resistance of children to several life-threatening infectious diseases and thus increases the risks of mortality among children (for an extensive review, see Pelletier, 1994). In India 54 per cent of the deaths among children below the age of five years is attributed to poor nutrition (Arnold et al., 2009, p. 14). Thus, the failure of India to reduce the levels of child nutrition as per its MDG commitments will likely have long-lasting impacts on its other development outcomes. This calls for urgent and effective policy action to attend to early-life needs of children in India.

The second indicator related to the proportion of people who suffer from the dietary energy deficits has had a rather controversial place in the

Indian policy scene. In its first-ever MDG country report in the year 2005, it was estimated that at the base year of 1990, 62.2 per cent of the Indian population was undernourished by this measure. According to this baseline estimate, the MDG target value of 31.1 per cent was set for the year 2015 (Ministry of Statistics and Programme Implementation, 2005). However, in the subsequent MDG reports published in 2007, 2009, 2011, 2014, 2015 and 2017, no proper estimates on this indicator were provided. The reasons for this are difficult to gauge, as the data on dietary energy consumption for the Indian population are collected periodically through the countrywide NSS. One plausible explanation why this indicator was dropped is that until 2009, calorie energy formed the sole basis of determining the poverty line in India. The individuals whose per-capita daily expenditure was lower than what it took to meet the *minimum dietary energy* of 2,400 and 2,100 calories in rural and urban areas, respectively, were classified as poor (Planning Commission, 1979, 1993). However, since the 1970s, there has been a constant decline in average calorie consumption across different income classes, and this has been the case in both rural and urban areas, even though poverty has declined and incomes have improved over the period (Rao, 2000; Patnaik, 2004; Radhakrishna et al., 2004; Radhakrishna, 2005; Sen, 2005; Deaton and Drèze, 2009). The recent evaluation of the declining trend of calorie consumption in India for the period from 1983 to 2004–05 by Deaton and Drèze (2009) also suggests a striking fact: calorie consumption has declined despite the fact that the relative prices of food have remained unchanged. There is no single explanation for these trends, and the plausible hypotheses include (*a*) improved epidemiological and health environment leading to enhanced conversion-efficiency of food (Deaton and Drèze, 2009), (*b*) increasing mechanisation of Indian agriculture as well as a shift in the workforce structure from farm to non-farm sectors, reducing the need for hard manual labour and, in turn, calorie requirements (Rao, 2000; Deaton and Drèze, 2009), (*c*) a voluntary transition from calorie-dense diets to better-tasting food with lesser calories (Banerjee and Duflo, 2011), (*d*) an involuntary reduction in food expenditure in order to accommodate non-food needs, such as better education and healthcare (Sen, 2005; Basu and Basole, 2012) and (*e*) an increase in out-of-home eating, the extent of which is not covered in the national surveys (Smith, 2015) (for a useful synthesis of calorie consumption puzzles, see Pritchard et al., 2014, pp. 34–39).

From the policy standpoint, however, the downward sloping calorie curve is subject to being interpreted as a sign of rising incidence of poverty in the country even though that may not be the case. In fact, this anomaly was highlighted in the India-MDG report for the year 2009, which suggested that while India was on track to reduce the number of people living below the poverty line (although this claim remains highly contested due to the low cut-off used to estimate poverty), the proportion of population with dietary energy consumption below the norms was on the rise – increasing from 64 per cent in 1987–88 to 76 per cent in 2004–05 (Ministry of Statistics and Programme Implementation, 2009, p. 30).

On the other hand, the FAO, in its annual *SoFI* reports, provides the cross-country estimates on this indicator to assess the progress of the world's nations on the MDG target on hunger. In these reports, the PoU is measured as a proportion of population whose actual dietary energy consumption is lower than the minimum dietary energy requirements (MDERs). The MDER norms vary by a person's age, sex, body weight and level of physical activity, and are calculated accordingly. Using these MDERs norms, the last MDG-stocktaking *SoFI* 2015 report showed that the proportion of undernourished people in India in the baseline period of 1990–92 was 23.7 per cent of the total population. By this yardstick, meeting the MDG required India to halve this number to 11.85. However, during 2014–16 – the MDG end-line period in the *SoFI* 2015 report – the proportion of undernourished people in India stood at 15.2 per cent of the total population (FAO et al., 2015, p. 46). This means India fell short of achieving this MDG target of hunger reduction (Figure 3.2).[5]

Additionally, in 2015–16, nearly a quarter (22.9 per cent) of Indian women of childbearing ages of 15–49 years had below normal BMI (IIPS and ICF International, 2017b, p. 332). The sheer magnitude of undernourishment in India is reflective of the lack of policy attention given to attending the basic needs of the country's population. Indeed, a decade ago, Drèze (2004, p. 1729) described the country's nutrition situation as a 'silent emergency'. Although recent years have witnessed reinvigoration of political interest on food and nutrition issues in India with the right to food now recognised as the constitutional right of every Indian citizen, much remains to be done. Moreover, the policy neglect of the past will take many years to make up for the current shortfalls.

In 2015, the global development community committed to the post-MDG development agenda in the form of SDGs. The SDGs comprise 17 goals and 169 targets, to be achieved by 2030. Food and nutrition security for all is a prominent goal within the SDG framework, and SDG 2 calls for

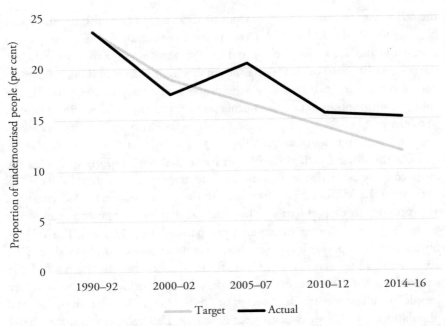

Figure 3.2 India's progress on the Millennium Development Goals (MDGs) indicator of the proportion of undernourished people, 1990–2016

Source: FAO et al. (2015, p. 46).

eradication of all forms of malnutrition from the face of the planet (United Nations, 2015). Importantly, unlike its MDG predecessor, the goal of food security is not tied with that of poverty reduction (and, implicitly, to achieving high economic growth); it is a separate, standalone goal. While this highlights the importance attached to eliminating undernourishment, this decoupling also seems inspired by the Indian experience where rapid economic growth did not translate into better food and nutrition outcomes – far from it.[6]

It is too early to assess India's progress on the SDG of food and nutrition security. At the time of writing, India released the *National Indicator Baseline Report*, 2015–16, which provides baseline values on all SDG targets at the beginning of 2016, and the first progress report in 2020. However, the progress report carried the same baseline data on child and maternal nutrition indicators from the NFHS 2015–16, as that was the latest complete available survey (and these data were also used in the last India-MDG report in 2017) (Ministry of Statistics and Programme Implementation, 2016, 2020).

Therefore, whether India will achieve its SDG target of eradicating hunger by 2030 remains to be seen. What is clear is that with India accounting for over a quarter of the world's undernourished people (FAO et al., 2020), progress in the country will be crucial for achieving the global SDG of hunger elimination.

SOCIAL, CULTURAL AND REGIONAL DIMENSIONS OF FOOD INSECURITY AND UNDERNOURISHMENT IN INDIA

The discussion in the preceding sections has attempted to highlight, in a broad sense, the overall magnitude of the problem of undernourishment in India. However, India is a huge and diverse country with widespread interstate and intrastate disparities, including in terms of food insecurity and undernourishment. Moreover, the widespread gender inequalities in the country mean that women are more prone to food insecurity. Indeed, India's failure to achieve the MDG targets on hunger is, in many ways, intimately related to these inequalities. The following section discusses these social, cultural (gender) and regional dimensions of food insecurity in India.

REGIONAL DIMENSIONS OF FOOD INSECURITY AND DEPRIVATION

Although the overall magnitude of undernourishment remains widespread in India, there is a substantial variability in the prevalence of food insecurity and deprivation across different states, districts within states and villages within districts. The past two decades have therefore witnessed enormous research on identification of the geographies of deprivation in India (inter alia, Debroy and Bhandari, 2003; Borooah and Dubey, 2007; Chaudhuri and Gupta, 2009; Drèze and Khera, 2012; Bakshi, Chawla and Shah, 2015).

At the state level, the mapping of food insecurity in 2009 by the IFPRI provides important insights on the broader regional geography of undernourishment in India. The IFPRI's assessment uses the SHI – a composite indicator, like the GHI, which measures the performance of individual Indian states on three interlinked indicators of proportion of population with inadequate calorie intake, proportion of underweight children below the age of five years and under-five mortality rate – to map the prevalence and severity of hunger in 17 large states of India. These states account for 95 per cent of the country's total population. The SHI assigns equal weights to all three indicators and, based on their average score, ranks the states into five categories that reflect the severity of hunger. These five categories are (*a*) low (score of below 5), (*b*) moderate (score between 5 and 9.9), (*c*) serious (score between 10 and 19.9), (*d*) alarming (score between 20 and 29.9) and (*e*) extremely alarming (score of 30 or more) (Menon, Deolalikar and Bhaskar, 2009). It is important to note that whereas the GHI is published every year to assess global hunger with the most recent edition being released in 2020, the SHI was a one-off exercise in 2009 (at least until the time of writing this book). In that way, the SHI is a bit dated. Nevertheless, it does provide useful insights on state-level differences in food insecurity.[7]

Based on the SHI values, Figure 3.3 presents the state-wise undernourishment prevalence in India. As is evident from the data in the map, not a single state falls in either the 'low' or 'moderate' hunger category. Furthermore, barring the states of Punjab, Kerala, Andhra Pradesh and Assam that are in the 'serious' category, the remaining have 'alarming' levels of hunger, with the situation in Madhya Pradesh in central India being 'extremely alarming'. It is likely that more recent data would show improvements in the hunger index values in all states, but this progress is likely to be moderate at best. This is because overall high scores for most Indian states in the SHI 2009 were largely because of the high prevalence of underweight children below the age of five years. Data on child underweight used in the SHI were from the NFHS 2005–06. The more recent round of the NFHS, conducted a decade later in 2015–16, shows persistently high levels of child underweight prevalence, which declined only marginally from 42.5 per cent to 37.5 per cent. Indeed, the mapping of the prevalence of undernutrition across Indian states shows a similar regional pattern, with 12 of the 17 states having alarming or extremely alarming levels of child underweight prevalence (Figure 3.4). This also suggests that the broad pattern that the SHI 2009 presented largely holds in recent years (Menon, Deolalikar and Bhaskar, 2009; IIPS and ICF International, 2017b).

In any case, the SHI provides important means for interstate comparisons of hunger, and a clear pattern of relative disadvantage can be discerned. In particular, the bottom four states (with SHI scores of 25) include Madhya Pradesh, Jharkhand, Bihar and Chhattisgarh; three of these four states (except Chhattisgarh) also have an extremely alarming prevalence of childhood underweight (over 40 per cent of under-five children in 2015–16). These Indian states are among the most backward states and form part of the undivided BIMARU states. (BIMARU is a Hindi acronym which

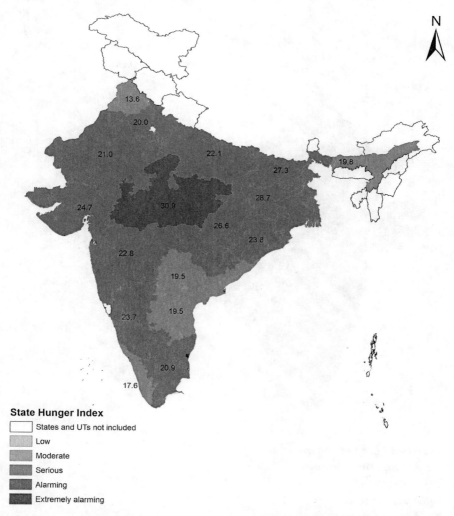

Figure 3.3 State-wise undernourishment prevalence in India according to the State Hunger Index (SHI), 2009

Source: Map by the author, with data from Menon, Deolalikar and Bhaskar (2009).

Note: Map not to scale and does not represent authentic international boundaries. The SHI 2009 predates administrative changes in the states of Andhra Pradesh, which was bifurcated to create a new state of Telangana in 2014, and Jammu and Kashmir, which was bifurcated to create a new union territory of Ladakh in 2019. This map reflects those changes. Since Andhra Pradesh and Telangana were included in the index, the SHI values of undivided Andhra Pradesh are applied on both.

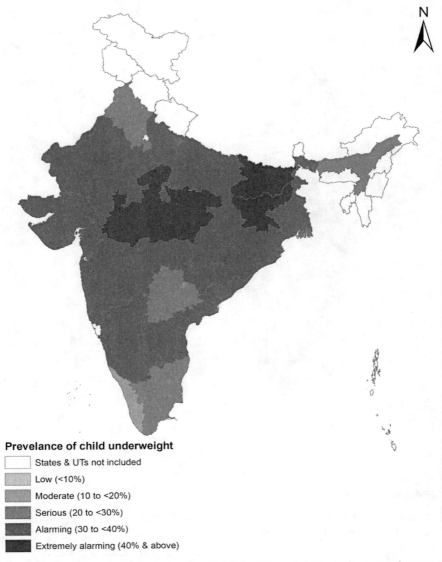

Prevelance of child underweight

☐ States & UTs not included

Low (<10%)

Moderate (10 to <20%)

Serious (20 to <30%)

Alarming (30 to <40%)

Extremely alarming (40% & above)

Figure 3.4   State-wise prevalence of child underweight in India according to the National Family Health Survey (NFHS), 2015–16

Source: Map by the author, with data from IIPS and ICF International (2017b).

Note: Map not to scale and does not represent authentic international boundaries. Telangana was carved out of Andhra Pradesh as a separate state in 2014, and the NFHS 2015–16 follows these official administrative changes. Since this map uses the NFHS 2015–16 data, it also shows Telangana as a separate state and uses data provided by the NFHS for both states.

means morbid; it was originally derived from the first letters of the four most socio-economically and demographically backward states of Bihar, Madhya Pradesh, Rajasthan and Uttar Pradesh. In 2000, the states of Jharkhand and Chhattisgarh were carved out of Bihar and Madhya Pradesh, respectively, and included as separate states in the Indian Union. Later, the state of Odisha was also added to the list, and the acronym became BIMARUO.)

In a recent exercise by the Planning Commission that ranked the districts and sub-districts (or district blocks) of the country in the order of their backwardness, 35 of 50 most backward districts were from these four states (and the number increased to 47 districts when the adjacent states of Odisha, Rajasthan and Uttar Pradesh were included) (Bakshi, Chawla and Shah, 2015, annexure A).[8] Similalrly, in the multidimensional poverty index, which captures acute deprivations in health, education and living standards that people face simultaneously, the states of Bihar, Jharkhand, Madhya Pradesh and Chhattisgarh ranked among the bottom-five states and had over 35 per cent of their populations in multidimensional poverty (Alkire, Kanagaratnam and Suppa, 2021). With the exception of Bihar, all these states have a significantly large proportion of Scheduled Tribe (Advasi) populations who, having suffered historical neglect, remain extremely marginalised. Indeed, the Planning Commission study quoted earlier finds a strong correlation between concerntration of tribal population and backwardness of the region (Bakshi, Chawla and Shah, 2015, pp. 48–50). The reasons for the backwardness of Bihar, which is the broader case-study setting for the present study, are somewhat different and lie in a slew of problems, including the burden of faulty colonial land settlement and revenue policies, historical caste-based inequalities in land and asset ownership (also a perennial cause of tensions and occasional violence), high demographic pressures and governance deficits (see Chapter 4 for a detailed discussion of the reasons for Bihar's backwardness).

The SHI index is useful in that it points to the high interstate disparities in the prevalence and severity of hunger in India. However, the prevalence of hunger and deprivation also varies across different districts within the state. Indeed, pockets of backwardness and deprivation exist even in India's most developed states. As the Planning Commission study by Bakshi, Chawla and Shah (2015, p. 46) found: '... the remarkable characteristic of regional disparities in India is the presence of backward areas even within states that have grown faster and are at relatively high income levels on average.' In terms of hunger, the authors noted:

Intrastate disparities are not just in terms of income, but also non-income indicators such as hunger ... India's richest states include some of our 'hungriest' districts. These include East Godavari, Khammam and Mahbubnagar in Andhra Pradesh, Fatehabad and Hissar in Haryana, Gulbarga in Karnataka, Malappuram, Palakkad, Thiruvananthapuram and Thrissur in Kerala and Kolhapur, Ratnagiri, Satara and Sindhudurg in Maharashtra. This is also true of other indicators such as infant mortality and literacy. (Bakshi, Chawla and Shah, 2015, p. 46)

The undivided BIMARUO-belt states (including Jharkhand and Chhattisgarh), however, remain the bigger problematic zone in terms of hunger and deprivation. Indeed, district-wise mapping of rural food insecurity in India by the World Food Programme (WFP) and the Institute of Human Development (IHD), India, show that seven of the eight states in which this exercise was performed were from the BIMARUO group, suggesting their significance (WFP and IHD, 2008a, 2008b, 2008c, 2008d, 2009a, 2009b, 2010).[9] Also, 89 of the 100 most backward districts identified by Bakshi, Chawla and Shah (2015) are from the undivided BIMARUO states. A similar assessment by Drèze and Khera (2012) on the district-wise patterns of human and child deprivation, using two composite measures of the Human Development Index (HDI) and the Achievement of Babies and Children (ABC) Index, also finds similar patterns of deprivation, with most of the districts in the seven states falling in the bottom and second-bottom quintile of the HDI and ABC indices.[10]

It is also important to note that some of the districts within the BIMARUO group are intensely backward and the most hunger-prone regions of India. In particular, the Kalahandi–Balangir–Korutput (KBK) region of the eastern Indian state of Odisha and the Baran district in Rajasthan are places where hunger and starvation deaths, particularly among the lower-backward caste and tribal communities, continue to be reported (Banik, 2007; Mishra, 2010; Dutta, 2014; Nayar, 2014). Their low-caste and tribal status makes these communities even more vulnerable to hunger and starvation, an issue to which we now turn.

SOCIAL CORRELATES OF POVERTY AND FOOD INSECURITY

In India, remarkable disparities exist in the levels of food and nutritional deprivation across different social groups. In particular, the Scheduled

Caste and Scheduled Tribe populations face a disproportionately higher burden of hunger and undernourishment. Although the Scheduled Castes and Scheduled Tribes have been accorded special status in the Indian Constitution, and the post-independence development planning in India has sought to uplift their social and economic standing, a significantly large majority of their population continues to be at the lowest rung of the economy and society. Poverty, hunger, illiteracy and landlessness among Scheduled Castes and Scheduled Tribes remain exceptionally high (Planning Commission, 2013b). Indeed, to bridge this gap, the Government of India operates several social support programmes, such as income support in the forms of pensions, scholarships for children, and so on. However, their implementation on the ground remains ineffective. By the virtue of their low social and economic status, they often lack the voice and representation to claim what is rightfully owed to them and are cheated frequently (Chapter 5 discusses this issue based on field-research findings in rural Bihar).

Table 3.1 presents the NFHS data on the differentials in the nutritional status among under-five children and women and men aged between 15 and 49 by social groups in India. Although the undernutrition prevalence remains

Table 3.1 Percentage of undernourished children and adults by social groups in India, 2015–16

Social groups	Undernutrition among children aged 0–59 months*			Undernutrition among adults aged 15–49 years**	
	Stunted	Wasted	Underweight	Women with BMI > 18.5	Men with BMI > 18.5
Scheduled Tribe	43.8	27.4	45.3	31.7	25.2
Scheduled Caste	42.8	21.2	39.1	25.3	22.9
Other Backward Caste	38.7	20.5	35.5	22.9	20.3
Other	31.2	19.0	28.8	17.8	16.3

Source: IIPS and ICF International (2017b, pp. 304, 330–31).

Note: *Children with height-for-age, weight-for-height and weight-for-age are two standard deviations below the median of the World Health Organization (WHO) international reference population. **Body mass index (BMI) is measured as weight (in kilograms) divided by height (in metres square) (or, BMI = kg/m2).

high among all the social groups, compared to 'other' castes (a residual category comprising all non-backward caste groups), a significantly higher proportion of children, women and men belonging to the Scheduled Caste and Scheduled Tribe groups are undernourished. For example, at 45.3 per cent, the proportion of under-five underweight children among the Scheduled Tribes is 16 per cent higher compared to other groups. Similarly, 31.7 per cent of Scheduled Tribe women of childbearing ages have a below normal BMI of 18.5, and the corresponding proportion of the women in the other category is almost half of that.

The NFHS's categorisation of social groups in India, useful as it may be in understanding the health and nutrition disparities across different social groups in broad terms, does not, however, provide insights into the inequalities within castes and tribes in the levels of nutritional deprivation. Indeed, within the Scheduled Castes and Scheduled Tribes, some communities are more disadvantaged than others. As an example, one such caste group is Musahars who live in the parts of backward Indian states of Uttar Pradesh and Bihar. Also known as the 'rat eaters', Musahars are undoubtedly one of the most resourceless and disadvantaged caste groups in India. In an important book that brings together the stories of persistence of hunger and destitution among the most marginalised communities in India, Mander (2012) provides a gut-wrenching narrative on the life circumstances of the Musahars living in eastern Uttar Pradesh and argues that hunger is an inseparable part of their lives, which they have come to embrace as their life-long companion. The children in Musahar households are taught to live without food from an early age. Citing his conversation with Musahar womenfolk who told him what they do when their children cry for food, Mander (2012, p. 6) recounts:

It is difficult for us to bear their weeping. When the wailing of infants gets too much, we lace our fingertips with tobacco or natural intoxicants and give our fingers to the babies to suck. We give them cannabis or khaina (local tobacco for chewing) or cheap country liquor. It helps them sleep even with nothing in their stomachs. If they are small, we sometimes beat them until they sleep. But as they grow older, we try to teach them how to live with hunger. We tell them this lesson will equip them for a lifetime. Because we know that hunger will always be with them. It'll be their companion for the rest of their lives.

Similarly, the Sahariya tribe in the Baran district of Rajasthan is another case. Since 2002, the tribe has witnessed a wave of deaths among children due to starvation and undernourishment (Drèze and Khera, 2014; Dutta, 2014; Nayar, 2014). Reporting on the severity of undernourishment among Sahariya children, a piece in a leading Indian daily described the situation of these tribal children as follows:

Two-and-a-half-year-old Prince Sahariya cries uncontrollably as his grandmother Shanti tries to make him stand but gives up as his weak and spindly legs refuse to cooperate. *'Hamara Prince bahut kamzor hai'* [My grandson Prince is severely undernourished], the doting grandmother offers apologetically, having brought him to the community health centre in Shahabad block in Baran district, Rajasthan ... There are 18 other children with Prince in the 12-bed malnutrition ward, most exhibiting signs of severe malnutrition – from bloated stomachs to stunted growth. Without adequate medical staff, the health centre clearly has more than its fair share of young patients it can look after. Some children have even been accommodated in the entrance gallery, where they are being given nourishing food supplements to get them back on their feet. It's a scene that repeats itself across other health centres in the district, their malnourished children's wards filled to capacity, and then some more. (Dutta, 2014)

Not surprisingly, nutritional and health deficits remain a perennial feature of the lives of a majority of India's socially disadvantaged communities, stretching from one generation to another. In addition to the categories of caste and tribe, the other social markers of vulnerability to hunger include factors such as old age, widowhood and gender. And when combined with low socio-economic status, these factors can further exacerbate one's proneness to poverty and food insecurity (Photo 3.1).

GENDER AND FOOD INSECURITY

The aggregate caste and class differentials in food and nutrition deprivation need further assessment by within-class gender categories. Within the household, differentials in food and nutritional outcomes of men and women can and often do exist. In many parts of the world, the weak social

Photo 3.1   An old widow from a lower caste: multiple layers of vulnerabilities

Source: Photo taken by the author during fieldwork in Siwan, Bihar.

and economic status of women often makes them more vulnerable to food insecurity. Indeed, the evidence suggests that women are overrepresented among the food insecure people (FAO et al., 2020). Although these differences may be in part due to the varying biological needs of men and women, more often than not they reflect the societal construction of gender and varying bargaining positions of different sexes within the household (Sen, 1987).

The pervasive gender inequalities in India mean that the issue of sex differentials in food and nutrition has particular relevance in the Indian context. A range of studies has pointed out that the widespread persistence of son preference, particularly in the northern part of India, often manifests into intra-household distribution of food favouring male children over female children, and it has been invoked as the possible reason for explaining the relative survival disadvantage of women vis-à-vis men (Bardhan, 1974; Miller, 1981; Das Gupta, 1987; Sen, 1987, 1990; Sen and Sengupta, 1983).

However, the relationship between gender, undernourishment and excessive female mortality often takes differentiated and complex forms and is influenced by a range of other intersecting variables, such as level of household wealth, landholdings and inheritance rights, sociocultural norms around the participation of women in economic activities and their perceived economic worth vis-à-vis men, and so on. For example, in her study in rural Punjab, a state with a strong son preference and excessively skewed SRs in favour of males, Das Gupta (1987) found that while girls fared worse than boys in the allocation of expenditure on food, clothing and healthcare, there were differentials across households by landholding status (a proxy of household wealth in rural India), and girl children among landless households fared worse than households with land (Das Gupta, 1987, pp. 86–88). In other words, even though girls got a disproportionate share in household wealth vis-à-vis boys in overall terms, the bigger resource pie worked to the advantage of the girls in the intra-family distribution of resources. As Bardhan (1974, p. 1301) suggests: 'Where there is more food to go around in the family, the female may have better chances.' On the other hand, other researchers suggest that because the patriarchal norms related to intergenerational land transfers favour men over women, the landed families may have an added pressure to favour sons over daughters to inherit property (Kishor, 1993, p. 249; also see Miller, 1981). Using the nationally representative NFHS-3 survey data, Arokiasamy and Goli (2012, p. 89) found that the likelihood of women having an ultrasound test (sought often for sex determination and female feticide) and induced abortion as well as female-child mortality rose with the increase in the size of landholding. Indeed, the SRs are much more masculine in Punjab, a state with higher average landholding sizes and per-capita incomes compared to other states. As Das Gupta (1987, p. 89) also notes:

> … female children may be neglected because their parents are poor, and, faced with difficult choices in allocating resources among their children, they give priority to children of the preferred sex. This does not tally, however, with the fact that the marked regional differences within India in sex ratio imbalances in no way correspond to regional differences in per capita income.

Similarly, Rosenzweig and Schultz (1982) also found these discrepancies between micro- and macro-level data on the linkages between wealth and sex differentials in child survival rates. While their analysis of the household-level data involving 1,331 rural households suggested that an increase in household wealth positively influenced the survival prospects of girls, the district-level data on landholding showed quite opposite results, and female children relative to males were higher in districts where a greater proportion of population was landless.

These contrasting findings make it difficult to ascertain the extent to which gender-based discrimination in intra-household allocation of food leads to excessive female mortality. Indeed, some researchers have questioned this claim. Drawing on the primary survey data on anthropometrics of children belonging to Uttar Pradesh and Tamil Nadu – two culturally diverse states with different gender norms – who lived in a slum in Delhi, Basu (1993) found no clear gendered pattern of undernourishment. The author argued that attributing gender imbalances in food distribution to survival disadvantage of female children is a hastily arrived conclusion and is often a product of an assumption that 'if women do badly on one count, they must do badly on all other counts as well' (Basu, 1993, p. 35). Another study by Griffiths, Matthews and Hinde (2002) on child undernutrition among under-five children in the states of Maharashtra, Tamil Nadu and Uttar Pradesh found no differences in underweight prevalence (weight-for-age Z-scores) by gender. However, as Udry (1997), Rose (1999), and Maitra and Rammohan (2011) have suggested, the failures to statistically unpack the gendered basis of undernourishment could be due to the fact that gender-based discrimination is manifested in higher mortality rates among girls during infancy, and that for surviving girls, there are no substantive gender differences. It is difficult, however, to completely rule out gender-based discrimination in intra-household food allocation, and recent evidence points to gendered pattern of diets. Using primary data from 3,600 households from the three Indian states of Bihar, Odisha and Uttar Pradesh, Gupta, Sunder and Pingali (2020) found that women consumed less diverse diets than other household members. Moreover, women's diets consisted of cereals, pulses and other vegetables, while the consumption of micronutrient-rich food groups, including green leafy vegetables, fruits and vegetables, dairy, and poultry and meat, was particularly low among women.

Although the existence of treatment differentials in intra-household food allocation between boys and girls in India remains contested, there is no dispute and much evidence that female undernourishment has substantial intergenerational costs. When undernourished women reach their reproductive age, they are likely to bear ill-nourished children. Indeed, it has been invoked as one of the possible explanations for the South Asian enigma – the fact that the region fares worse on child nutritional outcomes than Sub-Saharan Africa, which has considerably higher levels of poverty and deprivation than the former (Ramalingaswami, Jonsson and Rohde, 1996). Within South Asia, gender inequalities are more pervasive in India than in many other countries in the region. In fact, on many indicators of gender inequality, such as the proportion of women with secondary education, women's labour-force participation and political representation of women, India fares worse than its poorer neighbours of Bangladesh and Nepal (UNDP, 2020, pp. 361–64) that now also have lower levels of child undernutrition than India (WHO, 2021). India's laggard performance vis-à-vis other South Asian countries on curbing the widespread gender inequalities means that over time the South Asian enigma has increasingly become an Indian enigma.

AGRARIAN STRESS, CHANGING RURAL LIVELIHOOD TRAJECTORIES AND DYNAMICS OF MIGRATION AND URBANISATION IN INDIA

The foregoing discussion has attempted to highlight the perilous performance of India on meeting the MDG targets on hunger and undernourishment, and how this correlates with, and in fact in many ways is underpinned by, concentration of hunger in select geographies and sociocultural groups, mainly including the country's Scheduled Caste and Scheduled Tribe populations and women. Following the advent of rapid market reforms since the early 1990s, the Indian economy has grown at remarkably high rates. And although the faster growth rates of the past three decades are associated with a decline in poverty and improved income and consumption levels, its impact in addressing the deep regional, social and cultural inequalities (including those represented through nutrition) has been slow (for a useful account on this, see Drèze and Sen, 2013, pp. 72–80). Moreover, the evidence from successive rounds of the nationally representative NFHS suggest that in the post-reform period, disparities in child nutritional outcomes have widened between the rich and the poor and across the geographical regions and states of India (Pathak and Singh, 2011, p. 8).

Accompanying these inequalities is another important issue – and one that cuts across these dimensions – of rural–urban disparities in food insecurity and undernourishment. In India the problem of food insecurity is characteristically rural in nature. As noted in Chapter 1, through own-account agriculture or wage labour, a large majority of the rural population has been traditionally dependent on the agriculture sector to meet their income and food security needs. However, the growth trajectory taken by India over the past three decades has weakened the role of agriculture as a primary source of income and food security. The economic growth in the post-reform period has been highly urban-centric in nature, with over 60 per cent of the national income now emanating from urban centres (Planning Commission, 2011, p. 378). And between 1990–91 and 2019, the share of agriculture in the national income declined from 33 per cent to 16 per cent (Mehrotra et al., 2013; World Bank, 2021a). Added to this is the progressive fragmentation of landholdings over this same period. Between 1970–71 and 2015–16, the average landholding size in the country declined by more than half – from 2.28 hectares to 1.08 hectares (Ministry of Agriculture, 2019). These developments have profound implications for the rural livelihood systems and, by implication, for the food security of rural populations. Indeed, research suggests that there exists an agriculture–nutrition disconnect in India (Headey, 2011; Gillespie and Kadiyala, 2012).

Not surprisingly, these processes are leading to a restructuring of rural livelihood trajectories. As a consequence of stress on farm-dependent livelihoods, the significance of work migration, mainly to urban areas, has grown over time. The national population census data on employment trends provide some evidence in this regard, though recent trends remain confusing. Using data from the last two decennial population censuses conducted in 2001 and 2011, Table 3.2 shows the number of main and marginal cultivators and agricultural labourers in rural India. The Indian census enumerates the population in the two main employment categories of *main workers* and *marginal workers*, based on their duration of work. The main workers are defined as those who worked for a period of 180 days or more in the year preceding the census enumeration. And as a residual category, the marginal workers refer to those who worked for less than 180 days in the past year. These workers are then classified by the type of employment activity, such as cultivators, agricultural labourers, household industry workers, and so on (Census of India, 2011a).

The analysis of this data suggests that during this inter-censal period, the *main cultivators* declined by over 8.60 million and *marginal cultivators* decreased by 1.14 million. In percentage terms, the decline in main cultivators was of over 9 per cent, and marginal cultivators declined by 5 per

Table 3.2 Cultivators and agricultural labourers in rural India, 2001–11

Census year	Cultivators		Agricultural labourers	
	Main	Marginal	Main	Marginal
2001	101,345,252	23,374,495	60,517,788	41,913,430
2011	92,737,696	22,230,802	80,958,300	56,036,151
Absolute change during 2001–11	-8,607,556	-1,143,693	20,440,512	14,122,721
Percentage change during 2001–11	-9.28	-5.14	25.25	25.20

Source: Census of India (2001c, 2011c). The calculations of the decadal percentage change are by the author.

cent (Table 3.2). More recent data from the NSS and the PLFS suggest an even more profound shift: between 2004 and 2016, the agriculture sector witnessed a loss of 40 million workers (see Van Duijne and Nijman, 2019).

On the other hand, the census data also show that in the past decade the number of *agricultural labourers* increased steeply by over 20 million in the main-worker category and 14 million in the marginal category – an increase of over 25 per cent in both categories. This increase in the proportion of agricultural labourers in rural India is rather puzzling. It does not add up with the evidence on shrinking of agriculture-dependent livelihoods. Thus, while there were over 8.5 million less main cultivators in 2011 compared to 2001, which would generally be expected to be associated with a decline in agricultural employment opportunities for the landless and land-poor populations, the number of main agricultural labourers has increased by more than twice as much. This increase could plausibly be explained by two interlinked reasons.

First, it is perhaps the case that increasing land fragmentation and the concomitant decline in the average landholding sizes is pushing the land-poor rural households to supplement their agricultural income by allocating household labour in wage work on others' land locally. Secondly, it may be that with the decline in land sizes, cultivator households are moving away from direct farming and leasing out their land to the landless and land-poor households for sharecropping farming. Field research confirms the intensification of land-leasing and sharecropping arrangements in the case-study district of Siwan (see Chapter 6). At all-India level too, there is evidence that land-leasing in Indian agriculture has increased over the period, which has given rise to a new category of farm households in rural

India. This new category is labelled as 'non-cultivating peasant households'; their proportion doubled between 1981 and 2002, and they now account for around 20 per cent of rural households in India (Vijay, 2012, p. 40). Although the census definition classifies an agricultural labourer as 'a person who works on land owned by another person for cash or in-kind wages, with no right of lease or contract on land on which she/he works' (Census of India, 2011a), the informal nature of much of the land-leasing arrangements in India means that the census enumeration is inadequately equipped to capture the nuances of these arrangements. It is therefore not inconceivable (and perhaps likely) that sharecropper farmers are classified as agricultural labourers in the census. This also means that those who are leasing out land to pursue non-farm jobs are not classified as cultivators anymore as they are no longer engaged in direct farming, and hence the drop in the number of cultivators.[11] In any case, the decline in the number of cultivators and a surge in the number of agricultural workers point to rising pressure on agriculture-dependent livelihoods.

An expected manifestation of these developments in the country's rural employment landscape would be a rise in rural–urban migration for employment. Do national statistics indicate increasing levels of rural–urban mobility? At the outset, it is important to note that in India labour migration among the rural poor characteristically takes the form of seasonal and circular mobility, and the national-level datasets are ill-equipped to capture these flows in their entirety. The two major sources of migration data at the national level include the decennial population census and the quinquennial round of the NSS. However, they usually cover long-term movements and severely underestimate temporary migration flows (Breman, 1996, 2010; Deshingkar and Farrington, 2009; Tumbe, 2018).[12] Nonetheless, the findings from the 2011 population census suggest a significant rise in the urban population growth in India over the last decade, compared to previous decades. Whether or to what extent this can be attributed to rural–urban migration is a question that deserves attention.

There is no standard definition of the term 'urban', and different countries use varying criteria to classify places as either rural or urban. It is therefore important to first understand how urban is defined in India. The Indian census classifies areas as either rural or urban based on a combination of administrative, demographic and economic indicators. Since 1961, the definition of 'urban' followed in the Indian census includes the following criteria: (*a*) all places with a municipality, corporation, cantonment board or notified town-area committee, or the like; or (*b*) all other places which satisfy the following criteria: (*i*) minimum population of 5,000, (*ii*) at least 75 per cent of the male main working population engaged in non-agricultural pursuits and (*iii*) population density of at least 400 persons per square kilometres (Census of India, 2011e, p. 1). While the former includes *statutory towns* with urban governance, the latter type of settlements, also known as *census towns*, are small settlements at the bottom of the urban hierarchy that lack proper urban systems and infrastructure.

In an insightful analysis of urbanisation trends in India, Bhagat (2012, p. 27) showed that for the first time since independence, population increase in urban India was higher than in rural areas of the country. However, the urban population growth is not just the product of rural–urban migration but several other factors as well. The four important components of urban population growth include: (*a*) natural increase (births minus deaths), (*b*) rural-to-urban migration, (*c*) classification of rural areas as urban towns and (*d*) changes in jurisdictional and municipal boundaries. Of all these factors, the natural increase has always played the most significant role in urban population growth in India.

Figure 3.5 shows the trends in urban population growth from 1951 to 2011, and Table 3.3 presents the population growth in rural and urban areas during the recent inter-censal period. As is evident from the data, the total urban population has grown steadily since 1951, and in 2011 it accounted for 377 million people. When the long-term urbanisation trends are compared with the data on population size and growth rate in rural and urban areas pertaining to the most recent inter-censal period of 2001–11, important findings emerge.

Thus, between 2001 and 2011, the urban population increased from 286 million to 377 million, whereas the population in rural areas grew from 742.5 million to 833 million. Although this difference in the population increase between rural and urban areas may not appear to be much (90.98 million in urban areas versus 90.97 million in rural areas) (Table 3.3), it is very significant when considering the fact that between 1991 and 2001, the rural population increased by 113 million, whereas the urban population grew by 68 million people (Census of India, 1991a, 2001c). It is important to note that the 2011 census data also suggest that there has been a reversal of trend of declining urbanisation growth of the last three decades of 1980s, 1990s and 2000s. The annual exponential rate of urban population was 3.79 per cent during 1971–81 (the highest since 1951–61), which declined to 3.09 per cent in 1981–91, and then further to 2.75 per cent in 1991–2001. However, during the past decade, the average annual exponential population growth

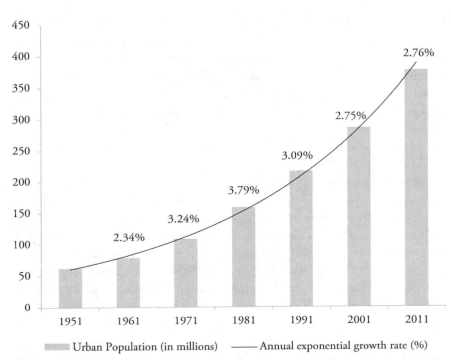

Figure 3.5 Trends in urban population size and urban growth, 1951–2011

Source: Bhagat (2012, p. 28).

Note: The annual exponential growth rates are based on the decadal census data, with 1951 as the starting period. Thus, the annual growth rate of 2.34 per cent in 1961 refers to the growth rate during 1951–61, 3.24 per cent in 1971 for the decade of 1961–71, and so on.

Table 3.3 Population size, distribution and growth by rural–urban residence in India, 2001–11

	Rural	**Urban**
2001	742,490,639	286,119,689
2011	833,463,448	377,106,125
Population increase during 2001–11	90,972,809	90,986,436
Average annual exponential growth rate during 2001–11 (per cent)	1.16	2.76

Source: Census of India (2001c, 2011f). The growth-rate calculations are by the author.

rate was 2.76 per cent, thus reversing the past trend (Figure 3.5). Importantly, this annual exponential growth rate of urban population was also more than double than that of rural population growth. This is despite the fact that a natural increase in population (births minus deaths), which, as noted earlier, has always played the most dominant role in urban population growth, was slower in urban than in rural areas (Bhagat, 2012). The data from the Sample Registration System show that in 2001, the natural growth of population in rural India was 17.3 persons per 1,000 people, which declined to 15.9 persons per 1,000 people in 2011 – a decline of 1.4 persons in a 10-year period. The natural increase in urban population was 14.4 persons per 1,000 people in 2001 which reduced to 12.2 persons per 1,000 people in 2011 – a drop of 2.4 persons, which is almost double that of rural population (Census of India, 2001e, 2011g). In the context of falling fertility, the pace of which is faster in urban than in rural areas, does this phenomenal rise in the urban population growth in the past decade indicate the rising rates of rural–urban migration?

The decomposition of incremental urban population by the relative contribution of its components suggests that of the 91 million people added to the urban population during 2001–11, 43.8 per cent (39.9 million) was from natural increase (of initial population plus inter-censal migrants), 20.6 per cent (18.7 million) from the net rural–urban migration and the remainder 35.6 per cent (32.3 million) was contributed by the net rural–urban classification. This latter factor contributed most significantly to the reversal of the trend of deceleration in urban population growth that characterised India's urbanisation story in the previous decades. Thus, whereas during 1991–2001, net rural–urban classification contributed 21.5 per cent (14.5 million) to the total urban population growth, its share jumped dramatically to 35.6 per cent (32.3 million) during 2001–11 (all data, Bhagat, 2012, p. 32, table 5). Indeed, the increase in the number of census towns during the last decade was almost equal to the growth of these towns in the last century: during 1901–2001, the number of census towns increased by 2,541 in all, whereas during 2001–11, 2,532 new towns were added in the census (Kundu, 2011, p. 15; Van Duijne, Choithani and Pfeffer, 2020). Recent research shows that even this phenomenal increase represents an underestimation of urban growth at the lower echelons of India's urban system. This underestimation occurs because of arbitrary administrative boundaries used in the Indian census do not consider the geographic clustering of places. Second, the local politics of the rural–urban classification often dictates that village leaders face democratic pressures to hold on to their rural status because urban status raises costs of living of residents and reduces rural development funding (Van Duijne, 2019; Van Duijne and Nijman, 2019).

The absolute share of net rural–urban migration in urban population growth also increased from 14.2 million during 1991–2001 to 18.7 million during 2001–11 (adding 4.5 million people in total), though in percentage terms the share declined moderately; it was 20.8 per cent during the previous decade and 20.6 per cent during 2001–11 (Bhagat, 2012, p. 32). In a nutshell, the evaluation of recent migration and urbanisation trends in India suggests that while the urban population growth has accelerated in the recent decade, the share of rural–urban migration in urbanisation has moderately slowed.

The population census data, however, capture the more permanent form of migration and severely underestimates the short-term mobility, as noted earlier. There is evidence that rural livelihoods are becoming increasingly multi-locational, and seasonal and circular migration has grown in recent years (Deshingkar and Farrington, 2009; Choithani, Van Duijne and Nijman, 2021). Estimates based on NSS data show that between 1993 and 2007–08, household dependency on remittances, as measured by the proportion of remittance-receiving households, increased significantly in India. In particular, the significance of domestic remittances rose considerably, and in 2007–08 internal remittance transfers amounted to USD 10 billion; and 30 per cent of all household expenditure among the remittance-receiving households (estimated at 10 per cent of all rural households in India) was financed by the remittances from migrants to their families (Tumbe, 2011). The rising significance of migration incomes can also be surmised from the data in Table 3.2 on the decline in cultivators and surge in agricultural labourers. In particular, the addition of 14.1 million agricultural labourers in the marginal category (those who worked for less than six months in the year preceding the census enumeration) in the last decade warrants attention. It would perhaps not be absolutely incorrect to state that a majority of these workers engaged in supplementary-income activities to make up for the employment deficits in the farm sector for the remainder of the year. And although the employment in the rural non-farm sector has also grown in recent years, acting as a buffer, urban areas have become more crucial in the overall framework of economy and job creation. Furthermore, the dominance of push factors notwithstanding, the more recent streams of temporary migration also involves new pulls, such as better urban incomes and improvements in infrastructure and communication networks. Using data from the NSS 2007–08 round that sought to capture temporary migration, Keshri and Bhagat (2012) estimated short-term migrants to be around 13 million in India. Other estimates peg the number of people on the move in any given year as between 40 million (Breman, 2010, p. 10) and 100 million (Deshingkar and Akhter, 2009; Government of India, 2017). Indeed, circular migration has dominated the mobility streams in India since the beginning of the twentieth century and is an important reason that has kept the overall levels of urbanisation low in India (de Haan, 1997a, 2002; Kundu, 2003, 2014). Thus, the decline in the relative share of net rural–urban migration in Indian urbanisation, on the other hand, may be indicative of rising circular migration. Recent research also shows that seasonal, short-term migration streams are being increasingly replaced with more permanent, long-duration forms of circular migration (Choithani, Van Duijne and Nijman, 2021).

The reasons for high circular labour mobility are complex. However, based on the available evidence and literature, there are four main explanations for this. First, the economic development trajectory in India has prevented a more permanent form of mobility. The structural transformation has not provided a smooth transition of labour from low-wage agriculture to salaried non-farm jobs. Informal employment accounted for over 90 per cent of 465 million jobs in 2017–18. In the period following the liberalisation reforms, most of the jobs have been created in this sector of the economy. Between 1999–2000 and 2017–18, informal employment has increased much more than formal jobs. Strikingly, moreover, increase in the job opportunities in the formal sector has mainly been for informal workers (NCEUS, 2007; Mehrotra, 2019). Urban employment in the lower echelons of the economy, which employ the poor and unskilled populations, has been almost exclusively in the informal sector. This has augmented circular mobility, for precariousness is one of the principal features of the informal sector (Breman, 1985, 1996, 2007, 2010). It must be noted that incomes from urban informal jobs are often higher than the rural wages. Indeed, urban informal employment still provides a valuable means of employment to a vast majority of poor and unskilled populations to make up for the livelihood deficits they face in rural areas. Moreover, more recent evidence shows an increase in the regular or wage salaried employment as opposed to casual employment (Mehrotra et al., 2013; Mehrotra, 2019).

The second reason pertains to the exclusive nature of Indian urbanisation in the post-reform period. According to Kundu (2003, 2014), the low rates of permanent rural–urban migration are because of the changing urban milieu, which has become increasingly hostile for rural poor. The increasing privatisation of land and civic amenities and consequent increase in the cost of living in urban areas is what has prohibited the rural populations from settling in the urban areas on a more permanent basis, which in turn has slowed down the tempo of urbanisation. In addition to that is the increasing hostility of urban residents to accept the rural poor in urban areas. For instance, in Mumbai, many citizen groups and resident organisations, such as Bombay First, CitiSpace, Khar Residents Association, Association of Clean and Green Chembur, have active and vociferous campaigns against street hawkers, most of whom are migrants from the poorer regions of India (Balakrishnan, 2003; Choithani, 2009).

These structural fissures that have come to characterise the contemporary Indian economy notwithstanding, a range of individual and social and cultural reasons also explain the low rates of permanent rural–urban migration. As explored in the work of Munshi and Rosenzweig (2016), the local, caste-based networks in rural India play an important role in restricting permanent mobility. A permanent change in residence implies less frequent interactions with natal villages and community. However, the absence of either comparable or more efficient insurance mechanisms acts as an incentive for the rural populations to stick to these networks for social insurance. This is particularly significant in the context of widespread prevalence of informal employment in India, as noted earlier. Finally, the social and cultural conventions in India pose restrictions on female mobility for work. In particular, in much of north India, labour migration is an exclusive preserve of men while women stay in the origin place. In turn, this provides an incentive for men to return (see Chapter 4 and Chapter 7).

CONCLUSION

This chapter has highlighted the broad dynamics of food insecurity, migration and urbanisation in India. Beginning with the assessment of the country's progress on the MDG target on hunger and undernourishment, the discussion has pointed out that India's performance has been highly dismal on this front. Undernourishment remains highly pervasive in India, and the rapid economic growth over the past two decades has not made any significant dent in curbing the levels of hunger, as experienced in other countries such as China. Indeed, India's experience has been crucial in triggering a shift in the official policy thinking that earlier rested on the assumption that economic growth will lead to an automatic decline in hunger and food insecurity. This shift in stance is reflected in the FAO's *SoFI* 2012 report, which bore the subtitle *Economic Growth Is Necessary but Not Sufficient to Accelerate Reduction of Hunger and Malnutrition* (FAO, 2012). For economic growth to reduce undernourishment, it has to be inclusive and pro-poor, which is far from true in the case of India. As the assessment of the factors underpinning India's laggard performance in reducing undernourishment has shown, the faltering progress of India in meeting the MDG target on hunger is, in many ways, linked to the uneven distribution of the benefits of economic growth across the lines of geography and sociocultural groups, mainly including the Scheduled Caste and Scheduled Tribe populations and women. The states in the undivided BIMARU belt still remain economically backward vis-à-vis other Indian states, with most districts in these states having a poor showing in terms of food security and key human development indicators; the impact of economic growth on improving the living standards of the country's marginalised social groups has been extremely slow; and the subjugated position of women within households has resulted in the perpetuation of poor nutritional outcomes in an intergenerational fashion.

In the final major section, the chapter has pointed out that the problem of food insecurity in India is largely rural in nature. Moreover, the changing contours of economic growth over the recent period, in which the overall significance of agriculture as a source of livelihood and food security has declined, is changing the sources of food security. Rural–urban migration for work is becoming increasingly significant in the lives and livelihoods of an increasing number of India's rural dwellers. An evaluation of the recent urbanisation trends in India, however, indicates low levels of permanent migration to urban areas and increased circular mobility because low incomes from urban informal jobs and prohibitively high costs of living in urban areas have prevented the rural poor from making cities their permanent homes. These processes have also has led to urbanisation becoming more exclusionary in nature. At the same time, it is also true that the urban informal sector provides a refuge to the millions of migrants who come to cities for work; without it, the migrants and their families at the origin villages would be much worse off.

This begs the question of whether and how migration relates to household food security outcomes. The next chapter discusses the research context before presenting empirical findings on the linkages between migration and food security.

NOTES

1. While the 1996 World Food Summit's goal was to reduce by half the number of people who were undernourished, the MDG 1 target was to reduce by half the proportion of undernourished people.

2. Originally, the MDGs consisted of 8 goals, 18 targets and 48 indicators. However, over time, new development targets and indicators to assess those targets were added.

3. It must be noted that in 2007, a new target, which was to 'achieve full and productive employment and decent work for all' was added to MDG 1. The assessment of progress on this new target was first reported in the 2008 report on the MDGs (United Nations, 2008), and this has figured in the annual MDG reports since then. This has altered the numbering of the targets, and in one of the recent annual MDG reports, the targets on poverty, decent employment and hunger were reported as 1.A, 1.B and 1.C, respectively (United Nations, 2013).

4. In recent years, there has been a shift away from using childhood underweight as the preferred indicator of child undernutrition. This is because underweight can cloak the co-occurrence of normal weight with stunting, which can give a false impression of progress in improving child nutrition outcomes. Stunting is increasingly the more preferred measure, as it indicates long-term growth retardations as well as long-term consequences of these growth imbalances (Wiesmann et al., 2015).

5. FAO-*SoFI* annual reports usually only provide the estimates on the proportion of undernourished people, and not the target. Since the MDG target was to halve the proportion of undernourished people in 2015 from the baseline figure, the target curve was plotted using this logic. The purpose here is not to assess time trends in divergence but overall progress till date, and this graph must be interpreted in that light.

6. In an MDG deadline-approaching appraisal, FAO's *SoFI* 2012 report, which carried the subtitle *Economic Growth Is Necessary but Not Sufficient to Accelerate Reduction of Hunger and Malnutrition*, cited in its foreword an article on India by Jean Drèze and Amartya Sen who distinguished between growth and development and called for a greater role of public policy to ensure inclusive, pro-poor growth (Drèze and Sen, 2011; FAO, 2012).

7. Note that in 2015, the GHI methodology was revised to include stunting and wasting indicators of child undernourishment instead of a single composite indicator of child underweight. The weight given to child undernourishment

component remains the same as that of other two components of child mortality and inadequate calorie intake, with each of the three dimensions assigned one-third weight. The one-third weight of child undernutrition component is shared equally between the two new indicators (Wiesmann et al., 2015).

8. To rank the districts and sub-districts in order of their backwardness, the authors used the population census 2011 data on seven indicators. These indicators include (*a*) agriculture workers as a proportion of total workers, (*b*) female literacy rate, (*c*) households without access to electricity, (*d*) households without drinking water and sanitary latrine within premises, (*e*) households without access to banking facility, (*f*) percentage of Scheduled Caste population and (*g*) percentage of Scheduled Tribe population. Given the availability of data at the sub-district levels, these indicators best captured three components of backwardness, including economic development, human development and infrastructure development. These indicators were assigned equal weights to compute the ranking (Bakshi, Chawla and Shah, 2015, 46–48).

9. The other state was Maharashtra. On the other hand, this was not done in Uttrakhand, a state which was carved out of Uttar Pradesh in 2000.

10. The HDI measures the average performance in the three dimensions of income, education and health. The District-level HDI computed by the authors used three indicators. These include (*a*) child mortality, (*b*) adult female literacy and (*c*) standard of living. The ABC index used four indicators of child survival and well-being that include: (*a*) probability of surviving until the age of five, (*b*) proportion of children fully immunised in the age group of 12–23 months, (*c*) proportion of children aged 12–35 months who are not underweight and (*d*) female literacy rate in the 10–14 age group (Drèze and Khera, 2012, 43–44).

11. It must be noted that these emerging land–labour dynamics may have a positive impact on the food security of the landless and land-poor households. By allowing access to land, land-leasing may reduce the dependence of poor households on the market purchase of food and, in turn, the food-price volatility that has characterised the global food markets over the recent years. This issue is discussed in Chapter 6 based on field research.

12. Some rounds of the NSS (55th and 64th rounds, conducted respectively in 1999–2000 and 2007–08) have, however, attempted to capture the extent of short-term migration in India.

4

THE CONTEXT OF MIGRATION

BIHAR AND SIWAN IN PERSPECTIVE

INTRODUCTION

Despite the fact that migration has traditionally been an integral part of the lives and livelihoods of rural communities in much of the developing world, all too often rural populations have suffered from the image of being *immobile* in the academic and policy discourse around rural development. This static image of rural societies is, in part, the result of the rural-equates-agriculture paradigm of thinking which, although fading, still remains prevalent. Although livelihoods for a large majority of rural populations in many low-income countries continue to depend on local, farm-based activities, the notion of an immobile peasantry is an unwarranted assumption and, with some risk of oversimplification, a myth. The inherently cyclical nature of agricultural work means that rural populations go through cycles of peak and lean seasons. In places where rural labour markets do not provide enough opportunities for non-agricultural income diversification throughout the year – which is often the case in most, if not all, countries of Asia and Africa – many households have traditionally employed migration as one of the livelihood diversification strategies to meet their income needs outside of the busy agriculture period. As de Haan (1999, p. 7) suggests, '... population movement [represents] the norm rather than the exception'.

Positing the significance of migration in rural livelihoods is important for it enables viewing rural livelihood systems as dynamic, comprising of not just farm-based activities but also a wide array of local and extra-local non-farm occupations. From the perspective of food security, this implies that in addition to land-based livelihoods, the issue of rural food security, or insecurity, has always been closely connected with access to, and gains from, the non-farm, migration incomes. In fact, in many instances the extent to which land facilitates a household's food security needs is contingent upon the extent of income from non-farm sources (Pritchard, Rammohan and Vicol, 2019).

The Indian state of Bihar, the geographic focus of this study, is a case in point, where a large majority of rural households have traditionally engaged in non-farm livelihood diversification to meet their income and food needs. Located in the Indo-Gangetic plains, Bihar is endowed with highly fertile soil and abundant water sources. However, persistently high population densities have almost always counterbalanced the capacity of rural land and resources to allow the state's inhabitants to adequately meet their food security needs. In particular, population densities in the western part of Bihar, where the case-study district of Siwan is located, have been much higher than in most other places in the country (O'Malley, 2007 [1930]; Yang, 1979, 1989). In the absence of non-agricultural local employment options, migration has always been central to the incomes and livelihoods of rural dwellers of this region.

The traditional importance of migration notwithstanding, economic reforms since the 1990s have changed the social, economic and infrastructural realties in India, which, in turn, are reshaping the very process of migration. New patterns and streams of migration are fast evolving. For example, rural–urban migration is gaining significance relative to rural–rural migration. By combining historical evidence with household survey data collected for the present study in Siwan, this chapter will discuss some of these changes in the later sections.

It is important to note that that in addition to high population pressures on land, Bihar as a whole has remained an economically backward region throughout the past two centuries. This has created heavy reliance on migration income among the rural communities of the state. In fact, continued lack of gainful opportunities at home seems to have created a culture of migration in rural Bihar. The economic decline of Bihar began during British rule and continued throughout much of the post-independence period. More importantly, market reforms initiated in India since the early 1990s largely bypassed Bihar until recently. Thus, although outmigration from Bihar has been historically widespread, village-level studies indicate that the incidence of migration from Bihar increased further in the 1990s (Karan, 2003; Sharma, 2005), a period which otherwise marks the watershed of Indian economy.

This trend of increased mobility from Bihar has continued in the following decades (Datta, 2016).

Against this background, this chapter aims to set out the research context as a precursor to the household-level analysis of the relationship between migration and food security. First, the chapter provides an overview of Bihar's economy and society and places it in the Indian map of development. Second, it attempts to briefly trace the reasons for Bihar's current backwardness and its relationship with high rates of outmigration. It then discusses the food security situation across different districts of Bihar and how this correlates with district-wise migration. Finally, it situates the case-study district of Siwan within Bihar and provides a brief profile of place, people and livelihoods in the district. For the discussion, the chapter combines the secondary data with some of the household survey data collected from Siwan.

A GEOGRAPHY OF DEPRIVATION: BIHAR ON THE INDIAN MAP OF DEVELOPMENT

A vast stretch of fertile alluvial land forming part of the Indo-Gangetic plain, the eastern Indian state of Bihar is among the most backward states in the country. The state is characterised by excessively high population pressures, an underdeveloped and weak economy, the highest proportion of population lacking access to bare minimum living standards, and dysfunctional education and healthcare infrastructure. Social inequalities along the lines of caste and gender, although by no means unique to Bihar, take a particularly potent form in the state.

Lagging far behind in demographic transition vis-à-vis most other Indian states, Bihar is affected by high population growth rates. The third largest Indian state in terms of population size, Bihar had a total population of over 100 million people in 2011, accounting for nearly 9 per cent of India's total population. During the most recent inter-censal period between 2001 and 2011 (for which data were available at the time of writing), the population in Bihar increased by 25 per cent. Although this represents a marginal decline from the decadal population growth rate of 28.6 per cent during 1991–2001, population growth in Bihar was still higher than the national average of 17.6 per cent. A predominantly agrarian society, Bihar has almost 90 per cent of its population living in rural areas. It is important to note that even though the urban population in Bihar grew at a faster rate during 2001–11, the levels

Table 4.1 Population size, growth and distribution

Place of enumeration	Total Population in 2011		Urban population (per cent)		Inter-censal change during 2001–11 (per cent)	
	Rural	Urban	2001	2011	Rural	Urban
Bihar	92341436	11758016	10.46	11.29	24.25	35.43
India	833087662	377105760	27.82	31.16	12.20	31.80

Source: Census of India (2001a, 2011c, 2011f)

of urbanisation barely moved upwards, indicating intensification of pressure on rural land and resources (Table 4.1).

With an economy characterised by little exposure to the urban manufacturing and service sectors, and a dearth of rural non-farm activities, agriculture remains the primary source of *local* livelihoods for a large proportion of Bihar's population. Indeed, the state is naturally endowed with highly fertile soil and abundant groundwater resources. Several tributaries of the river Ganges, including Mahananda, Kosi, Ghaghara and Gandhak, flow through different parts of the Bihar plain, making it one of the most fertile in the country. The real agricultural potential of the state, however, remains far from being adequately realised, which has prevented any meaningful decline in poverty and deprivation in the state. Fragmented landholdings, lack of irrigation facilities, and poor credit and extension services to farmers have impeded the achievement of the state's agricultural potential. This situation is best described in *A Report of the Special Task Force on Bihar*, which terms the Bihar plain a 'rich State inhabited by poor people' (Government of India, 2008, p. 11). Additionally, the large number of rivers also means that recurrent floods remain a perennial problem, affecting land-based livelihoods. The Bihar plain is among the most flood-prone areas of India. The calamitous floods in the state in 2008 from the Kosi river, considered 'the Hwang Ho of Bihar' (Ahmad, 1961, p. 265), took approximately 500 lives and rendered 2,73,000 acres of arable cropland fallow (Government of Bihar, 2008).

Until recently, Bihar suffered from a long spell of poor governance and economic stagnation, with each reinforcing the other. Prior to 2007, the state consistently ranked among the slowest growing regions of India (Basu, 2013; Sharma, 2013). While some of the factors for Bihar's laggard economic growth were related to internal problems such as governance deficits, it also suffered from discriminatory economic policies from the central government. For example, the Green Revolution, which brought about great economic prosperity in the northwestern states of Punjab and Haryana, largely bypassed Bihar even though the state seemed no less suited for it. The slow economic growth in the wake of rising demographic pressures has had a regressive impact on living standards and kept the incidence of poverty and deprivation high. In 2011–12, more than one-third of Bihar's population lived below the poverty line as against the national average of 25.7 per cent (Planning Commission, 2013a). On the multidimensional poverty index that captures acute deprivations in health, education and living standards, Bihar is the poorest Indian state with more than half of its population lacking adequate access to basic necessities (Oxford Poverty and Human Development Initiative, 2018). Poverty and deprivation take a particularly severe form in rural areas where much of Bihar's population lives, as noted earlier. This is also reflective of the highly unbalanced nature of the state's economy, hinging excessively on the rural end in the absence of any significant opportunities in the urban sector.

The accumulated damage of decades of slow economic growth in Bihar also acted as a detriment for the state to reap the benefits of market reforms initiated in India since the early 1990s. Following the liberalisation of its economy, India has registered impressive economic growth and has become one of the fastest growing economies of the world. Although the distributional aspects of increasing wealth in India remain troubling, the faster economic growth rates are nevertheless associated with overall poverty decline in India (Deaton and Drèze, 2002; Datt, Ravallion and Murgai, 2020). However, economic growth and poverty decline have hardly been uniform across Indian states and exhibit a regionally diverse pattern. Indeed, the evidence suggests that the new growth trajectory in India has resulted in a widening of regional inequalities in income and living standards. Findings of several studies indicate that the average incomes across Indian states have tended to diverge in the post-reform period, with income growth positively associated with the initial per-capita levels of income of the states. The Indian states with better human and capital resources and infrastructure have been able to attract more investments and grow faster in the post-reform period (see, inter alia, Rao, Shand and Kalirajan, 1999; Dasgupta et al., 2000; Kurian, 2000; Sachs, Bajpai and Ramiah, 2002; Kar and Sakthivel, 2007; Ghosh, 2012). The foreign capital flows are distinctly concentrated in a few advanced states, mostly in western and southern India. Between 2000 and 2012, just six states – Andhra Pradesh, Delhi, Gujarat, Karnataka, Maharashtra and Tamil Nadu – together cornered over 70 per cent of foreign direct investment (Mukherjee, 2011, p. 100).

With Bihar sorely lacking in human capital and physical infrastructure, it is not surprising that the state slipped further behind most Indian states. The per capita income in Bihar, which was close to 60 per cent of the Indian average during the 1960s, declined to nearly 40 per cent in 1993–94 and further to approximately 30 per cent in 2003–04 (Institute of Human Development, 2010, p. 1). In fact, in the first few years of market reforms, Bihar's economy contracted. Between 1992–93 and 1998–99, Bihar's per capita income turned negative at –0.2 per cent per year, whereas annual per capita income growth in Gujarat, for example, was 7.8 per cent (Sachs, Bajpai and Ramiah, 2002, p. 33). Although Bihar's economy has shown signs of revival since 2006, with the most recent data showing that during 2017–18 the state's economy grew at 11.3 per cent as against the national average of 7 per cent (Government of Bihar, 2019), its impact on poverty and living standards is still quite muted. The state still occupies the lowest rank on several key indicators of social and economic development.

Table 4.2 presents the HDI for 16 major Indian states from 1991 to 2019. The HDI is a summary measure which assesses average performance in the three interrelated dimensions of education, health and standard of living. As is evident, all states have witnessed improvement in the HDI value over the period, suggesting improvements in human development indicators. It is important to note that there is not much change in the HDI rankings of states throughout the whole period, and Bihar, although having witnessed some improvements in HDI values, has consistently occupied the lowest HDI rank among all major states.

FROM CIVILISATIONAL CORNERSTONE TO DEVELOPMENT CURSE: THE DECLINE OF BIHAR

It is important to note that Bihar was not always one of the backward states of India. In fact, it once represented an economically, socially and culturally advanced region of the country and indeed one of the cornerstones of the Indian civilisation. As it was the seat of the first all-India empire, the Mauryan dynasty, some commentators have argued that in many ways 'the history of ancient India [was] the history of ancient Bihar' (Thapar, 1966, cited in

Table 4.2 Trends in human development in India, 1991–2019

	1991		2001		2011		2019	
	HDI value	HDI rank	HDI value	HDI rank	HDI value	HDI rank	HDI value	HDI rank
Andhra Pradesh	0.426	10	0.483	11	0.587	9	0.649	9
Assam	0.412	11	0.491	10	0.570	11	0.613	12
Bihar	**0.379**	**16**	**0.437**	**16**	**0.520**	**16**	**0.574**	**16**
Gujarat	0.473	6	0.532	7	0.609	8	0.672	8
Haryana	0.469	7	0.552	5	0.641	6	0.708	5
Himachal Pradesh	0.482	4	0.596	2	0.669	2	0.725	2
Karnataka	0.447	8	0.522	8	0.611	7	0.683	7
Kerala	0.550	1	0.611	1	0.719	1	0.782	1
Madhya Pradesh	0.406	12	0.461	14	0.542	13	0.603	14
Maharashtra	0.497	3	0.562	4	0.651	5	0.697	6
Odisha	0.401	14	0.459	15	0.541	14	0.605	13
Punjab	0.500	2	0.581	3	0.664	3	0.724	3
Rajasthan	0.404	13	0.471	12	0.554	12	0.628	11
Tamil Nadu	0.474	5	0.549	6	0.655	4	0.709	4
Uttar Pradesh	0.397	15	0.465	13	0.537	15	0.594	15
West Bengal	0.443	9	0.507	9	0.577	10	0.641	10

Source: Radboud University's global data lab, 2021.

Mukherji and Mukherji, 2012, p. 2). The world's oldest university, Nalanda, was set up in Bihar, which for centuries served as a centre of knowledge and learning. Buddhism flourished in the state before it spread more widely in the countries of East and Southeast Asia. Furthermore, some of the earliest challenges to traditional hierarchies of caste and gender in India originated in Bihar (Sen, 2013, pp. 3–5). However, beginning from the late eighteenth century when the state came under British rule, Bihar declined in rank and clout. This fall of Bihar's fortunes continued throughout much of the post-independence period, so much so that it came to be viewed as a basket case in the Indian development discourse. It is perhaps not so much of a coincidence that the acronym BIMARU, a Hindi word meaning 'sick' or 'morbid', which is used to describe the backward Indian states of Bihar, Madhya Pradesh,

Rajasthan and Uttar Pradesh, begins with Bihar.[1] There are many reasons for why Bihar slid down to occupy the bottom ranks among all Indian states. The following section offers some of the explanations.

PERMANENT SETTLEMENT AND ITS FALLOUTS

Much of the current backwardness of Bihar could be traced back to the faulty economic policies imposed by the British Raj, which continue to impede its development even today. In particular, a great deal of the state's malaise can be attributed to the land revenue extracting system of the Permanent Settlement introduced by Lord Cornwallis in 1793, which planted the seeds of Bihar's decline. Under British rule, Bihar already received a disproportionately lower share of public investment in agriculture infrastructure compared to, say, the northwestern state of Punjab where the British made investments to restore and improve the canal systems for irrigation purposes (Timberg, 1982, p. 476).[2] The Permanent Settlement fixed the amount of taxes that the *zamindar*s – big landlords who controlled land and collected rents from cultivators – needed to pay to the British government. Unlike the Ryotwari System followed in the Madras and Bombay provinces, in which revenues were linked with agricultural output, this change in the tax system aggravated the woes of the discriminatory investment policies of the Raj. The Permanent Settlement, which was introduced against the backdrop of falling agricultural production in India, was intended to incentivise the *zamindar*s to invest in land, as any additional revenues coming to them from the land added after 1793 were not liable to be taxed. This also meant that the British government's taxes were now not to be affected by the variability in agricultural production on account of environmental vagaries such as droughts and floods. In other words, while agricultural production was still subject to vagaries of climate, the taxes became shock-proof (Banerjee and Iyer, 2005; Mukherji and Mukherji, 2012).

In the 30-year period between 1764 and 1793–94 before the Permanent Settlement was implemented, the tax revenues in Bihar had already increased by 300 per cent (Dutt, 1960, cited in Bhaduri, 1976, p. 45). Fixing of rents without due regard to the harvest conditions produced quite disastrous outcomes; it weakened Bihar's agriculture system and gave rise to new inequalities in land ownership. Far from encouraging investment in land, many *zamindar*s, particularly the smaller ones, defaulted while the others resorted to passing on the increased tax demand to the small peasants. The rural populations at the bottom of the social and economic strata were the worst affected; their poverty and food insecurity increased. As Mukherji and Mukherji (2012, p. 18) recount: 'The impoverishment of farmers and tillers continued throughout; small landowners sold out, farm labor became indentured, and the dismal situation of the already poor was made worse.' The big *zamindars* who largely belonged to the Hindu high castes of Brahmin, Rajput, Bhumihar and Kayastha appropriated more land, although a greater proportion of these high-caste Hindus were also landless or became so, along with other backward classes. In many places, men from upper-caste *zamindari* families who lost their land migrated out in search of employment and took up manual-labour jobs (de Haan, 2002, pp. 119–20), which were hitherto prohibited under the caste hierarchies.

In many districts of Bihar, the pauperisation of the peasant underclass, which comprised the large majority of the state's socially backward caste groups without access to land (Chakravarti, 2001; Sharma, 2005), was to the extent where they were unable to meet even their food needs. Added to this were recurrent famines. For example, the district of Saran in western Bihar (of which Siwan was earlier a part; see the discussion later) experienced five famines between 1770 and 1897 (O'Malley, 2007 [1930], p. 69). And while no large-scale famines have occurred in post-independent India, Bihar was one of the two states (the other being Maharashtra) which experienced a severe famine in 1966–67, affecting 34 million people in the state (Brass, 1986, p. 247). In many cases, the incidence of migration was intimately connected with food shortages, and oftentimes income from seasonal migration by household members, usually males, provided the only means to ensure the food security of the household. Not all migration was distress-induced, however, and colonial records suggest that many people migrated for better employment opportunities too (more on this in later sections of the chapter).

The Permanent Settlement debilitated Bihar's agricultural economy, on which the fortunes of a large majority of Bihari population directly depended. It also resulted in an even more exploitative agrarian structure, leading to widening of inequalities in landownership. In the post-independence years, efforts to remedy the colonial legacy of an inequitable agrarian structure through land redistribution policies in the state have remained beset with difficulties. Although Bihar was the first state in independent India to officially abolish the *zamindari* system in 1950, this did not translate into improved access to land among the very poor, particularly those belonging to the traditionally disadvantaged Scheduled Castes and Scheduled Tribes.

However, following the abolition of the *zamindari* system, social formation of agrarian relations based around caste did witness some change. Although the end of *zamindari* led to a mass eviction of sharecroppers and tenant cultivators who were the actual tillers of the land, big landlords from high castes also saw their landholdings diminish. A new class of landlords belonging to the upper-middle caste groups such as Kurmi, Koeri and Yadavs – officially categorised as *other backward classes* in contemporary Bihar – emerged. These were mostly small and middle peasants who were able to consolidate their landholdings and position in society in the midst of *zamindari* reforms (Wilson, 1999; Sharma, 2005).

Notwithstanding this shift in agrarian relations, land control still remained the prerogative of the upper castes. More importantly, the situation of the communities at the bottom of social strata did not change, as noted earlier. The rural underclass, including small peasants, sharecropper farmers and landless labourers saw their fortunes only deteriorate. Those who worked as farm labourers continued to be under-paid or not paid at all. Poor peasants whose incomes were so low to meet even the bare minimum consumption needs resorted to borrowing from the big landlords and entered into relationships of 'informal bondage' (Prasad, 1975, p. 931). Their social oppression, including sexual abuse of women, at the hand of landowning communities, continued unabated (Sharma, 2005).

This continuous oppression of the least privileged by the landowning elites provided an imperative for peasant mobilisation. Peasants organised themselves under several agricultural labour organisations such as Mazdoor Kisan Sangarhsh Samiti (Committee for Peasants' and Workers' Rights) and Bihar Pradesh Kisan Sabha (Bihar State Peasant Union) that emerged to represent their interests. By the late 1960s, radical ground-level politics, known as the Naxalite movement, had taken ground, which sought to challenge the existing order.[3] The Naxalite movement operated outside the purview of the constitutional framework of democracy, as it perceived the state not only to have ignored the plight of the lower castes but also viewed it as being responsible for further abetting and accentuating the feudal structures. Although the movement had a broad objective of addressing the historical oppression of the lower castes in all dimensions, including, for example, sexual exploitation of women, it was intimately connected with the issue of inequalities in land ownership. After all, control over land was the reason why the upper castes were able to rule.

These peasant movements provided confidence and hope to the oppressed class to regain their place and dignity in society. However, these hopes were soon dashed. Worried about the threat peasant resistance and mobilisation posed to the order of the day, the landowning elites, allegedly in connivance with the state apparatus, formed private armies and launched attacks on the oppressed masses. Peasant resistance was met with what Sushmita (2014, p. 41) terms as 'politics of massacres'. According to official estimates, in Bihar, between 1976 and 2001, the upper-caste militia and police killed nearly 700 people belonging to Dalit and lower-backward caste groups (Sushmita, 2014, p. 41). The most notorious of these landlord armies is Ranvir Sena, a militia of upper-caste Bhumihar landlords. Formed in 1995, Ranvir Sena allegedly perpetrated 29 massacres between 1995 and 2005, in which 287 people from the lower-backward castes were killed. In an incident that shocked the nation, on 1 December 1997, the members of Ranvir Sena massacred 61 people, including 27 women and 16 children, from the lower backward castes, mostly Dalits, in Laxamanpur Bathe village of Arwal district in central Bihar (Mahaprashasta, 2013).

The repression of the land and wage rights of the rural underclass by violent means instilled in them feelings of fear and insecurity. These continue to affect their everyday lives. Because the political and bureaucratic apparatus is largely dominated by the representation of the landowning communities, they have managed to prevent, to the extent possible, attempts that have sought to change the existing order. Although Bihar has undergone a major transformation in recent years, particularly after the election of a new government in 2005, remnants of feudalism still remain widely prevalent in the state. Rural populations at the bottom of the societal structure continue to be deprived of their rights. Following the election of the new government, the state constituted a Land Reforms Commission under the chairmanship of D. Bandyopadhyay, a former Indian Administrative Service official who was instrumental in the land reforms of West Bengal (a state which also carried a comparable colonial legacy of inequitable and exploitative land-tenure [Banerjee and Iyer, 2005]). The Bandyopadhyay Commission, after a detailed study, submitted its report in 2008. However, its recommendations have not yet been implemented due to lobbying by the upper-caste landlords (Bandyopadhyay, 2008, 2009). In 2010, the Indian media reported that the newly elected chief minister of Bihar, Nitish Kumar, who is widely credited for the state's revival, was warned by an upper-caste leader of his own political party, Prabhunath Singh, that passing a law that sought to protect sharecroppers' rights will push the state to the brink of civil war (*Deccan Herald*, 2010).

These class–caste tensions in the agrarian landscape of Bihar have had a huge impact on the development of the state in the post-independence period. Though it has been more than 70 years since the British Raj ended, the deep scars left by the Permanent Settlement continue to affect the society and economy of Bihar.

DISCRIMINATORY TREATMENT BY FEDERAL GOVERNMENT

If the faulty policies of the British government were responsible for pushing Bihar to the margins, the troubles of this eastern state were only compounded by the political indifference of, and even discrimination by, the federal government in much of the post-independence period. The disadvantage of Bihar was magnified, first, by the federal government's freight equalisation policy of 1948, which remained in place until 1993. In order to promote industrial growth in all the regions of the country, this policy subsidised the transportation costs of raw materials such as iron ore and minerals. In other words, the inputs for industrial development were to cost the same everywhere in India. Before the bifurcation of the state in 2000 into Bihar and Jharkhand (the southern part of the Bihar was carved out to create the state of Jharkhand), Bihar was rich in natural resources and minerals. However, with the freight equalisation policy, there was no incentive to set up industries in Bihar, which prevented industrial development in the state. This obliterated what might have been a source of competitive advantage for Bihar vis-à-vis other states (Singh and Stern, 2013, pp. xxi–xxii). With the agricultural sector already battling with the burden of high population growth and increasing class–caste tensions, this proved to be a double curse for Bihar.

On the other hand, despite the Indian planning vision of balanced regional development in which investments in underdeveloped regions have repeatedly figured as a development priority,[4] Bihar, for the most part after independence, has received inadequate fiscal transfers from the central pool. For nearly a decade and a half following independence (up until 1961), allocation of resources from the centre to states followed 'no definite formula' (Planning Commission, 1997, p. 2), and the funds allocated were at the discretion of the government at the helm. Although the formulae for fund allocations have subsequently been improved, Bihar has got a disproportionately lower investment vis-à-vis many other Indian states.

Guruswamy, Baitha and Mohanty (2013) compare the economic experience of Bihar and Punjab (the latter being one of the most developed Indian states) within the wider context of regional inequalities in India. They show that in 1965, the average per capita income in Punjab was INR 562, which was only 1.7 times higher than Bihar's INR 332. By 2001, Punjab's per capita income of INR 25,048 was five times than that of Bihar's INR 5,466. This widening income gap between the two states, the authors argue, is directly attributed to the differentials in public investment by the central government, with Punjab growing faster because of higher public investment. They estimate that over the course of the 10 five-year plans (1951–56 to 2002–07), whereas Punjab received INR 9,742.19 crore more than the projected allocation, Bihar got INR 77,161.5 crore less than what it should have received (Guruswamy, Baitha and Mohanty, p. 18, table 14). Furthermore, the additional allocation for Punjab does not factor in the huge investments in agricultural and irrigation facilities on which the success of India's Green Revolution rested.

INTERNAL GOVERNANCE DEFICITS

Added to this discriminatory treatment by the central government was the ineffective and corrupt political and bureaucratic administration that came to characterise Bihar since the 1990s. In that year, the Janata Dal party, headed by Lalu Prasad Yadav, formed the government. With its focus on narrow individual political gains rather than the development of the state, the Janata Dal rule, which lasted three terms (from 1990 to 2005), pushed Bihar farther behind the development curve vis-à-vis other Indian states. Under the garb of progressive politics for the backward classes, Lalu Prasad often played a tactic of divisive sectarian politics centred around caste.[5] More importantly, it is during this time that Bihar went into a mode of lawlessness; crime (murders, ransom kidnapping, dacoities, rapes) and corruption increased substantially, and criminals and corrupt officers enjoyed political patronage. In fact, crime, corruption and lawlessness became synonymous with Bihar. As Sinha (2011, p. 227) writes: 'When a daylight robbery or rape took place in Bengaluru, city residents would scream, "This is not Karnataka. This is Bihar."' The money that came for development projects was siphoned off by the corrupt political and bureaucratic apparatus, and no efforts were directed to improve the already deficient physical or human capital base. Kidnapping of rich industrialists by goons was so widespread that many of them fled to other parts of the country. Indeed, the governance deficits in Bihar were so acute that the state came to be known as 'Jungle Raj'. In an article in the *New York Times*, Polgreen (2010) notes the following about Bihar:

> Criminals could count on the police for protection, not prosecution. Highwaymen ruled the shredded roads and kidnapping was one of the state's most profitable businesses. Violence raged between Muslims and Hindus, between upper castes and lower castes. Its economy, peopled by impoverished subsistence farmers struggling through alternating floods and droughts, shriveled. Its government, led by politicians who used divisive identity politics to entrench their rule, was so corrupt that it required a newly coined phrase: the Jungle Raj.

MIGRATION AND FOOD SECURITY IN BIHAR

The aforementioned conditions produced a climate of social and economic insecurity, whereby a large proportion of the Bihari population was left with few livelihood options other than to migrate out of the state. Although some streams of work-related outmigration from Bihar were already well-established as early as the late nineteenth century (for example, migration to jute mills in Kolkata and adjoining areas [Sen, 1999]), in the 1990s the overall trend intensified.[6] Heightened pressures to migrate were closely related to acute food shortages in Bihar. The state's agriculture sector, already operating under intense population pressures, stagnated, and its capacities to ensure income and food security to the Bihari population dwindled.[7] The food-based safety net programmes, such as the PDS, were marred by huge problems of corruption.

Notwithstanding the political reinvigoration and higher economic growth in recent years, a rampant incidence of food insecurity persists in the state. Although food insecurity in India as a whole remains high as compared to many countries with similar and even lower levels of development, the situation in Bihar is even worse. A comparison of hunger and undernourishment in 17 Indian states by the IFPRI puts the food insecurity situation in Bihar as 'alarming'. In the IFPRI's SHI, Bihar ranks 15th out of 17 states, only ahead of two other highly food-insecure states (Jharkhand and Madhya Pradesh). Seen from an international perspective, Bihar's rank in the hunger index is lower than many extremely poor countries in the Sub-Saharan African region such as Mali, Malawi,

Mozambique, Tanzania and Rwanda (Menon, Deolalikar and Bhaskar, 2009, pp. 11–19).

Almost half of the 38 districts in the state currently suffer from food insecurity in varying degrees. Figure 4.1 presents the district-wise picture of undernourishment prevalence in rural Bihar using the Food Security Outcome Index (FSOI), as reported in the *Food Security Atlas of Rural Bihar* (WFP and IHD 2009a). The FSOI is a composite measure of food insecurity, which measures food deprivation using two key indicators of *underweight among under-five children* and *under-five mortality rate* (data on calorie undernourishment used in the SHI are not available at the district level, though the methodology of both indices is different too). Based on these parameters, the different districts are classified into five categories of (*a*) food secure, (*b*) moderately secure, (*c*) moderately insecure, (*d*) severely insecure and (*e*) extremely insecure. The index values range from 0 to 1, with low value corresponding to high food deprivation. As Figure 4.1 suggests, 18 districts fall in the categories of moderately food insecure and extremely food insecure. It is worth noting that food deprivation is largely concentrated in the northern part of Bihar (mostly in the areas above where the Ganges naturally divides the state into two unequal halves of north and south Bihar), which is relatively more backward than the southern part, though there are some clear outliers (WFP and IHD, 2009a, pp. 26–30).

Although there are no recent estimates of household-level food insecurity for the state as a whole, in 1999–2000 it was estimated that nearly a quarter of all households in Bihar did not 'get enough food all-year round', with this proportion increasing to 45 per cent among landless households and 65 per cent among households whose primary occupation was local agricultural labour (Sharma et al., 2000, cited in WFP and IHD, 2009a, pp. 36–37). The household survey data collected for this study in 2012 on 'regularity of eating' of 2,286 individuals from 392 households in Siwan suggested that 22 per cent of individual members consumed *two or less meals a day* during the month preceding the survey. This increased to 26 per cent among households with no land, compared with 15 per cent of households who owned land of an acre or more.

Does migration contribute to improving the food security situation at the household level in Bihar, where a large proportion of households simply do not have access to enough land and the rural and urban non-farm sectors remain characterised by a dearth of income and employment opportunities? Using household survey data collected from Siwan, this issue is explored in

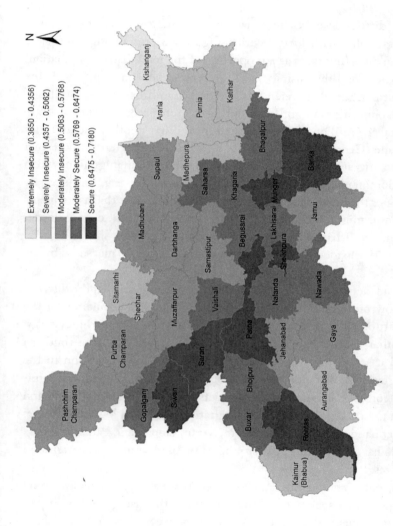

Figure 4.1 District-wise prevalence of food insecurity in rural Bihar according to the Food Security Outcome Index (FSOI)

Source: Map by the author, with data from WFP and IHD (2009a, p. 27).

Note: Map not to scale and does not represent authentic international boundaries. The map does not include Arwal district, which became the 38th district of Bihar in August 2001 when it was carved out from Jehanabad.

the analytical chapters that follow. Suffice to say at this point that though food security outcomes of migration are diverse for households positioned differently such as caste and landholding size, income from migration is very significant for household food security, particularly for the landless and land-poor.

At the district level, there is evidence to suggest that migration is positively associated with food security. Figure 4.2 presents the inter-state outmigration rates (migrants as a proportion of the total district population) for the districts of Bihar using the 2001 census data on migration.[8] The interstate outmigration here refers to migration from Bihar to places (village, towns, cities) in other states of India during the inter-censal period of 1991–2001. In total, 1.7 million people migrated from Bihar to other Indian states in that decade (Census of India, 2001a, p. 14). It is important to note that these data on migration do not take into account short-term migration, which is a more dominant form of labour mobility from the state, and severely underestimates the magnitude of migration. This also means that assessments based on census migration data are likely to underestimate the overall impact of migration. Yet district-wise outmigration rates, in general, show a positive association with the food security situation in the district, as measured by the FSOI.

The broad picture that emerges from Figure 4.2 suggests that the districts that have low outmigration are also the ones concentrated mainly in the northern part of Bihar, where food deprivation is high. As noted previously, northern Bihar is relatively more economically laggard than the southern region, and it seems that the low rates of livelihood diversification in the form of migration to distant places go some way in explaining the poor food-security outcomes. For example, the districts of Araria, Supaul, Purnia and Saharasa in the north-east have a low migration rate and a low FSOI value. On the other hand, the districts of Siwan, Saran, Gopalganj, Patna, Nalanda and Nawada have a relatively greater proportion of migrants and better food security scores.

Indeed, outmigration rate and food security have a reasonably strong *statistically* positive association. Figure 4.3 depicts this using the scatter plot with estimated linearity curve of association between these two variables. The adjusted R2 value of 0.263 – although not able to explain all the variation in FSOI values across districts, given that several other factors also influence child underweight and child mortality (variables that the FSOI uses) – seems reasonably well fitted still.

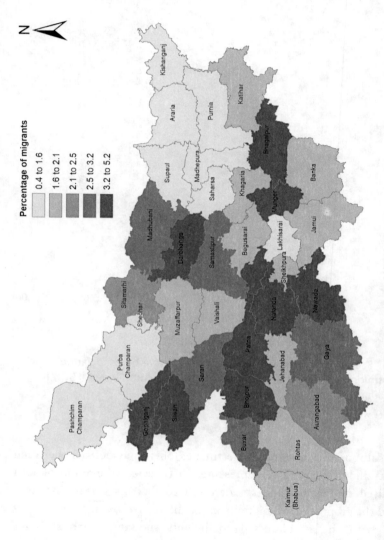

Figure 4.2 Interstate outmigration rates for the districts of Bihar

Source: Map by the author, with data from Census of India (2001b) on migration.

Note: Map not to scale and does not represent authentic international boundaries. The map does not include Arwal district, which became the 38th district of Bihar in August 2001 when it was carved out from Jehanabad.

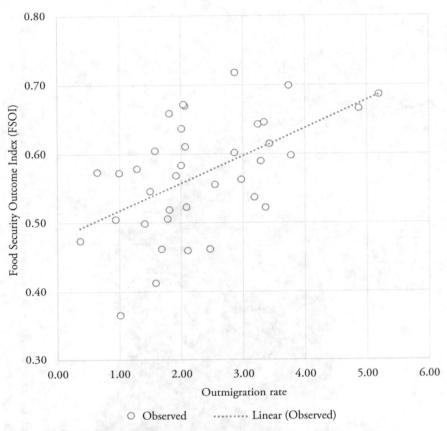

Figure 4.3 Scatter plot with estimated linearity curve on association between outmigration rate and the Food Security Outcome Index (FSOI) for districts of Bihar

Source: Author's work.

The results of linear regression estimates on the association between food security and outmigration are presented in Table 4.3. The results of both unstandardised coefficients and standardised coefficients reveal that food security and the proportion of migrants in the districts of Bihar are positively correlated, with the standardised coefficients showing much stronger association. In statistical terms, this suggests that one-unit change in the outmigration rate is positively associated with a five-unit change in the FSOI. The results are statistically significant with the *p* value of <0.001 and the *t–test* value of 3.67.

Table 4.3 Linear regression estimates on the association between outmigration rate and the Food Security Outcome Index (FSOI) for the districts of Bihar

Model	Unstandardised Coefficients		Standardised Coefficients	t	Sig.	95.0 per cent confidence interval for B	
	Beta	Std. error	Beta			Lower bound	Upper bound
(Constant)	.478	.028		17.312	.000	.422	.535
District outmigration rate	.40	.011	.528	3.676	.001	.018	.062

Source: Author's work.

CASE-STUDY DISTRICT: A BRIEF PROFILE OF SIWAN

The field research is focused on the district of Siwan in western Bihar, as noted earlier. This district was chosen because it exhibited a high rate of outmigration. Siwan came into existence as a separate district in 1972, prior to which it was one of the three sub-divisions of the larger district of Saran (the other two sub-divisions being Chapra and Gopalganj). The district of Siwan, which translates into 'border' in the local language, Bhojpuri – an apparent reference to its erstwhile geographic location when it formed the southern border of Greater Nepal – is one of the most densely populated districts of Bihar.[9]

In 2011, Siwan had a total population of 3.14 million people in a total land area of just 2,200 square kilometres (Government of Bihar, 2014a). To put these figures in perspective, there are nearly 400 more people on per-square kilometre of land in Siwan than the state average of Bihar, a figure which, in itself, is higher than the average population density of India as a whole. And the data over the longer period highlight that this density gap (Siwan vis-à-vis Bihar and India) has only increased over the years (Table 4.4). The level of urbanisation in Siwan remains unusually low, with close to 95 per cent of the population currently living in the rural areas. Though quite characteristic of Bihar – and, indeed, of most underdeveloped countries – this combination of high population density and low urbanisation makes it one of the poorest districts of India.

The district has been identified as one of the most backward districts of India, having low living standards and sub-par food security, education and

Table 4.4 Population density in Siwan, Bihar and India, 1981–2011

Year	Siwan	Bihar	India
1981	801	402	216
1991	978	685	267
2001	1223	881	325
2011	1495	1102	382

Source: Census of India (1981, 2011d, 2011e); Government of Bihar (2014b).

healthcare levels (Debroy and Bhandari, 2003; Bakshi, Chawla and Shah, 2015). The annual per capita gross district domestic product (GDDP) for Siwan is estimated to be INR 10,685, which is six times less than the capital district of Patna's GDDP of INR 63,063 (Government of Bihar, 2019, p. 17). Severely deprived of any major industrial activity, with no big private enterprises or public sector undertakings operating in Siwan, in 2011–12 the district had only 3,885 registered micro and small enterprises employing 13,120 workers, including their own family members,[10] of which close to one-third (1,246 units) were agro-based enterprises. However, the year-wise trends for the past quarter century in the number of micro and small enterprises registered and employment generated in the district show a decline – from 162 registered units employing 730 workers in 1984–85 to 65 units generating employment for 291 workers in 2010–12 (MSME Development Institute, 2012, pp. 11–12). Notwithstanding significant improvements in basic amenities such as roads and electricity in recent years, physical infrastructure in Siwan is inadequate, which has also, among other things, prevented any industrial development. Furthermore, the traditional forms of livelihoods such as pottery, brass work and embroidery, for which the district was once famous (Yang, 1998), have also gradually disappeared.

The *local* livelihoods in Siwan are heavily reliant on agriculture, with more than 60 per cent of the district's population working as either own-account cultivators or agricultural labourers (Census of India, 2011c). However, as is the broader case of Bihar, the nano-size of agricultural landholdings implies that for the large majority of rural dwellers, farming provides, at best, an option for subsistence and not a source of income. Furthermore, exponentially rising population pressures have undermined the capacities of agriculture-based livelihoods to enable the district's inhabitants to adequately meet their income and food needs. Already meagre in size, the average landholding size in Bihar has declined by half – from 0.75 hectare in 1995–96 to 0.39 hectare in 2015–16 (Ministry of Agriculture, 2021). Although similar time-series data are not available at the district level, the cross-sectional survey data collected for this study from 392 households in Siwan show that the average landholding size of the 265 households who owned any farmland was a little less than 0.25 hectare.

Poverty, coupled with lack of gainful employment opportunities in Siwan, means that a large majority of the district's population depends on wage-income options pursued in distant labour markets, usually outside the state. Although outmigration has been a key historical feature of the rural livelihood systems of Siwan (and indeed of Bihar in general), the significance of migration has increased over time. Not only is a greater number of rural dwellers seeking work outside, but migration is also increasingly becoming of longer duration; this is unlike the earlier predominant pattern of seasonal mobility that occurred in agriculturally lean seasons. It must also be noted that though much of the migration is induced by distress conditions at home, the decision-making matrices of households are complex and include, among other things, calculated strategies by households to spread income risks and accumulate savings. The next section attempts to place migration within the livelihood strategies of Siwani dwellers. The discussion draws on the history of migration from the district to highlight the nature and patterns of migration as well as some of the changes in mobility patterns and streams in recent years.

RURAL LIVELIHOODS AND CULTURE OF MIGRATION IN SIWAN: MOBILITY IN THE PAST AND PRESENT

A key feature of Siwan district throughout the past century and a half (as far as census records are available) has been high demographic pressures on land. Colonial records suggest that since the first synchronous population census of 1881, the former district of Saran was consistently ranked as one of the most densely populated districts of India; within Saran, the Siwan subdivision had the highest population density (O'Malley, 2007 [1930], p. 36; Yang, 1989). The high population pressures in western Bihar have meant that the region has historically lacked the ability to support its people. Furthermore, Saran's proneness to natural calamities, especially floods but also droughts, added to the woes. Harvest failures were not uncommon, leaving people starved and dead. Since Saran came under colonial rule in the late eighteenth century, the region witnessed five severe famines in 1769–70, 1783, 1866, 1874 and 1897 (O'Malley, 2007 [1930], p. 69). The famine of 1769–70 is considered to be the most severe one as, in some areas of the region, it wiped out 50 per cent of the total population (Yang, 1989, pp. 31–32). Nonetheless, the agricultural land under cultivation in the Saran region as a whole was evenly distributed among three harvests of the year, including *aghani*, *bhadoi* and *rabi* crops, which provided some protection against famines and recurrent food shortages.[11] Famines occurred only when two of the three harvests failed. The Siwan subdivision, however, did not enjoy this buffer, as it had a proportionally larger agricultural land dependent on the single *aghani* winter crop of rice (O'Malley, 2007 [1930]) and was thus among the most food scarcity-prone divisions of the district.

The implementation of the Permanent Settlement had wreaked havoc across different regions of Bihar. Agricultural production in the state suffered a blow and local livelihoods were disrupted, affecting, in particular, the class of small peasants and agricultural labourers. Because of its high demographic pressures on land, agricultural stagnation affected Saran district worse than virtually all other districts in Bihar, and at the beginning of twentieth century it became 'the first district [of] Bihar to reach the point at which it [could] no longer support an increase in its population in moderate comfort from the produce of the soil' (Fremantle, 1906, cited in Yang, 1979, pp. 47–48). Poverty and food insecurity among the rural underclass increased, and they resorted to migration in large numbers to other places in search of work. However, migration was not restricted to just the poor; it involved people from all socio-economic strata. Although the *zamindari* system meant that control over land determined one's power and position in society and hence migrating out implied loss of land and status, intense pressure associated with land-based livelihoods meant that many people in the region did not mind deserting their land parcels. In any case, the average land sizes were too small, and the region was characterised by 'petty zamindars' (Hagen and Yang, 1976, p. 77). As Yang (1989, p. 182) writes:

> Under the British Raj, when control of land became a fundamental source of power, wealth and status, flight became far less promising as alternative to the raiyats [peasants]. Its continuance … therefore, highlights the intense pressures on peasants in Saran's agrarian system.

Such was the extent of outmigration from Saran that in 1891, it was described as 'one of the greatest emigrating districts in Bengal' (Bourdillon, 1898, cited in Yang, 1979, p. 41).[12] In total, there were 364,315 Sarani migrants enumerated outside the district in 1891 (Yang, 1979, pp. 41–42). While many families from the region left their land and migrated permanently to other places, mobility from Saran was largely of *seasonal and circular* nature, which was connected closely with the local agricultural calendar and occurred outside the peak agricultural period. Yang (1979, p. 50) characterises the seasonal migrant from Saran as an 'optimizing peasant migrant' and suggests that seasonal migration was a deliberate strategy of the rural peasant populations of Saran, which provided them an effective means to supplement their agricultural incomes without incurring the potential costs (such as leaving behind the established life and family) that permanent migration involved. This pattern of migration has continued even after the end of British Raj (de Haan, 2002), though migration is now occurring for longer durations, as we will see later. Another defining characteristic of migration from the region has been that it has tended to be predominantly single-male migration because social and cultural norms regarding the roles of women restrict their mobility.

Though migration was largely a result of distress conditions at home, not all moves represented *push* migration. Many people simply responded to better work opportunities in order to improve their standards of living. Migration did, no doubt, involve huge risks, and Saranis willingly took onto them. In fact, the colonial administrators viewed the Bhojpuri-speaking population of Saran as distinctly different from the rest of Bihar when it came to their readiness to migrate. To quote Sidney Steward O'Malley, who served as the Collector of Bengal during the colonial rule:

The Bhojpuri speaking country is inhabited by a people curiously different from the others who speak Bihari dialects. They form one of the fighting nations of Hindustan. An alert and active nationality, with few scruples and considerable abilities, dearly loving a fight for fighting's sake, they have spread all over Aryan India, each man ready to carve his fortune out of any opportunity that may present itself. They have in former times furnished a rich mine of recruitment to Hindustani army and on the other hand they took a prominent part in the mutiny of 1857. As fond as Irishman of a stick, the long boned stalwart Bhojpuri with his staff in his hand is a familiar object striding over the fields far from his home. Thousands of them have emigrated to British colonies and have returned rich men; every year still larger numbers wander over Northern Bengal and seek employment either honestly as *palki*-bearers or otherwise as dacoits. The larger Bengal land-holders each keep a posse of these men, euphemistically termed *Darwans* [Doorkeepers] to keep his tenants in order. (O'Malley, 2007 [1930], p. 41)

Although there were numerous streams of migration from the region, as far as to the distant British colonies in Southeast Asia and Fiji in the South Pacific, much of the migration from western Bihar in the pre-independence era was to the neighbouring districts of Bengal, mainly Calcutta (now Kolkata). Following the development of the jute industry and railways in West Bengal towards the end of the nineteenth century, many labourers from Bihar migrated there to work in the jute mills or as coolies at the railway stations. The greater variety of employment in Calcutta and its neighbouring towns resulted in local labour shortages in the jute mills, and migrants from the poorer regions of Bihar and Odisha provided an easy source to fill this gap. In her study of the jute industry in Bengal, Sen (1999, p. 26) notes:

It is then not surprising that [jute] mills experienced periodic shortages of labour when they depended on local sources. Their problems were solved by the long-distance migrants. From the mid-eighteenth century, Bengal had begun to draw labour from Orissa and Bihar.

Jute mills supported a large number of migrants from Bihar and other eastern provinces. Saran district, of which Siwan formed a part, topped the chart in terms of the number of seasonal migrants coming to Calcutta to work in the mills (Sen, 1999, p. 27). However, the jute industry, which had already begun to stagnate by the late 1920s in some parts of West Bengal, hit a tipping point around the late 1960s, and employment opportunities in the sector dwindled (de Haan, 1997b).

The employment stagnation in the jute industry of West Bengal occurred contemporaneously with the advent of the Green Revolution reforms in the north-western states of Punjab and Haryana. These latter events generated massive agriculture employment in these states. The streams of migration from Bihar thus shifted to these north-western states, and a large number of people from Bihar migrated as agricultural labourers. A study carried out by Singh (1995) in 1980–81 in the districts of Ludhiana and Hoshiarpur of Punjab found that seasonal migrants from the north Bihar districts of Munger, Saharsa, Darbhanga, Muzzafarpur and Samastipur ranged between 400,000 and 500,000 workers in these two districts. Migration to Punjab involving the tribal populations from the southern Chotanagpur Plateau region of the state (currently the state of Jharkhand), although far less in numbers, was also significant (cited in Singh, 1997). It must be noted that seasonal migration from Bihar to Punjab occurred even during the decade of 1980–90, which saw insurgency in the state of which several migrant labourers were also the victims. Singh (1997, p. 519) notes: 'The flux of migrant labour from Bihar could never be deterred by the bullets of Sikh "militants" despite their massacre during the turbulent period of 1981–91.' Although there are no independent studies that track the migrant flows from Siwan to Punjab for agricultural work, personal histories of several current migrants confirmed that Punjab was one of their favoured work destinations. Many migrants also reported working in the knitting industry in the Ludhiana district of Punjab. Migration for farm work to Punjab and Haryana remained a predominant stream of migration from Bihar up until the early 1990s when agricultural productivity began to taper off, leading to an eventual reduction in demand for agricultural labour.

The high incidence of poverty and lack of productive employment opportunities in Bihar continue to be major *push* factors of migration from the state. However, more recent waves of migration involve new *pull* motives and destinations. Following the opening up of the Indian economy in the early 1990s, economic activities have largely come to concentrate in the country's urban centres and, in many ways, at the expense of rural areas where nearly 70 per cent of the country's population lives. Evidence suggests that the rural–urban income and expenditure gaps in India, although always persistent, have widened in the post-liberalisation period (Deaton and Drèze, 2002; Motiram and Vakulabharanam, 2011). The rising incidence of rural–urban inequalities in India has also resulted in a greater number of rural dwellers now migrating to urban areas for work. Although rural–rural migration still remains strong, work mobility to urban areas is becoming increasingly more important.

The household survey data collected for the present study on the current work destinations of migrants from Siwan suggest that most people moved to urban areas. Only two out of 280 migrants worked as agricultural labourers, and their average monthly income of INR 4,000 was the lowest among all the other occupational groups. In terms of urban work destinations, although migrants from Siwan were spread out across different parts of India, migration was found to be highly concentrated in the tier-1 cities that dominate the Indian economy.

Figure 4.4 presents primary survey data on major migration destinations from Siwan during 2011–12, as reported by their household members at the origin village. With the total migrants numbering 280, a *major migration destination* is defined here as a place where there were 15 or more migrants.

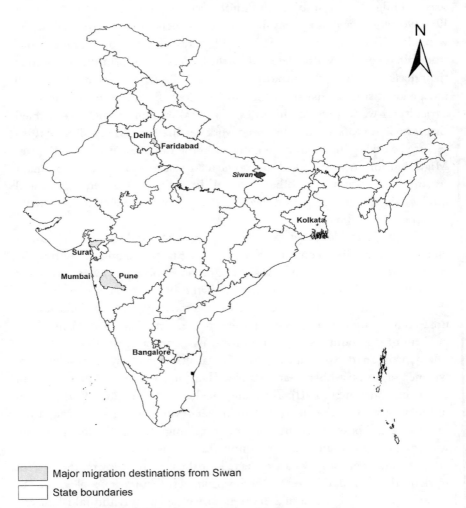

Major migration destinations from Siwan

State boundaries

Figure 4.4 Major migration destinations from Siwan, Bihar

Source: Primary household survey data.

Note: Map not to scale and does not represent authentic international boundaries.

In total, 161 migrants (65.4 per cent) were reported to be working in just seven cities. The national capital of Delhi had the highest number of Siwani migrants (51 migrants), followed by the age-old destination of Kolkata (26 migrants). Other migration destinations included Bangalore (20 migrants), Pune (16 migrants), Mumbai (16 migrants), Faridabad (16 migrants) and Surat (15 migrants). Labour migration to Pune, Faridabad, Bangalore and Delhi is connected with the increasing real-estate activities in these cities as most of the migrants were reported to be engaged in the construction sector.

Most migrants belonging to the sample household were engaged in casual work and lacked secure employment tenure. Yet, unlike the earlier pattern of short-term migration, which mostly coincided with the agricultural cycle at the place of origin, the household survey data suggest that a large number of Siwani households now have members who are spending more time away from their village for work.

Figure 4.5 presents the distribution of migrant households by their members' duration spent away from the village for work. Out of 197 migrant

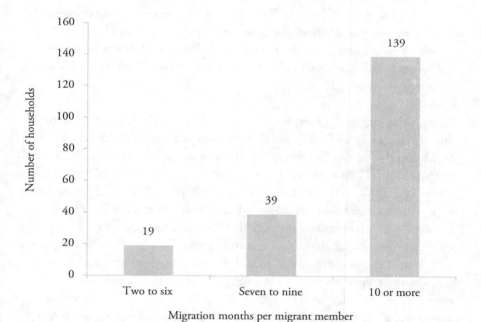

Figure 4.5 Distribution of households by migrant members' duration of stay away from their village, 2011–12

Source: Primary household survey data.

households, members of 178 households spent seven months or more outside the village for work, and 139 households reported that their migrant members were away for 10 months or more during the past year. This, of course, does not mean that migrants did not make visits back home. With the exception of 41 out of 280 migrants, all migrants returned home in the past year, with close to half of them (134 migrants) visiting home two times or more.

The fieldwork suggested that not all migrants, particularly those working in construction as masons or helpers, were able to find work on a regular basis. Nonetheless, in general, the average wages in the cities were more than the wages in the villages, which allowed most migrants to save and remit money home even after accounting for expenses at destinations, such as rent, electricity and food. In many cases, the motivation to migrate itself was deeply entrenched in the prospects of savings that migration allowed. As a migrant worker put it:

> It is not impossible to get work here [in the village]. While I may not get work all year round, work irregularity hangs on my head everywhere. But if I work in the village, I know I cannot save even a single penny. Saving is impossible from the little everyday earning here, whereas I am able to save working outside the village. At least, my children do not ask for pocket money when I am away, and you know how hard it is to refuse money to your children.

Though the longer duration spent away from home is driven by a complex mix of push and pull factors which vary from one household to another, it is also indicative of the increasing significance of migration in the livelihood systems of rural households in Siwan. That said, much of the migration from Siwan is still circular. Consistent with de Haan's (1999, 2002) findings in Saran district, the fieldwork suggested that most migrants in Siwan returned home to visit their families and friends although they now spent less time in the village than what the earlier research seemed to suggest. With migrants now spending more time away from home in non-farm activities, it seems that the dual 'optimising peasant migrant' character of rural dwellers from western Bihar, as suggested by Yang (1979, p. 50), is gradually weakening and that seasonal migration is now being replaced by more permanent forms of circular migration (also see Choithani, Van Duijne and Nijman, 2021). On the other hand, however, most migrants tended to invest their savings in household-owned land and agriculture in the origin village, which, in turn, allowed them to maintain their peasant identities. This carries important implications for food security, particularly in places of origin. How circular migration provides a potential pathway to influence household food security is discussed in Chapter 6.

Another defining feature of migration from Siwan is that it is almost exclusively undertaken by the male members of the household while the women stay behind. It is striking to note that this single-male pattern of migration has continued for a hundred years. Table 4.5 presents the general SR (females/1,000 males) of Siwan and Bihar from 1901 to 2011. As is evident, the number of females in Siwan has outnumbered males for a century (1901–2001), while the SR in Bihar began to decline after 1961 with 1931 being an exception. The data from the 2011 census show that the female–male ratio in Siwan has reduced to below 1,000 although it is still higher than Bihar's and the all-India figures of 918 and 943, respectively.

A number of studies have highlighted that the skewed SR in India favouring males is due to the strong preference for sons, which manifests into widespread treatment differentials and discrimination against girls in matters such as healthcare, food and nutrition and education, with the overall negative effect on survivorship of females (inter alia, Boserup, 1970;

Table 4.5 Sex ratio (SR) (females/1,000 males) in Siwan and Bihar, 1901–2011

Year	Bihar	Siwan
1901	1061	1199
1911	1051	1151
1921	1020	1066
1931	995	1038
1941	1002	1082
1951	1000	1118
1961	1005	1154
1971	957	1076
1981	948	1070
1991	907	1017
2001	921	1033
2011	918	988

Source: Census of India (2011d); Government of Bihar (2014c).

Bardhan, 1974; Miller, 1981; Das Gupta, 1987, 2005; Sen, 1990, 1992). In Siwan, the higher positive female–male ratio is not because of any absence of son-preference in the district; such a preference is deeply and rigidly entrenched in rural society in Siwan. The emanating difference owes largely to the effects of single-male migration outflows from the district which, in turn, are guided by the social and cultural conventions posing restrictions on the participation of women in distant labour markets. Not only do the societal norms prohibit women to take up employment outside the village, but the possibility of women joining their husbands at the place of destination is also considered socially unacceptable. In regard to the latter, while many migrants interviewed indicated that they found it economically unviable to bring their wives along, and economic reasons also figured prominently in the responses of migrants' left-behind wives surveyed at the origin, this is not the only explanation. During the fieldwork, many respondents alluded to the disruptions it can cause to the functioning of the households. For example, Ahmad (name changed), a migrant worker, narrated that when his daughter developed a major health problem, he decided to seek her treatment in Delhi as it had better healthcare infrastructure and services than Siwan. He brought his wife along to take care of the daughter so that he could continue to work and pay for his daughter's health expenses. The treatment, lasting around a year, required making periodic visits to the hospital. When the treatment was finally complete and the hospital visits were no longer required, Ahmad went to drop his wife and daughter back to the village. Upon their return, however, his mother separated his family from the joint household as she was of the view that Ahmad's decision to take his wife along to the city did not take into consideration that his wife is supposed to take care of his mother in her old age. In fact, interviews with many of the migrants' wives revealed a puzzling dichotomous response. When the stay-put wives of the migrants were asked if, given a chance, they would like to stay with their migrant husbands at the destination, many women expressed a strong desire for this living arrangement; at the same time, they wanted their daughters-in-law to stay in the village and take care of them. Equally important to note is that some women also suggested that they wanted to live in the village and take care of the family elders and children from which they appeared to derive their sense of self-worth (factors underlying the male-only pattern of migration are discussed in detail in Chapter 7). This provided a reason for the men to return home, and it explains, to some extent, the circularity of migration.

Male-only migration seems to also trigger fundamental changes in power relations at the household level. Absence of male members results in women assuming a more proactive role in household affairs, in matters financial and otherwise, which also has the potential to affect household food security. Whether and how this correlates with food security is explored in Chapter 7. It is rather surprising that despite male migration being the norm in many countries in the developing world, research evidence is scarce on how the resultant changing household gender dynamics may impact food security within the household.

CONCLUSION

This chapter has provided a broad overview of the economy and society of Bihar. The discussion has highlighted that a combined effect of discriminatory economic and investment policies, coupled with social tensions along the lines of caste and governance failures, has led the state to slide down from the commanding heights of the Indian civilisation to a 'basket case of irrelevance' (Singh and Stern, 2013, p. xvii). Decades of economic stagnation in the wake of high population pressures have produced a climate whereby migration has become an inseparable part of rural households of the state.

This chapter has also shown that mobility in Siwan (and in western Bihar in general) has been much more pronounced than the popular rural-equates-agriculture paradigm of thinking seems to suggest. It is worth noting that though the streams and duration of migration have undergone changes over the years, two central characteristics of mobility from western Bihar remain largely intact. These include (*a*) circular nature of migration and (*b*) male-dominated migration. These patterns of migration imply that there are two key pathways through which migration may have a potential bearing on household food security: first, the linkages that circular migration creates between rural and urban economies through remittances; second, the changes triggered by the single-male pattern of migration at the household level, with household responsibilities and decision-making invariably falling more on the women in the absence of the men. Chapters 6 and 7 discuss the ways in which these relationships between migration patterns and food security play out. The next chapter, however, addresses the connections between the institutional arrangements pertaining to the food and livelihood security in rural Bihar and migration.

The analysis of the government-run food and livelihood programmes is timely. As noted earlier, following the election of a new state government in 2005, a range of governance reforms has been initiated to revive the state. Indeed, some positive signs are already visible. The state of law and order has improved remarkably, and Bihar is no longer considered to be in the grip of 'Jungle Raj'. The growth rate of Bihar's economy has also surged, and basic amenities such as roads, electricity and water have improved. The arena of food and livelihood safety schemes has not been left untouched by these reforms to improve the food security of the rural poor. These governance reforms have led to claims on the decreasing incidence of migration from the state. Drawing from the household survey data collected from Siwan, these claims are examined in the next chapter.

NOTES

1. The acronym BIMARU was coined by Indian demographer Ashish Bose in 1980s to classify the states which were socially, economically and demographically the most backward in the country. Distinguishing Bihar in the BIMARU group states in one of his later papers, Bose commented that 'Bihar is a picture of anarchy' (Bose, 2000, p. 1699).

2. See Stone (1984) for a detailed account of canal irrigation in British India.

3. The Naxalite movement originated in 1967 in Naxalbari village in West Bengal, in response to the attack on a tribal farmer by the local landlords who tried to prevent him from farming on the land for which he had obtained judicial orders (Kujur, 2008, p. 2). Later, the movement spread to other parts of India. Currently, 90 districts of India are identified to be affected by Naxalism (Ministry of Home Affairs, 2020).

4. For example, the second five-year plan (1956–61) document noted: 'In any comprehensive plan of development, it is axiomatic that the special needs of the less developed areas should receive due attention … as development proceeds and large resources become available for investment, the stress of development programmes should be on extending the benefits of investments to underdeveloped regions' (Planning Commission, 1956, p. 36).

5. To Prasad's credit, the Janata Dal rule did have some positive impact on the emancipation of the backward castes. For instance, Witsoe (2013, p. 43) notes:

'While Lalu systematically destabilised the institutions of governance and state-directed development, I suggest that this also catalysed a meaningful, although partial empowerment of lower caste' (cited in Desai, 2013, p. 70).

6. For example, a follow-up study in six villages of the districts of Gopalganj, Madhubani and Purnea in north Bihar found that between 1982–83 and 1999–2000, the incidence of migration in the villages had doubled. In 1982–83, 27.69 per cent of households reported having one or more members working outside the village, and this proportion increased to 48.63 of all households in 1999–2000 (Karan, 2003, pp. 112–13; also see Sharma, 2005). Of course, not all of it was a result of the distress situation at home, and many people also responded to the better employment opportunities that emerged in other parts of India after the advent of market reforms in the early 1990s.

7. Population growth rates in Bihar have been much higher than in most states in the country. In 2011, 35 out of 38 districts in Bihar had a population size of more than a million people (Census of India, 2011b).

8. At the time of writing, migration data from the 2011 census were not released. Besides, the broad migration patterns relevant for present discussions are unlikely to be different.

9. Although Siwan no longer shares border with Nepal, the locals still signify the same Bhojpuri meaning of Siwan by loosely referring to the internal border the district shares with the other Bhojpuri-speaking districts of Deoria in its west and Balia in its south of the neighbouring state of Uttar Pradesh.

10. The evaluation report of the Ministry of Micro, Small and Medium Enterprises (MSME) Development Institute, cited earlier, does not clarify if the workers involved included family members. However, given most small-scale enterprises in India are family-run units, it is a reasonable assumption.

11. *Aghani* refers to the winter crop harvested in the months of November–December, which included mainly rice and sugarcane. *Bhadoi* was harvested in the autumn season (August–September), and the crops grown included millet, rice, *maura* rice, corn and indigo. And *rabi* crops mainly included wheat and pulses, harvested in the spring months of March–April (O'Malley, 2007 [1930]; Yang, 1989).

12. Until 1912, Bihar formed part of the Bengal Presidency.

5

CONNECTIONS BETWEEN FOOD SAFETY NETS AND MIGRATION

INTRODUCTION

A key issue facing a large majority of India's vulnerable rural populations is their inability to avail the benefits of state-assisted social protection schemes. Although public expenditure on social protection in India remains notoriously low compared to many other countries at similar stages of economic development (Drèze and Sen, 2013), numerous public assistance programmes – both in-kind and cash-income support – currently exist with the purpose of providing some form of social protection to the poor and vulnerable. Because of the exclusionary nature of economic growth in India in the post-liberalisation period, which has widened the gap between the haves and have-nots, the cause of strengthening social protection has been given further impetus in recent years. This is reflected in the dominant narrative of inclusive development that has come to characterise social and economic development policy thinking in India in the recent past. Social protection forms an integral feature of this broad-based vision of the development trajectory.

With India having among the worst food and nutritional indicators in the world, not coincidentally a major thrust of social protection policy in recent years has been on food-based safety nets, particularly for rural populations. It is important to note that the country has a long history of running an extensive set of food-based safety nets. For example, the PDS that provides subsidised food rations to poor families has been in place since the late 1960s. Yet, unlike earlier times, policy considerations of food security are now based on the recognition of the *right to food*. A landmark event in this regard is the passage of the NFSA in 2013, which enshrines the constitutional right to food for poor and vulnerable population groups (Government of India, 2013a). Thus, no longer is food security a matter of public policy discretion; instead, the state is now legally obligated to ensure that the minimum food needs of the poor and vulnerable are met.

The three major food-based safety net programmes in India are the PDS, the NREGS and the ICDS. The aim of this chapter is to review these interventions and ask how they interact with household food security and migration, the two core social processes at the heart of this book.

The chapter argues that notwithstanding the importance of these policy initiatives, the current state of these schemes in India is plagued by problems of maladministration, corruption and leakages, thereby preventing vulnerable rural populations from reaping the benefits of these programmes. These inefficiencies in the social protection system provide a strong imperative for the rural poor to devise their own livelihood security mechanisms. And migration can be viewed as one of the most important of these livelihood strategies.

Rural India is characterised by a preponderance of smallholder households whose already low farm output and income are subject to adverse shocks from erratic monsoon and several crop diseases. Such rural households, whose local livelihoods are subject to recurrent and transitory shocks and to whom social protection may not always be available, may seek to spread and mitigate income risks by geographic dispersion of their members across different economic activities. This is one of the central premises of the NELM which identifies risk aversion as a central determinant of migration decisions of rural households. A key starting point of the NELM is that in many developing countries, because the formal and informal institutional mechanisms (for example, financial, credit and labour markets) for managing risks are either weak or absent, smallholder households have strong incentives to send one or more members to distant urban locations to achieve a livelihood portfolio that lowers income risks. In other words, migration provides a risk-reducing and insurance-maximising strategy to rural households to allocate household labour more efficiently in order to achieve a diversified livelihood portfolio (Stark, 1991).

The entwined themes of migration and social protection have particular relevance in contemporary Bihar. As noted in Chapter 1, the administration of social welfare schemes is ironically the weakest in poor states and regions which need it the most. Bihar remains among the most economically backward states of India, notwithstanding the high economic growth in the state in recent years. The high incidence of poverty, coupled with lack of gainful livelihood options in the state, implies that safety nets such as the PDS, the NREGS and the ICDS represent crucial means of delivering food security to its most vulnerable citizens. At the same time, the ground realities of the functioning of these schemes suggest that they are riddled with massive corruption and maladministration. Notwithstanding the *culture of migration* from the state involving moves that are not necessarily caused by livelihood distress, it is reasonable to expect that the incidence of migration from the state would have been less in the presence of effectively functioning social safety nets.

Against this background, this chapter attempts to undertake a critical assessment of the three food-based safety nets of the PDS, the NREGS and the ICDS in the specific context of Bihar, drawing primarily on the field evidence collected from Siwan. In each case, while an overview of the scheme at the national level is provided, the focus is invariably centred more on Bihar. Placing the importance of these institutional arrangements for food security in the lives of disadvantaged rural populations of Bihar, the chapter highlights the wide discrepancies that currently exist between the design, attributes and intentions of these programmes and their on-ground implementation, ultimately leaving the rural poor to devise their own strategies to meet their food security needs.

THE PUBLIC DISTRIBUTION SYSTEM

The PDS is the largest permanent public welfare programme operated by the Government of India (Svedberg, 2012, p. 53). A producer-cum-consumer subsidy programme, the PDS serves the dual purpose of protecting farmers as well as poor and vulnerable households. Under the PDS, the government procures food grains (mainly wheat and rice) from the farmers at a minimum support price (MSP), thereby preventing them from market fluctuations; the MSP is often higher from the market price, which also acts as an incentive for farmers to produce. Then, through a vast network of approximately half-a-million government-licenced fair price shops (FPS), the PDS provides food grains at subsidised prices to the poor in order to help them meet their minimum calorie requirements.

Until 1992, the scope of the PDS was universal. Given the poverty-alleviation mandate of the programme and the high transaction costs of subsidising the non-poor (Parikh, 1994; Radhakrishna et al., 1997), the scheme was transformed, first in 1992 into the revamped public distribution system (RPDS) to reach out to the poor and vulnerable population segments located in geographically isolated and climate-prone regions, and then in 1997 into the targeted public distribution system (TPDS), which used economic status of the households to assess their eligibility for PDS benefits. In other words, while the RPDS targeted poor areas, the focus of the TPDS was on poor populations.

Under the TPDS, households were classified in accordance with a set of socio-economic parameters and provided with a ration card on this basis. Across India, the three core PDS card categories were Above Poverty Line (APL), Below Poverty Line (BPL) and Antyodaya (poorest of the poor). Originally, the changes implemented through the TPDS classified households into APL and BPL groups. The Antyodaya Anna Yojana (AAY) was started in 2000, with the aim of addressing the problem of hunger among the poorest BPL households. As per the last updated estimates by the central government, there were 40.9 million BPL households, 24.3 million Antyodaya households and 115 million APL households (Government of India, 2013b, p. 23). Following the changes introduced in 1997, the BPL and Antyodaya households were provided with subsidised food grains, while the central subsidies for APL households were done away with (Khera, 2011a, 2011b). Some states provided subsidies to APL households on food and non-food items, but the issue price was usually higher for them than for BPL and Antyodaya households.

The TPDS currently remains in operation albeit in a different avatar (and the common older acronym, PDS, is still widely used). As noted earlier, in 2013 the Indian government passed the NFSA, which provides constitutional guarantee to right to food. Subsidised food rations form part of this constitutional commitment, and the NFSA relies on the existing TPDS to deliver food rations. Following the passage of the NFSA, the scope and mandate of the TPDS have widened to cover more households. The NFSA provides legal entitlement to food to 50 per cent of the urban population and 75 per cent of the rural population. This expanded coverage is among the key reforms under the NFSA. Under the new system, the old categories of BPL and APL are done away with, and households are now classified into two groups of priority households (PHH) and AAY households. The AAY households are entitled to receive a monthly food-grain ration of 35 kilograms, which is a continuation of the earlier system. The monthly food rations of the PHHs are tied to household size, with each member in a household entitled to receive 5 kilograms of food grains per month. The prices of food grains include INR 3, INR 2, INR 1 for rice, wheat and coarse grains, respectively, for both categories of households. The TPDS under the NFSA covers a total of 813.5 million people from 165.7 million households. Different Indian states implemented the NFSA at different paces, and the NFSA was rolled out by all 36 states and union territories by the end of 2016 (Government of India, 2013a; OECD and ICIER, 2018).

Although the TPDS is a centrally sponsored scheme, independent Indian states enjoy considerable degrees of autonomy in programme management. By and large, the role of the central government ends at pegging the number of beneficiaries in each state, according to which central food-grain allocations are made. However, states can expend additional resources to widen the coverage, entitlement level and range of commodities offered to beneficiaries. For instance, the southern state of Tamil Nadu runs a universal PDS; Chhattisgarh also runs a near-universal PDS, including all vulnerable households such as those headed by widows or single women, and provides pulses and grams in addition to food grains (Government of Chhattisgarh, 2013; Drèze et al., 2019).[1]

The analysis of ground realties of the PDS in Bihar reported here uses the data collected in 2012, before the NFSA was rolled out. Notwithstanding the recent changes in the PDS, the primary field research provides insights that have continuing relevance to understand PDS delivery in India. The key argument put forth here is that understanding the on-ground operation of the PDS needs appreciation of the local political economy of resources and rights. In any case, given that the NFSA was implemented in full by the end of 2016, independent assessments of the PDS after the implementation of the NFSA are scarce. Bihar was among the earliest states to implement the NFSA in early 2014. An early assessment pointed to a revival of the PDS in Bihar (Drèze, Khera and Pudussery, 2015). However, more recent studies show problems (Drèze et al., 2019; Pradhan, Roy and Sonkar, 2019). Indeed, the evidence is mixed at best, and it is too early to draw any definitive conclusions about the impact of the NFSA on the PDS performance.

In Bihar, the state government has sought to implement the PDS under conditions of dire poverty. Bihar remains extremely poor, notwithstanding recent economic growth. In all Indian states, Bihar has among the highest proportion of people living below the official poverty line, with one-third of the state's population (36 million) classified as poor in 2011–12 (Planning Commission, 2013a).[2] The deep-rooted incidence of poverty in Bihar implies heavy reliance on PDS allocations throughout. In the pre-NFSA phase, the central government allocated Bihar with food grains of 35 kilograms per month for only 6.5 million households, whereas the state had listed 13.5 million households as BPL and a further 2.5 million households as Antyodaya (Government of Bihar, 2012). In other words, Bihar had an additional 9.5 million PDS beneficiary households on state rolls. To make up for this shortfall, the state allocated BPL households with only 25 kilograms of food grains per month, while Antyodaya households were nominally provisioned with 35 kilograms monthly. Notwithstanding this reduced allocation to the large cohort of BPL households in the state, the Government of Bihar was still required to incur ancillary expenditure on the PDS. The PDS in Bihar also provided a monthly allocation of 2.75 litres of subsidised kerosene to all beneficiary households, including those with APL cards who were only provided with kerosene through the PDS. After the implementation of the NFSA, the mandatory aggregate coverage of population for subsidised food rations is about 80 per cent, and this increases to 86 per cent for rural areas (Drèze, Khera and Pudussery, 2015). It is important to note that the NFSA coverage is for individuals, whereas PDS cards are usually allocated on a household basis. The Bihar government's latest post-NFSA beneficiary data show there were a total of 16.9 million AAY and PHH cardholders. Assuming an average household size of five persons per household, this translates to about 85 million individuals, which is as per the mandated coverage. However, this is only slightly more than 80 million people (16 million cardholding households with an average size of five persons per household) covered under the pre-NFSA arrangements. Indeed, the number of Antyodaya cardholders remain the same in both phases, while the number of PHHs (BPL households in the earlier system) increased marginally by 0.9 million after the NFSA (Table 5.1).

The household-survey sample in Siwan consisted of 191 households who were entitled to subsidised food and kerosene rations, 159 households who were entitled to only kerosene and 42 households who did not have any PDS card. For the purpose of analysis in this chapter, these households are grouped as *full beneficiary households*, *partial beneficiary households* and *non-beneficiary households*. As noted earlier, these data were collected before the NFSA was implemented. In the pre-NFSA terminology, full beneficiaries included the BPL (167 households) and the AAY (24 households) categories, partial beneficiaries comprised households in the APL category and non-beneficiary households were those excluded from the PDS and its benefits.

Table 5.1 Number of beneficiary households by the public distribution system (PDS) card category in the pre-National Food Security Act (NFSA) and post-NFSA phases in Bihar

	Number of households (in million)	
Type of household	Pre-NFSA	Post-NFSA
Antyodaya	2.5	2.5
Below poverty line/Priority	13.5	14.4
Above poverty line	2.9	N.A.

Source: Compiled from the online PDS data in Government of Bihar (2012, p. 229) and Government of Bihar (2020a).

Note: There are no official data on the number of above-poverty-line households in Bihar, and this figure is arrived at by subtracting the below-poverty-line and Antyodaya households from the total number of households in Bihar, which, in the 2011 census, was enumerated to be 18.9 million (Census of India, 2011c).

Table 5.2 presents the background characteristics of the study sample by their PDS beneficiary status. Of the households benefiting from the PDS (full and partial beneficiaries), the data show a close association between the PDS status on the one hand and poverty and deprivation on the other. For instance, by caste status, about 60 per cent of the households in the full beneficiary category were members of Scheduled Castes, Scheduled Tribes or extremely backward castes. However, of the households with partial beneficiary status, only 37.2 per cent were of Scheduled Castes, Scheduled Tribes or extremely backward castes. These differences are also apparent in other key socio-economic indicators of literacy, dwelling type, monthly per capita expenditure (MPCE) and landholding status. Nevertheless, reflective of the dire state of material circumstances in the study area, close to half of the partial beneficiary households had consumption expenditure levels lower than the official poverty line. This is suggestive of exclusion of deserving poor from PDS food benefits. Evidence from other studies also show that the TPDS routinely excluded the genuinely poor while including the better-off in its ambit (inter alia, Swaminathan and Misra, 2001; Hirway, 2003; Planning Commission, 2005; Khera, 2008; Ram, Mohanty and Ram, 2009; Drèze and Khera, 2010; Sahu and Mahamallik, 2011). This is further corroborated by the survey data pertaining to non-beneficiary households who lagged behind even the full beneficiary households in some indicators of material welfare: a greater proportion of them were landless, reported lower average consumption levels and fell below the poverty line. Yet they were excluded from the PDS

Table 5.2 Background characteristics of surveyed households by the public distribution system (PDS) card category

	Full beneficiary	Partial beneficiary	Non-beneficiary
Socio-demographics			
Average household size (in persons)	5.6	6.3	5.0
Women-headed households	26.2	25.8	57.1
Female respondents	48.2	45.9	69.0
Households where the head was illiterate	49.2	38.4	69.0
Caste			
Forward caste	6.8	10.1	0.0
Backward caste	33.5	52.8	54.8
Extremely backward caste	35.1	20.8	28.6
Scheduled Caste and Scheduled Tribe	24.6	16.4	16.7
Type of house occupied			
Kutcha	24.6	13.8	23.8
Semi-pucca	44.5	31.4	31.0
Pucca	30.9	54.7	45.2
Land, livestock ownership and migratory labour			
Landless households	39.8	17.6	54.8
Households with land size of less than an acre	52.4	67.3	40.5
Households with land size of an acre or more	7.9	15.1	4.8
Households who own any livestock	64.9	69.8	40.5
Households with one or more members working outside the village	42.9	55.3	64.3
Consumption expenditure and poverty			
Average MPCE (in INR)	810.7	996.3	746.7
Household with MPCE below poverty line	60.7	49.7	66.7
Total number of households (n)	**191**	**159**	**42**

Source: Primary household survey data.

Note: All data are in percentage terms unless specified otherwise. The 2009–10 revision of state-specific poverty lines, based on the Tendulkar committee's estimates, pegged the rural poverty line in Bihar at INR 655.6. The same has been applied to this survey data to estimate consumption poverty (Planning Commission, 2012).

benefits. The fieldwork suggested that many excluded households were from the marginalised groups in desperate need of PDS benefits (and other social protection measures) but were completely bypassed by the welfare system.

This problem persists on a large scale in rural Bihar where disadvantaged segments of the population often find it hard to press their claims on PDS eligibility due to powerful social hierarchies of caste and class. During the fieldwork in Siwan, a senior villager, aware of the PDS beneficiary identification process, remarked:

> People who have *pucca* houses, 2–3 acres of land, whose members are in stable jobs (some even in government jobs) have PDS cards. On the other hand, there are families left out whose stoves do not burn the day they do not find work.

Disappointed with the way PDS ration cards were distributed, another villager sarcastically suggested:

> I thought we were poor, but it seems all the upper-caste landlord families are poorer than us. After all, they all have PDS ration cards whereas we do not.

The widening of beneficiary coverage under the NFSA aimed at taming this problem of wrongful exclusion. Many Indian states, including Bihar, applied a simple *exclusion approach* under which all households were eligible for full PDS benefits except those who were better off, such as those households that had a government job, a four-wheeler or substantial landholding. While commendable, it is not clear whether this has led to inclusion of all deserving poor households in the PDS. A recent survey of PDS functioning in the six Indian states of Bihar, Chhattisgarh, Jharkhand, Madhya Pradesh, Odisha and West Bengal found that while in most states the NFSA's official lists of eligible households matched closely with their own lists, Bihar (and Jharkhand) had a 'significant proportion' (5–10 per cent) of untraceable households – households on official NFSA rolls but missing on the ground (Drèze et al., 2019, p. 37).[3]

The severity of this problem from the perspective of the role of the PDS in improving the food security of vulnerable households is reflected in the data on household food insecurity. Table 5.3 depicts various indicators of self-reported food insecurity by the type of PDS card held by the household.

Because the partial and non-beneficiary households did not receive PDS food rations, they are grouped together for comparison with full beneficiary households; this also allows for a larger (and roughly equal) sample size for comparison. The surveyed households were asked a range of questions to assess if at any time during the year preceding the survey they faced food shortages. The data in Table 5.3 refer to the proportion of households who reported having faced food inadequacy and food unavailability at least once in the past year.

Table 5.3 Household food security by the public distribution system (PDS) card category

	Full beneficiary households (per cent)	Partial and non-beneficiary households (per cent)
Food was not enough (defined by the following situations)		
Ate meals without vegetables	60.2	35.3
Could only afford to consume food from the PDS	38.2	N.A.
Consumed a single meal a day	17.3	17.4
Lacked all three main food categories (cereals, pulses and vegetables)	61.3	34.3
Lacked sufficient quantity of food to satiate hunger	50.3	30.3
Food was not available (defined by the following situations)		
Borrowed money from friends and/or relatives to buy food	22.5	17.4
Borrowed money from local traders or moneylenders or lifted ration on credit to acquire food	40.3	22.4
Sold jewellery or other personal assets to buy food	1.6	1.5
Ate less food than usual (consumption rationing)	59.2	32.8
Total number of households (*n*)	**191**	**201**

Source: Primary household survey data.

A few points from the data in Table 5.3 need consideration. First, while the percentage of partial and non-beneficiary households reporting food inadequacy and food unavailability is much less than that of full beneficiary households across most self-reported food-insecurity parameters, a considerable proportion of the former remain food insecure.[4] Second, lack of dietary diversity appears to be a major problem among both groups. More than 60 per cent of full beneficiary households and about 35 per cent of partial and non-beneficiary households reported having meals without vegetables and those that did not have the basic combination of cereals, pulses and vegetables. Village-based observation revealed that the day-to-day diets of many households comprised only rice and a potato-based meal of some form. Third, coping strategies were diverse and sometimes extreme, including selling valuable household assets like jewellery.

Furthermore, irrespective of the householder card status, the PDS in Bihar is afflicted by woeful delivery inefficiencies. It has historically been riddled with huge problems of pilferage and leakage. A nationwide performance evaluation of the scheme by the Planning Commission estimated that 75 per cent of PDS food grains did not reach the intended beneficiaries in Bihar, compared to the national average of 57 per cent (Planning Commission, 2005). Comparable NSS data analysed by Khera (2012) suggested that in the same year (2004–05), 91 per cent of the PDS food grains in Bihar were diverted from their eligible recipients. Five years later, in 2009–10, while most major states had improved their PDS performance (the incidence of grain diversion in Chhattisgarh, for example, fell from 52 per cent to 10 per cent between 2004–05 and 2009–10), the progress in Bihar was much slower, and in 2009–10, 75 per cent of the PDS food grains in Bihar still failed to reach their intended beneficiaries (Khera, 2012). The FPS-beneficiary interface is the core site where PDS leakage occurs (Planning Commission, 2005).

These contexts framed extensive attempts to reform the PDS in Bihar. The election of a new government in 2005 was widely interpreted as heralding an opportunity for dramatic institutional reforms within the state. It is certainly the case that since 2005 there have been wide-ranging governance reforms in Bihar (Sinha, 2011; Singh and Stern, 2013), and the arena of food-based safety nets has not been untouched by it. To contain corruption and illegal diversion of food grains from the PDS, in 2007, the chief minister of Bihar, Nitish Kumar, introduced a system of PDS coupons as a transparency measure. Under this system, every beneficiary household was annually provided with 12 coupons each for wheat, rice and kerosene, which specified their entitlements and the price they had to pay for each commodity (Photo 5.3). Every month, beneficiary households were to redeem one coupon against each of the specified PDS commodities at a local FPS (beneficiaries could ostensibly choose the FPS they use). Then the FPS owner forwarded coupons to the block- or district-level authorities in order to get the next month's supplies. Given much of the PDS leakages were found to occur at the FPS level, a guiding principle behind the introduction of the coupon scheme was that by tying the next month's supply of PDS commodities to coupons, it was considered that coupons would prevent the FPS owners from selling the PDS supplies in the open market as they would now need to have the requisite coupons to claim their stock. In an article published in *Economic and Political Weekly*, Bihar's coupon system was assessed in the context of wider national debates on whether the PDS should be strengthened or replaced by ostensibly transparent food coupons or cash transfers. This assessment noted that while coupons represented a well-intentioned reform attempt to prevent corruption and pilferage in the PDS, it hardly changed the ground realities of PDS operation and maladministration, and rent-seeking remained widespread and ubiquitous.

Household surveys in rural Siwan showed wide irregularities in the coupon-based PDS: Nearly 50 per cent of full-beneficiary households reported that they were not able to use all their food-grain coupons due to problems with late delivery of coupons (rendering them invalid), or because FPS owners did not honour the coupons citing an absence of stock. Nearly one-third (29 per cent) of these households had three or more unused coupons, meaning they had completely missed their food rations for those months in the past year. Additionally, it was often the case that FPS owners demanded two or more coupons for one month's food ration, and 60 per cent of full-beneficiary households reported such a practice. This translated into beneficiary households receiving less food grains than their entitlements (see Choithani and Pritchard, 2015 for a greater explication of Bihar's coupon system).[5]

In the survey, information was collected from households on their PDS use during the three months (January–March 2012) preceding the survey. This included full and partial beneficiary households as they were entitled to the PDS. Table 5.4 presents a summary of survey findings on PDS functioning. Only 10.5 per cent of full beneficiary households reported that they received food grains in each of the past three months, and just 1 per cent (a mere two out of 191 full beneficiary households) reported getting their full food-grain

Table 5.4 Functioning of the public distribution system (PDS): a summary

	Full beneficiary households (per cent)	Partial beneficiary households (per cent)
Food grains		
Received food grains in each month in the past three months	10.5	–
Received full food-grain entitlements in the past three months	1.0	–
Average purchase–entitlement ratio (PER) for food grains for the past three months	38.1	–
Kerosene		
Received kerosene in each month in the past three months	58.1	82.4
Received full kerosene entitlements in the past three months	0.5	5.0
Average PER for kerosene for the past three months	70.9	82.6
Total number of households (*n*)	**191**	**159**

Source: Primary household survey data.

entitlements. The average purchase–entitlement ratio (PER), which is the proportion of full entitlement obtained by beneficiary households (Khera, 2011b, p. 40), for the past three months for food grains was less than 40 per cent. In other words, 60 per cent of the entitled food grains did not reach the beneficiaries. The reason why the surveyed households were unable to obtain their PDS rations on a regular basis was because of maladministration at various layers of PDS governance.

Field research showed that FPS owners rarely honoured their commitments. It was often the case that they provided PDS beneficiaries with their food-grain rations only for seven–eight months a year and skipped four–five months completely. In months when food rations were distributed, beneficiaries did not receive their full quota – far from it. The most common reason FPS owners gave to their patrons was 'insufficient stock'. While some of the FPSs genuinely faced shortages in the supply from the higher end of the PDS supply chain, on occasions these claims were bogus. According to informal testimonies from a number of village stakeholders, it was still common for many FPS owners to sell PDS grains in the open market, thus inducing deliberate shortages for legitimate beneficiaries.

A greater proportion of households reported getting kerosene in the past three months, and the PER for kerosene was also higher. This suggests a considerably higher incidence of pilferage or leakage in food grains than for kerosene. This was a rather striking finding because discussions with the FPS owners revealed that the price differential between PDS-subsidised and open-market kerosene was greater than that for food grains, which suggests that kerosene would be a more profitable item to pilfer than food grains.[6]

A likely explanation for the differing PERs between food grains and kerosene is the fact that the allocations of these two items are connected to quite different local politics. Kerosene was available to all households, except those without PDS cards (that is, the non-beneficiary category). This included high-caste, better-off households who commanded greater voice and representation in local affairs. These households had a direct stake in the operational efficiency of the PDS, and this stake translated into strong pressures on FPS owners to ensure high kerosene allocations. Whereas a large majority of households entitled to food grains were from poor socio-economic strata, notwithstanding high exclusion errors. The qualitative evidence gathered during the fieldwork supports this observation. In most of the study villages, FPS owners tended to class and caste allegiances that were separate from those of beneficiaries. In one GP, all five dealers were from the upper castes of Bhumihar and Rajput who gave in to pressures from members of their own castes but often cheated lower-caste households on their food-grain rations. Lower-caste communities such as Musahars and Harijans were particularly prone to exploitation because of the caste power structures. This might also be the case in much of rural Bihar. Bihar has a large number of most-backward districts of India (Debroy and Bhandari, 2003; Bakshi, Chawla and Shah, 2015). In these pockets of deprivation, poor households are often ill-equipped to understand or assert their rights, and for FPS owners, ignorance and disempowerment represent avenues for exploitation. Indeed, one key lesson from the fieldwork is that the widespread failures of the PDS to reach its intended beneficiaries are situated within the local political economy of resources and rights that operates through social power structures.

The fieldwork, however, also revealed that the positions of the FPS owners, while culprits, were connected, in turn, to wider anomalies in the operation of the PDS in Bihar. For example, in one of the study villages, when the villagers united to demand from the FPS owner their full ration entitlements, he got his licence transferred to another village nearby because the bribes he was compelled to pay to the higher authorities in the PDS chain meant that distributing actual entitlements was not possible if he were to stay in the business. A GP *mukhiya* very candidly suggested:

> All the dealers [FPS owners] have to pay bribes to higher authorities to keep themselves in the business. It's not the dealer's fault. He cannot possibly pay from his own pocket. These bribes then are ultimately passed on to the PDS beneficiaries.

Most of the FPS owners informed us that each bag of 50 kilograms of wheat and rice obtained from PDS depots typically weighs around 44–46 kilograms. Furthermore, FPS owners alleged they did not receive adequate compensation for the costs of transporting rations from depots to village ration stores. In one instance, PDS supplies were disrupted at the local level because an assistant manager of a PDS warehouse at the sub-district (block) was arrested for corruption. This meant that all PDS dealers in that area now had to go farther to the district headquarters to procure monthly supplies but were not compensated for the higher transportation costs. The sister of a PDS dealer in one study village, who was also the headmistress of a high school in a nearby village, remarked:

> Everyone is wise enough to understand that nobody will pay this transportation cost from their pocket. The government must fix it if they have to set the system straight.

Nevertheless, as the survey data indicate, where local circumstances contrive in ways that give greater scope for FPS owners to exploit their powers, this will occur with greater abandon, and those most in need of the PDS will suffer the most. Not surprisingly, fieldwork showed a marked preference among PDS beneficiaries for cash transfers in lieu of food rations. In the survey, when beneficiary households were asked to indicate their preference between food rations from the PDS store or cash money in lieu of subsidized food grains, nearly 80 per cent opted for the cash option (Figure 5.1). Beneficiary households cited various reasons in support of their preferences, including irregularity in the functioning of the ration shop and lesser quantity of ration

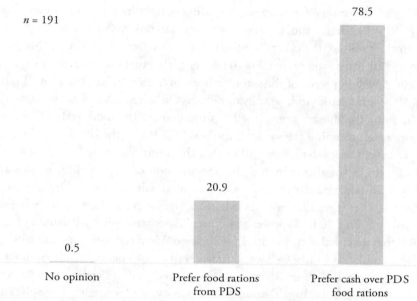

Figure 5.1 Food versus cash: the public distribution system (PDS) preferences among full-beneficiary households (per cent)

Source: Primary household survey data.

received than actual entitlements; given PDS only provided wheat and rice, some beneficiaries also noted that cash would give them more choice on what to eat. In one way or the other, most of these reasons were linked with the systematic failures of the PDS to provide food and nutritional security to the beneficiary households (also see Photos 5.1–5.3).

This discussion has tried to engage with PDS system in its various avatars, including the recent changes brought about by the NFSA. However, as noted earlier, the field research reported here was carried out in 2012, before the NFSA was implemented. One might ask if these findings have relevance in the post-NFSA phase, given that the food law was implemented to address some of these issues. It is definitely the case that the PDS in Bihar has shown some signs of improvement in recent years. At the same time, many of the problems highlighted earlier persist still. This is corroborated by some recent studies that throw light on Bihar's PDS blues. Drèze, Khera and Pudussery (2015) conducted surveys with 997 households in four districts of Bihar in December 2014, soon after the NFSA was implemented in the state, and found major positive changes, including correct inclusion of households on PDS rolls, better functioning, more regular ration distribution, and so on. In the two months preceding the survey (October–November 2014), the reported PER for food grains was 70 per cent. Two years later, another survey in 2016, involving some of the same authors, in the six Indian states of Bihar, Chhattisgarh, Jharkhand, Madhya Pradesh, Odisha and West Bengal found Bihar to be the most laggard in PDS functioning. The food-grain PER for two months preceding the survey (April–May 2016) for the Bihar sample was 44 per cent, the lowest among all states. The study also noted the problems with the PDS supply chain and the phenomenon of 'gap months' in Bihar, where no food-grain distribution occurred in an entire month (Drèze et al., 2019, p. 41), an issue that primary fieldwork in Siwan also highlights, which, in turn, is rooted in local power structures. Another study by Pradhan et al. (2019) that included surveys with 1,600 households in the three states of Bihar, Odisha and Uttar Pradesh showed that overall just 40 per cent of households received their full PDS entitlements, and this declined to 35 per cent in Bihar. Furthermore, the findings also suggested that over 50 per cent of households in Bihar rated the PDS as either 'average' or 'poor', and that there was a clear preference for direct cash transfers across social groups and genders. The positive changes in the early phase of the NFSA's implementation were perhaps due to the assembly elections in 2015, whereby political leadership showed interest in the PDS to garner electoral gains, but this political interest seems to have waned recently. Whether democratic politics will assert itself to permanently fix the PDS blues in Bihar remains to be seen. What is clear is that the problems of PDS governance run deep through the various layers of administration, with the overall effect being that they prevent deserving poor households from benefitting from this important safety net.

NATIONAL RURAL EMPLOYMENT GUARANTEE SCHEME

The NREGS is a public-works, social safety-net programme, which emanated from the Constitutional act of the same name, the National Rural Employment Guarantee Act (NREGA), passed by the Indian Parliament in 2005. The scheme was first implemented in early 2006 in the 200 poorest districts of India and later extended to the whole nation in 2008. The main aim of the NREGS is to enhance the livelihood security of rural households in the country while also creating productive assets in rural areas. It is premised on the principle of a legal right to work and provides a Constitutional guarantee of at least 100 days of wage employment per year to every rural household who demands this. The NREGS provisions stipulate that the employment is to be provided within 15 days of a household submitting its application for work, upon which they are provided with a job card. In the event of failure to provide employment within this period, the applicants are entitled to receive the daily unemployment allowance in lieu from the relevant state government. Aiming also at the financial empowerment of rural women, upon its inception the NREGS envisaged having women constituting one-third of the total beneficiaries. The projects undertaken through the NREGS include, inter alia, rural connectivity through road building, water conservation and irrigation, community land development and social forestry, with the overall purpose of creating common assets at the village level. The administration of the scheme is highly decentralised, with village councils, or GPs, being the principal planning and implementation authorities. The GPs are responsible for identifying suitable projects and reviewing their progress, and they also act as intermediaries between the beneficiaries and the higher echelons of bureaucratic apparatus. As per official statistics, in 2018–19 the total government expenditure on the scheme amounted to INR 69,619.5 crore, generating INR 268 crore (USD 2.68 billion) person–days of employment. During the same period, 5 crore (50 million) households worked under the NREGS, of which more than one-third (38 per cent) belonged to the Scheduled Castes (10.4 million) and Scheduled Tribes (8.5 million). More than half (54 per cent) of the NREGS beneficiaries were women in terms of their share in total person–days of employment (Government of India, 2005; Ministry of Rural Development, 2020).

Although the NREGS is a rural employment programme, it holds crucial significance for rural food security. Most of the beneficiaries of the scheme belong to socially and economically marginalised sections of the population who often lack the land and financial resources to meet their food and nutrition needs all year round. In fact, the genesis of the NREGS was closely connected with heightened concerns around persistently high levels of food insecurity and undernutrition in rural India. The scheme was implemented in a context when the sustained economic growth for nearly a decade and a half had failed to bring about significant improvements in the living standards in rural areas. Contrarily, the first few years of economic reforms were characterised by rising rural distress in many parts of India. While the 1990s, the first decade of systematic economic reforms, were in general characterised by the phenomenon of 'jobless growth' – faster economic growth associated with low employment elasticity (Bhattacharya and Sakthivel, 2004) – deceleration in the growth of employment and wages in the rural areas was sharper. Agricultural growth more than halved from an average of 3.2 per cent per year observed between 1980 and 1996–97 to 1.5 per cent per annum subsequently (Planning Commission, 2006, p. 5). This had a detrimental effect on the growth of rural employment as the sector provided livelihood to over a half of India's labour force. The two large rounds of the NSS suggested that the overall rural employment grew at an average rate of merely 0.6 per cent per year between 1993–94 and 1999–2000 (Patnaik, 2005, p. 203). The sluggish growth of the farm sector meant that poor households dependent on agricultural wage work saw their fortunes deteriorate further. Added to this was the drought of 2002 that exacerbated woes. Measured as the third largest drought in India in the past 100 years (Bhat, 2006), the Indian drought of 2002 intensified the rural livelihood and food security crisis. Numerous cases of hunger and starvation deaths among rural households were reported in many parts of the country around this time (Jha, 2002), and distress migration characterised the rural landscape of many Indian states. This occurred amidst the climate of an overall faster economic growth. These events disillusioned the then popular belief of 'shining India' (a slogan of the then ruling coalition, the National Democratic Alliance, led by the Bharatiya Janata Party) and triggered a rethinking around the need to initiate effective income redistribution measures. A strong civil society action around the right to food, and more broadly *right to life*, which had already gained significant momentum by then (for example, the PUCL petition in the SC seeking government's intervention to prevent starvation deaths in Rajasthan by initiating drought-relief measures [see Chapter 1]), furthered the cause of the NREGS. In key ways, the implementation of the NREGS was thus tied to the politics of food security in India. Indeed, by providing an assured wage employment for 100 days per year, the scheme envisaged to (*a*) provide the poor households with a livelihood option that would boost their income and consumption levels and food security, (*b*) reduce the incidence of distress migration from rural areas and (*c*) have a multiplier effect on the rural economy by the means of job and asset creation.

The NREGS has been instrumental in galvanising a politics in which the rights and entitlements of the rural poor have acquired greater significance. It has also strengthened local democracy, whereby the poor and vulnerable populations in the countryside increasingly assert their rightful claims on what is owed to them by the state and demand accountability from their local representatives.[7] Nevertheless, the extent to which the programme has met its desired objectives appears quite mixed. Several implementation issues such as irregularity of work availability, delayed payment of wages to beneficiaries and issuance of bogus job cards, resulting in misappropriation of wage payments, beset the effective functioning of the scheme. The performance outcomes of the NREGS vary markedly, depending on the choice of indicators used. Important from the perspective of the current discussion is the fact that the performance of the scheme is not wholly uniform and exhibits great regional variation across the states, an issue connected with uneven, state-based governance (Drèze and Oldiges, 2011; Khera, 2011c; Dutta et al., 2012a, 2012b; Ministry of Rural Development, 2012; Pritchard et al., 2014).

Using the official data for the year 2018–19, Table 5.5 presents some summary indicators of the NREGS's performance for 20 major Indian states. It is apparent that the states rank differently on the different outcome indicators. For example, the southern Indian states of Kerala and Tamil Nadu lead the way when it comes to the share of women in total person–days of employment, with women accounting for 90 per cent and 85 per cent of total beneficiaries, respectively. Punjab has the highest proportion of Scheduled Caste population (73 per cent), followed by Odisha where the combined share of Scheduled Caste and Scheduled Tribe population accounts for 52 per cent.

Given that the NREGS is essentially a demand-driven programme, the proportion of rural households demanding work and the proportion of those availing work under the scheme provide crucial parameters to evaluate the importance of the scheme from the perspective of rural livelihood security. When looked at in terms of the importance of the scheme, a sad irony of the NREGS's performance is that the demand for work as well as the participation of rural households in the scheme appears relatively weaker in some of the most economically backward Indian states. In particular, in the two large backward northern states of Uttar Pradesh and Bihar, less than a quarter of the rural households demanded work during 2018–19. Furthermore, a mere 10 per cent of households were able to complete 100 days of work at the national level, and the person–days employment per household in these northern states is even below the already abysmal national figure.

These current shortfalls in the provisioning of NREGS employment notwithstanding, trends in the functioning of the scheme suggest improvements over time. In 2006–07, the first year of the NREGS's

Table 5.5 Some summary indicators of the performance of the National Rural Employment Guarantee Scheme (NREGS) for selected Indian states, 2018–19

State	Share of rural households that demanded work under the NREGS (per cent)	Share of rural households that worked under the NREGS (per cent)	Total person-days of employment per employed household	Share of employment in total person-days (per cent)			Households under NREGS completing 100 days of work (per cent)
				Scheduled Castes	Schedule Tribes	Women	
Andhra Pradesh	30.9	29.7	58	21.5	10.2	59.9	20.5
Assam	35.5	32.1	31	5.1	20.0	41.1	1.1
Bihar	21.8	17.3	42	19.8	1.6	51.8	0.8
Chhattisgarh	64.5	55.9	57	9.7	36.7	50.1	17.5
Gujarat	15.4	13.5	46	5.9	38.9	44.5	3.7
Haryana	9.1	7.6	34	45.6	0.0	50.1	1.6
Himachal Pradesh	45.1	42.2	52	27.5	8.5	63.3	12.7
Jammu & Kashmir	46.8	42.0	57	3.6	15.1	30.0	5.8
Jharkhand	33.2	26.9	42	11.2	26.7	39.2	2.0
Karnataka	29.7	26.5	50	15.5	9.6	48.6	10.0
Kerala	39.3	35.6	66	15.9	5.5	90.4	29.9
Madhya Pradesh	41.3	35.4	52	16.3	34.3	36.5	2.0
Maharashtra	15.0	13.6	47	10.5	20.0	44.9	10.7
Odisha	29.4	26.6	39	16.1	35.5	42.0	2.2
Punjab	24.8	20.1	30	73.4	0.0	60.7	1.0

Rajasthan	61.1	54.4	57	21.3	22.3	66.1	11.4
Tamil Nadu	61.2	58.7	46	26.8	1.4	85.4	4.6
Uttar Pradesh	22.7	19.6	42	31.3	1.0	35.3	1.4
Uttarakhand	37.1	34.3	45	16.9	3.8	55.1	5.3
West Bengal	34.4	31.8	77	31.4	8.4	48.1	30.4
India	**33.2**	**29.7**	**51**	**20.7**	**17.4**	**54.2**	**10.0**

Source: Calculated from the official data posted by the Ministry of Rural Development on the NREGS's public data portal, http://nrega.nic.in (accessed in March 2020).

Note: All figures pertain to the Indian financial year of 2018–19. The first two columns are calculated using the 2011 census data on the total number of rural households. The total number of rural households likely increased between 2011 and 2018–19. This means that the lower denominator likely overestimates the share of rural households who demanded work and those who worked.

implementation, the person–days employment generated through the scheme was merely 17 days per rural households at the all-India level (Drèze and Oldiges, 2011). The current figure of 51 days is three times higher. Additionally, the available evidence suggests that, through its direct and indirect benefits, the NREGS seems to be gradually transforming the contemporary social and economic landscape of rural India with overall positive impacts, particularly on the lives of disadvantaged sections of the rural populations.

First, the fact that nearly a half of the NREGS participants come from the historically marginalised groups of the Scheduled Castes and Scheduled Tribes is significant in itself. In many places, these populations traditionally depended on upper-caste families for their survival in arrangements that were highly exploitative and degrading. These involved landless poor from the lower castes working as permanent labour in the fields (and homes) of upper-caste landlords for their basic food needs. This economic dependence often came at the expense of caste-based humiliation and even violence. To be sure, these feudal economic arrangements began to fade away much before the NREGS's inception. The wider availability of non-farm jobs following the advent of market reforms in the early 1990s significantly weakened these relationships in rural India as the lower-caste households turned to non-farm futures as a means to both achieve upward economic mobility and break free of caste oppression (Jodhka, 2014). Yet not all lower-caste households are equally positioned to access these non-farm jobs. By providing work locally to marginalised groups, the NREGS provides an additional challenge to entrenched caste structures and freedom from caste-based oppression that characterised the life-worlds of socially disadvantaged populations.

Second, the scheme seems to be playing a crucial role in attracting women from poor households to join the labour force. As is evident from Table 5.5, in 2018–19 over a half of the total employment went to women. Moreover, there are no overall differentials in the wages of men and women working under the NREGS, and the wages of women working under the scheme are much higher than in other casual work (Jandu, 2008; Azam, 2012; Dutta et al., 2012b;). Given the well-established role of economic independence of women in enhancing their bargaining position within the household (Boserup, 1970; Sen, 1987), the NREGS seems to represent an important tool towards curbing gender inequality.

Third, Drèze and Sen (2013) note that by guaranteeing a statutory minimum wage, the NREGS has positively altered wage relations in rural areas, particularly for unskilled casual labour and women. Between 2005–06 and 2010–11, the real wages of rural labourers grew at an average annual rate of 1.82 per cent for men and 3.83 per cent for women, which was substantially higher compared with the annual growth rate of real wages of merely 0.01 per cent for men and −0.05 per cent for women in the pre-NREGS period (between 2000–01 and 2005–06). Furthermore, the annual growth rate of real wages of unskilled labourers increased even faster at 3.98 per cent and 4.34 per cent for men and women, respectively. Given that NREGS participants generally belong to socially and economically fragile groups, this could be viewed as enhancement of the income and livelihood security of poor rural households. Indeed, the evaluations of household-level impacts of NREGS highlight the positive impacts of the scheme. For example, a study by Ravi and Engler (2009), which used a baseline survey data of 1,066 households supplemented with a subsequent panel of 320 households in a single district (Medak) of the state of Andhra Pradesh, found that participation in the scheme was associated with enhanced household welfare. They found that the two most significant household welfare impacts of the NREGS were that the programme (*a*) improved household food security, as reflected in increases in household expenditure on food and (*b*) decreased the level of emotional distress and anxiety among participating households.[8]

Fourth, while the popular perception of the productive value of assets created under the NREGS is negative, recent research suggests that is not always the case. A study by Ranaware et al. (2015), based on a detailed survey of over 4,100 NREGS jobs across 100 villages in Maharashtra, found that 87 per cent of sample jobs were functional and 75 per cent contributed to supporting the local agriculture with benefits accruing largely to small and marginal farmers. In some places, the NREGS jobs also include construction or renovation of GP offices and local *anganwadi* centres that provide important local infrastructure.

The extent to which these positive attributes of the schemes are realised, however, varies widely across the states depending upon how successfully the programme is implemented on the ground. That there is a strong geographical dimension to the scheme's performance is reflected in the data in Table 5.5. In many places, the NREGS remains utterly dysfunctional, which acts against rural households joining the programme, thereby undermining its effectiveness. The case-study district of Siwan is one such place. Drawing on field-research evidence, the discussion now turns attention to the on-ground functioning of the NREGS in Siwan.

In general, Bihar fares rather poorly on most parameters of the NREGS's performance. It ranks among the bottom-five states in terms of work demand and participation of rural households and among the bottom-eight in terms of total person–days of employment per household. Bihar also fares poorly in terms of women's share in total employment. Furthermore, independent assessments of the NREGS in the state paint an even more dismal picture. For example, a performance audit conducted in 100 extremely backward villages spread across 10 districts of Bihar, which covered a sample of 2,500 households, revealed that in the six years (2006–11) of the NREGS's implementation, (a) the scheme completely bypassed 17 of the 100 villages during the entire period, (b) 36 per cent (892 households) of the sample households across all villages did not receive even a single day of work under the scheme, (c) the actual average annual employment was merely five days per household per year, (d) 73 per cent of the wage component was completely misappropriated and (e) the combined effect of these anomalies was that of the total amount of INR 8,189 crore spent on the scheme during 2006–11, nearly INR 6,000 crore (73 per cent of the total spending) was fraudulently malversated (Rai, 2012). However, the functioning of the scheme is not uniform across the different districts of the state and villages within the districts.

In the case-study district of Siwan, the small agricultural landholdings and a dearth of non-farm livelihood options meant that wage-employment under NREGS was vitally important, and it was indeed perceived so by many landless and land-poor households. The fieldwork, however, suggested that the on-ground implementation of the scheme was extremely weak, with the overall effect being that it did not constitute a significant livelihood component of a large majority of rural households. Poor governance and maladministration of the programme provided a disincentive for households to seek work under the scheme. The survey data collected from rural Siwan indicate that of the 47 households who reported having a NREGS job card, 46 worked under the scheme during 2011–12, a participation rate of nearly 100 per cent among those who had a job card. However, the overall outreach of the programme seemed insignificant when looked at in terms of the total sample of rural household surveyed. Only 11.7 per cent of the total sample of 392 households worked under the NREGS. This figure comes close to the official data on rural households' work participation rate of 10.2 per cent for Siwan in the same year (Ministry of Rural Development, 2020).[9]

The survey data on the socio-economic characteristics of sample NREGS-participating households in Siwan show that these households invariably involved the poorer sections: the households' average monthly per-capita expenditure was 35 per cent lower than that of non-participant households, they had lower food security and diversity than their counterparts, and all households were from either backward castes or Scheduled Castes and Scheduled Tribes (not a single household from a forward caste worked under the NREGS). This is consistent with the evidence at the national level that a significant majority of NREGS participants belongs to poor socio-economic groups. However, as noted before, with only 12 per cent of the total rural households participating in it, the overall work participation in the scheme was very limited.

The reasons why the scheme has not been able to provide an effective source of livelihood for a large majority of rural households are rooted in its implementation. In the survey, nearly a quarter of the sample (100 households) reported that they had asked for but not provided NREGS job cards. On the other hand, most of those households who held cards and worked under the scheme reported facing multiple issues. First, work under the scheme was highly unpredictable, and none of the NREGS-participating households was provided with 100 days of work. Only nine households were able to avail more than 60 days of employment in 2011–12 (Figure 5.2). Irregularity and uncertainty of work were common complaints, which discouraged rural households from seeking employment under the scheme. To quote one of the respondents:

> Work under the NREGS is never regularly available. There is hardly two–three days of work in a month. Moreover, we are unsure when we will get work. The government launches many schemes and then stops them. In such a situation of uncertainty, we cannot rely on the NREGS if we are to survive.

This quote calls attention to the problem, identified by Dutta et al. (2012b), that the NREGS's effectiveness must be assessed against considerations of forgone employment and income by recipients. In Siwan, uncertainty of employment under the scheme meant that many households, particularly those who had other occupational choices available, found NREGS employment less lucrative.

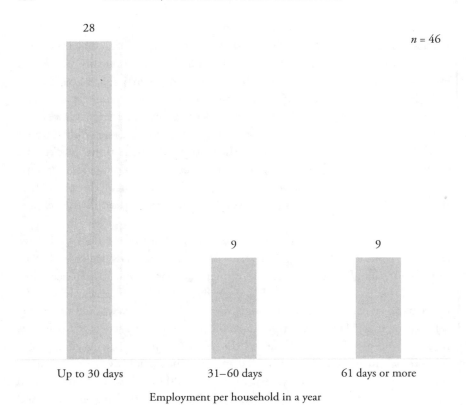

Figure 5.2 Distribution of the National Rural Employment Guarantee Scheme (NREGS)-participating households by person–days of employment availed in the past year, 2011–12

Source: Primary household survey data.

Some households did not, however, have a choice but to depend, and significantly so, on the NREGS. This included, for example, a household headed by a widow of over 60 years old whose son died young and daughter divorced at an early age and whose shoulders now bore the responsibility of feeding seven other people (an unmarried daughter, widowed daughter-in-law, divorced daughter and four grandchildren). There were three young, able-bodied women in the family, but cultural norms did not permit their participation in wage-work outside the domestic space. Across different caste and religious groups, young women usually stayed indoors even when faced with financial hardship. In this case, separation from male partners owing to death and divorce curtailed the mobility of two young women even more. The old widow had little choice but to rely on NREGS employment. However, she, too, complained of inadequate workdays allotted to her. In her words: 'I get 14 days of work in a year and earn in total INR 2,000. Why can't the government provide me with more work?'

The lower than mandated person–days of employment provided to households is often the result of malpractices of the rent-seekers. In one of the study villages, for example, many respondents complained that machines, such as backhoe loaders, were used for road-digging work, and then bogus attendances were registered on beneficiaries' cards and money claimed. This defeated the very purpose of the scheme. In the words of a respondent:

> If a job requires 30 days of work from 10 labourers, the machine does it in five days or less with just one operator. That is not the end of it. Our job cards are taken, and though I cannot read, people tell me that my attendance is registered too. The only thing missing is the payment.

Second, many households who worked under the NREGS reported long delays in payment of their wages, with some households not receiving their wages for as long as six months after the work. A few households even reported that they were waiting for their wages for the work they did a year ago. One such NREGS worker who was not paid for two years of work bitterly recounted:

> My dues for 84 days of work have not been paid to me. And I am not the only one around here. There are many workers whose outstanding dues have not been cleared. But people here are too scared to complain to the higher authorities because we fear that whatever little we earn from the NREGS will be snatched away from us. For now, we are making do with the hope of getting our wages someday.

While payment delays were a widespread problem, the extent of delays varied widely across the study villages, and often from one worker to another within the same village. Even though the rent-seekers often manipulated and undermined the entitlement franchise of poor workers by fraudulent means, the fieldwork also revealed that the NREGS at the same time provided a tool in the hands of the rural poor to understand their rights and entitlements better than before. The bargaining power of the poor vis-à-vis actors at the higher echelons, however, was weaker, which prevented any meaningful assertion of their rights.

Finally, in terms of the impact of the NREGS in reducing outmigration and improving food security of rural households – the two key objectives of the scheme as well as the main themes of relevance to this book – the evidence from Siwan suggests that the NREGS has not made any significant dent on either counts in the district. The job-cardholder households were asked if any of their members who were earlier working outside the village returned to work under the NREGS. Only two households replied in the affirmative. NREGS wages were certainly higher than the wages earned locally from farm and non-farm casual work. However, long delays in payment diminished the real value of NREGS employment. Furthermore, not only were migration incomes higher, but remittances also provided a steady source of income for migrant households. The participation of migrant households in the scheme was contingent on the number of adult members, usually males, present in the household, and if the timing of NREGS work did not coincide with the other kinds of farm work in the village. The latter applied to the non-migrant households as well. Even though the wages offered by agricultural work were significantly lower, households tended to view them as more certain than NREGS wages. With regard to gender, barring women from the Scheduled Castes and Scheduled Tribes, most women viewed manual labour jobs offered under the NREGS (other than plantation work) as *culturally inappropriate* and instead preferred to work as agricultural labourers on a daily wage rate of INR 50 that was nearly one-third of NREGS wage of INR 144.

As far as the NREGS's impact on improving the food security situation of the households is concerned, four out of the 46 households perceived that the wage-income from the scheme provided a vitally important source to meet their food needs, and 14 households said that even though the scheme did not directly affect their food security, it had made life easier for them. Notwithstanding the massive operational inefficiencies, the fact that nearly 40 per cent of the NREGS-participant households perceived the scheme in positive terms highlights its relevance for poor households. At the same time, the NREGS had no perceptible impact on the food security of 60 per cent of the households who undertook work under the programme (Figure 5.3).

In conclusion, because of the multiple issues, described earlier, which beset the effective functioning of the NREGS in Siwan (which presumably applies to many other districts in Bihar) and act as deterrents for households to accrue its benefits in a meaningful sense, many rural households also seemed

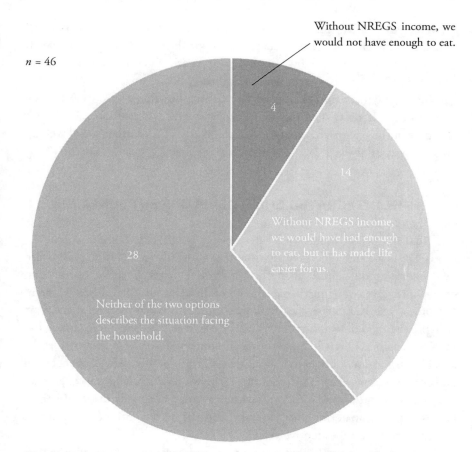

Figure 5.3 Perceptions of the National Rural Employment Guarantee Scheme (NREGS)-participating households on the impact of the scheme in improving food security, 2011–12

Source: Primary household survey data.

to be becoming increasingly indifferent to the scheme. Interviews with a number of local NREGS stakeholders, including the elected representatives of village councils, block development officers, NREGS programme officers and, most importantly, numerous rural households and NREGS workers themselves (including those who did not form part of the household sample), revealed that although there appeared some signs of the rural poor pressing hard to make their rightful claims, their pleas often went unheard. Due to their low socio-economic status, the power equation was so negatively skewed against them that they were unable to turn things around. In overall terms, real benefits of the scheme for the poor thus seemed quite muted. It is in this context that many households increasingly detached themselves from NREGS work. On the other hand, those who are unable to access other gainful employment options, locally or outside the village, continue to stick with it in the hope that things will change someday (see Photos 5.4–5.7 for glimpses of the on-ground operation of the NREGS and other social welfare programmes in Siwan).

THE INTEGRATED CHILD DEVELOPMENT SCHEME

The final important food-based safety net is the ICDS. Launched in 1975, the ICDS is a crucial intervention that seeks to address nutrition and health deficiencies among children in their formative years, with an overall aim of the programme being achievement of healthy childhood-development outcomes. The ICDS specifically targets children below the age of six years and pregnant and lactating mothers. More recently, the programme has involved in its ambit adolescent girls in some states. These groups are the specific targets for the scheme because of alarmingly high levels of maternal and child undernutrition in the country, with each reinforcing the other in an intergenerational fashion: undernourished women are likely to give birth to babies with below normal birth weight, and the cycle continues when these babies reach their reproductive years.

The ICDS was first launched on a pilot basis covering only 33 sub-districts or blocks in India, but it is now operational countrywide. The scheme currently operates through a nationwide network of nearly 1.35 million ICDS centres, popularly known as *anganwadi*s. The term *aaganwadi* means 'courtyard' in Hindi and originated from the idea that effective early childcare could be provided through low-cost local projects with minimal infrastructure. The *anganwadi* centres form part of the broader public-health infrastructure in India. The current norms for *anganwadi*s provide for setting up one centre catering to a population of 400–800 people. Each *anganwadi* usually includes two staff members of *sevika* (centre in-charge) and her assistant called *sahayika*. These staff report to the Child Development Programme officer (CDPO), who is responsible for the monitoring of *anganwadi*s at the local level. The services provided to eligible women and children through the *anganwadi*s include (*a*) supplementary nutrition, (*b*) immunisation and

Photo 5.1   A village public distribution system (PDS) shop where beneficiaries wait to receive their monthly food-grain rations

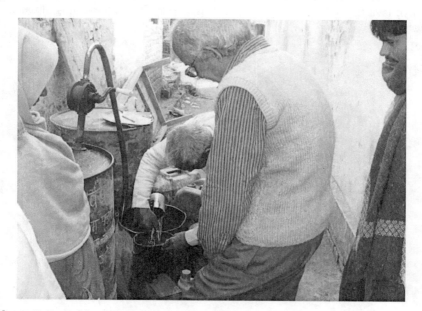

Photo 5.2   Public distribution system (PDS) beneficiaries receiving their monthly kerosene quota

Photo 5.3 Public distribution system (PDS) food-grain coupons of an Antyodaya family entitled to 21 kilograms of rice and 14 kilograms of wheat per month

Photo 5.4 A display board with information on the tree-plantation work carried out under the National Rural Employment Guarantee Scheme (NREGS)

Photo 5.5 A representative of the National Rural Employment Guarantee Scheme (NREGS) explaining the employment scheme and registration process to villagers

Photo 5.6 National Rural Employment Guarantee Scheme (NREGS) workers carrying out construction work for a community land-development project

Photo 5.7   A sub-district official taking a woman's thumb impression to register her in a welfare scheme

Photo 5.8   An *anganwadi* centre in one of the study villages – with a yellow board displaying information on the beneficiaries' entitlements, including a weekly menu of meals served to children and adolescent girls

Photo 5.9   A makeshift kitchen in an *anganwadi* where *khichadi* (a dish comprising a mixture of rice and lentils) is being prepared for lunch, which is indicative of many other such *anganwadi*s lacking basic infrastructure for operation

Photo 5.10   Children in a local *anganwadi* where they get preschool education and food

Source: All photographs taken by the author during fieldwork in Siwan.

health check-ups, (c) preschool education for children between three and six years of age and (d) nutrition and health education to expectant and lactating mothers. In 2017, the Government of India launched the National Nutrition Mission, also called Poshan in short, which aims to contribute to the goal of a malnutrition-free India by 2022. Planned in a phased manner with a three-year budget of about INR 9,000 crore, Poshan seeks to attain greater convergence across different health and nutrition programmes pertaining to women and children, such as supplementary nutrition, immunisation, safe pregnancy and delivery, sanitation, and so on. The *anganwadi* system forms a crucial pillar of Poshan (Ministry of Women and Child Development, 2020).

Although the ICDS provides various nutrition-related health services for women and children, as stated earlier, provision of free supplementary nutrition to the target women and children forms a crucial component of the programme. It must be added that providing free food was not originally as integral a feature of the ICDS, and the focus was more on the non-food aspects of child nutrition and development (Ghosh, 2006). However, with cases of malnutrition deaths among children due to lack of food surfacing from time to time in many parts of the country, direct provisioning of food for children has acquired a greater political significance concerning the right to food and child rights (see the various SC interim orders since 2001: Right to Food Campaign, 2020). Indeed, the NFSA that provides constitutional guarantee to right to food also includes provision of free food for children as well as women. And because the ICDS forms an important component of the newly launched Poshan mission, supplementary nutrition is also key to the malnutrition-free-India strategy (Government of India, 2013a; Ministry of Women and Child Development, 2020). The following discussion thus focuses more on this food provisioning aspect of the ICDS, based on the fieldwork in Siwan.[10] However, in discussing the operational aspects of the programme, it also provides some general overview of the broad features of the scheme.

Under the ICDS, children aged 6 to 36 months and pregnant and lactating mothers are provided with a certain quantity of take-home food rations per month, and children aged between three and six years are provided with a cooked meal for six days a week in the *anganwadi* where they also receive preschool education. The entitlement norms for the take-home rations as well as cooked-food menus vary across states. The programme currently covers about 83 million children under the age of 6 years and 19 million women of child-bearing ages (Ministry of Women and Child Development, 2020).

Several studies have documented the positive impact of the ICDS on the nutritional status of children (Tandon, 1989; Avsm et al., 1995; Jain, 2015). Recent evidence also suggests that the uptake of ICDS benefits increased significantly between 2005–06 and 2015–16 (Chakrabarti et al., 2019). However, like the PDS and the NREGS, the impact of the ICDS varies across states depending on the financial and implementation capacities of the relevant state government.

Although the ICDS is largely a federally-funded scheme, with the central government bearing 90 per cent of the total programme cost, the supplementary nutrition component of the programme is funded 50:50 between the centre and each state, except in the seven north-eastern states where the same 90:10 format applies (Ministry of Women and Child Development, 2020). The budgetary arrangements imply that varying financial capacities of the individual states play an important role in explaining the differential impacts of the programmes on child food and nutrition outcomes across states.

In many ways, Bihar suffers from severe deficits in terms of both budgetary capabilities and operational efficiency. Table 5.6 presents the picture of ICDS finances during 2011–12 and 2016–17. The 2011–12 period corresponds to the primary-survey reference period, and 2016–17 is the latest year for which reliable data were available at the time of writing.

Table 5.6 Snapshot of the finances of the Integrated Child Development Scheme (ICDS) in Bihar, 2011–17

	2011–12	**2016–17**
Number of *anganwadi* centres (ACs)	91,677	91,677
Budget versus spending (INR crore)		
Total annual budget	1,255.87	1,494.10
Total funds released by the centre	767.40	987.30
Actual spending	945.09	893.50
Budget versus spending per AC (INR crore)		
Average annual budget per AC (total budget/number of ACs)	136,989	162,974
Average monthly budget per AC ([total budget/number of ACs]/12)	11,416	13,581

Source: Compiled from Government of Bihar (2013, 2018).

The data for Bihar show that there were 91,677 operational *anganwadi*s covering all the 38 districts and 534 blocks of the state – a number that remained unchanged in the five-year period.[11] In 2011–12, the total annual ICDS budget of the Government of India for Bihar was INR 1,256 crore; the state received 61 per cent (INR 767 crore) of these sanctioned funds and spent over 75 per cent of the total budget. In 2016–17, the central budget increased to INR 1,494 crore (an increase of about INR 240 crore in a five-year period); the state was provided with INR 987 crore, but the actual spending on the ICDS in Bihar declined by INR 50 crore between 2011–12 and 2016–17 (from INR 945 crore to INR 894 crore). This downfall notwithstanding, analysis of trends in ICDS finances suggests that compared to previous years, the amount of funds received and utilised for the ICDS by the Government of Bihar are indeed significantly higher. For instance, the ICDS budget for Bihar increased from INR 484 crore in 2007–08 to INR 1,494 crore in 2016–17. Similarly, actual spending rose from about INR 350 crore in 2007–08 to INR 894 crore (Government of Bihar, 2013, 2018). Indeed, when looked at in aggregate terms, these are no mean figures. However, in terms of the funds per *anganwadi*, and after factoring in the number of beneficiaries and their monthly entitlements, the ICDS appears to be chronically under-funded in the state. The average monthly budget per *anganwadi* in Bihar was INR 11,416 and INR 13,581 in 2011–12 and 2016–17, respectively.[12]

From this amount, the *anganwadi*s are mandated to provide (*a*) a monthly take-home ration of 3 kilograms of rice and 1.5 kilograms of pulses each to 16 pregnant and lactating mothers, (*b*) a monthly take-home ration of 2.5 kilograms of rice and 1.25 kilograms of pulses each to 28 children identified as malnourished, and 4 kilograms of rice and 2 kilograms of pulses each to 12 severely malnourished children in the age group of six months to three years, (*c*) morning refreshments or breakfast and hot-cooked lunch for 25 days per month to 40 children aged between three and six years who attend *anganwadi*s for preschool education, and (*d*) cooked lunch for 25 days per month to three adolescent girls aged between 11 and 18 years (Table 5.7). More recently, Bihar has also started providing milk and eggs to women and children as part of supplementary nutrition services.

During the fieldwork, a common complaint of *sevika*s and *sahayika*s interviewed across all the study villages in Siwan was that this amount was often inadequate to honour these commitments. Many also complained that they did not receive the official sanctioned amount to begin with. Yet the

Table 5.7 Supplementary nutrition norms in Bihar

| Beneficiary group | Number of beneficiaries | Take-home food entitlement | | Cooked-meals days per month |
		Rice (kilograms)	Pulses (kilograms)	
Children aged six months to three years				
Malnourished children	28	2.5	1.25	—
Severely malnourished children	12	4	2	—
Children aged three to six years	40	—	—	25
Pregnant or nursing mothers	16	3	1.5	—
Adolescent girls	3	—	—	25

Source: Government of Bihar (2020c).

scheme operated. For most *anganwadi* women workers, the scheme provided the sole source of income and, with it, self-esteem. Many of the ICDS centres visited during the fieldwork were found to be operating from the *sevikas'* own homes without the government paying any rent. Many workers stick with the job and offer their premises in the hope that the government will make these jobs permanent, and they will be provided with tenure security and benefits that accompany it. However, and not surprisingly, the on-ground operation of the scheme, from the perspective of the beneficiaries, was hardly without problems. Not all problems were because of the practices of *sevikas* or *sahayikas*.

The household survey data revealed that of the total 170 households who were eligible for the ICDS benefits in 2011–12 across all study villages (those with children aged between 6 and 72 months and/or pregnant and lactating mothers), 37 per cent (63 households) did not receive any supplementary nutrition benefits under the scheme. It must be added that the cap on the number of beneficiaries per *anganwadi* means that the *sevikas* are supposed to screen the households and provide benefits to only those from low socio-economic strata; mothers and children are monitored for their anthropometric status, and those who are undernourished are provided with nutrition benefits. This means-test aspect of the scheme was addressed in the NFSA that universalised supplementary nutrition through *anganwadi*s to all pregnant and lactating mothers and children aged between six months and six years (Government of India, 2013a). In reality, however, this does not happen. Notwithstanding the low population norms for setting up *anganwadi*s, as indicated earlier, fieldwork revealed that this often excluded a large majority of households where women and children were in genuine need of supplementary food benefits (also see Kaur, 2019; Sarkar, 2019). Indeed, the survey results suggest that of the 63 households who did not receive ICDS benefits, only six households opted out of choice. In other instances, the deserving poor households from the Scheduled Castes and Scheduled Tribes were largely untouched by the scheme because the *anganwadi* centres were often distant from their settlements. Furthermore, caste-based discrimination meant that oftentimes children from these low-caste groups were not allowed to enter the *anganwadi* premises. To quote a women respondent from the surveyed household: 'The children are often chased away by the *anganwadi* madam. But when there is a checking, she comes home and takes our children to the centre.'

Furthermore, hardly any of those 107 households who reported receiving ICDS benefits received them regularly or for the entire duration (usually women get take-home rations from the time of pregnancy till six months after childbirth, after which the take-home food entitlements get transferred to children up until they are three years old). The ICDS beneficiaries in the 107 households included 56 members (women and children below the age of three years) who were entitled for monthly take-home rations, and 89 children aged between three and six years who received meals with preschool education at the *anganwadi* (a few households had both women and child beneficiaries). In all the study villages, the distribution of take-home ration to eligible members was highly errant and often occurred before the monitoring visits of senior district, state or central government officials. Furthermore, the only sub-district-level CDPO who could be interviewed (see the discussion later) was of the view that the idea that providing take-home ration every month to undernourished children and pregnant and lactating mothers would improve their nutritional status was wrongheaded. In her words:

The monthly take-home ration for combating nutritional deficiencies among women and children is a big failure. Because most beneficiaries come from poor households, the ration given to women and children

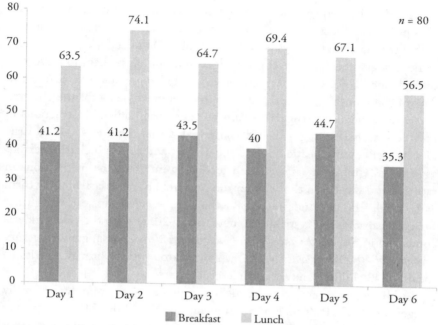

Figure 5.4 Percentage of children provided meals at an *anganwadi* in the past week when the survey was conducted, 2011–12

Source: Primary household survey data.

is often consumed by the entire household. It makes sense for the poor households for it translates into households not having to buy ration for a day or two in a month. But that is not what take-home ration aims at.

One aspect of the ICDS that seemed to be working relatively better was the meals provided to children who attended *anganwadi*s. In the survey, information was collected on whether the *anganwadi*-attending child(ren) from the household got their breakfast and hot-cooked lunch meals for each of the past six days. Figure 5.4 presents the distribution of these children. Out of the 89 children from 107 households, 80 reported going to the *anganwadi* regularly. Fieldwork showed that children went to the *anganwadi* mainly for the food, and not necessarily for preschool education. Most respondents reported that children were provided with something to eat at least once a day, as the data suggest. However, oftentimes the meals provided to children were inadequate and different from the prescribed norms. In none of the study villages did the frequency of cooked meals served to children exceed three days per week, effectively implying that these meals were provided for only half of the mandated 25 days per month (Table 5.7). Indeed, many *anganwadi* workers suggested that watertight budgets did not allow them to serve hot-cooked lunches every day, nor were they ever able to provide two meals on all days of the month. The breakfast or morning refreshments for the children *routinely* included two sugary biscuits as against the official instructions to provide seasonal fruits (fieldwork also revealed that there was also an issue of a lack of communication: while the district authorities included 'carrots' as seasonal fruits, the *sevikas* often tended to interpret the instructions in rather literal ways even though they did or could not necessarily follow them as strictly). The demands placed on the *anganwadis* often exceeded their financial capacities. It is striking to note that in 2012, when the fieldwork was conducted in Siwan, *the daily official budget provided to each* anganwadi *for the breakfast of 40 children was INR 22*, which was too little to provide nutritious meals for 40 children and three adolescent girls.[13]

Additionally, there were frequent complaints that from the monthly budget, many CDPOs took a monthly cut of INR 1,000–2,000 from each *anganwadi* centre. The *anganwadi* workers did not openly say this fearing action against them, but they did allude to it. Indeed, failures to pay bribes often resulted in more monitoring visits to the *anganwadi* by the CDPO that often had the purpose of intimidation. During repeated visits to the block development offices which house the CDPOs' offices, only one of the nine CDPOs could be met during their official working hours. Each time their office staff claimed that the field-oriented nature of their work required them to stay in the villages for monitoring of the *anganwadis*. However, they could not be found in the *anganwadi* centres visited during the course of the fieldwork either. To be fair, it was impossible for these officers to visit all *anganwadis* under their watch. In Siwan, the number of *anganwadi* centres assigned to each CDPO ranges from 73 to 255 (Government of Bihar, 2020c). Some *anganwadis* got their turn for a CDPO visit every quarter a year; places distant from the block office were particularly badly affected by the lack of supervision and monitoring. But a greater number of centres also meant that where money passed hands, collective bribes from *anganwadi* centres were often more than their official salaries. *Anganwadi* workers were also complicit, but their positions were connected with the authorities in the higher rung.

In a nutshell, there is no dispute that the programmatic objective of the ICDS to improve the food and nutrition security of women and children through supplementary nutrition is well intended. Indeed, evidence suggests that in many states with well-functioning *anganwadi*s, the ICDS is helping women and children to meet their food and nutrition needs. The southern state of Tamil Nadu has been a leading example of running a successful nutritious meal programme for children at *anganwadi*s (Rajivan, 2006; Drèze and Sen, 2013, pp. 164–66). Moreover, the concerted policy action on women and child undernutrition in recent years, reflected in initiatives such as Poshan, has resulted in significant overall improvements in the ICDS at the national level. Recent assessment of the programme by IFPRI researchers show that ICDS service receipts by women and children increased significantly between 2005–06 and 2015–16 in India, with service uptake rising particularly for supplementary nutrition – from 9.6 per cent to 37.9 per cent in the 10-year period. The programme's reach also improved among the traditionally disadvantaged caste groups belonging to the Scheduled Castes and Scheduled Tribes. At the same time, the programme also excluded poor households, particularly in the economically backward Indian states. Bihar is one such state which performed poorly (Chakrabarti et al., 2019). The field research has thrown light on the operational realities of the ICDS in Bihar that show why that is the case. Budget deficits, coupled with maladministration of the scheme, make the ICDS a weak engine to spur improvements in nutritional outcomes of children. According to the NFHS 2015–16, 44 per cent of under-five children in Bihar were underweight, and 30.4 per cent of women in the age group of 15–49 years had a below-normal BMI of 18.5 (IIPS and ICF International, 2017a). Indeed, although the ICDS has been in operation in the country for nearly 45 years, India has among the worst levels of child and maternal nutrition in the world. This research has attempted to highlight some of the systematic issues with the scheme. Unless these issues are fixed, the ICDS will continue to underachieve upon its objectives (see Photos 5.8–5.10 on the functioning of the ICDS in Siwan).

CONCLUSION

This chapter has provided an assessment of the food and livelihood safety nets in Bihar, based primarily on the fieldwork in Siwan district. The persistently high incidence of poverty in Bihar means that the state-assisted safety-net programmes hold vital significance in the lives of vulnerable rural populations. At the same time, they are affected by woeful delivery failures.

The evidence presented in this chapter suggests that the PDS, the NREGS and the ICDS are all plagued by severe maladministration and corruption. The operational inefficiencies in these schemes severely undermine their effectiveness in making significant contributions towards the food security needs of the rural poor.

That corruption is endemic in most social protection schemes in Bihar is not a secret – far from it. It is, however, encouraging to note some signs of a political will to revamp the dire state of social provisioning in the state in recent years. The experiments with coupon-based PDS reforms reflect this tendency. There are other important non-state, citizen initiatives as well. In Siwan, for instance, a popular community radio called *Radio Snehi* at the time of this fieldwork had a programme which, based on people's complaints, attempted to name and shame the corrupt officials. In one of the prank-playing show formats, Snehi's radio jockey, R. K. Rana, made phone calls to the village-level providers of social services, such as *anganwadi sevika*s, school headmasters, and so on, and pretended to be a monitoring officer from the state or central government. The usual conversation that followed is that he had received complaints that the concerned official was not dispensing his duties as mandated. Not surprisingly, prank calls by Rana wreaked havoc until he revealed his true identity. What is striking is that many officials, unaware of the prank at first, admitted to the alleged wrongdoings (of not honouring their duties) and vouched to not repeat the mistakes in the future. The significance of such initiatives notwithstanding, solutions to curb the corruption to bring about a meaningful change are yet to emerge.

Positing this issue in terms of India's landmark right-to-food legislation, the corruption and rent-seeking in the food-based safety nets pose a significant challenge to the effective realisation of this right. One manifestation of this, as echoed by Chatterjee (2004, p. 38), albeit in a slightly different context, is that 'most of the inhabitants of India are only tenuously and only then ambiguously and contextually rights-bearing citizens in the sense imagined by the constitution' (cited in Witsoe, 2012, p. 53).

This is not to say that these safety-net programmes are not important. The importance of these schemes in the lives of resource-poor households was all too apparent from the village-level observations and interviews carried out with them. Consistent with the arguments of Drèze and Sen (2013, p. 212), this chapter does not intend to suggest that leaving poor people on their own is a good policy; and as the recent assessment of social security initiatives by Drèze and Khera (2017) show, over the past 15 years there has been a major expansion of social security programmes in India. Instead, the overall argument pursued here is that the current institutional arrangements on social safety nets in Bihar (and in some other states of India) do not provide a robust food security anchor for a large majority of rural populations. The research findings from Siwan are in sync with evidence from other parts of the state. For example, reporting the findings of a longitudinal study that traces the development contrasts in two socially and economically heterogeneous villages in north Bihar over three decades (since 1980), Datta et al. (2014, p. 1198) note:

> In both villages, state social policies, previously notable mainly by their absence or ineffectiveness, are now increasingly visible ... But this progress in social policy did not seem to be an important source of the differences in development path between the two villages.

In Siwan, the inefficiencies in the social protection nets leave little option for a large majority of rural poor households but to fend for themselves. However, dejected as they may be with the current state of social provisioning, the rural poor do not appear to be passive actors. They devise multiple strategies to mitigate risks to their income and food security. The weak capacity of the land-based livelihoods and the underdeveloped state of the rural non-farm sector means that migration figures as an important strategy within the rural livelihood systems in Siwan. While migration, in large part, represents a response to the broader livelihood deficits that characterise the life-worlds of a large majority of the rural dwellers in the district, the inadequacy of social protection further aggravates their vulnerability to income and food insecurity and provides a strong incentive for migration. The complex dynamics of household decision-making matrices make it difficult to precisely decompose the relative effects of a lack of proper social protection in guiding the households' migration decisions. However, it is certainly the case that the incidence of migration would have been less in the presence of effectively functioning social safety nets.

Ironically, however, migration appears to further deprive many of the poor households of access to these social safety nets. This occurs mainly in two ways. First, the predominantly single-male nature of migration from Siwan means that most households have their adult men outside the village for a major part of the year. And the cultural norms restricting the participation of women in the affairs outside the household often result in left-behind women finding it hard to register their claims over their entitlements; those who try to do are often ignored and manipulated. Second, the local authorities in charge of administering the safety nets often regard households with migrant members as having steady income streams and thus consider them ineligible for the benefits of these schemes. Interviews with various village-level stakeholders pointed towards this tendency. The household survey data also capture these dynamics. The data suggest that whereas the average percentage share of government benefits (such as pensions, scholarships, and so on) in household income was 4 per cent for non-migrant households, it was less than half (1.9 per cent) for the households with migrants, though it must be noted that the latter had higher average incomes than the former because of the higher urban incomes.

Thus, while the dire state of social protection acts as an incentive for migration, the act of migration also appears to result in the exclusion of rural households from the safety-net benefits. However, it is equally pertinent to invert the equation and ask whether and how migration helps rural households to cope with perennial conditions of economic distress to meet their income and food security needs. Fieldwork suggested that while the economic circumstances of many households remained dire, without migration incomes most of the surveyed households would be worse off. Furthermore, in cases where remittances were significant, they also enabled households to improve their overall economic standing. The positive impacts of migration were perhaps most pronounced on household food security, and regardless of the background circumstances of the households, migration did seem to improve the households' access to food. The next chapter discusses the role of migration and remittances in influencing food security among rural households.

NOTES

1. Chhattisgarh implemented its own Food Security Act in 2012 even before the NFSA (Government of Chhattisgarh, 2013).
2. This figure is based on the NSS's quinquennial consumption expenditure data for 2011–12. Poverty estimates are updated periodically using this survey data. The recent round of consumption expenditure survey was conducted in 2017–18. However, results of this survey indicated a decline in consumption demand. This was the first fall in consumption expenditure in four decades,

an unprecedented finding. The Government of India, headed by the Bharatiya Janata Party (BJP), scrapped the 2017–18 survey report and data arbitrarily instead of releasing it for public discussion and analysis.

3. Not all untraceable households mean bogus or ghost cards, and some of these errors may also be due to location errors and family migration.

4. On almost all food security indicators, non-beneficiary households fared worse than those in the partial beneficiary category; they also reported worse food security outcomes than did full beneficiary households on indicators of 'consuming single meal a day', 'borrowing money from friends or relatives' and 'borrowing from local traders and other lenders'. This is consistent with the data in Table 5.2 that shows that many of the households left completely out of the PDS were among the poorest. However, because of their smaller sample size, they do not affect the partial-beneficiary category as such. In other words, many of the overall better-off partial beneficiary households that were part of the PDS but did not receive food rations also reported high food insecurity.

5. This coupon scheme was discontinued after the implementation of the food security legislation.

6. In some areas of India, a low PER for food grains could be indicative of low food-grain quality, which encourages households to not take up their PDS rations (Khera, 2012, p. 40). However, in the study villages, this process was extremely unlikely because of the extreme poverty of most surveyed households. As the data in Table 5.3 show, nearly 40 per cent of food-grain beneficiary households reported that there were times in the past year when they could only afford to buy food from the PDS.

7. Details of public works under the NREGS are displayed publicly on signboards in the local area as a measure to increase transparency, including information on funds sanctioned and spent. Local residents can use this information to hold their GP leaders accountable. In reality, this rarely happens because leaders are often too powerful, though these measures have helped strengthen grassroots democracy and workers now increasingly assert their voice for their social protection entitlements (see Photo 5.4).

8. For an extensive review of the literature on the impacts of the NREGS, refer to Ministry of Rural Development (2012) and the contributions in Khera (2011c).

9. The work participation for Siwan is arrived at by dividing the official NREGS figure on the number of households that worked under the scheme (52,113 households) in 2011–12 by the total rural households in Siwan district

(507,055 households), as enumerated in the 2011 census (Ministry of Rural Development, 2020; Census of India, 2011c). Household work participation rate in 2018–19 is even less at 7.5 per cent (38,238 households).

10. Children in local *anganwadi* centres also get preschool education, though because most children come from socio-economically disadvantaged backgrounds, they attend *anganwadi*s primarily for food. But another important but *understated* contribution of these spaces is that they also take some load of childcare duties off parents, usually women.

11. These figures include only the operational *anganwadi* centres. In 2016–17, the total number of sanctioned *anganwadi* centres was 114,718, but only 91,677 centres were functional.

12. Field research in Siwan in 2012 showed that the actual amount *officially* received by *anganwadi* centres was INR 10,950 a month, which was less than the average budgeted sum.

13. This is based on interviews with several *anganwadi sevika*s and *sahayika*s, and the sub-district (block)-level Child Development Programme officer.

6

MIGRATION, REMITTANCES, LAND AND HOUSEHOLD FOOD SECURITY

INTRODUCTION

The development experience of most countries in the world suggests that economic growth is accompanied by structural transformation. As economies advance, the share of population chiefly dependent on agriculture declines. However, the outcomes of this structural transformation on rural and urban economies and societies are far from uniform, and they depend on the ways in which 'the complexity of national diversity asserts itself' (Timmer, 2007, p. 4).

The Indian experience of structural transformation appears peculiar. The market reforms from the 1980s (though beginning in earnest only in the early 1990s) put the Indian economy on the path of higher growth and are associated with increased overall prosperity. This has been accompanied by a structural shift in which the non-agricultural sector vis-à-vis the agricultural sector and urban areas vis-à-vis rural areas have gained significance in terms of their shares in national income. However, changes in employment patterns have not followed at an expected pace. The rural–urban transition is far from complete, and nearly 70 per cent of the country's population still lives in the countryside. And despite the fast-growing non-agricultural sector of the economy, the share of labour in agriculture has declined at a slower rate than the contemporary experience of other Asian countries suggests. The source of this apparent contradiction lies in the fact that much of the economic growth of the recent past is accounted for by more capital and skill-intensive business and service sectors, constraining the opportunities for the poor and unskilled populations to alter their livelihood pathways more fully.

India's distinctive structural transformation notwithstanding, the fundamental shifts that have characterised the Indian economy over the past three decades are rapidly altering rural livelihood trajectories in the country. Although agriculture still remains the single largest employment provider, the relative importance of agriculture as a *primary* source of income and food security has weakened. Between 2004 and 2016, there has been a net loss of 40 million jobs in agriculture with effects extending to 200 million rural dwellers (see Van Duijne and Nijman, 2019; Choithani, Van Duijne and Nijman, 2021).

Jobs and economic output are now increasingly concentrated in cities and towns. Most urban jobs are informal, but they provide an important buffer against livelihood losses in the rural agriculture sector. This means urban areas have assumed greater significance in the overall framework of the economy and job creation. Indeed, it is the spillover effects of urban growth on rural incomes and employment that seem to have become increasingly more crucial for rural poverty reduction in recent years (World Bank, 2011b; Datt, Ravallion and Murgai, 2020).

This chapter explores what implications these broad changes have in shaping household livelihood pathways and how they correlate with household food security. The focus here is on the ways in which migration as a livelihood strategy affects household food security. To engage with these questions, the discussion draws on primary survey data from the case-study district of Siwan. Needless to say, the impact of these national, macro-level changes is unlikely to be uniform across and within different states of India, possibly varying even from one village to another, and thus they necessitate a place-based contextualisation and understanding. In Siwan, rural–urban linkages, although never absent due to the long history of migration, have assumed greater significance in recent years and are fundamentally altering social and economic relations at the village and household levels with direct implications for household food security. The decreasing returns from agriculture-based livelihoods suggest the increased importance of migration incomes for rural livelihoods. Yet the precariousness and uncertainty of urban jobs and a complex mix of sociocultural reasons mean that migrants continue to maintain close relations with their origin villages; they invest their earnings and remittances in the origin villages. In turn, this implies that rural land and resources continue to play a vital role in households' incomes and food security. At the same time, the capacity of rural land and agriculture to meet household food security needs is becoming increasingly contingent on urban remittances. In other words, complex interactions between rural and urban economies exist at the household level, which warrant examination to understand more fully the food security outcomes of migration. Given the rising significance of migration in livelihoods across rural India (Choithani, Van Duijne and Nijman, 2021), lessons from Siwan have wider significance to understand livelihood change in India and its impacts on household food security.

The layout of the chapter is as follows: The next section explores the decision-making matrices of households in terms of whether livelihood diversification occurs locally or at a distance. Not all households migrate, and it is important to understand the factors shaping migration decisions. The second section discusses whether there are differential gains from diversification within the rural and urban sectors. The third section then looks at the type of linkages that migration creates between rural and urban economies and how they relate to food security at the household level in Siwan. In particular, the focus here is to understand whether and how remittances correlate with household food security. The fourth section turns attention to the village-level changes in land and agrarian relations and their significance for food security. The final section concludes.

WHO MIGRATES, WHO STAYS AND WHY? CONDITIONS, INTENTIONS AND MOTIVATIONS TO MIGRATE AND STAY PUT

The economic landscape of rural Siwan is marked by the notable absence of gainful employment opportunities. Average landholdings are exceptionally small, and the cash-income generating potential of land and farming is very limited. Moreover, despite some growth in rural non-farm employment in recent years, the rural non-farm sector still remains highly underdeveloped; the jobs in this sector are errant and less remunerative. The few regular, better-salaried non-agricultural jobs, particularly in the social service sector run by the government (such as teachers, doctors, clerks, health workers, and so on), presuppose a certain level of education and skills which most poor households do not possess, and are thus cornered by the socially and economically better-off groups, mainly upper castes.[1] Additionally, while the return to normalcy of law and order and the high growth rates of the Bihar economy after the election of a new state government since 2005 has led to an increase in the number of the rural poor commuting daily to the district and block headquarters to engage in activities such as vending and hawking, rickshaw pulling, picking up labouring duties in construction work, and so on, local labour supply far exceeds the work demand and employment availability. As a result, a considerable proportion of rural households engage in long-distance, interstate migration. The survey data show that out of the 280 migrants belonging to 197 migrant households, only three migrants worked in another districts within Bihar. Much of the interstate outmigration from the district is to the tier-1 Indian cities which dominate the country's economy (see Figure 4.5 in Chapter 4).

Table 6.1 presents the socio-economic characteristics of surveyed households in Siwan by migration status. The data suggest minimal differences in the propensity to migrate across most socio-economic variables, with the notable exception of household type. Nuclear households were much more likely not to include one or more migrants, when compared with joint households.

Fieldwork, however, also pointed towards important new developments in household composition in rural India. At one level, it is not surprising that joint families with more members provided a migration-facilitating structure. In these cases, it has traditionally been the case that remittance incomes were jointly shared, with the left-behind wives and children of migrants looked after by the stay-put members, mainly the elderly parents. However, this is no longer always the case. Interviews with households indicated an increased reluctance of migrant individuals, and their wives, to share the remittances with the less productive members of the family. In turn, this led to increasing intra-household tensions over cash management, which had an impact on family structure. The upshot was that many migrants separated themselves from joint households, leading to new types of familial arrangements which could be characterised as ones where the roof is shared, but income and financial responsibilities are separated (see Chapter 7).

A second issue, evident in Table 6.1, is the association between household's economic status and propensity to migrate. Survey data suggest that migrant households fared relatively better than non-migrant households on measures of economic well-being. The average monthly per capita income (MPCI) and MPCE among households with migrant members were approximately 30 per cent more than those of their non-migrant counterparts; 66 per cent of the non-migrant households had MPCE below the state poverty line as compared to 47.7 per cent of that

Table 6.1 Background characteristics of surveyed households by migration status

	Migrant household	Non-migrant household
Household size (in person)*		
Average household size	7.3	5.7
Average number of persons aged 20–50 years	2.9	2.1
Average number of males aged 20–50 years	1.6	1.0
Religion of the household		
Hindu	77.7	79.5
Muslim	22.3	20.5
Caste of the household		
Forward caste	7.1	7.7
Backward caste	46.7	40.4
Extremely backward caste	28.4	28.7
Scheduled Caste or Scheduled Tribe	17.8	23.1
Type of household		
Nuclear	47.2	74.4
Joint or extended	52.8	25.6
Type of house occupied		
Kutcha	16.2	24.1
Semi-pucca	37.1	38.5
Pucca	46.7	37.4
Agricultural land ownership		
Landless households	33.0	31.8
Households with land size of less than half an acre	66.7	67.7
Households with land size of less than an acre	83.3	85.7
Average land size (in acre)	0.65	0.58
Income and expenditure		
Average monthly per capita income (in INR)	970	654
Average monthly per capita expenditure (in INR)	1021	735
Household with monthly per capita consumption expenditure below poverty line**	47.7	66.2
Total number of households (*n*)	**197**	**195**

Source: Primary household survey data.

Note: All data are in percentage terms unless specified differently. *Includes migrant members. **The 2009–10 revision of state-specific poverty lines, based on the Tendulkar committee's estimates, pegged the rural poverty line in Bihar at INR 655.6. The same has been applied to this survey data to estimate consumption poverty (Planning Commission, 2012).

of the migrant households; a higher proportion of migrants lived in *pucca* (concrete) houses than non-migrant counterparts. However, these data reflect post-migration economic outcomes, and they alone cannot be used to infer pre-migration differentiated propensities to migrate. Thus, whereas previous studies have pointed out that the poorest households are often least able to migrate because of their inability to bear the initial costs of migration (Connell et al., 1976), which in turn increases intra-village inequality among the households (Lipton, 1980), field research in Siwan did not suggest that the initial economic position of the household was a major explanatory variable for migration.

While many households faced difficulties in financing the initial costs of migration, this did not deter migration among the poorest. For example, the wife of one migrant informed us that for her husband's first trip to the city 10 years ago, they mortgaged her silver anklets to borrow money from the local moneylender. Similarly, other households borrowed money from their relatives and friends to send their members to the cities; in turn, having a member in the city enhanced the creditworthiness of migrant households who were able to borrow money in months when migrants did not send remittances. In any case, the high incidence of poverty in Siwan meant that economic constraints to migration applied almost equally to all households. Like their rural counterparts, most migrants worked in casual jobs in the urban informal sector. However, the average migration incomes were higher than the local earnings, which allowed households with migrants to fare better economically than their non-migrant counterparts. The survey data suggest that the average annual income of households with one or more migrant member from remittances alone was INR 43,563, which was slightly higher than the total income of INR 43,507 among non-migrant households; and households with primary dependence on remittances as a source of income had higher incomes and expenditure as compared to the households that chiefly depended on local farm and non-farm incomes (see Table 6.2 and Figure 6.2).

Most households reported that their migrant members had been going to the cities for work for a long time. Of the 280 migrants, 85.7 per cent had at least two years and more of migration history, with 64 per cent (197 migrants) having a duration of stay-away since the first migration as five years or more. The higher urban incomes and the savings they allowed meant that it is the repeated trips to the city for a few years that affected these income differentials between migrants and non-migrant households. Research based on longitudinal village surveys conducted over the course of 30 years

(1975–2005) in Maharashtra and Andhra Pradesh that collected systematic information on temporary work migration from 1992 onwards corroborates this finding. The research shows that while differences in income and assets between migrants and non-migrant households were insubstantial at the time of migration in 1992, the income and assets per capita of migrant households were respectively 30 per cent and 50 per cent higher than those of non-migrant households by 2002 (Badiani, 2011).

Furthermore, it is important to note that the incidence of migration in Siwan did not vary much by mutually interlinked categories of landholding size and caste – two key predictors of poverty and migration in India. Evidence from large-scale surveys and village studies suggests that in many parts of India, it is generally the landless and land-poor communities of lower castes who partake in unskilled seasonal or circular migration (Breman, 1996, 2010; Mosse et al., 2002; Srivastava and Sasikumar, 2003; Keshri and Bhagat, 2012; Srivastava, 2019). However, survey data from Siwan show no significant differences in the proportion of migrant and non-migrant households by their caste status, and migrants came from all castes. Studies from other parts of Bihar also suggest the same (Sharma, 1997; Karan, 2003). However, the gains of migration varied, with households from upper castes faring slightly better than the lower-caste households in Siwan. Indeed, colonial records of migration from western Bihar suggests that migration was widespread across different caste groups (Hagen and Yang, 1976; Yang, 1979, 1989; de Haan, 1997a, 1997b, 2002). Long history of migration from the western Bihar region has further loosened the caste basis of migration over time. In fact, while the landless and land-poor communities belonging to lower castes have traditionally relied more on the income from menial jobs elsewhere (de Haan, 2002), in recent years the incidence of migration has increased among the upper castes. Following the abolition of the *zamindari* system and related, albeit partial, land reforms carried out in Bihar in the post-independence period, the land-loss among the upper castes has been greater. Further diminishing the capacity of land-based livelihoods has been the continuous fragmentation of landholdings due to high population pressures. Village studies from other parts of Bihar suggest that landholdings of upper castes have reached a point where farming no longer provides a viable income option (Sharma, 2005, p. 965; Datta, 2016). By reducing the wage-income opportunities locally, this has also propelled migration among the traditionally disadvantaged communities of the Scheduled Castes, Scheduled Tribes and extremely backward caste groups, though it should be noted that the lower-caste communities of Bansfor and Musahar (two traditionally marginalised caste groups in Bihar) did not show a high migration propensity.

Personal histories of many lower-caste households in Siwan revealed that many had members who earlier worked as attached labourers in the fields of forward-caste landowners. However, this is no longer the case. In none of the 10 study villages was the incidence of labour bondage reported. Studies from other parts of Bihar confirm that attached labour no longer characterises agrarian and land relations in the state. Reporting the findings of a longitudinal study that traced the changes in socio-economic relations in two contrasting villages in norther Bihar over a 30-year period, Datta et al. (2014, p. 1199) found that between 1981 and 2009, both 'attached labour' and 'pure landlords' disappeared in the two villages. In Siwan, the progressive reduction in the already meagre size of landholdings has weakened the erstwhile feudal relations. At the same time, new land dynamics are emerging, whereby the landowning communities are leasing out their land to pursue more remunerative non-local, non-farm livelihoods in the cities. How these land relations have a bearing on food security of the land-poor households is discussed in a later section of this chapter.

At this stage, however, it is important to note that the motivations to migrate as well as to stay put in the village were complex. In the case of migrant households, although economic reasons figured prominently in most and almost exclusively in many households' migration decisions, they conflated with several other motivations such as personal desires of the migrants to experience the outside world. That said, connections with family and village at the place of origin remained strong, and most migrants showed a strong leaning towards village life.

To most households, long-distance migration to urban areas inevitably provided the route to make up for livelihood deficits in the origin villages. The predominance of push induced by unemployment notwithstanding, higher urban incomes also provided the pull motives to many households. In fact, in myriad instances, the classic push–pull dichotomy was often obscured, as the responses of most respondents often reflected a combination of the distress-push and income-pull factors. In interviews with migrants in cities, a common response to the question of the migration trigger was that 'we don't have much employment available there [in the village]', often followed by, at times in the same breath, 'incomes here [in the city] are much better'. In other words, the escape from the economic drudgery in the village often coincided with the inherent desire among migrants to better themselves.

Furthermore, and this is important, there was a great degree of differentiation in the ways in which different migrants and households perceived and pursued the economic gains of migration. To some households, often the very poor with no land and other assets in the place of origin, migration served the immediate goal of meeting food consumption needs. For Ahmed (name changed) and his family, for instance:

> I often wonder what would happen if I did not come and work here. My family would die of starvation ... My daughter died two-and-a-half years ago when she was just two-and-a-half years old. She had jaundice, and I asked my wife if I should come back so that we could see a good doctor for her, but she told me not to. A few days later, she called me to inform that my daughter is no more, and I must come now. If I had gone earlier, she could have been saved. But I could only go to bury her. I do not blame my wife either, as she probably thought that me not earning for a month (or may be longer), and thus not sending money home, would have killed her anyway.

For others, migration provided a way to save and accumulate money for long-term goals, such as dowry for daughters' wedding, via the mechanism of buying a piece of land (a few migrants bought land when their daughter(s) were growing up and sold it later to meet dowry demands). Thus, to quote another respondent:

> My family's day-to-day expenses are provided by the cash income from the milk we sell. But selling milk can never pay for my daughter's marriage. So the money that I earn here is used for bigger expenditure ... whatever I have been able to do is from the money I earn here. I married off two daughters, spent money on my parents' treatment and funeral, and I am now educating my younger children.

In a handful of other cases, work migration, although occurring due to distressing circumstances at home and with the broader purpose of maximising household welfare, also coalesced with individual migrants' desire to experience the outside world away from the watchful eyes of family and village elders. Seen this way, mobility also provided an avenue for *partial individualisation* of migrant members' lives. Personal narratives of such migrants revealed that they often combined broad household goals with their own aspirations, though the former were almost always more important than the latter. To quote another migrant:

> My father did not have much, and so I had to start working even before I hit puberty. But I wanted to move out of the village and experience the outside world. I was always curious to meet and interact with people from other regions and cultures. But I had to earn some money to support my aspirations and, more importantly, I had my family to support. So I started working outside. But now I realise that I have been away from the village and my family forever.

The lack of gainful employment opportunities in Siwan notwithstanding, most of the migrants interviewed were of the view that while they could find work in and around the village, migration allowed savings that local work did not. Indeed, saving was the single biggest reason reported by the migrants. As Bhim (name changed), who worked as a carpenter in Faridabad, Haryana, put it:

> I know here in the village I can earn as much money as I make staying 500 miles away from home. But I will not ever be able to save a single penny here, whereas in Faridabad I save between INR 4,000 and INR 5,000 every month. This money helps my family when they need it. What is the point of earning and not saving anyway?

Not all migrants (and the households they belonged to) were able to improve their economic standing over time in any significant manner (for example, Ahmed's case). Most migrants worked in the urban informal sector and had precarious jobs. Indeed, it is one of the important reasons why migration from this region (and from Bihar as a whole) has remained circular as well as intergenerational in nature, with old members in the household passing the baton to the younger members of employable age. However, it is also true that without migration the rural populations of western Bihar would be much worse off. Furthermore, remittances played an important role in the lives and livelihoods. From the specific perspective of food security, while nutritional circumstances were dire across the survey sample, having a member outside was invariably associated with improved access to food and dietary diversity.

On the other hand, decisions by some respondents not to migrate were not because they were better off and thus did not have any need. It was also not always the case that they lacked the requisite information and networks.

In all the 10 study villages, the ubiquity of migration (and of its circular nature) meant that information on work availability, destinations and wages flowed quickly, and the long history of migration from the region meant that networks were well established. Yet many households stayed in their village. This was because, first, as noted earlier, a larger proportion of non-migrant households came from nuclear families and had a lower average family size. For instance, Munni Lal (name changed), a 45-year-old man from the Kushwaha community (cultivator caste), who combined cash incomes from farming and sharecropping with repairing irrigation pumps, told us: 'I wanted to go and work in the city, but I couldn't do it because I was alone. But when my son grows up, I want him to go and live in one of the big cities.' Households with fewer members found it difficult for someone to move out. Second, attachment with village life, local networks and agricultural land kept several households embedded in the village economy and society.

Third, some non-migrant households earlier had members who migrated but returned because they either developed health problems or faced exploitation and abuse in the city. The latter reason was particularly true for some of the most disadvantaged households, such as Bansfors and Musahars (see Box 6.1 and Photos 6.1–6.6). Many had no networks and depended on the work agents or contractors to change their fortunes. The way agents recruited men from these lower castes was to provide an advance sum of a few thousand rupees to the cash-starved poor families. Although this advance amount varied from one village to another and, within the village, from one household to another, it ranged between INR 3,000 and INR 8,000. As per the verbal contract and commitment by the agent, it was meant to be the payment worth one month of work. However, in many cases, this amount was all that was paid for the duration of work ranging between six and eight months, in addition to the weekly sum of a few hundred rupees for their food expenses. High levels of exploitation at the destination, also often including long working hours, less-than-promised pay and sometimes no pay at all, reduced the benefits of migration for these households. To quote one such migrant who returned:

I am a poor and illiterate man. When it came to settling my account towards the end of the working period, my contractor would show me a huge paper and tell me that instead I owed him money which I must return. Upon hearing that, my heartbeat would stop. I worked with four different agents in Kolkata, Chennai, Guhawati and Cochin [Kochi], but this happened with me each time. So I am better off living in the village.

Box 6.1   Bansfors and Musahars: a brief profile

Socio-economic conditions

Officially recognised as the Scheduled Castes in the Indian Constitution, the Bansfor and Musahar caste groups are mainly found in the two Indian states of Bihar and Uttar Pradesh. Fieldwork in rural Siwan suggested that in a village structure, members from these lower-caste communities formed the contingents of socially marginalised, economically and educationally backward and geographically isolated people. As outcasts, they lived on the village margins and were segregated from the main village habitations. Most families had subhuman living conditions, dwelled in kutcha (mud/bamboo) houses and had no land or any other productive resources. The incidence of food insecurity and hunger was extremely high among the Bansfors and Musahars, and most families were seldom able to eat three meals a day every day. Due to the lack of resources and networks, migration was very low among these caste groups, and most families depended on local income options.

Livelihoods

Also known as 'rat eaters', Musahars occupy the lowest rung of caste hierarchy in India. The livelihoods of Musahars are gender-segregated. Most Musahar men work in the local brick kilns for about five months per year (February–June). During interviews with Musahars in one of the study villages, it was revealed that they received INR 300 for every 1,000 bricks they made. On an average, an adult man makes between 500 and 700 bricks every day, thus earning close to INR 150 as daily wages. During the peak agricultural season, women work as agricultural labourers in the fields of landowners at the daily wage rate of INR 30–50 per day for four–five hours of work. In the slack period when work is available under the National Rural Employment Guarantee Scheme (NREGS), both men and women work under the scheme.

The main livelihood activity of Bansfors is making bamboo-based small products by hand, such as baskets. Bans is a Hindi word for bamboo, and Bansfors are commonly known as 'bamboo workers'. Whole families, including young children, are involved in making baskets, and a family can

(Contd)

(Contd)

> usually make between five and eight baskets per day. Depending on the size, type and quality, each basket is sold for anywhere between INR 10 and INR 30. Like Musahars, Bansfors women also work as agricultural labourers, earning the similar daily wages of INR 30–50 per day. Interviews with some of the Bansfor households also revealed that oftentimes they beg for food from neighbours in their village.

Photo 6.1   A settlement of the Bansfor community in one of the study villages

In a nutshell, the decisions of households to migrate as well as stay put were complex, and were also guided by a range of non-economic factors. However, it is pertinent to understand how migrant households fare vis-à-vis non-migrant households, an issue taken up in the next section.

Photo 6.2   A Bansfor family making baskets

Photo 6.3   A Bansfor woman making bamboo-based baskets (the neighbours' children wanted to be in the frame too!)

Photo 6.4 A settlement of the Musahar community near a brick kiln where they worked

Photo 6.5 Musahar men working in a brick kiln

Photo 6.6   Musahar children who owned one pair of shirts each which their mothers had washed that day

Photo 6.7   An intrastate bus from Patna to Siwan, with many men on board being migrants who are returning to their native villages by sitting on the roof instead of in the main chamber as it costs less

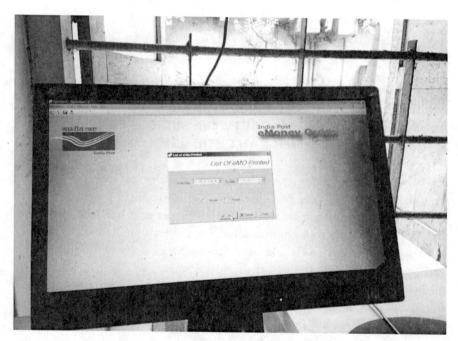

Photo 6.8   A postal money order carrying the value of INR 100

Photo 6.9   A computer screen in a Siwan post office showing the e-money order interface that postal officers now increasingly use for money transfer

Photo 6.10   A Western Union money-transfer centre in Siwan

Source: All photographs taken by the author during fieldwork in Siwan.

LANDHOLDING PATTERNS, NON-FARM INCOME DIVERSIFICATION AND INCOME DIFFERENTIALS BETWEEN MIGRANT AND NON-MIGRANT HOUSEHOLDS

In Siwan, landholdings are sub-economical. Out of the 392 surveyed households, 32.4 per cent of households had no land, 57.4 per cent owned landholdings of less than an acre and only 10.2 per cent had land sizes of an acre or more (Figure 6.1). These landholding patterns implied that for a large majority of surveyed households, the productive capacity of land to provide cash income was quite limited, though land was invariably valued highly by all households as a critical livelihood asset, a source of security and a vital foundation for the provisioning of food security. Indeed, as discussed later, farm and non-farm livelihoods were tightly linked. Non-farm cash incomes were important not only to supplement the gains from land-based livelihoods, but also to maintain and sustain the small land parcels that most of the poor households owned. In other words, small landholdings provided a strong

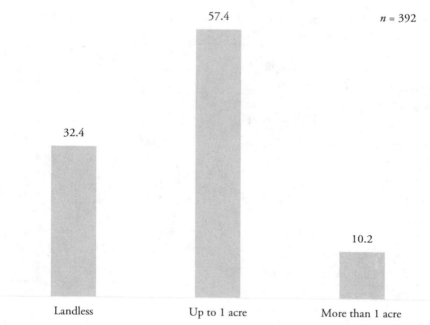

Figure 6.1 Percentage distribution of households by land-ownership status in Siwan

Source: Primary household survey data.

incentive for migration, but remittance incomes were crucial for household agriculture.

Most households relied on non-farm sources for their cash needs that contributed over three-quarters of the households' annual incomes. For migrant households, the combined share of rural and urban non-farm incomes accounted for more than 90 per cent of the average annual income. Migrant households had higher incomes than their non-migrant counterparts, largely because earnings in urban areas were higher than rural incomes. The annual per capita income of migrant households was 32 per cent higher than that of households without any migrant members (Table 6.2).

Another important point is that while households had their incomes spread across multiple sources, they varied in terms of the degree of dependence. The relative contribution of the source had important bearing in terms of explaining the income differentials between households with

Table 6.2 Average percentage share of income by source among migrant and non-migrant rural households in Siwan

Source of income	Migrant households (n = 197)	Non-migrant households (n = 194)*
Farm	1.5	7.7
Livestock	1.6	4.3
Rural non-farm	17.4	76.2
Off-farm	1.4	5.6
Remittances	75.4	0.0
Government benefits	1.9	4.0
Others	0.8	2.1
Total	100.0	100.0
Average annual income (INR)	60,232	43,507
Average annual per capita income (INR)	11,629	7,844

Source: Primary household survey data.

Note: *The total non-migrant sample included 195 households, but one of them did not share their income details.

and without migrants. The distribution of households across MPCI tertiles (division of households into three equal parts based on their income) by their *primary source of livelihood* is presented in Figure 6.2. The primary source of livelihood is defined here as the sector or occupation which accounted for 50 per cent or more of the total household income in the year 2011–12. This has been classified into three broad categories that include (*a*) agriculture and livestock (including off-farm wages from agriculture work and tending animals), (*b*) rural non-farm and (*c*) remittances. The logic of such classification was that together they accounted for 96 per cent of the average household income. The cut-off points for MPCI tertiles obtained from the survey data include INR 485.12 and INR 767.12. Using these cut-off points, the classification is as follows: (*a*) low (INR 0–485.12), (*b*) medium (INR 485.13–767.12) and (*c*) high (INR 767.13 and above).

These data suggest that while a relatively small proportion of the overall sample (32 households) depended on income from farm and livestock, a greater proportion (62.5 per cent) among them was in the low-income category, suggesting that farm incomes were low. Compared to them, a much smaller proportion of those who relied chiefly on rural non-farm incomes

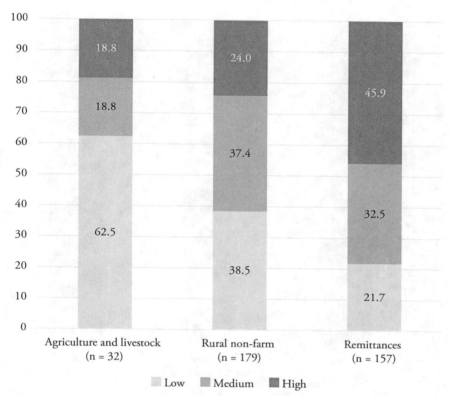

Figure 6.2 Percentage of households in tertiles of monthly per capita income (MPCI) by the primary source of livelihood

Source: Primary household survey data.

and remittances were in the low tertile. Importantly, nearly a half of 157 households that depended primarily on remittances were in the high-income category. This dependency on remittances provided migrant households an edge vis-à-vis their non-migrant counterparts. Comparing households in the same income tertiles by migration status shows that the proportion of non-migrant households in the low-income category is almost double than of migrant households (34 per cent and 66 per cent, respectively), and these percentages reverse in the high-income tertile (Figure 6.3).

Furthermore, other data comparing migrant and non-migrant households along the axis of castes also suggest that migration status exerts a positive force on household income: households with migrant member(s) fared better than non-migrant households across all caste categories.

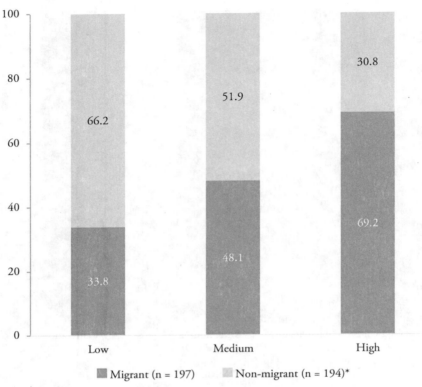

Figure 6.3 Percentage of households in income tertiles by migration status

Source: Primary household survey data.

Note: *One non-migrant household did not report its income.

However, the extent to which migration benefited the households varied by castes, whereby a larger proportion of migrant households in high-income group was from the forward castes, followed by backward castes, extremely backward castes, and Scheduled Castes and Scheduled Tribes. This is despite the fact that there were virtually no caste-based differences in the educational and occupational status of the migrants, and most had low levels of education and worked in the urban informal sector as low-skilled workers. But this caste structuring of income gains is not entirely surprising. Notwithstanding the general precariousness of the urban informal occupations most migrants are engaged in, the weak social status of the Scheduled Castes and Scheduled Tribes and the extremely backward castes often makes them more vulnerable to exploitation and discrimination.

It is important to note the two-way interconnectedness between non-farm livelihood pathways and migration. While the rural non-farm sector in Siwan remains underdeveloped, the potential of this sector to offer employment and income seemed to be connected, in part, to the flow of remittances into the district. This is unlike some other parts of India, such as Punjab, where agricultural growth provided the key stimulant to the growth and development of rural non-farm employment (Bhalla, 1993; Tripathy, 2009). In Siwan, average landholdings are small, and farming is largely family-based.

While much of the outmigration from the district tends to take place within the national boundaries (albeit mostly outside the state), the outflow of labour migrants to the Gulf countries is significant as well. In recent years, the Saran sub-division in western Bihar that comprises the three districts of Chapra, Gopalganj and Siwan has emerged as an important hub of labour migrants to the Persian Gulf; within western Bihar, Siwan sends the largest number of migrants to the Middle East. In some areas such as Chandpali village in the Ziradei block – the birthplace of the first president of independent India, Rajendra Prasad – almost every household has at least one member working abroad. In many villages across the district with a high incidence of international migration, having a member abroad has become a symbol of social status; families who do not have any members in *bidesh*, a common local metaphor for the Gulf countries (though in the local Bhojpuri folklore, the term is also used loosely to refer to far-off destinations within the country as well; see Chapter 7), are often looked down upon within the village. International remittances flows are significant and are growing, which is reflected in the proliferation of Western Union money-transfer centres that could be spotted throughout the district (Photo 6.10). Presently, at the time of writing, the author's estimate is that there are about 100–50 such centres in Siwan. The post office of Siwan, where the first Western Union centre was set up, was ranked as one of the richest post offices in Bihar for three consecutive years of 2009, 2010 and 2011, receiving the highest number of international money orders in the state (Pandey, 2011). Latest available data show that in 2014–15, Bihar received INR 1,800 crore through post offices alone, and Siwan was estimated to have among the highest migrants (Chaudhary, 2016).

International remittances have had significantly positive impacts on living standards. In-depth personal histories of families with members abroad revealed that even though investment in migrants' moving often required families to sell assets such as jewellery and land, a trip of three years allowed many households to quickly achieve upward economic mobility; most households were able to not only reclaim the assets sold to finance migration but also accumulate additional ones. Remittances have allowed many households to become petty entrepreneurs, engaged in a range of trading and service activities. For instance, some of the district blocks in Siwan with high international migration, such as Barharia in the north-east and Hasanpura and Hussainganj in the south, have witnessed a huge growth of local markets and trading activity in recent years. Earlier, households had to go to the urban market in Siwan for basic needs such as clothing. Now, local markets flaunt modern consumption goods – from LED television sets to automatic washing machines. *Knowledge transfer* from international migration has led to some households investing in water purifiers, a rarity in rural Bihar. Many households with members abroad have invested in housing, which has generated employment in the rural construction sector (also see Choithani, Van Duijne and Nijman, 2021).

International migration, however, is not the option for all, and most of the poor households resort to domestic migration. Given the high magnitude of these within-country flows, domestic remittances are perhaps several times more than international remittances. While remittances are playing an increasingly diverse role in rural households' lives and livelihoods, their effects on the food security – the main concern of this research – are perhaps the most discernable. The next section therefore discusses the role of remittances in influencing household food security.

REMITTANCES, RURAL–URBAN LINKAGES AND HOUSEHOLD FOOD SECURITY

To gauge the magnitude of remittances, data on postal money orders can provide important insights. Postal money orders have long been a popular mode of income transfer used by migrants from the western Bihar region to remit their earnings and savings in the home villages (Yang, 1989). Postal money orders have traditionally involved paper-based *challan*s (receipts), available in many denominations. The sender fills in the payee details and keeps a part of the order as proof. But paper-based postal orders are now fast being replaced by electronic modes of money transfer such as online banking and mobile wallets. Increasing penetration of rural banking in Bihar, coupled with growing financial literacy among the rural populations of the state in recent years, has diminished the overall importance of money orders. India's post offices are also responding to these changes and now offer electronic money orders (Photos 6.8 and 6.9).

Figure 6.4 presents the district-level data on the amount of money paid by the Siwan postal office in money orders for the period of 2002–03 to 2009–10. This data is dated but provides an important basis for inferences on remittance flows at the macro level. These figures pertain to internal transfers to the district post office from different parts of India and do not include transfers from overseas (which, as noted previously, are significant too). While not all transfers are remittances, the share of non-remittance transfers would presumably not be very high. Indeed, domestic money orders have historically been associated with migrants' remittances (Tumbe, 2015b), and Bihar is often described as a 'money-order economy' (Deshingkar et al., 2009). But as noted earlier, the growth of modern alternatives to money orders means that they are now used by a relatively small proportion of migrants.

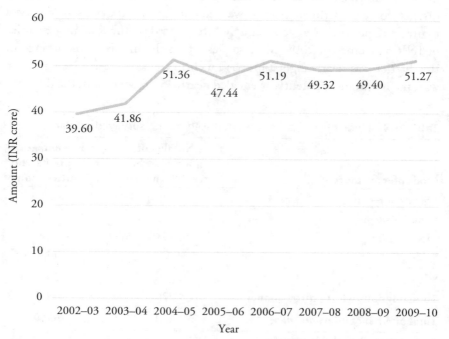

Figure 6.4   Value of money orders paid by post offices in Siwan, 2002–09
Source: Siwan Head Post Office (2012).

Trends in remittance flows in the district suggest that the amount of postal money orders paid by the Siwan post office increased in absolute terms – from INR 39.6 crore in 2002–03 to INR 51.2 crore in 2009–10. This represented approximately 2 per cent of the GDDP of Siwan in 2009–10.[2] However, as noted earlier, postal money orders represent a small fraction of the overall remittance flows in the district.

The household survey data suggest that of the 280 migrants, 275 migrants from 192 households remitted money home in the past year; among those who sent money, only 12 per cent (33 migrants) used the postal money orders as against 34 per cent (95 migrants) who used banks to transfer their incomes. An even greater proportion of migrants (36 per cent) remitted money home through their friends and fellow villagers. This latter mode of remittances has always been, and continues to be, the most important means of remittances transfer among Siwani migrants, and is indeed one reason why the precise magnitude of remittances is hard to arrive at.

Nonetheless, if one were to combine the household survey data on the mode of remittances with the formal data on the postal money orders in the district, some guesstimates can be worked out. Thus, if the household survey figure of 12 per cent were to be simply extrapolated on the total money order of INR 51.2 crore in 2009–10, it suggests that the inflow of remittance in the district was nearly eight times as much in the same year. Seen another way, the remittances potentially equaled nearly 15–16 per cent of the district's

Table 6.3 Mode of remittance transfer used by the surveyed migrants

Mode of remittance	Number of migrants who remitted money	Percentage of migrants who remitted money
Friends or relatives	101	36.1
Bank transfers	95	33.9
Money orders	33	11.8
Self	29	10.4
Others	17	6.1
Total migrants who remitted money*	**275**	**98.2**
Total number of migrants (n)	**280**	**100.0**

Source: Primary household survey data.

Note: *Five of the 197 migrant households reported receiving no remittances from their members; all five households had only one migrant member working outside the village.

GDP. While there are methodological issues in combining these two sources of data, the total magnitude of remittances is unlikely to be less (and quite likely to be more).[3]

Within this large remittance flow, the magnitude of informal channels warrants consideration. In Bihar, several informal networks of money-transfer agents operate. Originating around the late 1970s when migration from Bihar was directed to the Green Revolution-belt states of Punjab and Haryana, these informal networks filled the void created by the virtual absence of rural banking in Bihar at that time (though rural banking still remains quite patchy in many places in the state). These networks still operate and deliver huge sums of money to migrants' families. Indeed, in a conversation with a person who was earlier part of one such network in Siwan, it was found that three years ago (before the fieldwork in 2012), he was one of the 30 individuals in Siwan district who distributed between INR 2 lakh and INR 3 lakh *every day* as remittances sent by the migrants to their families.

Rural households' increased reliance on remittances notwithstanding, migrants' connections with their village of origin remain strong in Siwan. This is because circular mobility still dominates the outmigration flows from the district. While a section of better-off, usually upper-caste Siwani rural households is seeking more permanent mobility to urban towns, a vast majority of households still engage in seasonal and circular migration, usually involving male members (Photo 6.7). Most of the surveyed migrant households had members who worked in the informal sector where they earned low wages and lacked employment security. The precarious jobs in the informal sector prohibited, in large part, a more permanent form of migration from the district, though various sociocultural reasons, such as restrictions on the mobility of women, also coalesced with economic reasons to produce this form of migration. For example, when a migrant respondent, who got married two years ago and spent eight–nine months away from the village, was asked if it was financially feasible for him to take his wife along in the city and maintain his family, he replied:

> Of course, I am capable to take my wife in the city and start a life there. I do feel lonely after work, and I miss my wife. But I would not ever take her there. I would like her to stay in the village. The culture in the city is not as good as the one we have in the village. In the village, people have respect for each other, but in the city the conversations are filled with abuses. I do not want my wife to pick up those bad things.

Not all migrants, however, were suitably placed to maintain their families at their place of work, and economic reasons often outweighed social and cultural considerations (see Chapter 7). The low average wages earned from informal-sector jobs, coupled with increased urban unaffordability, did not allow most migrants to bring their families to the cities and settle there on a more permanent basis (also see Kundu, 2003, 2014). In turn, the left-behind families in the rural hinterlands augmented circular mobility. To several migrants, the city provided a livelihood avenue, but the village was where life belonged. It is important to note that even migrants who successfully trudged the stern demands of work life in urban areas and were able to achieve upward economic mobility showed a strong inclination towards the rural way of life. In an interview with a migrant who worked his way up from being a manual labourer in his first migration-job to an assistant manager in an export garment factory in Panipat, Haryana (where the author interviewed him), and who now had 30 people working directly under his watch, he suggested:

> No matter how much we suffer in the village, it is still better. I have my family and friends there … Sitting under the tree in the village is better than the air-conditioned office here.

While most migrants worked in low-paying jobs in the urban informal sector, migration nonetheless provided a crucial livelihood strategy to cope with employment deficits in the village. Importantly, most migrants sent nearly half of their monthly income home. Even for the very poorest households, remittances as low as INR 1,000 per month often helped them to stave off hunger and illness at the very least.

Data on income earned and remittances sent by migrants by occupation establish the importance of these transfers (Table 6.4). The migrant members worked across diverse casual and semi-casual occupational categories – except 12 migrants who held permanent government jobs, mainly in the army and the police. As noted in Chapter 4, all migrants, except the two who were agricultural workers, worked in the urban areas. The urban construction sector provided the single largest occupational category, absorbing 40 per cent of the surveyed migrants. This was followed by various forms of salaried employment in small and medium private firms (for example, export garment factories in the National Capital Region) accounting for a quarter of all migrants; and a similar proportion worked as casual labourers (for

Table 6.4 Occupation, income and remittances of migrants (*n* = 280)

Occupation	Number of migrants (*n* = 280)	Average monthly income (INR)	Average remittances per month (INR)	Percentage of monthly income remitted
Government service	12	14,750	7,292	49
Salaried employment in private firms with fixed monthly income*	71	5,528	2,688	49
Self-employment in petty business	14	4,964	2,263	46
Construction work	114	5,925	2,546	43
Driving	20	6,100	3,254	53
Other casual labour	47	4,715	2,169	46
Agricultural labour	2	4,000	625	16

Source: Primary household survey data.

Note: *Fixed income salaried jobs were not permanent and lacked tenure security too.

example, security personnel and drivers).[4] While the average monthly income of migrants working in casual and semi-casual jobs may appear to not vary much across occupations, ranging from INR 4,000 for agricultural laborers to INR 6,100 for drivers, they often made huge differences for the recipient households. The difference of INR 2,000 often allowed the households to invest in land and agriculture (for example, purchasing farm inputs such as fertilizer or lease-in land).

Importantly, most of the migrants remitted nearly half the share of their income back home. It must be added that migrants' incomes were reported by their households in rural areas, and thus it is likely that they represent an underestimation of the total earnings of the migrants as well as the remittances. Indeed, in the interviews conducted with migrants in cities, all of them reported incomes which were between one-and-a-half to two times more than what was reported by their rural counterparts. Given that most were single-minded about earning and saving more money, many of them often worked overtime and made extra incomes; the pressures to save and send money home also meant that many cut down on their own expenditure even when it came to the most basic needs such as food.

Most migrants also brought little hoards of cash when they came home. Another point that deserves a mention is that these are income and remittances by individual migrants, but some households had more than one migrant member, and thus the collective remittances for such households were significantly higher. Households with two migrant members received an average annual amount of INR 58,789, which was nearly 40 per cent more than the remittances received by households with one migrant member, while remittances received by households with three or more migrants were more than double than those of one-migrant households (Figure 6.5).

The extent of remittances also varied by duration spent working outside the village. While most (90 per cent) of the remittance-receiving migrant households had members who spent more than half of the year at their destinations, with 70 per cent (135 out of 192) among them having members who spent 10 months or more in the destinations, the remaining 10 per cent of households with shorter migration durations of two–six months had

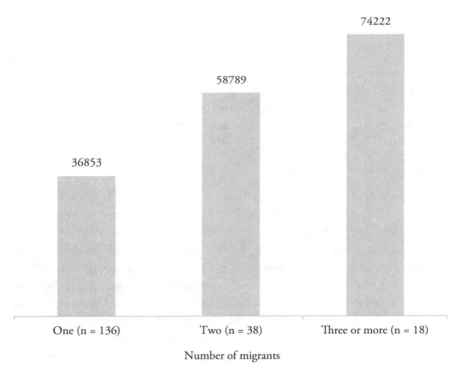

Figure 6.5   Average annual remittance income (in INR) of migrant households by number of migrants

Source: Primary household survey data.

invariably lower remittance incomes (Figure 6.6). Indeed, the average yearly remittances received by these households were almost three times less than those who spent more than six months away.

This is not surprising as migrants who worked for longer durations outside the village were inevitably better positioned to remit more. When the data on remittances by the number of migrants and duration spent outside the village are viewed in conjunction with each other, it implies that having more migrants in the household does not necessarily mean higher remittance incomes. Other things being equal, the household with three migrant members with each spending two months outside the village would fare worse than the household with one migrant member who spent more than six months.

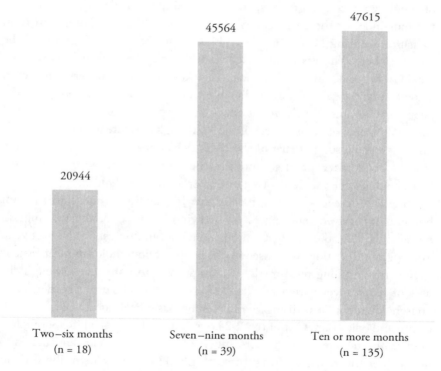

Figure 6.6 Average annual remittances (in INR) received by households by number of migration months per migrant member

Source: Primary household survey data.

While most migrants spent a major part of the year outside the village for work, as the data suggest, interviews with migrants also revealed that many also made needs-based, short trips to the cities. For example, a migrant interviewed at a construction worksite in Noida reported that his length of stay outside the village never exceeded more than five months in a year in the seven years since he first migrated. In his words:

> I work here for as long as required. If I feel I have earned enough to get my family by for the whole year, I go back to my village. Why stay away from the family when one can be with them? I come back again here when I need money. And this goes on.

Indeed, despite higher average returns of longer-duration migration, some of the very poorest migrants spent considerably less time in the cities. For the remainder of the period, they often worked as wage labourers in rural agriculture during harvesting for in-kind wages of a few kilograms of the crop they helped harvest, and picked up other odd jobs, such as construction, outside the peak farming seasons. This kept them in poverty, however. Importantly, the generally unpredictable availability of local employment and poor wages meant that the remittances still accounted for more than half of the total income of many households even though absolute incomes were low. The survey data suggest that of the 18 households with per capita migration months between two and six months, the share of remittance in the total household income was 50 per cent or higher for 11 households.

These differences in remittances notwithstanding, almost all migrant households received remittances from their members. Of the 197 migrant households, 192 households reported receiving remittances in the past year. The migrants' earnings were used by the recipient households to meet various short-term and long-term goals. It is important to note that although the uses of remittances varied markedly from one household to another, most households reported utilising the money on basic livelihood needs of food, health and education. Out of the 192 households, almost all (188 households) used remittances on food, 85 per cent (162 households) spent remittances to finance healthcare expenses, and two-thirds (133 households) utilised them for the education of household members. For the very poor households, these remittances allowed them to not only stave off the exigencies of starvation and ill-health but also invest in future livelihood assets, such as children's education. The average annual expenses on the education of children aged between 6 and 18 years among migrant and non-migrant households was INR 1,570 and INR 907, respectively, suggesting the important role remittances played. The other uses of remittances included buying durables such as kitchen utensils, radios and bicycles, spending on weddings and other ceremonies (for examples, funerals and religious functions), renovating and/or building houses, saving money for the future, and buying agricultural land (Figure 6.7).

As noted earlier, nearly 98 per cent of the remittance-receiving households used the money on food. Indeed, remittances provided the most crucial means of food security for households across socio-economic categories. While the poorest households without any land or financial assets spent a larger share of their cash receipts on food (indeed, food insecurity was one of the key drivers of migration among these households) compared to relatively better-off households, the latter also spent part of the remittances on food often to improve their diets, such as by eating meat or fish more often in a week. Migration-income-induced changes in diets were also often guided more by taste than by nutritional considerations.

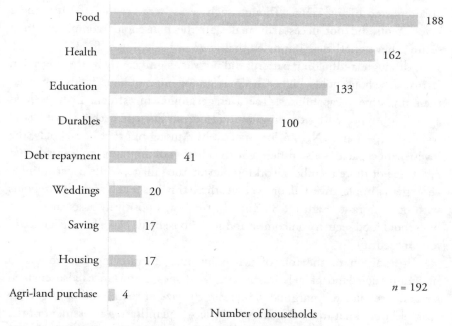

Figure 6.7 Uses of remittances among migrant households

Source: Primary household survey data.

Additionally, remittances also allowed many of the households to invest money in land and agriculture. Seen this way, the relationship between migration on the one hand and land and agriculture on the other was two-way: land-poverty and inadequate farm incomes provided a crucial prompt for migration, but migrants' earnings were recycled into family-owned agriculture. Indeed, in many cases, migrants' remittances were crucial for maintaining and sustaining the little land parcels that households owned. In cases where remittances were significant, they also allowed households to buy and accumulate more land and derive better gains from farm work. Out of the total 128 migrant households who owned some land and received remittances, more than half (56 per cent) reported that they invested money to boost household agriculture.[5] However, because of the small landholdings, the investments were also very small. Most households spent money to buy agricultural inputs, such as seeds, fertilisers and pesticides, and pay the rents for hiring water pumps for irrigation for the paddy crop in times when monsoon was weak and bleak; remittances were also used by some households, often the very poor, to lease in land for sharecropping farming. Some of the migrant households with no young men to tend to household agriculture also reported hiring labour, though such cases were very few. While these investments did not necessarily make all the households completely food secure, they nonetheless improved their own provisioning of food.

Although landholding patterns did not vary significantly by the migration status of the households, higher incomes among migrant households enhanced their investment capabilities. The average annual investment in household agriculture reported by the migrant and non-migrant households with land was INR 8,454 and INR 7,615, respectively. Among migrant households, the investment capacities also differed by the number of migrants: households that had three or more members working outside the village, while constituting a very small sample, invested, on average, three times as much as the households with one migrant (Figure 6.8). This, in turn, was positively associated with household food security outcomes, and such households had a low incidence of food insecurity.

In addition to the role of urban incomes in allowing households to maintain their land parcels in the origin villages, remittances also enabled some households to (marginally) increase the size of their landholdings. The cross-sectional nature of the survey restricts a quantitative assessment of the consolidation of landholding. However, interviews with rural households and

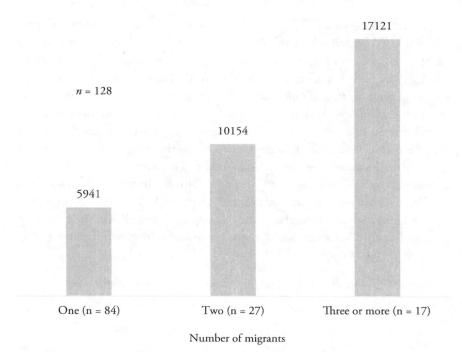

Figure 6.8 Average annual investment (in INR) in agriculture among migrant households with land by number of migrants

Source: Primary household survey data.

their migrant members provide strong evidence in this regard. At the same time, although urban incomes were higher than rural earnings that enabled some households to save, these savings were small; consequently, it often took a long time for households to enhance the size of their landholdings. For instance, a 45-year-old migrant who was working in Faridabad, where he was interviewed, recounted that after two decades of recurring work trips outside the village, he had been able to accumulate 2 acres of land. The data presented in Figure 6.7 on the uses of remittances show that only four households reported buying agricultural land. However, the survey recorded the households' utilisation of remittances in the past year (April 2011–March 2012), which means that land bought by the households before the survey reference period, when the savings so allowed, was not recorded, and thus the number of households who made land purchases through savings from migration income is likely to be greater than four.

A great degree of differentiation in savings existed within migrant households. Households with two or more members working outside the village were able to save more and quicker than those with only one migrant member; moreover, information on the landholding status of remittance-receiving migrant households suggests that the former had a relatively lower incidence of landlessness and bigger landholdings than the latter (Figure 6.9).

Given the cross-sectional nature of the survey, it is not methodologically feasible to attribute these differences in landholding status to savings from urban incomes over the period. At the same time, this relationship – households with more migrants having relatively better land status – is hardly surprising. Evidence from other parts of India also suggests that poor migrants often invest the money to save and consolidate their existing landholdings. In his study on southern Gujarat, for instance, Breman (1985)

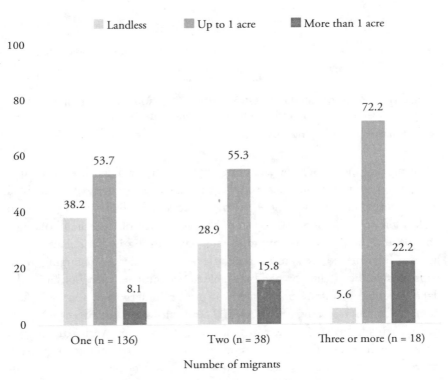

Figure 6.9 Size of agricultural landholding (in acre) among remittance-receiving households by number of migrants

Source: Primary household survey data.

found that migration incomes were indispensable for small-cultivator households to prevent them from sliding down into landlessness. He notes:

> The income earned outside during their temporary absence from home becomes indispensable for the consolidation of the small peasant holdings which have reached the level of semi-proletarianization; while the departure itself, either temporary or permanent, quite frequently helps to mask the transition to a completely landless existence among those already vulnerable. (Breman, 1985, p. xvii)

In Siwan, households with higher urban incomes did not stop pursuing farming; on the contrary, higher urban incomes were associated with increasing cash incomes from agriculture. Indeed, given the generally smaller landholdings across the survey sample, much of the investments in land and agriculture was for the households' own consumption. However, households that were favourably positioned, in terms of the number of migrants, were also able to derive higher incomes from own-account agriculture. The data showed that while the amount of remittances increased with the number of migrant members, the farm income also improved (Figure 6.10).

Importantly, while farm income was twice as much among households with two migrants as compared to households with one migrant, the households with three or more migrants had significantly higher agriculture incomes. It is also important to note that while the categorisation of farm incomes included income from off-farm labour, no household with three or more migrants engaged in manual agricultural labour, and thus its share in the total farm income was zero for these households. In other words, all the farm income came from selling the agricultural produce grown on the land owned by the households. Another important dynamic that emerges from this data is that the degree of dependence on rural non-farm incomes also decreased slightly among the households with three or more migrants, in both absolute and proportional terms (Figures 6.10 and 6.11). Thus, higher remittances did not result into households' withdrawing from land- and farm-based livelihoods; contrarily, they allowed households to engage with agriculture much more actively and derive better income gains. This is an important finding. It points to the fact that the dynamics of rural livelihoods often involve these backward–forward linkages between farm and non-farm sectors, and they need to be understood much more holistically than what the simple *structural transformation* and *deagrarianisation* theses allow.

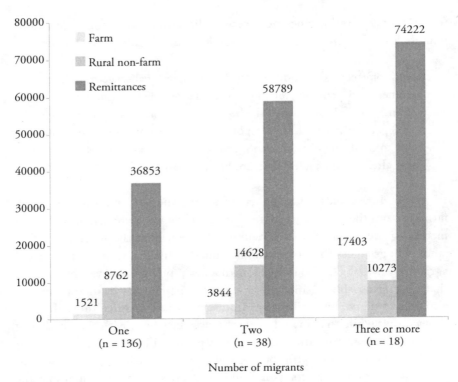

Figure 6.10 Average annual income (in INR) of remittance-receiving migrant households by source and number of migrants

Source: Primary household survey data.

The effects of remittances played out quite differently on the food security of the households, depending on the total amount of money received, size of land owned (and acquired) and money invested in land and agriculture. However, in general, remittances improved the purchasing power of the households which, in turn, was associated with better household food security.

Table 6.5 compares the migrant and non-migrant households on the self-reported parameters of food security. As noted in Chapter 5, the surveyed households were asked a series of questions to assess if at any time during the year preceding the survey (April 2011–March 2012) they experienced food insecurity and food shortages. This data refers to the percentage of households who reported having experienced food inadequacy and food unavailability at least once in the survey reference period. As the data suggests, on most food

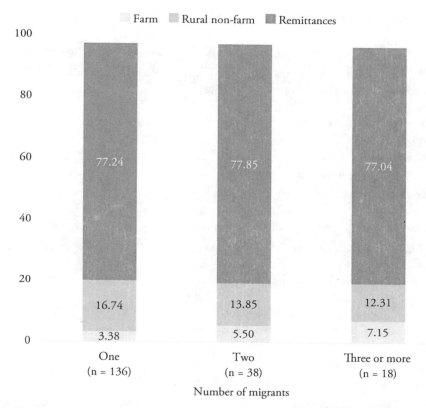

Figure 6.11 Average annual percentage share of the income (in INR) of remittance-receiving migrant households by source and number of migrants

Source: Primary household survey data.

security indicators, the proportion of non-migrant households is nearly 10 per cent higher than the migrant households.

Food security also varied by the landholding status of the household; a greater proportion of landless households reported having faced food insecurity as compared to households with some land. And within the landed category, the incidence of food insecurity differed by land size. Land provided an important source of own-provisioning of food security, as households with more land were better able to avoid food shortages. However, the positive effects of landholding on food security were much more evident among the migrant than the non-migrant households. In other words, while land ownership generally exerted a positive role on household food security,

Table 6.5 Household food security by migration status

	Migrant households (per cent)	Non-migrant households (per cent)
Food was not enough (defined by the following situations)		
Ate meals without vegetables	41.1	53.8
Could only afford to consume food from the public distribution system (PDS)	36.6	39.4
Consumed a single meal a day	13.7	21.0
Lacked all three main food categories (cereals, pulses, vegetables)	41.6	53.3
Lacked sufficient quantity of food to satiate hunger	35.5	44.6
Food was not available (defined by the following situations)		
Borrowed money from friends and/or relatives to buy food	15.2	24.6
Borrowed money from local traders or moneylenders or lifted ration on credit to acquire food	28.9	33.3
Sold jewellery or other personal assets to buy food	0.5	2.6
Ate less food than usual (consumption rationing)	39.6	51.8
Total number of households (*n*)	**197**	**195**

Source: Primary household survey data.

migrant households fared better than their non-migrant counterparts across all the landholding categories. Thus, no migrant households with land size of an acre or more reported consuming 'single meal a day' and having to 'borrow money from friends and/or relatives to buy food', whereas the proportion of non-migrant households for the same land-size group was 11 per cent and 17 per cent, respectively (Table 6.6).

MIGRATION, CHANGING AGRARIAN RELATIONS AND HOUSEHOLD FOOD SECURITY

Another important dimension of the relationship between migration and food security that deserves attention is the system of sharecropping farming.

Table 6.6 Household food security by migration status across the different landholding categories

	Landless households (per cent)		Up to 1 acre (per cent)		More than 1 acre (per cent)	
	Migrant	Non-migrant	Migrant	Non-migrant	Migrant	Non-migrant
Food was not enough (defined by the following situations)						
Ate meals without vegetables	64.6	72.6	33.6	48.7	9.1	22.2
Could only afford to consume food from the public distribution system (PDS)	26.2	35.5	10.0	17.4	9.1	5.6
Consumed a single meal a day	13.8	25.8	16.4	20.0	0.0	11.1
Lacked all three main food categories (cereals, pulses, vegetables)	61.5	71.0	35.5	48.7	13.6	22.2
Lacked sufficient quantity of food to satiate hunger	47.7	59.7	33.6	40.9	9.1	16.7
Food was not available (defined by the following situations)						
Borrowed money from friends and/or relatives to buy food	18.5	22.6	16.4	27.0	0.0	16.7
Borrowed money from local traders or money lenders or lifted ration on credit to acquire food	44.6	53.2	22.7	26.1	13.6	11.1
Sold jewellery or other personal assets to buy food	1.5	3.2	0.0	2.6	0.0	0.0
Ate less food than usual (consumption rationing)	58.5	72.7	33.6	45.2	0.0	0.0
Total number of households (*n*)	**65**	**62**	**110**	**115**	**22**	**18**

Source: Primary household survey data.

The agrarian relations in Siwan (and in Bihar as a whole) have traditionally involved a widespread prevalence of various forms of land-leasing and tenancy contracts, and the system of sharecropping, known locally as *bataidari*, is one of the most common forms. Traditionally, sharecropping arrangements have involved landless and land-poor households from the lower castes leasing land for cultivating purpose from the landowning communities, usually the upper-caste Brahmin, Bhumihar and Kshatriya households. In return for the cultivation rights, sharecropper farmers pay a certain percentage of the total crop produce to the landowners as rent, though cash as a form of rent is also practised in many places and is becoming increasingly popular. The input costs of production, including labour, are borne by the cultivating farmers, and the ratio of crop shared with the landlords typically amounts to 50 per cent of the total produce. Because much of the sharecropping happens on an informal basis, there are no data sources or studies that provide systematic estimates on the incidence of sharecropping. However, the report of the Bihar Land Reform Commission, 2006–08, estimated that nearly 35 per cent of all cultivable land in Bihar is under sharecropping, and 15 to 20 per cent of all cultivating peasants are engaged in *bataidari* (Bandyopadhyay, 2008, 2009). The household survey data collected from Siwan for this study suggest an even higher incidence: of the 302 households who reported having been engaged in farming in 2011–12, nearly half of them (48.3 per cent) had leased in part or whole of their land (there were 37 landless households who had leased in all of the land they cultivated). The ubiquity of sharecropping in Siwan suggests that it holds crucial significance in the livelihoods and food security of many of the rural households. How the dynamics of sharecropping arrangements play out to influence the food security outcomes of rural households and how migration correlates with these rural production relations are key questions explored in this section.

At the outset, it is important to note that the patterns of landholding and sharecropping arrangements have had a regressive impact on the agricultural growth in Siwan and Bihar and, indeed, on the overall economic performance of the state. This is because the primary sector has traditionally been the main source of income in Bihar. In 2017–18, the agriculture sector still accounted for more than one-fifth of the state's overall income (Government of Bihar, 2020b). Under the present system, neither the cultivating farmers nor the landlords have an incentive to improve the productive capacity of the land. Bihar's agriculture sector is marked by a notable absence of innovation and, despite the natural endowments of high soil fertility and abundance of water resources, the land productivity in the state remains among the lowest in the country (Government of India, 2008; Joshi, Tripathi and Gautam, 2012). Additionally, in Bihar, land is not just an economic asset but also a symbol of power and status, and sharecropping has often been used by the upper-caste landowning communities as a means to maintain and assert their dominance without necessarily engaging in primary production. In various pockets of the state, sharecropping arrangements have been highly exploitative, with landlords often placing extortionate rent demands on poor peasants, with little or no regard to the land and crop rights of tillers. These issues were appropriately raised by the Bihar Land Reform Commission, 2006–08, headed by D. Bandyopadhyay, a retired civil servant who is credited with successful land reforms in the state of West Bengal. The commission recommended wide-ranging reform measures. Important among them were recognising and protecting the land rights of sharecroppers, which, in the commission's view, will bring about wider efficiency gains in the sector, with overall positive impacts on the living standards in the state. However, powerful lobbying by the landowning communities against the reforms means that the commission's recommendations have not been implemented (Bandyopadhyay, 2008, 2009). This issue remains significant in the politics of contemporary Bihar.

The potential of sharecropping reforms to improve the operational efficiency of the agricultural economy notwithstanding, it is important to understand how these arrangements are inserted into the life-worlds of the poor households. It is certainly the case that the existing arrangements need reform in order to provide the sharecropping families with adequate land rights and improve their bargaining position. At the same time, the lack of adequate livelihood options and the absence of effectively functioning safety nets, such as the PDS (see Chapter 5), in the state makes it an obvious choice for many landless and land-poor households. Although sharecropping arrangements largely favour the landlords, the fact that they have continued unabated is also because they offer the poor access to scarce land resources.

Fieldwork in Siwan suggested that by allowing access to land, unprotected and vulnerable as it may be, sharecropping played an important supplementary role in the food security of poor households, particularly those belonging to the socially and economically marginalised caste groups. Furthermore, although the cross-sectional nature of the household survey data does not allow a quantitative assessment of changes in the incidence of sharecropping in Siwan over the period, numerous interviews with households belonging to different socio-economic strata and village-level observations suggested intensification of sharecropping arrangements across all the 10 study villages. Evidence from other parts of Bihar also suggests a similar situation (Sharma, 2005).

The growing importance of sharecropping within the local livelihoods systems is primarily due to two mutually interlinked processes of increasing land fragmentation and migration. First, the progressive reduction in landholding size over the period has provided an impetus for an increasing number of rural households to migrate out of villages to earn cash income. Second, at the same time, in many instances, higher urban incomes are leading to households withdrawing themselves from direct farming. However, there are important caste dynamics to sharecropping. The survey data do not adequately capture the caste basis of sharecropping relations, as they also involved land lease-in and lease-out transactions outside the survey sample. However, field observations and qualitative interviews suggested that it is mainly the upper caste who increasingly disassociated themselves from direct farming; many of them also sought to sell their land to seek more permanent forms of mobility in urban towns. Village-level studies from other parts of Bihar also support these observations. For example, a study by Sharma (2005), which traced changes in agrarian dynamics over a period of 18 years (between 1981–82 and 1999–2000) in 12 villages of Bihar, suggested an increase in the phenomenon of non-agriculturalist households among the upper-caste peasants and, with it, a rising tendency of land leasing during this period. As noted earlier, land loss among the upper caste has been steeper, reaching a point where farming no longer provides a (viable) livelihood option for them. As Sharma (2005, p. 965) notes:

The upper-caste peasants, who have lost their land to the point where the land cannot produce a surplus, find themselves in a dilemma as a member of the upper caste. They can neither meet wage demands nor take to the plough for fear of caste opprobrium. However, in recent years, a significant trend towards ploughing and other menial agricultural activities on the part of poor upper-caste males appears to be emerging (although the upper caste women even from very poor families do not venture to work outside the home in their own fields, leave aside in those of others for wages). Hence, they opt for renting out land and migrate.

Additionally, some of the upper-caste landowner households interviewed for the study perceived risks to directly partaking in agriculture as being very high. Across India, farming is largely rain-fed and depends on the mercy of monsoon. Many households who faced crop failures in the past considered it better to transfer the risks while sharing the rewards in the form of half the produce via the mechanism of sharecropping. For instance, Rajveer Singh (first name changed), a well-to-do Rajput by caste – with his son working with the IBM corporation in Delhi, and daughter-in-law being the democratically-elected judicial head of the GP (though she lived with her husband in Delhi, and Rajveer acted on her behalf) – who had earlier cultivated 4 of the 6 acres of land owned (with hired labour), but had now leased out 4 acres to six different poor families (including one Scheduled Tribe Gond household and five Rajput families), remarked: 'Agriculture is like gambling, except that in gambling there is a degree of excitement. The amount of hopelessness is the same in both.'

In some villages, sharecropping had a strong caste element embedded in it in the sense that members of one caste often preferred to lease out their land to the land-poor families belonging to the same caste (for example, Brahmins obliging fellow caste men), and resource-less and land-poor families from upper-caste Hindus and Muslims also engaged in sharecropping. However, a larger proportion of the households who engaged in *bataidari* were from extremely backward castes and the Scheduled Castes and Scheduled Tribe because of their relatively weaker land position.

Data on landholding status by caste show these connections. The small landholdings in Siwan notwithstanding, there is a clear patterning of landownership by caste. A greater proportion of landless households were from the Scheduled Castes and Scheduled Tribes and the extremely backward castes, while the percentage of forward-caste and backward-caste households (the latter were able to appropriate land following the abolition of *zamindari* and related land reforms; see Chapter 4) was higher in landed categories. Similarly, the data on average landholding size by caste also suggest the same (Figures 6.12 and 6.13).

In terms of how these landholding arrangements reflect the caste basis of sharecropping dynamics, survey data suggest that the incidence of leasing in land was much higher among households from the extremely backward castes and the Scheduled Castes and Scheduled Tribes, compared to the forward-caste and backward-caste households. Conversely, the proportion of the former two caste groups leasing out land was much lower than the latter:

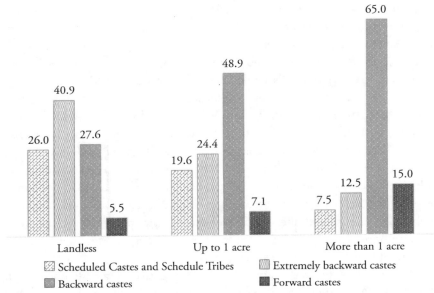

Figure 6.12 Landholding status by caste (percentage of households)

Source: Primary household survey data.

the proportion of forward-caste and backward-caste households leasing out land, respectively, was five times and two times as much as the extremely backward castes and the Scheduled Castes and Scheduled Tribes. It should also be noted that among the backward castes, the prominent sub-castes such as Kushwaha and Koeri have traditionally been the cultivators whose attachment to land remains strong. This explains in part why, compared to upper-caste households, a lower proportion of them leased out land and a higher percentage leased in. In fact, fieldwork suggested that some backward-caste households with significant larger landholdings also leased in land for sharecropping (Table 6.7)

As regards to the impact of sharecropping on household food security, the ability to access land and grow food enhanced the food security situation of households, though because the leased-in landholdings were too small in most cases (less than an acre for all households), the impact of sharecropping alone in bringing about sustained improvements in the household food security was still quite limited. Thus, while sharecropping resulted in improved own-production entitlements from the land, its positive impact

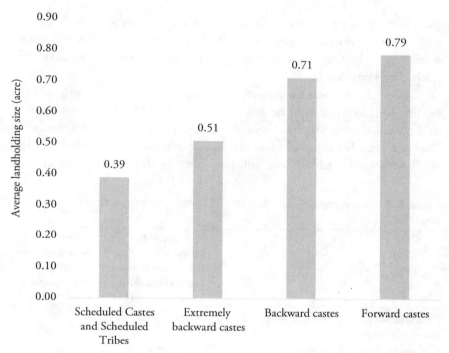

Figure 6.13 Average size of landholding (in acre) owned by caste

Source: Primary household survey data.

Table 6.7 Sharecropping dynamics by caste

	Number of households	Percentage of landless households	Percentage of landed households that leased out land	Percentage of households that leased in land
Forward castes	29	24.1	31.8	32.0
Backward castes	171	20.5	11.0	43.8
Extremely backward castes	112	46.4	5.0	62.5
Scheduled Castes and Scheduled Tribes	80	41.2	6.4	49.2

Source: Primary household survey data.

was much greater for households that were able to effectively combine this with other productive non-farm sources. Nonetheless, in overall terms, sharecropper households still fared much better than the landless non-cultivating households.

Table 6.8 compares the self-reported indicators of food inadequacy and food unavailability among households that cultivated 50 per cent or more land on a sharecropping basis with the non-cultivating landless households. The logic of such a comparison is that households that leased in half or more of the total cultivated land are land-poor households and, in many respects,

Table 6.8 Sharecropping and household food security (percentage of households)

	Cultivator households with 50 per cent or more cultivated land leased in (*n* = 116)	Non-cultivator landless households (*n* = 90)
Food was not enough (defined by the following situations)		
Ate meals without vegetables	50.9	72.2
Could only afford to consume food from the public distribution system (PDS)	22.4	26.7
Consumed a single meal a day	17.2	18.9
Lacked all three main food categories (cereals, pulses, vegetables)	50.9	68.9
Lacked sufficient quantity of food to satiate hunger	37.9	56.7
Food was not available (defined by the following situations)		
Borrowed money from friends and/or relatives to buy food	18.1	23.3
Borrowed money from local traders or moneylenders or lifted ration on credit to acquire food	32.8	52.2
Sold jewellery or other personal assets to buy food	0.9	2.2
Ate less food than usual (consumption rationing)	46.6	67.8

Source: Primary household survey data.

similar to landless households. Additionally, choosing households that leased in 50 per cent or more of total cultivated land reflects their sharecropper status better. The purpose is to understand whether access to land, in whatever small way, had an impact on food security. The small agricultural holdings notwithstanding, the data suggest that the non-cultivating landless households fared worse than their sharecropper counterparts on all parameters of food security. The differences in some of these indicators are quite significant. For example, the proportion of households that 'ate meals without vegetables', 'had less food than needed to satiate hunger' and 'reported borrowing money from local traders or lenders' was almost 20 per cent higher among the non-cultivator landless households than those that cultivated leased-in land.

The issue of land access assumes greater significance in the context of high food volatility that characterises contemporary food systems. Importantly, the fieldwork for this study was conducted in early 2012, when food-price inflation in India, and indeed around the world, was at record levels. The unprecedented surge in the prices of food commodities since 2007, which eventually culminated in a global food crisis, had severely negative impacts on the ability of the rural poor to access food in many poor countries. Not only did the food-price spikes stall global progress on hunger reduction, but they also reversed the progress made thus far, and in 2009 the number of undernourished people crossed, for the first time in human history, the one-billion mark (FAO, 2009). In particular, the non-agriculturalist poor households had a greater exposure to the risks posed by high food prices, as their complete reliance on market-purchase of food meant they found their food budgets squeezed by the high food prices. In other words, the same amount of money now bought less food (Pritchard, 2014). Global food prices are still much higher compared to the period before the 2006–08 food crisis. In 2019, the FAO's food price index, which measures change in the international prices of food commodities, was at 171.4 (from its base of 100, at 2002–04 prices), indicating high food inflation (FAO, 2020).

In such circumstances, sharecropping farming can be considered as providing a means for poor households to reduce their exposure to market purchases and, in turn, food insecurity. In his entitlement theory, Sen (1981b, p. 5) also noted:

The agricultural labourer paid in money terms will have to depend on the exchange entitlement of his money wage. When famines are accompanied by sharp changes in relative prices – and in particular a sharp rise in food prices – there is much comparative merit in being a share-cropper rather than an agricultural labourer.

Fieldwork suggested that sharecropping provided a useful buffer against food shocks and that households with access to land were able to cope with the food price rises relatively better as compared to non-agriculturalist landless households. In the survey, households were asked whether they perceived that the relative price of food changed in the past year (April 2011–March 2012). Analysis of this data by land and sharecropping status suggests some differences. Of the 116 households that leased in 50 per cent or more of cultivated land, the proportion of households that perceived food prices 'increased a lot' in the reference period was 66.4 per cent for cereals and pulses, 73.3 per cent for eggs, milk, ghee, and meat, and 79.3 per cent for fruits and vegetables. The corresponding proportions for 90 non-cultivator landless households were 73.3 per cent for cereals and pulses, 83.3 per cent for eggs, milk, ghee, and meat, and 86.7 per cent for fruits and vegetables.

These differences were small, presumably because the sizes of land leased in by the sharecropper households, although constituting half or more of the total cultivated land, were still small (less than an acre for all households). In turn, this meant that even these households were dependent on the market for food purchases, with the degree of dependence varying in accordance with the land leased in and crops grown. Nonetheless, they point to the role of access to land for the food security of the very poor. The discussion here outlines the sharecropping–food-security linkage which remains a relatively unexplored issue. More research is needed, particularly in contexts with similar land dynamics but where the sizes of the leased-in land are relatively bigger, in order to understand more fully the impact of sharecropping on food security.

CONCLUSION

Using a livelihood-centred analysis that weaves together insights from the changing contours of economic and agrarian landscapes at the macro level in India and the dynamics of household decision-making at the micro level (though they are not mutually exclusive), the discussion in this chapter points to the growing importance of migration and remittances for rural households' income and food security in the case-study district of Siwan. However, the relationship between migration and food security is not straightforward – far from it. The processes of progressive fragmentation of agricultural land on the one hand and the rising significance of urban areas in the overall framework of economy and employment generation on the other are leading to increased reliance among rural poor households on urban incomes. At the same time, the trajectory of economic growth in India, and a complex mix of individual choices and sociocultural reasons, have prevented a complete shift away from the rural-agrarian to urban-industrial mode of life and work, contrasting with the popular theses of *structural transformation and deagrarianisation*. The resultant effect of these processes is to create complex linkages between rural and urban economies, which have much significance from the perspective of understanding food security among rural households, and the discussion in this chapter has highlighted how these linkages play out to interact with household food security in rural Siwan.

First, the diminishing capacity of land-based livelihoods over the period (which is an important push for migration) has led to a growing significance of remittances in the lives and livelihoods of rural Siwani households. The most direct impact of remittances is to equip households with the purchasing power to source food from the market. As the data presented earlier show, most migrant households used the remittances on food, and compared to their non-migrant counterparts they fared better on income and food security outcomes.

The second important finding is that the relationship between migration and land was rarely one-way. In other words, while landlessness and land-poverty prompted rural outmigration, urban remittances provided much-needed cash incomes for household agriculture, prevented households to slide down into the state of complete landlessness, and, in some cases, also allowed households to buy and accumulate more land, with the overall effects on household food security being *positive*. And while land provided a critical asset in the livelihood portfolios, and thus attachments to rural land were strong, the uncertain nature of urban jobs made holding on to land even more attractive. Indeed, the economic security offered by land was unmatched by any other asset. Interviews with many respondents on the land question also indicated that land provided a means through which households reduced long-term livelihood and income risks. In the words of a respondent:

> If you [so] want me to tell you what land means to us, I shall put it simply for you. I hope you are following the news about increasing

border tensions with China [in the north-east India]. Suppose if China invades our country and changes the currency here, all the money we have will be of no value. But no one can change the value of our land.

Indeed, higher urban incomes did not stop households from pursuing farming. On the contrary, they allowed many rural households to maintain their peasant identities. Far from discouraging rural households from farming, higher remittances only deepened their engagement in farm work. This finding assumes importance and suggests that an analysis of rural livelihoods must take into account these backward–forward linkages between farm and non-farm incomes more than the inexorable deagrarianisation thesis allows. Findings of research conducted by Yaro (2006) in three villages in northern Ghana, involving 600 households surveys (200 households from each village), also found these connections between farm and non-farm income and flexibility of rural livelihoods. Thus, as Yaro (2006, p. 125) argues: '[D]eagrarianisation should be seen as a process embedded in social change, bearing in mind the reversibility between farm and non-farm livelihood strategies used by households (reagrarianisation?).'

A third emergent dynamic of the migration–land–food-security relationship is the (growing) incidence of sharecropping farming in Siwan. Some households, particularly erstwhile upper-caste landowners, are also increasingly detaching themselves from direct farming and leasing out land to the land-poor households, with important implications on the food security of the latter. The household survey data and other fieldwork suggest that by allowing landless and land-poor households access to land, temporary and precarious as it may be, sharecropping farming was associated with relatively lower incidence of food insecurity. Sharecropping assumes particular significance in the wake of high food-price inflation, for it strengthens the own-production food entitlements of households and reduces, in a relative sense, the households' dependence on market-purchases of food. .

These findings assume significance, particularly in the wake of recent evidence on the rising significance of migration in rural livelihood systems across a number of developing countries. In many developing economies, such as India, China and Brazil, the recent patterns of economic growth have led to a weakening of rural households' self-provisioning capabilities from local land and resources (Pritchard et al., 2016, p.2). Recent economic growth has occurred largely in the urban centres, leading to an increasing number of rural households engaging in work migration to cities. This means that these findings have significance beyond the immediate research settings of Siwan, and thus they warrant wider attention to understand the role of migration in influencing household food security. As the analysis in this chapter has shown, migration and remittances structure and restructure economic and land relations in the origin village, with direct implications for the food security of households that engage in migration as well as those who stay put (for example, through sharecropping). This inter-household comparison provides a useful way to delineate the impact of migration on food security. However, the migration–food-security nexus also involves important intra-household dynamics of altered production and reproduction roles and responsibilities. In large parts of rural India, where migration is predominantly undertaken by men, this implies alteration in gender relations at the household level. The next chapter discusses the connections between gendered livelihoods and household food security.

NOTES

1. Although the positive-discrimination policy of reserving a quota of jobs has somewhat reduced this imbalance, it is the better-off within the lower-caste groups that have an edge. Equally, a considerable proportion of resource-less upper-caste households also find it difficult to access these jobs.

2. The GDDP was arrived at by extrapolating Siwan's per capita GDPP of INR 8,111 for the year 2009–10 (at 2004–05 prices) over the district's total population, which in the 2011 census was estimated at 3.31 million (Census of India, 2011c; Government of Bihar, 2013).

3. The NSS 2007–08 data show that at all-India level, the share of the post office in remittances was nearly 20 per cent. But this has declined in recent years due to competition from other entrants offering cheaper and faster digital payment transfer options. In 2015, the post office was estimated to have 10 per cent of the current market share in India (Tumbe, 2011, 2015b). This closely corresponds to 12 per cent of households using money order in Siwan in 2012.

4. In addition to agricultural labourers, construction workers and drivers who are also casual workers in many respects, sample migrants were found to be performing a number of other casual jobs such as those of sweepers and cleaners, security personnel in urban residential complexes, and so on. Since

they were widely spread across occupations, they have been grouped into this single category for analytical purpose.

5. Out of the sample of 197 migrant households, 192 reported receiving remittances, and 132 owned land. Four of the 132 migrant households with land did not receive any remittances, and hence this question applied to 128 households.

7

OPENING THE HOUSEHOLD BOX

MIGRATING MEN, LEFT-BEHIND WOMEN AND HOUSEHOLD FOOD SECURITY

INTRODUCTION

In India, labour migration is highly gendered. Rigid social and cultural norms restricting women's participation in income-earning activities in distant labour markets means migration is more commonly undertaken by men, leading to a phenomenon of *left–behind women*. Nationwide data show that male migration is prevalent in regions covering over 200 million people, including places as diverse as coastal Maharashtra and mountainous Uttarakhand. In large parts of the two northern states of Uttar Pradesh and Bihar that account for a significant bulk of migrants in the country, labour mobility is almost exclusively a male-only activity. Strikingly, this migration pattern has persisted for over a hundred years (Tumbe, 2012, 2015a).[1] Independent estimates of the left-behind women are wanting, but rising significance of migration in rural lives means that their numbers may be on the rise and so may be the households headed by them. Some evidence of this shifting gender composition in the familial sphere is provided by the NFHS data that show that in just seven high outmigration states in the eastern and central regions of the country, over 10 per cent of women were not staying with their husbands (Ganguly and Negi, 2010), and that between 1992–93 and 2014–15, women-headed households increased from 9.1 per cent to 14.9 per cent in rural India (IIPS, 1995; IIPS and ICF International, 2017b). Available research shows that women-headed households are at a disadvantageous position in terms of access to land and livestock, agricultural credit and extension services, and assets, and are thus often overrepresented among the poor and vulnerable (Buvinić and Gupta, 1997; King and Mason, 2001; FAO,

2011). Patriarchal systems can confer a gender-based disadvantage to left-behind women and create more vulnerabilities.

Vulnerability to food insecurity is a key challenge. Indeed, despite women's crucial role as *food producers* in the farms and *food providers* in the families, their own food and nutritional needs are often ignored, and they share a disproportionate burden of undernourishment (FAO, 2011; FAO et al., 2020). This discrimination often starts at the household level where social arrangements determining the access to productive economic opportunities and control over household resources often favour men. This results in a weak bargaining position of women with intra-household distribution of food favouring men over women (Sen, 1987), reinforcing gender inequalities in an intergenerational fashion.

An understanding of intra-household gender power relations is particularly important for the analysis of the relationship between migration and food security. Male-only pattern of migration has the potential to alter the social systems that underpin gender differentials in food security. The absence of men requires women to assume the role of household heads, which carries implications for household food security. Male migration can result in improved autonomy and access to resources among women, which can positively influence food security outcomes. On the other hand, absence of men can also lead to increased responsibilities of the household's productive and reproductive functions for women, which can undermine nutritional well-being. This relationship is, however, complicated, and other factors such as the structure of the family also mediate to produce varied household welfare (or ill-fare) outcomes.

Against this background, the aim of this chapter is to highlight interconnections between male migration, left-behind women and household food security. With a focus on gender social roles, the discussion here engages with conceptual pathways of 'improved autonomy', 'increased responsibility' and 'household structure' to explain migration–gender–food-security linkages. The chapter uses the primary data collected from Siwan to contextualise these relationships. Siwan provides an apt setting to understand the broader processes of gendered social change. As noted in Chapter 4, labour migration from Siwan is largely the preserve of men, while the women stay behind. And this pattern of migration has remained virtually unchanged throughout the past century. Fieldwork suggests that while cultural norms still guide the role of women within and outside the household, the long history of male-only pattern of migration from Siwan has transformed gender relations. The aim of this chapter is to understand the bearing of these altered gender relations on household food security.

GENDERED LIVELIHOODS

Labour migration from Siwan district (and Bihar more generally) is almost exclusively a male-only activity. Women stay behind in the origin villages and rarely accompany the men. The analysis of the 2011 census data from 1,435 villages in Siwan on the sex composition of population aged six years and above suggests that although villages varied widely in the intensity of migration, nearly half of them (681 villages) had SRs skewed in favour of females (at least 1,000 females per 1,000 males), suggesting a male-dominated pattern of outmigration (Census of India, 2011c).[2] In some villages with a high incidence of migration, it is difficult to sight young men of employable age, and many rural families comprise only women and children. It is only during festivals, such as Chhath and Holi, when a large majority of the migrants return home that the households' sex and age compositions appear more balanced (Photo 7.1).

This gender-based segregation of rural livelihoods finds vocal expressions in local Bhojpuri folk tradition and culture. Folk-song genres such as *bideshia*, which translates as 'foreigner' (and is an affectionate term used mainly for male members of a household living in far-off destinations), and *birah*, which means 'separation' from the beloved, reverberate widely in the culture. Originating around the mid-nineteenth century when migration from western Bihar began to gain momentum, these folk songs still remain hugely popular in the region and beyond.[3] They depict the left-behind women as celebrating the earnings of their husbands in *bidesh* (destination places), mourning the separation that follows their men's migration, expressing scepticism about their men's sexual fidelity and loyalty towards them while they are away, and worrying about shielding their own modesty from other men in the origin villages (de Haan, 2002; Jassal, 2012).

These Bhojpuri folklore genres developed around the time when transport and communication infrastructure was weak, which often meant that it took days of travel to reach work destinations, and while away male migrants could seldom make any contact with their families at the origin village; many who went to the British colonies abroad never returned.[4] The huge advancements in transportation and communication networks in recent years, however, follow that this is no longer the case. Travel has become increasingly easier, and technology such as mobile phones – which most rural Siwani households, including many of the very poor, possessed – have enabled the Siwani migrants and their families to keep in regular touch with each other. While mobile phones also provide means by which male migrants assert and maintain their authority in the household affairs from a distance, the physical absence of men often results in a restructuring of family relations and realigning of households' productive and reproductive roles and responsibilities, at least for the duration men are away. Indeed, with an increasing number of Siwani migrants now spending more time away from their place of origin (Chapter 4), the issue of intra-household gender relations in the study of migration, and rural livelihoods more broadly, assumes even greater significance.

In order to contextualise the impacts of male migration on intra-household gender relations, it is useful to first understand the factors underlying male-dominated patterns of migration and the characteristics of women who stay behind. Table 7.1 provides the background household characteristics of 144 left-behind women respondents. Important characteristics include: First, half of the households were below the poverty line, and more than half lived in non-permanent (*kutcha* and semi-*pucca*) dwellings. Second, nearly two-thirds of women lived in households that owned livestock and land, though average land size was small. These characteristics are broadly reflective of the socio-economic situation in Siwan. Third, close to half of the women lived in nuclear households, and almost all reported to be the *de facto* household heads in the absence of their husbands. Finally, migrant households had almost all men aged 20–50 years living outside the village for work, meaning male labour was largely absent in these households.

In terms of the reasons for the male-only pattern of migration from Siwan, fieldwork revealed the primacy of two factors. First and foremost, the social and cultural norms posed restrictions on the mobility and participation of women in the distant labour markets for cash incomes. As dutiful daughters, wives and mothers, women were expected to stay in the village and manage the rural end of the household. Single-woman migration for work is almost non-existent from Siwan, and the idea of married women joining their husbands on their departure is also considered socially unacceptable. Of the total 144 left-behind wives surveyed, 85 women (59 per cent) reported that they had never visited their husband's place of work.

Second, interviews with some long-term male migrants indicated that although years of migration to the cities brought about attitudinal changes

Table 7.1 Household characteristics of left-behind women

Household characteristics	Left-behind women
Household demographics (in person)*	
Average household size	7.5
Average number of persons aged 20–50 years	3.0
Average number of men aged 20–50 years	0.4
Caste	
Forward caste	6.3
Backward caste	42.4
Extremely backward caste	30.6
Scheduled Castes and Scheduled Tribes	20.8
Religion	
Hindu	72.2
Muslim	27.8
Living arrangements and household headship	
Nuclear	50.7
Joint or extended	49.3
De facto head of the household	46.5
Type of house occupied	
Kutcha	15.3
Semi-*pucca*	37.5
Pucca	47.2
Land and livestock ownership	
Average land size (in acre)	0.6
Landless households	34.0
Households with land size of less than an acre	56.9
Households with land size of an acre or more	9.0
Income, expenditure and poverty	
Average monthly per capita income (INR)	938
Average monthly per capita expenditure (MPCE) (INR)	959
Households with MPCE below the poverty line**	50.0
Total number of households (*n*)	**144**

Source: Primary household survey data.

Note: *Includes migrant members. **The 2009–10 revision of state-specific poverty lines, based on the Tendulkar committee's estimates, pegged the rural poverty line in Bihar at INR 655.6. The same has been applied to this survey data to estimate consumption poverty (Planning Commission, 2012).

among them on the acceptability of their wives' mobility, financial difficulties precluded realistic opportunities for families to live together in cities. Most migrants worked in urban informal jobs with low incomes and no benefits. Though poverty and unemployment in villages meant urban incomes were significant, high costs of urban living and the inability of many migrants to access government-run education and health services at destinations made maintaining families in cities difficult. Some migrants had earlier brought their wives at the destinations, but they returned to the villages after a few years, most of them after the birth of their first child. During the village surveys, a woman respondent who never visited her migrant husband remarked: 'My husband tells me that in the city he even has to pay for water. Is it not a joke? Look at that government handpump over there; it is all free water.' Similarly, a migrant worker interviewed in his rented room in Faridabad district of Haryana, approximately 30 kilometres south of Delhi, commented:

> In the village, we have our own house. Cooking fuel and water are also free. But here, expenses on these heads cost fortunes; the rent alone for this shabby room costs me INR 1,000 a month. It is simply not affordable for a single earner like me to maintain a family of five people here [in the city].

The pressure to save money meant that most migrants lived in cheap, shared accommodation with other labour migrants, with two–three migrants living in a single room. For migrants engaged in construction industry – a sector that absorbs a large number of migrants – uncertain job and wage schedules and constant movement from one site to another added to the challenge of bringing the wives and children to the cities. The newlywed migrants made recurrent trips to home villages to see their wives but did not bring them to work destinations. One such migrant engaged in construction work explained:

> When I do not get my wages on time, I borrow money from my friends and fellow villagemen. But this cannot happen when my wife is around. I need to have sufficient money so that I do not have to worry about it … Besides, my job requires shifting from one place to another. I can just carry my bag and baggage and move, but not my wife.

These are reflected in the data in Table 7.2 on women respondents' reasons for not ever visiting their husband's place of work. Of the 85 women who reported never having visited their husband's place of work, 62 per cent cited financial

Table 7.2 Women respondents' reasons for not ever visiting their husbands' place of work

Reason	Left-behind women
Financial problems	42 (49.4%)
Housing problems at the destination	11 (12.9%)
Domestic and childcare responsibilities	10 (11.8%)
Husband's mobile job	6 (7.1%)
Need to look after family land	5 (5.9%)
Husband says 'I must stay home'	4 (4.7%)
Others	7 (8.2%)
Total number of left-behind women (*n*)	**85**

Source: Primary household survey data.

(49 per cent) and housing (13 per cent) problems as the reasons. Other women cited their role in caring for rural land and resources.

Some women also preferred to stay in the villages and, in fact, showed a strong desire to stay put. In interviews with these women, many suggested that while they did miss their husbands, village is where they belonged and where they wanted to be. Staying put in the village meant that they could look after the household resources and take care of children and in-laws. It is certainly the case that cultural expectations about gender roles guided such preferences, and oddly, though not surprisingly, there was an intergenerational aspect to it. For instance, younger women of the household were expected to take care of their in-laws, and they, in turn, expected their future daughters-in-law to do the same; nonconformity to these expectations often led to intra-household tensions and also changes in the familial structure – from joint to nuclear. But it was also clear that some women derived their sense of self-worth from managing the rural side of the family. In other words, factors underlying gendered livelihoods were complex, and economic and cultural constraints also coalesced with women's personal choices.

IMPACTS OF MALE MIGRATION ON INTRA-HOUSEHOLD GENDER RELATIONS

Male migration led to increased presence of women in all spheres of rural life, manifested in women's enhanced intra-village mobility and greater participation in village affairs (Photo 7.6).[5] However, the effects of male migration were much more pronounced at the household level. Women's participation in household decision-making increased, with many women in migrant households acting as the household managers in the absence of men. On the other hand, this also resulted in a greater burden of work for women in both the domestic and non-domestic spheres. Additionally, migration and remittances also seemed to cause intra-household conflicts over cash management. All of these have implications for household food security. The next section discusses these effects.

WOMEN'S PARTICIPATION IN HOUSEHOLD DECISION-MAKING

Male migration enhanced women's participation in household decision-making. The field research suggested that in many families, women acted as the *de facto* household heads in the absence of men. The survey data confirm this: 52 per cent of 197 migrant households were reported to be headed by women, whereas the corresponding figure among 195 non-migrant households was 7 per cent. It is important to recognise, however, that migrants' wives still regarded the men as the *de jure* household heads and consulted them before they took any major decisions. However, they single-handedly managed the household for a large part of the year. The degree of participation of women within the household varied by the type of familial arrangement, and generally women in nuclear households enjoyed greater autonomy and decision-making vis-à-vis joint or extended families.

In the survey, women were asked about household decision-making processes on different aspects of their family lives when their husbands were around and when their husbands were away. Table 7.3 presents these results. A greater proportion of women reported making decisions alone in the absence of their husbands, compared to when they were around. Some of these differences were large, such as those pertaining to their own and children's health, children's education and household finances. While these data suggest that the effects of male migration on women autonomy lasted as long as the men were away, it should be noted that most migrants spent a large part of the year away. Out of 197 migrant households, 139 reported their migrant members were away for 10 months or more during the past year. This means women in these families, particularly in the nuclear units, had greater decision-making authority for a greater part of the year. Indeed, a few women

Table 7.3 Participation of migrants' wives in household decision-making when their husbands are around and when they are away

Decision type	Husband around (per cent) ($n = 144$)			Husband away (per cent) ($n = 144$)		
	Woman alone	Woman not involved*	Joint decision**	Woman alone	Woman not involved*	Joint decision**
Own and children's health	10.8	49.6	39.6	60.2	26.8	13.0
Children's education	16.5	40.6	42.9	54.1	23.3	22.6
Visits to relatives and friends	11.2	44.4	44.4	30.3	36.6	33.1
What food to be cooked	44.3	45.1	10.6	71.1	25.4	3.5
Daily HH household purchases	32.6	42.6	24.8	64.6	24.8	10.6
Large HH household purchases	5.7	50.3	44.0	37.6	31.9	30.5
Overall money management	6.3	42.0	51.7	26.6	29.4	44.0

Source: Primary household survey data.

Note: *This includes decisions taken by the husband and/or in-laws which did not involve the woman. **This includes decisions taken by all household members, including the women respondents.

respondents were very vocal about their role within the household. To quote one such woman aged 42 years from the Muslim Sabzifarosh caste:

> Our men only bring home money, but we are the ones responsible for managing it, for spending it as wisely and stingily as possible. And besides, we have a whole lot more of other family responsibilities on our plate than men do.

Some migrant men praised their wives for their contribution in the smooth functioning of the household. Besides, exposure of migrants to the cities brought about some attitudinal shifts among some men regarding women's roles. To quote a migrant who had worked in cities for 12 years but later returned:

> At first, I was shocked to see how women in the cities carried themselves. The women in the cities were so different from the women in my village. But honestly speaking, I liked it. Given the societal norms, I may not allow my wife to be as modern as an urban woman, but I know that she is not supposed to be confined to the four walls of the house either.

Rigid social structures, however, precluded opportunities and expressions of progressive social change. Many women respondents suggested that they did not lack the freedom to take decisions when their husbands came back, and yet considered it culturally inappropriate to decide on things on their own when their husbands were around. The spread of mobile phones has at once aided in enhancing the role of women in managing the household affairs and curtailed their autonomous decision-making abilities. Thus, while many women indicated they phoned their husbands to seek advice (for instance, how to use banking services to withdraw money that their husbands sent), the utility of mobile phones also meant that women hesitated taking independent decisions. In families where the male migrants did not share cordial relations with their in-laws, the wives called their husband and sought permission beforehand each time they visited their natal places. In other words, male migration did not usher in absolute freedom for women, but it seemed to enhance their role within and outside the household and contributed to their improved agency, at least for the time that the men were absent.

INCREASING WORK BURDEN ON WOMEN

On the negative side, male migration also brought about significant hardships for many rural women, particularly those from very poor households. In addition to single-handedly managing the household affairs and caring for dependent children and elders, women were required to perform an increased number of tasks in household agriculture. In many cases, managing the family farms was solely done by women. High incidence of poverty, coupled with small landholdings, meant very few migrant households were able to hire outside labour for agriculture work. This was particularly the case in families belonging to lower-backward caste groups where women performed all the tasks – from sowing to harvesting – on their own, and in some cases with the help of their young children. Most male migrants spent a large part of the year outside their origin villages for employment. This meant that male labour for agriculture work was not available for much of the crop cycle. And while most men made at least one trip back to their origin villages in a year, and many timed the visit to coincide with the tasks of *buwai* (sowing) and *katai* (threshing), working on the farm was *not* the 'main reason for the trip back home'. Of the 239 migrants who were reported to have made at least one trip back home in the past year, only 34.7 per cent returned to help or work on the farm, whereas for the remaining 65.3 per cent, this was not the *main* purpose of visit. Instead, after a long work trip to the cities in which many migrants also worked overtime to earn and save more money, the home villages provided an escape from the hardship they endured in the cities. As one migrant, who worked as a spinning operator in a cotton mill in Hoshiarpur, Punjab, but whom we spoke to in his home village when he was on a break, put it:

My work is very demanding. My daily shift is of eight hours, but I often work between 10 and 12 hours every day of the week to earn overtime money. Sometimes I do a double shift of 16 hours. And when I go to my room after work, I do not have anyone to interact with. Besides, the *seth* [employer] I work for keeps changing my work shifts. One day I find myself working in the morning shift, and the next day I am asked to do the night shift. This constant changing of shifts disrupts my body rhythm, and I feel tired all the time. When I feel too tired and lonely, I come to my village to relax. But I cannot stay here forever because I need money to run my household. So I go back again.

Similarly, the woman respondent from the Muslim Sabzifarosh caste, quoted earlier, grudgingly remarked:

> My husband's job starts and ends at earning money, but I am the one who has to do multiple jobs here, including cooking, cleaning, washing, feeding kids, taking care of their education and health, and managing the land and animals. Though he is out of the village for work for a major part of the year, even when he is around, he does not do anything.

Table 7.4 summarises survey data on the amount of time women spent on household agriculture and domestic activities *before* and *after* their husbands' migration. The number of women varied for each activity, as not all women reported performing all tasks, and the numbers for the categories of before and after husband's migration also varied, as some women reported performing some tasks only after their husbands' migration. The sample for the before and after categories, respectively, included 85 and 86 for collecting water, 26 and 29 for animal care, 34 and 37 for agriculture work, 72 and 79 for childcare, 35 and 47 for collecting fuel or wood for cooking, 116 for cleaning in both, and 114 for cooking and washing in both.

Table 7.4 Average minutes spent daily on different activities by migrants' wives

	Average time spent daily (in mins)	
Activity	Before husband's migration	After husband's migration
Collecting water	27	27
Cleaning and mopping the house	45	46
Cooking	100	99
Washing clothes	62	62
Collecting cooking fuel or wood	56	61
Taking care of animals	80	84
Childcare	72	79
Agriculture work	120	148
Leisure	165	157

Source: Primary household survey data.

Core household activities like cleaning, cooking, and so on, remained the same, but those activities in which husbands and wives were more likely to share responsibilities (like childcare and, particularly, agriculture) increased noticeably. Also, leisure time fell. These data, however, do not fully capture the participation of women in agriculture. Only 37 out of 144 migrants' wives reported that after their husbands' migration they did agriculture work, which is a gross underestimation. Qualitative accounts on women's participation in agriculture revealed that, barring some women from forward castes, most women engaged and laboured in household agriculture in varying degrees; some women reported managing the farm was solely their responsibility. The source of this contradiction in survey data and qualitative insights may lie in the fact that many women in rural Siwan considered work in agriculture as rather ancillary and often part of their domestic responsibilities. To quote a 45-year-old woman from the Kushwaha caste who worked on family land, but did not think it needed to be counted separately from her domestic duties: 'I do tend to our agricultural

Photo 7.1   Two children fixing a flat bicycle tyre with village elders in the background

Photo 7.2   A woman returning home after tending to her family-owned land

Photo 7.3   Women sorting out onions they harvested from their family farm

Photo 7.4 A Kushwaha woman working on her family farm alongside her husband

Photo 7.5 A woman sorting out crop residue to use as fuel for cooking dinner for her family

Photo 7.6 A *gram panchayat* meeting where women participate in equal measure as men

Photo 7.7 A woman receiving her monthly food rations from a local shop under the public distribution system (PDS) – a common occurrence among women in the absence of men though they often face great difficulties on account of their gender

Photo 7.8   A man in one of the study villages selling traditional palm wine, locally known as *tadi*, with eggs available for purchase as snacks on a stand nearby

Photo 7.9   The Bihar government's scheme to provide free bicycles to girls attending grade 9 acts as an incentive for more girls to enroll in higher education and helps improve their mobility

Photo 7.10   A dwelling inhabited by three brothers and their families with different kitchens, indicative of emerging familial arrangements in Siwan

Source: All photographs taken by the author during fieldwork in Siwan.

land. But just like this house, that is our land, too. So it is part and parcel of my domestic work. Is not it?' Indeed, there was some degree of *feminisation of agriculture* across rural Siwan.

However, participation of women in agriculture varied by familial structure, caste, economic class and age. Young women in joint families largely remained indoors. And usually women from relatively richer and upper-caste households did not do agriculture work; instead, the family land was leased out to the lower-caste families in the same village. Women from the lower-backward castes were most visible in farm work, tilling the land as family farmers, agricultural labourers and sharecroppers. The participation of women from the cultivator caste groups of Koeri and Kushwahas (officially classified as backward castes in contemporary Bihar) was no less significant, and many among the non-migrant households also worked alongside their husbands in the fields (Photos 7.2–7.5).

And while men tended to send their remittance earnings home, this was not universal. Crucially, moreover, the amount of remittance varied widely, and households from the disadvantaged castes groups of Scheduled Castes, Scheduled Tribes and extremely backward castes reported, on

Box 7.1 More autonomy or greater responsibility? Understanding the different impacts of male migration through the tales of two women

Meena Devi

Meena Devi (name changed) is a 32-year-old married woman from village A of Maharajganj block, Siwan. She was born in an upper-caste Rajput family and is married to a man from the same caste. Her husband, Rajbinder Singh (first name changed), is a migrant. Rajbinder first migrated for work to Delhi after marriage. He spent six years in Delhi, and Meena lived with him for the most part (Rajbinder and Meena were 18 and 16 years old, respectively, when they got married). However, two years after the couple had their first child, a daughter, they moved back to the village; they now have four children (three daughters and one son). Rajbinder inherited 2 acres of agricultural land from his father, and savings from six years of migration allowed him to add another half an acre. The family lived off the cash income from the agricultural land. However, Meena said that Rajbinder did not like farming, and for the past three years he had been working in a cellular company in Patna while she and children stay in the village. Being from the Rajput caste, Meena does not work on farms, and the agricultural land has been leased out to three different lower-caste families for sharecropping farming. The family gets half of the total produce in return.

Patna is approximately 150 kilometers south of village A. Given the short distance, Rajbinder comes to the village at least once in two months. In fact, his decision to work in Patna was so that he could be close to his wife and children as there are no other elder members in the family. However, his visits are short, lasting only for a few days; he mostly visits on the weekends. In the absence of her husband, Meena manages the household. She does not work on the farms and in any other cash income activities, but she feels more independent now than before. She now goes to the village market to make household purchases which she would not do earlier when her husband was living in the village. She also takes decisions on major family matters, such as children's education and household finances, though she calls her husband and takes his opinion. She keeps him in the loop to keep their relations cordial and harmonious. In her words: 'Do aadmi mein agar rai ho jaye toh behtar hai' (It's always better if the two of us discuss and decide on things jointly).

(Contd)

(*Contd*)

Meena is also a *gram–panchayat* (GP) ward member (member of the village council), and she participates in the GP activities and meetings. But her husband is looking for a house in Patna, and their long-term plan is to move and settle there. They intend to sell part of their agricultural land to buy a house in Patna and keep some land for the dowry for their daughters' marriage.

Noorjahan Begum

Noorjahan Begum (name changed), a 45-year-old woman, is from the same village as that of Meena. She belongs to the Mahadalit caste of Muslim *dhobis* (washermen), a socially and economically backward caste and occupational group. Her current family includes her partially disabled husband, three daughters and two sons. The family of seven has a hand-to-mouth existence, and they live in their *kutcha* bamboo hut. Following her wedding, Noorjahan's life has been full of economic hardships. Her husband was a migrant construction worker, but a few years ago he met with an accident at the work site. The accident caused severe injuries to one of his legs, and he has been in the village ever since. He is also an alcohol addict, and even when he earned money, he spent most of it on drinking and seldom sent money home. He has recently been diagnosed with a damaged liver. Two months ago, Noorjahan sent her 20-year-old son to Delhi for work. But he has not yet started remitting money.

Noorjahan alone has the responsibility of feeding seven members on her shoulders. As the family's sole breadwinner, she single-handedly does multiple on-farm and non-farm jobs. She farms five *katthas* (0.1 acre) of family-owned land, sharecrops a land parcel that she has leased in from a Rajput family in the village, works as an agricultural labourer at the wage rate of INR 30 per day (for four–five hours) and, being from the washerman caste, also washes the clothes of families in the village (her daughters help her in this work). Despite all the work, rarely does Noorjahan's family have days when they eat three meals a day, and there are days when they do not eat any food at all. The family has a ration card under the public distribution system (PDS), which allows them access to subsidised food grains. However, food rations are *never* regularly distributed.

Noorjahan's bigger concern, however, is the dowry money for the marriage of her three daughters. She told us that earlier her caste had the

(*Contd*)

(*Contd*)

> practice of *mehar* (bride-price) in which the girl's side received the money. This, however, has changed in recent times. Initially started by wealthy Muslim families who considered dowry as a gift to their daughters, the practice has now trickled down to the poor families. Noorjahan's only hope is her son who has recently migrated to Delhi. She wishes that he does not follow the footsteps of his father. Despite all these difficulties, Noorjahan wore a smile. At the end of the interview, she said: 'I feel defeated, but crying does not help. So, I try to make peace with my situation which I know will probably not change anyway.'

average, smaller income receipts vis-à-vis forward-caste and backward-caste households. For instance, the average monthly remittance amount of INR 4,135 among forward-caste households was about 25 per cent more than that of INR 3,170 received by extremely-backward-caste households. Women in such low- or non-remittance-receiving households had an added burden of providing for their families. Thus, the outcomes of male migration were not uniform – far from it. The individual experiences of women differed widely, and whether migration of men brought about greater freedom in decision-making or more work was guided by several intersecting variables such as social caste and economic class (see Box 7.1).

CHANGES IN THE FAMILY STRUCTURE

An emergent dynamic of the effects of migration from Siwan that deserves particular attention here is that migration is also leading to changes in familial structure and living arrangements due to intra-family tensions over cash incomes. Migration of young male members was still largely undertaken within the broader context of a joint-family structure, and remittances (and local incomes) were jointly shared by all household members. This is, however, no longer always the case. Fieldwork also pointed to reluctance among migrants and their wives to share the remittances with the economically less productive or unproductive members of the households such as the migrants' brothers and their families. This was particularly the case among the poor families that had no land or other resources in the origin village, and thus sharing of remittances did not bring any benefits to the immediate

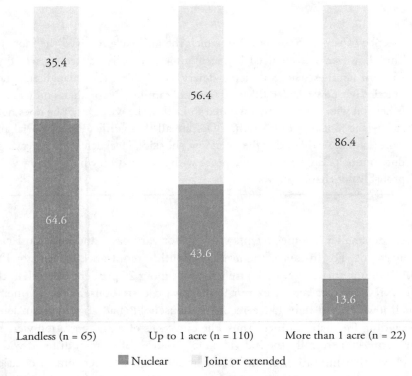

Figure 7.1 Percentage of migrant households by family type and landholding status

Source: Primary household survey data.

family. The household survey data also provide some insights on this issue. Figure 7.1 shows the type of family by the landholding status of the surveyed migrant households. Whereas 65 per cent of households with no land were nuclear entities, households in the land-size category of an acre or more were predominantly joint or extended ones.[6]

These cross-sectional survey data are not adequate to infer the long-term changes in the family organisation. However, detailed personal histories of several households provide evidence in this regard (see later). Findings of longitudinal studies conducted in other parts of India also suggest that the emergence of disparate incomes and divergent economic interests are associated with changes in family type and living arrangements. In her longitudinal ethnographic study of the two villages of Dalena and Mangala in Mysore district in the southern Indian state of Karnataka, carried out at the interval of a 15-year period (1955 and 1970), Epstein (1973, p. 201) noted:

> Landless families and those with insignificant size landholdings have for the most part remained elementary units. On the other hand, growing cash income has increased the tensions within joint families in the middle range. A considerable proportion of families which during the last fifteen years have extended to three generations have either already been partitioned or are on the verge, or in the process, of breaking up.

In rural Bihar, these changes in the family structure – from joint or extended to nuclear – also occurred among households where all the young men, brothers in this context, were earning migrants in the cities but had differences in their earnings. These households typically included the ones without the old male patriarch. For instance, in an interview with Kanti Devi (name changed), a 60-year-old widow whose three sons all worked outside the village (the eldest one in a textile mill in Kolhapur, Maharashtra, the middle son as a truck driver with a base in Delhi, and the youngest one as a tempo driver in Ranchi, Jharkhand), said that her middle son made the most money and contributed the most to the family, which was not acceptable to his wife. Kanti's daughter-in-law wanted the extra money to be spent on her children's education instead of contributing to the family pool that had to be equally distributed among all members. This led to family squabbles, and all the brothers separated later.[7]

The story of Bhola Prasad's (first name changed) family is another case of intra-household conflicts over incomes. An old man in his early 60s from the cultivator Kushwaha caste, Prasad owned four *beegha* (roughly 2.5 acres) land. His three married sons all worked in cities. While two of the sons (and their wives and children) lived with him as part of the joint family and helped him on family farms, the youngest son – who spent the most time in the city and earned more than the other two brothers – separated from the joint family a few years ago. The wife and children of this son lived with his in-laws, and whenever he returned to the village, he also stayed there. Prasad recounted that all was well in the family until his wife fell ill. For the treatment of his wife (who later died), Prasad had to mortgage 11 *katthas* (0.4 acre) of land to take a cash loan from the local moneylender, which he had not been able to repay. While the family earned some cash income from the agricultural produce from the owned land, it was not enough to repay the loan. (Over the years, the family size also increased, which meant that more of the agricultural produce was used for their own consumption.) From the remittances he received, Prasad was saving money to get the family land back. However, his youngest daughter-in-law asked her husband to not contribute anything to the joint-household income pool over which tensions erupted. While two other sons continued to remit to Prasad, his youngest son now sent remittances to his wife at her natal place. The youngest son had also started asking for his share of land from the joint property. Prasad, however, thought that after what his son did, he was not bound to give him any land. His decision to not give his son any land, however, it appeared, was an effort to save the household from being broken down further, as that would mean that he would then have to give his other two sons their shares of land as well. Prasad thought it was inevitable after he dies, but he did not want that to happen as long as he was alive.

Similarly, the story of a joint family of Sahs (from a backward caste), a relatively wealthier household which stood on the verge of a break-up, is another example. The Sah household comprised three brothers and their families, who, at the time of this fieldwork in 2012, all lived under the same roof, and had a shared kitchen and joint income and expenditure. Two of the elder brothers lived in the village with their families and minded the family-owned farmland of 10 acres. The youngest one worked as a labour migrant in Saudi Arabia, but his wife and son lived in the same joint household. He remitted money home to his eldest brother, who is the head of the household, and also some of his earnings to his wife. However, his wife's spending patterns and money management caused suspicion that the migrant brother sent more money to his wife than to his brother for the joint household pool. As an example, whenever her son caught cold or had fever, she took him to the state capital of Patna (160 kilometres south of Siwan) to seek treatment, whereas the children of her two brothers-in-law saw the doctor in the block hospital for the same health conditions. This bubbled tensions in the family, and they had agreed that after the migrant brother returns, they would divide the shared property and split.[8]

There were numerous other stories of families splitting up due to rising tensions over cash management. As one survey respondent summed up:

The number of families in the village increases almost every day. How do you think that happens? These are not new families settling in the village from the outside (who would come here to live?) but the old ones who are splitting among themselves. And money is the biggest evil.

It is important to note that separation did not mean that families moved away from the house they previously lived in. While a few migrants with money and homestead land elsewhere moved out of the house, and some also moved to their in-laws' places (for example, Prasad's son, as noted earlier), most of them dwelled in the same house, albeit each family now managed their own finances and had separate kitchens. These new forms of familial relations in rural Siwan could be most aptly characterised as the ones in which *the roof is shared but income and financial responsibilities are separated* (Photo 7.10).

FOOD SECURITY AMONGST HOUSEHOLDS HEADED BY LEFT-BEHIND WOMEN

Alterations in intra-family relations and gender roles as a result of migration of men have a bearing on household food security outcomes. This section highlights the ways in which the phenomenon of left-behind women and women-headed households relate to household food security. To this end, three interlinked factors through which the gender of the household head mediates food security outcomes deserve mention. These include (*a*) income or economic status of the household, (*b*) women's participation in cash-earning activities and (c) family structure.

INTERACTIONS OF INCOME AND GENDER

Studies indicate that women tend to spend a greater share of their income on food than men do (Guyer, 1980; Engle, 1988). This is often a reflection of an overall higher incidence of poverty among women-headed households. Generally, poor households tend to spend a larger proportion of their income on food (Alderman, 1986; Mahapatro et al., 2017). To understand how the gender of the head and the household income interact with the food expenditure patterns of the surveyed migrant households, Table 7.5 presents the data on (*a*) average total MPCE, (*b*) average MPCE on food and (*c*) average share of food expenditure in the total MPCE, by gender of the household head and living standard.[9]

The data confirm a decline in the proportional share of food expenditure with a rise in living standards among both women-headed households and men-headed households. At the same time, the absolute food expenditure increases

Table 7.5 Average food expenditure (in INR) among the migrant households by living standards and the gender of the household head

Living standard	Households headed by men (n = 95)			Households headed by women (n = 102)		
	Total average MPCE (INR)	Average MPCE on food (INR)	Average share of food in total MPCE (per cent)	Total average MPCE (INR)	Average MPCE on food (INR)	Average share of food in total MPCE (per cent)
Low	587	265	45	511	231	45
Medium	743	274	37	792	293	37
High	1473	400	27	1380	479	35

Source: Primary household survey data.

from the low to high-living-standards categories, which is a product of income. Importantly, for this study, the data show that the gender of the household head appears to significantly affect food expenditure in the high-living-standard group, but not for the low and medium ones: women-headed households in the high-living-standard group had average MPCE on food which was 20 per cent higher than that of households headed by men. Fieldwork suggests two possible explanations for these expenditure differentials.

First, the effects of women spending on food were realised only in households that were economically better off because women in these households had less pressure to use and save money for non-food items or future needs, such as daughters' weddings, as compared to women from poorer households (see Box 7.1). Another important reason for women spending more on food than men do is related to men out-spending women on alcohol, a finding that is corroborated in studies elsewhere (Peters, Herrera and Randolph, 1989; Duflo and Udry, 2004). The WHO's study revealed that 90 per cent of Indian women abstain from alcohol throughout their lives, compared to 60 per cent of Indian men (Sinha, 2014). In Bihar, rural women's political mobilisation against the rampant alcohol abuse by men, which left little money for other household needs, led the state government to implement a total alcohol prohibition in 2016 (Photo 7.8).

In households where women had some control over money, spending on food was prioritised (Table 7.6). Detailed interviews with some women revealed that when their husbands were outside the village, they went to local

Table 7.6 Average food expenditure (in INR) among migrant households by women's control over money

	Households where women managed money independently	Households where women did not manage money independently
Total average monthly per capita expenditure (MPCE) (INR)	1022	933
Average MPCE on food (INR)	396	338
Average share of food in total MPCE (per cent)	39	36
Total number of households (*n*)	**38**	**106**

Source: Primary household survey data.

Note: This categorisation is based on women's responses on whether or not they alone took decisions on overall money management in their household when their husbands were away (see Table 7.3).

markets to buy fresh and seasonal vegetables, but they did not venture out of the house much when their husbands were around.

However, women-headed households in the high-living-standard group spending a greater share and amount of money on food did not necessarily translate into better food security. Table 7.7 presents data which refer to the proportion of households who reported having faced food inadequacy and food unavailability at least once in the past year. The effects of better economic status of the household on food security are quite discernible, irrespective of the gender of the household head. However, a comparison of food security by the gender of the household head suggests that on virtually all indicators and across all three living-standard categories, a greater proportion of women-headed households reported facing food inadequacy and food unavailability than did households headed by men.

EFFECTS OF FAMILIAL STRUCTURE AND LIVING ARRANGEMENTS

The structure of a family has complex interactions with household food security. Generally, women in nuclear families enjoyed greater autonomy and had a greater role in household decision-making compared with those in joint or extended families where men were present. Also, the average per capita monthly food expenditure of women-headed nuclear households was higher

Table 7.7 Household food security among migrant households by the gender of the household head and living standards

| | Living standard | | | | | |
| | Low | | Medium | | High | |
	MHHs	WHHs	MHHs	WHHs	MHHs	WHHs
Food was not enough (defined by the following situations)						
Ate meals without vegetables	46.4	93.8	50.0	54.1	17.1	26.5
Could only afford to consume food from the public distribution system (PDS)*	14.3	18.8	23.1	18.9	14.6	8.2
Consumed a single meal a day	32.1	18.8	11.5	18.9	4.9	6.1
Lacked all three main food categories (cereals, pulses, vegetables)	53.6	87.5	46.2	56.8	14.6	28.6
Lacked sufficient quantity of food to satiate hunger	53.6	68.8	42.3	48.6	14.6	18.4
Food was not available (defined by the following situations)						
Borrowed money from friends and/or relatives to buy food	17.9	37.5	19.2	21.6	4.9	8.2
Borrowed money from local traders or moneylenders or lifted ration on credit to acquire food	39.3	43.8	38.5	40.5	12.2	18.4
Sold jewellery or other personal assets to buy food	0	0	0	2.7	0	0
Ate less food than usual (consumption rationing)	60.7	81.3	46.2	51.4	14.6	22.4
Total number of households (n)	**28**	**16**	**26**	**37**	**41**	**49**

Source: Primary household survey data.

Note: All data are in percentage terms. 'MHHs' stands for households headed by men; 'WHHs' stands for households headed by women. *This applies to only those households with PDS cards. But there were many households that did not have the cards to access PDS food rations. Given women-headed households were over-represented among those without PDS cards, these data likely conceal their gender-based disadvantage.

than that of women-headed joint households; it was also greater than those of both the nuclear and joint households headed by men (Figure 7.2)

However, the food security outcomes were better among joint and extended households. Table 7.8 shows different self-reported food security indicators for women-headed migrant households by the type of living arrangements. Although nearly three-quarters of all women-headed migrant households were nuclear units, the women-headed joint or extended families fared better than the nuclear households on virtually all parameters of food security.

There are at least three explanations for why this may be the case. First, as noted earlier, joint families fared better than nuclear families in terms of land-size (Figure 7.1), which provided a crucial supplementary source of food security. Second, the nuclearisation of rural households in Siwan over income tensions notwithstanding, joint-household structure seemed to provide a greater buffer against income and food shocks. Joint households also had more

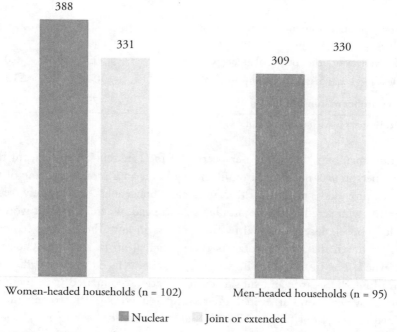

Figure 7.2 Average expenditure (in INR) on food by living arrangements and the gender of the household head

Source: Primary household survey data.

Table 7.8 Household food security among women-headed migrant households by type of living arrangements

	Nuclear households (per cent)	Joint households (per cent)
Food was not enough (defined by the following situations)		
Ate meals without vegetables	52.0	33.3
Could only afford to consume food from the public distribution system (PDS)	13.3	14.8
Consumed a single meal a day	16.0	3.7
Lacked all three main food categories (cereals, pulses, vegetables)	50.7	40.7
Lacked sufficient quantity of food to satiate hunger	42.7	22.2
Food was not available (defined by the following situations)		
Borrowed money from friends and/or relatives to buy food	21.3	7.4
Borrowed money from local traders or moneylenders or lifted ration on credit to acquire food	30.7	29.6
Sold jewellery or other personal assets to buy food	1.3	0.0
Ate less food than usual (consumption rationing)	45.3	33.3
Total number of households (*n*)	**75**	**27**

Source: Primary household survey data.

migrant members. From the perspective of food insecurity, this meant that if one person was not able to remit money home in a month, income of the other(s) provided a cushion. Third, in nuclear households, it was the wives of migrants who acted as the *de facto* household head, whereas in joint women-headed households, it was mainly the mothers-in-law. The age and seniority of the women mattered insofar as the participation in affairs outside was concerned. For instance, while women in general faced greater difficulties in availing PDS cards and subsidised food rations compared with men, the younger wives found it even harder compared with older women due to sociocultural reasons (Photo 7.7). Also, as noted earlier, many young women did not work outside the home in any income-generating activities or on their family land, which might have affected food security negatively. Almost all women who engaged in wage labour were aged over 35 years, though it should be noted that the households these women belonged to were invariably among the poorest and most disadvantaged, an issue taken up in the next section.

WOMEN'S WORK PARTICIPATION AND FOOD SECURITY

In the survey, 26 of the 144 migrants' wives reported working in income-generating activities outside of own-account agriculture, though most worked as agricultural labourers. Of the 26 women, 17 worked as agricultural labourers, three worked as sharecroppers, and six engaged in non-farm occupations such as bamboo-based basket-making. Women's work participation in cash-earning activities is generally associated with their improved bargaining power (Sen, 1987). Table 7.9 presents data on the proportion of households on various dimensions of food inadequacy and unavailability. A comparison shows that the households where women reported working had invariably higher incidence of food insecurity than the ones where women did not work.

Looking at these figures in conjunction with other data reveals that the households where women had to work were invariably among the poorest. For instance, barring one household from a forward caste, all of them were from the lower-backward caste groups, with 58 per cent from the Scheduled Castes and Scheduled Tribes and the extremely backward castes. It is not that these households did not receive remittances from their migrant members; 24 of these 26 households reported receiving remittances. But the average monthly remittances received by these households were smaller – INR 2,474 in comparison to INR 4,326 received by families where women did not work (a difference of 75 per cent). In other words, poverty and low remittances forced the women from these poor households to work outside household agriculture. This evidence corroborates the findings of other village-level studies in India that suggest that when remittances are not adequate, women often have to take on the roles of income earners to fend for their families (Jetley, 1987; Paris et al., 2005). However, due to unavailability of gainful employment opportunities, women's work did not positively influence the food security outcomes. These women worked for an average of nearly five months in the past year and 18 days per month. Moreover, 16 of 26 women reported getting a certain quantity of crop they helped cultivate as in-kind wages, while 10 received low-cash wages (around INR 150 per day), though these often helped avoid starvation. While women's work participation is viewed as a precursor to improving their bargaining

Table 7.9 Household food security among women-headed migrant households by women's involvement in income-earning activities

	Households where wives did not work in income-earning activities (per cent)	Households where wives worked in income-earning activities (per cent)
Food was not enough (defined by the following situations)		
Ate meals without vegetables	39.8	61.5
Could only afford to consume food from the public distribution system (PDS)	13.6	15.4
Consumed a single meal a day	13.6	19.2
Lacked all three main food categories (cereals, pulses, vegetables)	39.8	69.2
Lacked sufficient quantity of food to satiate hunger	32.2	57.7
Food was not available (defined by the following situations)		
Borrowed money from friends and/or relatives to buy food	13.6	30.8
Borrowed money from local traders or moneylenders or lifted ration on credit to acquire food	27.1	46.2
Sold jewellery or other personal assets to buy food	0.0	0.0
Ate less food than usual (consumption rationing)	38.1	61.5
Total number of households (*n*)	**118**	**26**

Source: Primary household survey data.

position, these findings reveal that socio-economic contexts, households' background circumstances and employment characteristics often mediate these outcomes. Feminist scholars have argued that gender intersects with other vectors such as social context, caste and class (Valentine, 2007; Ramnarain, 2015; Rodó-de-Zárate and Baylina, 2018). These findings show that the most marginalised (poor, lower-caste women) experience the intersectional effects of migration, gender relations and food insecurity most intensely.

CONCLUSION

By opening the *household box* to understand the impacts of migration, this chapter has discussed the ways in which male-only migration restructures and realigns gender dynamics and power relations at the household level. In terms of the key themes, the discussion has shown that two major, and in many ways simultaneous, impacts of male-migration from rural Siwan include the increased participation of women in household affairs and decision-making and an accompanying increase in the work burden of left-behind women. These two themes of *improved autonomy* and *increased responsibility* provide conceptual pathways to understand the migration–gender–food-security relationship. Another important, and much less explored, issue highlighted here is the impact of migration in changing the traditional family form – from joint to nuclear households – as a result of increasing tensions over cash incomes from migration. Although this latter outcome is not explicitly the result of male migration, the cases of the households presented in the chapter suggest that stay-behind women appear to negotiate with other family members control over their husband's earnings and the ways these earnings should or should not be spent.

Through the lens of gender, the discussion in this chapter has also attempted to establish the linkages between these changes in gender social roles and household food security. The analysis presented, however, highlights that the connections between male migration, gender and household food security are highly complex. Thus, while greater women's autonomy and their enhanced involvement in household affairs as a result of male migration are associated with an increased household food expenditure among women-headed households compared to those in households headed by men, the effects of the gender of the household head on food expenditure are discernable only in the high-income category; for the households at the lower end of the income spectrum, no clear relationship emerges from the survey data. This finding notwithstanding, across the living-standard categories, women-headed households fare worse than the households headed by men on food security, a finding which is indicative of gender-based disadvantage that women-headed households suffer in patriarchal societies.

Second, the structure of the family also appears to have a contradictory relationship with food security. Thus, while women living in nuclear households enjoyed greater financial autonomy than their counterparts in the joint or extended households, and women who controlled household finances spent a greater share of money on food, the food security outcomes of women-headed households are better among joint families. Perhaps this is because of the buffer that a joint family provides in times of income shocks. Extrapolating these findings to draw their implications on the changing family organisation in Siwan, it appears that nuclearisation of families in the district, although reflective of the *agency* of women in many ways, is not always a healthy development.

Finally, and this is important, the discussion also highlights that women-headed households were heterogeneous, and the migration–gender–food-security nexus was influenced by a range of intervening variables such as caste, landholdings, type of family, and the amount of remittances received by the household. In regard to the latter, the women who did not receive adequate remittances had to work to supplement their household income. However, in settings where employment opportunities are rather scarce and wages low, this makes it even more difficult for the left-behind women, and their work participation does not appear to positively influence the household food security. Importantly, this also highlights the crucial role of remittances for left-behind women to manage their households. Whether or not the lack of decent jobs and incomes *locally* would dislodge the restrictions on women's mobility and propel women migration among poor households remains to be seen.

NOTES

1. It should be noted, however, that in India, while the population census and large-scale national surveys severely underestimate the true extent of labour migration in general, women migrants are more likely to be underestimated because respondents are often asked to give one reason for migration, and female migration is mostly associated with marriage. However, many women work after marriage. Second, cultural norms often prevent women from emphasising their economic role (Santhi, 2006; Mazumdar, Neetha and Agnihotri, 2013).

2. Ideally, choosing population aged 10 years and above would have been more suitable. But the Indian census does not permit the same at the village level.

3. An extremely influential Saran-born Bhojpuri singer, playwright and lyricist of all time, and the one who is considered to be the originator of *bideshia* folk

and theatre, is Bikhari Thakur. In 2012, London-based musical label EMI/ Virgin Records released a *bideshia* folk album of Thakur titled 'The Legacy of Bikhari Thakur' with Assamese-Bhojpuri singer Kalpana Patowary as the lead vocalist. This album was released by the vice-prime minister of Mauritius (Borah, 2012), a country where many men from Bihar migrated as indentured labourers to work on plantations and settled on a more permanent basis.

4. In the mid-nineteenth century, many people from Bihar migrated as indentured labourers to British colonies such as Fiji, Mauritius and British Guiana (now Guyana) to work on plantations (Gillion, 1956; Smith, 1959) and settled there. Indeed, these countries now have a significant presence of Bihari-origin people, and Bhojpuri is one of the national languages of Fiji and Guyana and is spoken widely in Mauritius.

5. It should be noted that gender relations in Bihar are also in flux because of recent policy reforms, including the reservation of 50 per cent of the seats in GPs and promoting higher education among girls through incentives such as providing free bicycles to girls who attend grade 9 (Photo 7.9).

6. Some poor households also separated in order to avail themselves of separate ration cards and benefits such as subsidised food under the PDS scheme that accompanied it.

7. Kanti did not reveal any of this in the first hour of the interview. In the beginning, she appeared content with her family and situation. But after some rapport was built, she burst into tears and narrated this story of her family break-up. Individual interviews with two of her three daughters-in-law (the third one was not present at the time of the interview) also suggested the primacy of money matters as the cause of changes in the family structure, though, unlike Kanti, they expressed happiness over this change.

8. Households with international migrants were not a part of the fieldwork, but some of these households were spoken to for insights on broader migration dynamics. As noted in the previous chapter, international migration from Siwan to the Gulf nations is significant too, which is transforming the gender social relations (also see Choithani, Van Duijne and Nijman, 2021).

9. Sample households were divided into three equal tertiles of low, medium and high based on their income. The cut-off points for the MPCI tertiles obtained from the survey data include INR 485.12 and INR 767.12. Using these cut-off points, the classification of living standards is as follows: (*a*) low (INR 0–485.12), (*b*) medium (INR 485.13–767.12) and (*c*) high (INR 767.13 and above).

8

CONCLUSION

This book has argued that despite the obvious connections between migration and household food security, little attention, and even scarcer direct evidence, has been marshalled towards the linkages between them in development policy research and practice. The preceding seven chapters of the book have attempted to highlight these connections, and primary data from the case-study district of Siwan in western Bihar provided empirical evidence on how the relationship between the two plays out. The findings reveal that food insecurity is a critical driver of rural households' migration decisions, and the act of migration, in turn, influences the households' food security outcomes. In other words, there is a two-way relationship between migration and household food security. However, these connections are not straightforward – far from it. They manifest at various levels, as the primary research findings presented in the three empirical chapters (Chapters 5, 6 and 7) establish. These include: (*a*) the interactions of the wider institutional and policy environment with rural households' food security status and migration decisions; (*b*) the effects of migrants' remittances on household food security and inter-household differences among migrant and non-migrant households in income, assets and food security; and (*c*) within-household dynamics of migration and food security.

The primary research findings from the rural hinterlands of Bihar provide important insights of national and international significance that need attention. This final chapter brings together the main insights of this research, identifies the key findings that may have wider policy significance and comments on the direction of future research. As a way of introduction, the discussion that follows first revisits the main research premise and rationale and summarises the narratives told in the previous chapters.

RETURNING TO THE BEGINNING

This book began by summarising the key question it pursues: what role does internal migration play as a livelihood strategy in influencing food security outcomes among rural households in India? The broad rationale for this work is provided by the disconnect that currently exists in the academic and policy discussions on migration and food security. Migration has become a key component of livelihood strategies of an increasing number of rural households across the developing world. During recent years, academics and prominent global policy-making bodies have increasingly argued for the need to encourage migration to promote sustainable human-development outcomes. However, despite food insecurity being a growing global development challenge, barring a few notable exceptions (Zezza et al., 2011; Crush, 2013; Craven and Gartaula, 2015; Crush and Caesar, 2017), there appears to be virtually no discussion on the potential role migration plays in household food security. In part, this neglect emanates from invariably more focus devoted to international migration and remittances in recent development policy and research practice, and consequently, the discussions have tended to centre around their wider development impacts. At the level of food policy, the tendency to treat rural households as homogenous groups engaged solely in farming is also an important reason for this disregard. Using a case-study approach, involving surveys and interviews with rural households from the high outmigration district of Siwan in western Bihar, and their urban-based migrant members, this book has sought to contextualise this less-investigated relationship.

In alignment with the key question, the previous seven chapters have been developed with a view of generating a holistic understanding of the links between migration and food security. To briefly recap, Chapter 1 establishes the global significance of India as an appropriate setting to study this relationship. Despite the abundant food availability at the national level and a rapid increase in the nation's overall wealth following economic reforms, chronic food insecurity and hunger remain pervasive in India, the burden of which is disproportionately shared by the country's rural masses. Looking through the headline national statistics on agricultural production and economic growth in India, it clearly emerges that the issue of food insecurity in India is intimately related to the wider set of livelihood circumstances of the country's food-insecure populations. In turn, this necessitates an understanding of those lives and livelihoods. Recent evidence points to a growing significance of migration, particularly to urban areas, in the rural livelihood systems in India (Deshingkar and Farrington, 2009; Government of India, 2017; Nayyar and Kim, 2018; Choithani, Van Duijne and Nijman, 2021). However, pre-existing research on whether and how migration influences household food security in India is virtually non-existent.

Chapter 2 contextualises the links between migration and food security in a broader context. It argues that the relationship between migration and food security is best understood through the prisms of 'entitlements' and 'livelihoods'. These frameworks provide people-centred perspectives on how and why differently placed individuals and households choose the means and livelihood strategies they do and how, in turn, they connect people with food on their plate or lack thereof (Sen, 1981; Chambers and Conway, 1991; Scoones, 1998). With a focus on migration as a livelihood strategy, the discussion also conceptualises and lays out the potential pathways of linkages between migration and food security that deserve empirical scrutiny.

Chapter 3 sets the scene for field-based evidence by addressing the broad dynamics of food insecurity, migration and urbanisation in India. It assesses India's progress on the MDG on hunger and undernourishment and discusses its various socio-spatial dimensions. It also illustrates how the failure of India on meeting its MDG targets is, in many ways, intimately related to the failure of economic growth to strengthen the food entitlements of disadvantaged population groups. The discussion also briefly reflects on the post-2015 development agenda that seeks to eliminate all forms of malnourishment from the planet. While it is too early to assess India's progress on SDGs, the preliminary findings from the recent round of the NFHS 2019–20, which indicate a reversal of child nutritional outcomes in many large states, is clearly a matter of concern. These findings also suggest that elimination of food insecurity and undernourishment, as envisaged by SDG-2, requires a policy approach that considers pursuit of faster economic growth as not an end in itself but rather a means to achieve better human development (Drèze and Sen, 2013). Indeed, the Indian experience of disconnect between economic growth and nutritional well-being has led to a change in global policy thinking that now views *economic growth as a necessary but not a sufficient condition* to meet the challenge of global hunger reduction

(FAO 2012). The discussion in the chapter also shows that the problem of food insecurity in India is predominantly rural in nature. Moreover, rising demographic pressures on land, expressed through progressive reductions in the average landholding sizes in rural areas, are weakening the capacity of land-based livelihoods to allow the rural households to meet their income and food needs. The evaluation of these trends in India's economic and employment landscape suggests that non-farm, non-local, urban incomes are becoming increasingly crucial for rural households' incomes and food security.

These broad national-level trends, however, need contextualisation in their place-based settings. In order to understand how these macro-level changes are shaping rural households' livelihood pathways (migration decisions in particular) and food security at the local level, this book draws on primary fieldwork with rural households and their urban migrant members from Siwan district in western Bihar. Chapter 4 provides a detailed discussion of the context of Bihar and Siwan and establishes the significance of the research context to study the relationship between migration and food security. For over 200 years, Bihar has remained a geography of deprivation on the Indian map of development. Consequently, livelihoods in the state have traditionally involved a frequent engagement of rural households in distant labour markets. While much of the rural outmigration from Bihar has been, and continues to be, distress-induced, income-pull factors have also been, and are becoming increasingly more, significant. Mobility has been much more pronounced in the western Bihar region, and food (in)security has often acted as one of the critical drivers of migration. These were considerations that crucially informed the selection of Siwan as a case-study site. A close examination of the colonial records and district gazetteers points to a culture of migration from Siwan (Gupta, 1923; O'Malley, 2007 [1930]; Yang, 1979, 1989), which contrasts with the *static peasant* image that has dominantly been used in academic and policy discourses to characterise the rural populations of developing countries. Strikingly, however, core dimensions of mobility from Siwan have been highly static over the years. These include (*a*) circular migration and (*b*) male-dominated mobility. These patterns notwithstanding, fieldwork suggests that in recent years the importance of migration among Siwani dwellers has increased, and migration is now occurring for longer durations.

The next three chapters provide empirical insights on the three key conceptual pathways of linkages between migration and food security, as set out in Chapter 2, namely (*a*) interactions of institutional arrangements with rural households' food entitlements and migration decisions, (*b*) role of migrants' remittances in influencing food security at the place of origin and (*c*) given the male-dominated migration, the effects of gender on household food security.

Focusing on the first of these pathways, Chapter 5 assesses the three important food-based safety nets of the PDS, the NREGS and the ICDS in their grounded contexts in order to understand whether and how these institutional arrangements relate to rural households' food security status and their migration decisions. Following the governance reforms initiated since 2005, important initiatives have been taken to improve the government-run food-based safety nets. That there is a political will to change the status quo cannot be denied and, indeed, deserves much appreciation. At the same time, assessment of these schemes points to widespread institutional failures. These programmes remain plagued with massive corruption and maladministration which, as things stand, have not meaningfully improved the food entitlements of rural populations of the state. Given the high incidence of poverty and a general lack of gainful employment opportunities all around the year in the case-study villages, the widespread operational inefficiencies in these schemes mean that they do not provide an effective substitute to migration. It is in these contexts that interstate labour migration remains an important strategy of rural Siwani households to meet their income and food needs.

Chapter 6 then examines the role of migration and remittances in household food security in Siwan. The discussion points out that sub-economical landholding and a lack of adequate employment in the *local* non-farm sector means that remittances now form a significant component of rural migrant households' overall income portfolios. At the same time, a range of factors, including precarious nature of urban informal jobs, migrants' attachment to origin villages and sociocultural norms, have prohibited permanent mobility. Thus, the nature of migration involves circular moves. In turn, from the perspective of the food security of origin members, circular migration has created complex rural–urban linkages. To most households, migrants' remittances provided the cash income to buy food. In other cases, sending of a member to the city prevented the households to slide down to a state of absolute landlessness. A few households were able to also increase their landholdings over the period from the savings accumulated from the urban incomes. Moreover, those households with relatively large landholdings, and with more members working in the cities, invested their remittances in family agriculture and were able to derive better income gains from land and agriculture. While the usage of remittances varied, depending on the background circumstances of the households, its positive impact on the food security of members at the origin villages were highly discernable: households that had one or more migrant members were invariably more food secure than those without migrants, though the incidence of poverty and food insecurity across the survey sample was still high. The primary evidence suggests that without access to remittances, the income and food security of most household would have been even worse; and for some households, migration encouraged an upward spiral of land acquisition and livelihood enhancement.

Chapter 7 finally takes the debate on these issues within the household itself. The chapter shows that migration of men has created a space for women to participate more proactively in household decision-making when their husbands are not around and has improved their autonomy. In terms of food security, in households where women received adequate and regular remittances and controlled them, food expenditure was generally higher compared to households where women had less autonomy. However, despite this, women-headed households did not have a better food security status as compared to those headed by men, a finding which points to the added disadvantage that comes from being a woman in a patriarchal setting such as Siwan. Indeed, while their men were away, women faced numerous challenges in accessing the government food-based safety nets. On the other hand, male migration has also brought significant hardship for women, and those who did not receive adequate remittances fared even worse as, in addition to the domestic duties, they also had to find work and employment to make ends meet. Additionally, migration incomes are leading to disputes over cash within the families, with the resultant effect being evidenced in the breaking up of joint households into nuclear units. Importantly, it is the left-behind wives of migrants who are increasingly seeking to stake claims on their migrant husband's earnings. This is reflective of women exercising their agency. At the same time, this also means erosion of traditional support for the left-behind women which, given the generally high incidence of poverty, is not necessarily a healthy development. In overall terms, the positive effects of gender on household food security are highly contingent on the flow of migrants' remittances, and their intersection with household arrangements.

KEY FINDINGS, POLICY RELEVANCE
AND FUTURE RESEARCH

These findings point to a number of issues of broader policy significance.

First, attention needs to be given to the empirical insights on how institutional arrangements on social protection relate to household food security and migration. The evidence from the villages in western Bihar shows that although households' decisions to migrate were not always guided by their inability to access social protection, it nonetheless further aggravated their vulnerability to food insecurity. It is important to emphasise that the issue of food-based safety nets is of contemporary significance in India. As noted in Chapter 1, in 2013 the GoI passed the right-to-food legislation to address the problem of chronic food insecurity. One of the most important features of this legislation is that it establishes a constitutional right of the country's marginalised populations to subsidised food through the existing PDS. However, the past history of leakages in the existing PDS means that different Indian states are experimenting to improve its operational efficiency. The food security legislation also stipulates reforming the PDS to honour the beneficiaries' food entitlements. Some influential commentators in India have argued that efficiency gains would be optimised if the in-kind food provisioning through the PDS was replaced with coupons or direct cash transfers, which can help eliminate pilferage, save costs and empower beneficiaries (Basu, 2011; Kotwal, Ramaswami and Murugkar, 2011; Gangopadhyay, Lensink and Yadav, 2012), and the proposed reforms in the right-to-food law include introducing food coupons and cash-transfer schemes (Government of India, 2013a). In these contexts, this book draws on field evidence to assess the coupon reforms in Bihar to engage and inform this larger national debate on the right to food (also see Choithani and Pritchard, 2015). The PDS basket in Bihar includes subsidised food rations and kerosene. As the discussion in Chapter 5 has highlighted, a rather confounding finding that emerges from the primary survey data is that incidence of pilferage for food grains is higher than for kerosene despite the fact that the latter is a more profitable item to pilfer. An important difference is that while the subsidised food grains are only available to selected households from marginalised socio-economic backgrounds, kerosene is available to all households. These differences suggest that perhaps the universality in kerosene distribution helps induce a local politics of the PDS in which there is a less scope to suppress the rights of disadvantaged populations. Drèze and Sen (2011), drawing from the Tamil Nadu case, argue that universality in PDS entitlements, despite its obvious higher initial costs, ultimately generated budgetary and public efficiencies because of its role in eliminating the potential for inclusion and exclusion errors. The primary evidence from western Bihar reinforces these arguments by calling attention to the capacity for universality to help instigate a local politics in which the improved PDS delivery is an issue of common concern across class and caste constituencies. From the perspective of the migration–food security relationship, the improved food-based social protection can act as an effective supplement, if not a substitute, to migration to support rural livelihood systems and vulnerable households' efforts to improve their lot in the long run.

Second, it is clear that decreasing returns from land-based livelihoods are leading to remittances becoming increasingly crucial to rural households' income portfolios. In terms of the impact of remittances on food security, the evidence presented in Chapter 7 shows that migrants' remittances had a generally positive impact on the food security of the household members in Siwan. Indeed, the food security of surveyed migrant households was highly dependent on remittances from the migrant members. Remittances equipped most households with the purchasing power to source food needs from the markets. Across the different categories of land size, assets, caste and class, the households with migrant members had invariably better food security outcomes than the non-migrant households. A recent study in India, which used nationally representative NSS data, corroborates this finding: it showed that 8 per cent of households in the country received remittances from their domestic migrant members, and food expenditure was the leading usage of remittances, with over 75 per cent of these remittance-receiving households spending migration receipts on food (Mahapatro et al., 2017). Systematic evidence on domestic remittances and food security in the contexts of developing countries is scarce. But in the wake of evidence on the rising levels of rural outmigration in many developing countries (Deshingkar and Grimm, 2005; World Bank, 2009; UNDP, 2009; Meng, 2012; Rigg, Salamanca and Parnwell, 2012; Cole and Rigg, 2019; Bryceson and Jamal, 2018; Choithani, Van Duijne and Nijman, 2021), these findings suggest that the aim of the development policy must be to recognise that remittances can, and indeed do, play a potentially important role in improving food access among vulnerable rural households.

Third, beyond the immediate impact of remittances in providing cash to rural households to meet their food needs, the evidence in this study also suggests that they allowed several rural households to invest in land and agriculture at their places of origin. Seen this way, the relationship between migration and landholding was mutually reinforcing. Land-poverty pushed households to engage in migration, but remittances allowed the households to maintain and, in a few cases, improve their landholdings at the place of origin and also provided the money to pursue farming, with the overall effect being that it strengthened the own-production food entitlements of households. Importantly, the rising significance of non-local, migration incomes notwithstanding, rural households' attachments with their land remain intact. The precarious jobs in the urban informal sector only increased the importance of land in rural lives, and it is viewed as a long-term safety net. Furthermore, and this is important, higher urban incomes were purposely recycled by some households into land and agriculture to derive better income gains from farming. The wider significance of these findings is that they suggest that the dynamics of rural livelihoods often involve these backward–forward linkages between farm and non-farm sectors, and, in turn, they warrant the need for rural livelihood analysis to take into account these linkages rather than what the simple thesis of deagrarianisation permits.

Fourth, the primary research findings also point to the intensification of sharecropping arrangements in the case-study villages in Siwan, which have important caste dynamics. Some households, particularly the forward-caste landlords, are increasingly withdrawing from direct farming and instead leasing out land to the landless and land-poor families, particularly belonging to the historically disadvantaged communities of the Scheduled Castes and Scheduled Tribes. These have important implications for the food security of the latter groups. The field evidence suggests that although their access to land remains precarious and sharecropping arrangements are exploitative, it nonetheless provides these vulnerable rural households important supplementary means to partially meet their food needs. Moreover, these arrangements have particular relevance in the wake of high food-price volatility that has characterised the global food system after the 2007–08 food-price crisis. There is ample evidence in the survey and related fieldwork that sharecropping farming reduced, in a relative sense, the landless and land-poor households' dependence on market-purchases of food and, in turn, their vulnerability to food shocks. However, because the average size of land leased in was too small for most households, they needed additional supplementary income streams. These findings call for more research on these dynamics, particularly in rural settings where there are similar land and caste dynamics but landholdings are relatively bigger in size, to evaluate the bearing of these arrangements on the disadvantaged rural populations' food security.

The fifth key finding pertains to mediating effects of gender on household food security. The stronghold of traditional gender norms that place restrictions on the mobility of women in many parts of India and, indeed, in much of South Asia, means that migration is predominantly undertaken by men while women stay behind to look after the family and resources. This phenomenon of left-behind women has important implications for household food security. The evidence presented in this book demonstrates that migration of men transforms gender relations and contributes to increased presence of women in affairs within and outside the household. In the absence of men, women proactively participate in household affairs, including the management of household finances. While the evidence suggests that women prioritise expenses on food, and improved female autonomy is associated with increased household food expenditure, the widespread gender discrimination means that the positive effects of increased women's autonomy are not fully realised. This is an important finding and warrants a need to better understand and address the gender-based vulnerability to food insecurity facing households headed by left-behind women. Indeed, many poor women face an uphill battle to avail the benefits of various government welfare programmes on account of their gender. Importantly, the left-behind women are becoming increasingly more vocal about wanting to control their husband's earnings. In turn, this is leading to households becoming more nuclearised. The effects of these changes on household food security are not very clear. However, given that the urban earnings of their husbands are precarious (significant though) and gender discrimination is widespread, the erosion of economic and social support provided by the joint families would probably have negative implications for the food security of left-behind women and their children. More research is needed on this phenomenon.

As a final set of observations, the relationship between household food security and migration would assume much greater significance in the context of climate change. Climate change would likely exert further negative effects on the already fragile farm-dependent livelihoods because of heightened flood risks and forecasted higher incidences of temperature spikes. In turn, this would exacerbate the vulnerability of poor populations to food insecurity. Climatic change would affect the rural poor's food security directly through reduction in crop yields and impacts on livelihoods, as well as indirectly through increased food prices (IPCC, 2014). Rural populations in many tropical countries, including India, are particularly vulnerable to climate-induced food insecurity because of high exposure to climate risks and low adaptive capacity (Ericksen et al., 2011). There is growing evidence that migration already represents an increasingly important adaptation strategy by rural households in the developing world to deal with climate-related hazards, though migration decisions remain complex (Dun, 2011, 2014; Jülich, 2011; Wodon et al., 2014; Singh et al., 2018; Maharjan et al., 2020). As climate change's adverse impacts on rural livelihoods intensify, seasonal and long-term migration would become *necessary* for livelihood sustainability in many parts of the developing world (World Bank, 2018). There is thus a pressing need to better integrate migration and food security agendas in development research and practice.

REFERENCES

Abraham, V. (2017). 'Stagnant Employment Growth. Last Three Years May Have Been the Worst'. *Economic and Political Weekly* 52(38): 13–17.

Adams, R. H. (1991). 'The Economic Uses and Impact of International Remittances in Rural Egypt'. *Economic Development and Cultural Change* 39(4): 695–722.

Agarwal, B. (1994). *A Field of One's Own: Gender and Land Rights in South Asia.* Cambridge, MA: Cambridge University Press.

Ahluwalia, M. S. (1978). 'Rural Poverty and Agricultural Performance in India'. *Journal of Development Studies* 14(3): 298–323.

Ahmad, E. (1961). 'The Rural Population of Bihar'. *Geographical Review* 51(2): 253–76.

Ahmed, S. (2020). 'Women Left Behind: Migration, Agency, and the Pakistani Woman'. *Gender and Society* 34(4): 597–619.

Alderman, H. (1986). *Effect of Food Price and Income Changes on the Acquisition of Food by Low-Income Households.* Washington, DC: International Food Policy Research Institute. http://ageconsearch.umn.edu/bitstream/42910/2/The%20Food%20price%20and%20income%20changes.pdf. Accessed on 7 April 2020.

Alkire, S. (2002). *Valuing Freedoms: Sen's Capability Approach and Poverty Reduction.* Oxford: Oxford University Press.

Alkire, S., U. Kanagaratnam and N. Suppa (2021). *The Global Multidimensional Poverty Index (MPI) 2021: MPI Results by Subnational Regions.* OPHI MPI Methodological Notes 51. Oxford: Oxford Poverty and Human Development Initiative, University of Oxford.

Alston, M., and B. Akhter (2016). 'Gender and Food Security in Bangladesh: The Impact of Climate Change'. *Gender, Place and Culture* 23(10): 1450–64.

Arnold, F., S. Parasuraman, P. Arokiaswamy and M. Kothari (2009). *Nutrition in India: National Family Health Survey III (2005–06), India.* Mumbai: International Institute for Population Sciences.

Arokiasamy, P., and S. Goli (2012). 'Explaining the Skewed Child Sex Ratio in Rural India: Revisiting the Landholding-Patriarchy Hypothesis'. *Economic and Political Weekly* 47(42): 85–94.

Avsm, Y. S., N. Gandhi, B. N. Tandon and K. S. Krishnamurthy (1995). 'Integrated Child Development Services Scheme and Nutritional Status of Indian Children'. *Journal of Tropical Pediatrics* 41(2): 123–28.

Azam, M. (2012). 'The Impact of Indian Job Guarantee Scheme on Labor Market Outcomes: Evidence from a Natural Experiment'. IZA Discussion Paper No. 6548, May. Institute of Labor Economics, Bonn, Germany. http://ftp.iza.org/dp6548.pdf. Accessed on 6 July 2020.

Azzarri, C., and A. Zezza (2011). 'International Migration and Nutritional Outcomes in Tajikistan'. *Food Policy* 36(1): 54–70.

Badiani, R. (2011). 'Temporary and Permanent Migration in Six Villages in the Semi-Arid Tropics'. Research Bulletin No. 22. International Crops Research Institute for the Semi-Arid Tropics, Andhra Pradesh.

Bakshi, S., A. Chawla and M. Shah (2015). 'Regional Disparities in India: A Moving frontier'. *Economic and Political Weekly* 50(1): 44–52.

Balakrishnan, S. (2003). 'Move on Hawking Zones Slammed'. *Times of India*, 15 October. http://timesofindia.indiatimes.com/city/mumbai/Move-on-hawking-zones-slammed/articleshow/233679.cms. Accessed on 13 March 2020.

Balla, S., S. Goli, S. Vedantam and A. Rammohan (2021). 'Progress in Child Stunting across the World from 1990 to 2015: Testing the Global Convergence Hypothesis'. *Public Health Nutrition* 24(17): 5598–5607.

Bandyopadhyay, D. (2008). *Report of the Bihar Land Reforms Commission*, vol. 1. Patna: Government of Bihar.

———. (2009). 'Lost Opportunity in Bihar'. *Economic and Political Weekly* 44(47): 12–14.

Banerjee, A., and L. Iyer (2005). 'History, Institutions, and Economic Performance: The Legacy of Colonial Land Tenure Systems in India'. *American Economic Review* 95(4): 1190–1213.

Banerjee, A., and E. Duflo (2011). *Poor Economics: Rethinking Poverty and Ways to End it*. Noida: Random House.

Banerjee, D. (2022). 'Regional Divergence in Farmers' Suicides'. In *Dynamics of Difference: Inequality and Transformation in Rural India*, edited by N. Pani, pp. 164–76. London and New York: Routledge.

Banik, D. (2007). *Starvation and India's Democracy*. Oxon: Routledge.

Bardhan, P. (1974). 'On Life and Death Questions'. *Economic and Political Weekly* 9(32–34): 1293–1304.

Barrett, C. B., T. Reardon and P. Webb (2001). 'Nonfarm Income Diversification and Household Livelihood Strategies in Rural Africa: Concepts, Dynamics, and Policy Implications'. *Food Policy* 26(4): 315–31.

Basu, A. M. (1993). 'How Pervasive Are Sex Differentials in Childhood Nutritional Levels in South Asia?' *Biodemography and Social Biology* 40(1–2): 25–37.

Basu, D., and A. Basole (2012). 'The Calorie Consumption Puzzle in India: An Empirical Investigation'. PERI-UMASS Working Paper 285, https://peri.umass.edu/publication/item/476-the-calorie-consumption-puzzle-in-india-an-empirical-investigation. Accessed on 20 August 2020.

Basu, K. (2011). 'India's Foodgrain Policy: An Economic Theory Perspective'. *Economic and Political Weekly* 46(5): 37–46.

———. (2013). 'The Bihar Economy: An Overview and Some Field Notes'. In *The New Bihar: Rekindling Governance and Development*, edited by N. K. Singh and N. Stern, pp. 9–19. Noida: HarperCollins Publishers India.

Bell, C., and R. Rich (1994). 'Rural Poverty and Aggregate Agricultural Performance in Post-Indepdence India'. *Oxford Bulletin of Economics and Statistics* 56(2): 111–33.

Bhaduri, A. (1976). 'The Evolution of Land Relations in Eastern India under British Rule'. *Indian Economic Social History Review* 13(1): 45–53.

Bhagat, R. B. (2012). 'A Turnaround in India's Urbanization'. *Asia–Pacific Population Journal* 27(2): 23–39.

Bhalla, S. (1993). 'Patterns of Employment Generation'. *Indian Journal of Labour Economics* 39(1): 1–12.

Bhat, G. S. (2006). 'The Indian Drought of 2002: A Sub-Seasonal Phenomenon?' *Quarterly Journal of the Royal Meteorological Society* 132(621): 2583–2602.

Bhattacharya, B. B., and S. Sakthivel (2004). 'Economic Reforms and Jobless Growth in India'. Working Paper Series No. E/245/2004, Institute of Economic Growth, Delhi. http://iegindia.org/upload/publication/Workpap/wp245.pdf. Accessed on 29 August 2022.

Bigsten, A. (1996). 'The Circular Migration of Smallholders in Kenya'. *Journal of African Economies* 5(1): 1–20.

Borah, P. (2012). 'Assamese Singer Kalpana Patowary Resurrects Bhojpuri Shakespeare'. Eastern Fare Music Foundation. http://www.easternfare. in/2012/06/assamese-singer-kalpana-patowary.html. Accessed on 22 December 2020.

Borooah, V. K., and A. Dubey (2007). 'Measuring Regional Backwardness: Poverty, Gender and Children in the Districts of India'. *Journal of Applied Economic Research* 1(4): 403–40.

Bose, A. (2000). 'North–South Divide in India's Demographic Scene'. *Economic and Political Weekly* 35(20): 1698–1700.

Boserup, E. (1965). *The Conditions of Agricultural Growth: The Economics of Agrarian Change under Population Pressure*. New York: Aldine Publishing Company.

———. (1970). *Woman's Role in Economic Development*. London: George Allen and Unwin Ltd.

———. (1981). *Population and Technology*. Oxford: Basil Blackwell.

Brass, P. R. (1986). 'The Political Uses of Crisis: The Bihar Famine of 1966–1967'. *Journal of Asian Studies* 45(2): 245–67.

Breman, J. (1985). *Of Peasants, Migrants and Paupers: Rural Labour Circulation and Capitalist Production in West India*. New Delhi: Oxford University Press.

———. (1996). *Footloose Labour: Working in India's Informal Economy*. Cambridge: Cambridge University Press.

———. (2007). *Poverty Regime in Village India: Half a Century of Work and Life at the Bottom of the Rural Economy in South Gujarat*. New Delhi: Oxford University Press.

———. (2010). *Outcast Labour in Asia: Circulation and Informalization of the Workforce at the Bottom of the Economy*. Oxford: Oxford University Press.

Brenner, N., and C. Schmid (2014). 'The "Urban Age" in Question'. *International Journal of Urban and Regional Research* 38(3): 731–55.

———. (2015). 'Towards a New Epistemology of the Urban?' *City* 19(2–3): 151–82.

Bryceson, D. F. (1997). 'De-agrarianisation in Sub-Saharan Africa: Acknowledging the Inevitable'. In *Farewell to Farms: Deagrarianisation and Employment in Africa*, edited by D. F. Bryceson and V. Jamal, pp. 3–20. Aldershot: Ashgate.

———. (2002). 'The Scramble in Africa: Reorienting Rural Livelihoods'. *World Development* 30(5): 725–39.

Bryceson, D. F., and V. Jamal (eds.). (2018). *Farewell to Farms: De-agrarianisation and Employment in Africa*. Oxon: Routledge.

Buvinić, M., and G. R. Gupta (1997). 'Female-Headed Households and Female-Maintained Families: Are They Worth Targeting to Reduce Poverty in Developing Countries?' *Economic Development and Cultural Change* 45(2): 259–80.

Care India (2012). *Prioritizing Nutrition in India, The Silent Emergency: A Strategy for Commitment Building and Advocacy.* New Delhi: Care India.

Castaldo, A., P. Deshingkar and A. McKay (2012). 'Internal Migration, Remittances and Poverty: Evidence from Ghana and India'. Working Paper 7, Migrating Out of Poverty Research Programme Consortium, University of Sussex, Brighton. http://www.migratingoutofpoverty.org/files/file.php?name=wp7-internal-migration-remittances-and-poverty.pdf&site=354. Accessed on 2 December 2019.

Census of India (1981). *District Census Handbook 1981 (Siwan District).* Patna: Directorate of Census Operations, Bihar.

——— (1991a). *Final Population Totals*, Series 1, Paper 2 of 1992. New Delhi: Registrar General and Census Commissioner of India.

——— (1991b). *Primary Census Abstract (Series 1, Part 1).* New Delhi: Registrar General and Census Commissioner of India.

——— (2001a). *Data Highlights: Migration Tables (D1, D2 and D3 Tables).* New Delhi: Registrar General and Census Commissioner of India. https://censusindia.gov.in/Data_Products/Data_Highlights/Data_Highlights_link/data_highlights_D1D2D3.pdf. Accessed on 7 July 2014.

——— (2001b). *Migration Tables (D-series).* New Delhi: Registrar General and Census Commissioner of India. Accessed through CD-ROM.

——— (2001c). *Primary Census Abstract.* New Delhi: Registrar General and Census Commissioner of India. http://www.censusindia.gov.in. Accessed on 28 March 2014.

——— (2001d). *Provisional Population Totals: Sex Composition of the Population.* New Delhi: Registrar General and Census Commissioner of India. https://censusindia.gov.in/Data_Products/Library/Provisional_Population_Total_link/PDF_Links/chapter6.pdf. Accessed on 25 July 2014.

——— (2001e). *Sample Registration System Bulletin*, 35(2) (October 2001). New Delhi: Registrar General and Census Commissioner of India. https://www.censusindia.gov.in/vital_statistics/SRS_Bulletins/SRS_Bulletins_links/Bulletin_2001_Vol_35_No_2.pdf. Accessed on 3 February 2015.

——— (2011a). *Concepts and Definitions, Census 2011: Online Metadata.* New Delhi: Registrar General and Census Commissioner of India. http://www.censusindia.gov.in/. Accessed on 9 May 2014.

———— (2011c). *Primary Census Abstract*. New Delhi: Registrar General and Census Commissioner of India. http://www.censusindia.gov.in. Accessed on 17 July 2020.

———— (2011d). *Provisional Population Totals for Bihar*. Patna: Office of the Director of Census Operations. http://censusindia.gov.in/2011-prov-results/data_files/bihar/Provisional%20Population%20Totals%202011-Bihar.pdf. Accessed on 30 May 2014.

———— (2011e). *Provisional Population Totals: Urban Agglomerations and Cities (Paper 2)*. New Delhi: Registrar General and Census Commissioner of India. https://censusindia.gov.in/2011-prov-results/paper2/data_files/India2/1.%20Data%20Highlight.pdf. Accessed on 5 February 2015.

———— (2011f). *Rural–Urban Distribution of Population*. New Delhi: Registrar General and Census Commissioner of India. http://censusindia.gov.in/2011-prov-results/paper2/data_files/india/Rural-UrbanDataSheets_paper2.pdf. Accessed on 2 April 2014.

———— (2011g). *Sample Registration System Bulletin*, 46(1) (December 2011). New Delhi: Registrar General and Census Commissioner of India. http://www.censusindia.gov.in/vital_statistics/SRS_Bulletins/SRS_Bulletin_December_2011.pdf. Accessed on 3 February 2015.

———— (2011h). *Single-Year Age Returns by Residence and Sex, 2011 Census*. New Delhi: Registrar General and Census Commissioner of India. http://www.censusindia.gov.in/. Accessed on 19 January 2020.

Chakravarti, A. (2001). 'Caste and Agrarian Class'. *Economic and Political Weekly* 36(17): 1449–62.

Chakrabarti, S., K. Raghunathan, H. Alderman, P. Menon and P. Nguyen (2019). 'India's Integrated Child Development Services Programme: Equity and Extent of Coverage in 2006 and 2016'. *Bulletin of the World Health Organization* 97(4): 270–82.

Chambers, R. (1983). *Rural Development: Putting the Last First*. Essex: Pearson Education Limited.

Chambers, R., and G. R. Conway (1991). 'Sustainable Rural Livelihoods: Practical Concepts for the 21st Century'. Discussion Paper 296, Institute of Development Studies, Brighton.

Chatterjee, P. (2004): *The Politics of the Governed: Reflections on Popular Politics in Most of the World*. New York: Columbia University Press.

Chaudhary, P. (2016). 'Maximum Remittances from Gulf in Bihar's Siwan and Gopalganj'. *Times of India*, 3 April. https://timesofindia.indiatimes.

com/city/patna/Maximum-remittances-from-Gulf-in-Bihars-Siwan-and-Gopalganj-districts/articleshow/51671720.cms. Accessed on 9 April 2020.

Chaudhuri, S., and N. Gupta (2009). 'Levels of Living and Poverty Patterns: A District-Wise Analysis for India'. *Economic and Political Weekly* 44(9): 94–110.

Choithani, C. (2009). *Entry of Corporate Retail and Its Impacts on Hawkers and Small Retailers: A Case Study from Mumbai*. Mumbai: Focus on the Global South.

Choithani, C., and B. Pritchard (2015). 'Assessing Bihar's Coupon-Based PDS: Importance of Local Context'. *Economic and Political Weekly* 50(3): 61–68.

Choithani, C., R. J. van Duijne and J. Nijman (2021). 'Changing Livelihoods at India's Rural–Urban Transition'. *World Development* 146: 1–17. https://doi.org/10.1016/j.worlddev.2021.105617. Accessed on 20 August 2021.

Christiaensen, L., L. Demery and J. Kuhl (2010). 'The (Evolving) Role of Agriculture in Poverty Reduction: An Empirical Perspective'. UNU-Wider Working Paper 36, United Nations University's World Institute for Development Economics Research, Helsinki.

Cole, R., and J. Rigg (2019). 'Lao Peasants on the Move: Pathways of Agrarian Change in Laos'. *Australian Journal of Anthropology* 30(2): 160–80.

Connell, J., B. Dasgupta, R. Laishley and M. Lipton (1976). *Migration from Rural Areas: The Evidence from Village Studies*. New Delhi: Oxford University Press.

Corbett, J. (1988). 'Famine and Household Coping Strategies'. *World Development* 16(9): 1099–1112.

Craven, L. K., and H. M. Gartuala (2015). 'Conceptualising the Migration–Food-Security Nexus: Lessons from Nepal and Vanavatu'. *Australian Geographer* 46(4): 455–71.

Crush, J. (2013). 'Linking Food Security, Migration and Development'. *International Migration* 51(5): 61–75.

Crush, J., and M. Caesar (2017). 'Introduction: Cultivating the Migration–Food-Security Nexus'. *International Migration* 55(4): 10–17.

Das Gupta, M. (1987). 'Selective Discrimination against Female Children in Rural Punjab, India'. *Population and Development Review* 13(1): 77–100.

———. (2005). 'Explaining Asia's "Missing Women": A New Look at the Data'. *Population and Development Review* 31(3): 529–35.

Dasgupta, D., P. Maiti, R. Mukherjee, S. Sarkar and S. Chakrabarti (2000). 'Growth and Interstate Disparities in India'. *Economic and Political Weekly* 35(27): 2413–22.

Datt, G., and M. Ravallion (2011). 'Has India's Economic Growth Become More Pro-Poor in the Wake of Economic Reforms?' *World Bank Economic Review* 25(2): 157–89.

Datt, G., M. Ravallion and R. Murgai (2020). 'Poverty and Growth in India over Six Decades'. *American Journal of Agricultural Economics* 102(1): 4–27.

Datta, A. (2016). 'Migration, Remittances and Changing Sources of Income in Rural Bihar (1999–2011).' *Economic and Political Weekly* 51(31): 85–93.

Datta, A., G. Rodgers, J. Rodgers and B. Singh (2014). 'Contrasts in Development in Bihar: A Tale of Two Villages'. *Journal of Development Studies* 50(9): 1197–1208.

de Brauw, A. (2011). 'Migration and Child Development during the Food Price Crisis in El Salvador'. *Food Policy* 36(1): 28–40.

de Brauw, A., and R. Mu (2011). 'Migration and the Overweight and Underweight Status of Children in Rural China'. *Food Policy* 36(1): 88–100.

de Haan, A. (1997a). 'Migration as Family Strategy: Rural–Urban Labour Migration in India during the Twentieth Century'. *History of Family* 2(4): 481–505.

———. (1997b). 'Unsettled Settlers: Migrant Workers and Industrial Capitalism in Calcutta'. *Modern Asian Studies* 31(4): 919–49.

———. (1999). 'Livelihoods and Poverty: The Role of Migration – A Critical Review of the Migration Literature'. *Journal of Development Studies* 36(2): 1–47.

———. (2002). 'Migration and Livelihoods in Historical Perspective: A Case Study of Bihar, India'. *Journal of Development Studies* 38(5): 115–42.

de Haan, A., K. Brock and N. Coulibaly (2002). 'Migration, Livelihoods and Institutions: Contrasting Patterns of Migration in Mali'. *Journal of Development Studies* 38(5): 37–58.

de Waal, A. (2015). 'Armed Conflict and the Challenge of Hunger: Is an End in Sight?' In *Global Hunger Index: Armed Conflict and the Challenge of Hunger*, edited by K. von Grebmer, J. Bernstein, N. Prasai, S. Yin and Y. Yohannes, pp. 23–29. Washington, DC: International Food Policy Research Institute.

Deaton, A., and J. Drèze (2002). 'Poverty and Inequality in India: A Re-Examination'. *Economic and Political Weekly* 37(36): 3729–48.

——— (2009). 'Food and Nutrition in India: Facts and Interpretations'. *Economic and Political Weekly* 44(7): 42–65.

Debroy, B., and L. Bhandari (eds.) (2003). *District-level Deprivation in the New Millennium*. New Delhi: Konark Publishers.

Deccan Herald (2010). 'Nitish Kumar Threatened for Wanting to Protect Sharecroppers'. 19 February. https://www.deccanherald.com/content/53604/ nitish-kumar-threatened-wanting-protect.html. Accessed on 18 June 2020.

Desai, S., and M. Banerji (2008). 'Negotiated Identities: Male Migration and Left-Behind Wives in India'. *Journal of Population Research* 25(3): 337–55.

Desai, M. (2013). 'Equity, Growth and Governance: The Bihar Story'. In *The New Bihar: Rekindling Governance and Development*, edited by N. K. Singh and N. Stern, pp. 69–78. Noida: HarperCollins Publishers India.

De Schutter, O. (2012). *A Rights Revolution: Implementing the Right to Food in Latin America and the Caribbean*. Briefing Note 6, September. Olivier De Schutter, UN Special Rapporteur (2008–2014). http://www.srfood.org/ images/stories/pdf/otherdocuments/note06-septembre2012-en-v2.pdf. Accessed on 27 March 2014.

Deshingkar, P., and S. Akhter (2009). 'Migration and Human Development in India'. Human Development Research Paper 2009/13. United Nations Development Programme, New York. http://hdr.undp.org/sites/default/ files/hdrp_2009_13.pdf. Accessed on 1 April 2014.

Deshingkar, P., and E. Anderson (2004). 'People on the Move: New Policy Challenges for Increasingly Mobile Populations'. Working Paper 92, Overseas Development Institute, London.

Deshingkar, P., and J. Farrington (2009). *Circular Migration and Multilocational Livelihood Strategies in Rural India*. New Delhi: Oxford University Press.

Deshingkar, P., and S. Grimm (2005). 'Internal Migration and Development: A Global Perspective'. IOM Migration Research Series Paper 19. Geneva: International Organisation for Migration.

Deshingkar, P., S. Kumar, H. K. Choubey and D. Kumar (2009). 'Circular Migration in Bihar: The Money Order Economy'. In *Circular Migration and Multilocational Livelihood Strategies in Rural India*, edited by P. Deshingkar and J. Farrington, pp. 139–76. New Delhi: Oxford University Press.

Devereux, S. (2009). 'Why Does Famine Persist in Africa?' *Food Security* 1(1): 25–35.

DFID (2001). *DFID Sustainable Livelihoods Guidance Sheets*. London: Department for International Development. https://www.livelihoodscentre.org/ documents/114097690/114438878/Sustainable+livelihoods+guidance+ sheets.pdf/594e5ea6-99a9-2a4e-f288-cbb4ae4bea8b?t=1569512091877. Accessed on 17 February 2021.

——— (2007). 'Moving Out of Poverty: Making Migration Work Better for Poor People'. London: Department of International Development. http://

www.sussex.ac.uk/Units/SCMR/drc/publications/other_publications/
Moving_Out_of_Poverty.pdf. Accessed on 17 February 2021.

Drèze, J. (2004). 'Democracy and Right to Food'. *Economic and Political Weekly* 39(17): 1723–31.

Drèze, J., and R. Khera (2010). 'The BPL Census and a Possible Alternative'. *Economic and Political Weekly* 45(9): 54–63.

———— (2012). 'Regional Patterns of Human and Child Deprivation in India'. *Economic and Political Weekly* 47(39): 42–49.

———— (2014). 'Water for the Leeward India'. *Outlook*, 24 March. https://www.outlookindia.com/magazine/story/water-for-the-leeward-india/289801. Accessed on 5 March 2020.

———— (2017). 'Recent Social Security Initiatives in India'. *World Development* 98: 555–72.

Drèze, J., and C. Oldiges (2011). 'NREGA: The Official Picture'. In *The Battle for Employment Guarantee*, edited by R. Khera, pp. 21–39. New Delhi: Oxford University Press.

———— (2011). 'Putting Growth in Its Place'. *Outlook India*, 14 November. https://www.outlookindia.com/magazine/story/putting-growth-in-its-place/278843. Accessed on 11 October 2021.

———— (2013). *An Uncertain Glory: India and Its Contradictions*. London: Allen Lane.

Drèze, J., R. Khera and J. Pudussery (2015). 'Food Security: Bihar on the Move'. *Economic and Political Weekly* 50(34): 44–52.

Drèze, J., P. Gupta, R. Khera and I. Pimenta (2019). 'Casting the Net: India's Public Distribution System after the Food Security Act'. *Economic and Political Weekly* 54(6): 36–47.

Duflo, E., and C. Udry (2004). 'Intrahousehold Resource Allocation in Cote d'Ivore: Social Norms, Seperate Accounts and Consumption Choices'. NBER Working Paper 10498, National Bureau of Economic Research, Cambridge, MA. http://www.nber.org/papers/w10498.pdf. Accessed on 7 September 2021.

Dun, O. (2011). 'Migration and Displacement Triggered by Floods in the Mekong Delta'. *International Migration* 49(s1): e200–e223. DOI: 10.1111/j.1468-2435.2010.00646.x.

————. (2014). 'Shrimp, Salt and Livelihoods: Migration in the Mekong Delta, Vietnam'. PhD thesis in Human Geography. University of Sydney.

Dutta, P., R. Murgai, M. Ravallion and D. van de Walle (2012a). 'Does India's Employment Guarantee Scheme Guarantee Employment?' *Economic and Political Weekly* 47(16): 55–64.

——— (2012b). 'Rozgar Guarantee? Assessing India's Biggest Anti-Poverty Program in India's Poorest State'. Presentation organised by the Social Protection Group, World Bank, Washigton, DC, April 2012. http:// siteresources.worldbank.org/SAFETYNETSANDTRANSFERS/ Resources/281945-1131468287118/BREGS.pdf. Accessed on 6 August 2014.

Dutta, S. (2014). 'Tribe Has Been Reporting Similar Child Deaths for Over a Decade'. *Indian Express*, 23 September. http://indianexpress.com/article/ india/india-others/tribe-has-been-reporting-similar-child-deaths-for-over- a-decade-2/99/. Accessed on 27 January 2015.

Ellis, F. (1998). 'Household Strategies and Rural Livelihood Diversification'. *Journal of Development Studies* 35(1): 1–38.

———. (2000a). 'The Determinants of Rural Livelihood Diversification in Developing Countries'. *Journal of Agricultural Economics* 51(2): 289–302.

———. (2000b). *Rural Livelihoods and Diversity in Developing Countries*. Oxford: Oxford University Press.

Elmhirst, R. (2002). 'Daughters and Displacement: Migration Dynamics in an Indonesian Transmigration Area'. *Journal of Development Studies* 38(5): 143–66.

Engle, P. (1988). 'Women-Headed Families in Guatemala: Consequences for Children', in *The Determinants and Consequences of Female-Headed Households* (notes from seminars 1 and 2). Washington DC: Population Council and International Center for Research on Women.

Epstein, T. S. (1973). *South India: Yesterday, Today and Tomorrow – Mysore Villages Revisited*. London: Macmillan.

Ericksen, P., P. Thornton, A. Notenbaert, L. Cramer, P. Jones and M. Herrero (2011). *Mapping Hotspots of Climate Change and Food Insecurity in the Global Tropics*. CCAFS Report No. 5. CGIAR Research Program on Climate Change, Agriculture and Food Security. Copenhagen, Denmark: CCAFS. http://ccafs.cgiar.org/publications/mapping-hotspots-climate- change-and-food-insecurity-global-tropics. Accessed on 11 November 2021.

FAO (2000). *The State of Food Insecurity in the World: When People Live with Hunger and Fear Starvation*. Rome: Food and Agriculture Organization.

——— (2003a). *The State of Food Insecurity in the World: Monitoring Progress towards the World Food Summit and Millennium Development Goals*. Rome: Food and Agriculture Organization.

——— (2003b). 'Trade Reforms and Food Insecurity: Conceptualising the Linkages'. Rome: Food and Agriculture Organization.

——— (2005). *Voluntary Guidelines to Support the Progressive Realisation of the Right to Adequate Food in the Context of National Food Security*. Rome: Food and Agriculture Organization.

——— (2006). *Food Security*. Policy Brief 2 (June 2006). Rome: Food and Agriculture Organization. http://www.fao.org/forestry/13128-0e6f36f27e0 091055bec28ebe830f46b3.pdf. Accessed on 1 January 2020.

——— (2009). *The State of Food Insecurity in the World: Economic Crises – Impacts and Lessons Learned*. Rome: Food and Agriculture Organization.

——— (2010). *The State of Food Insecurity in the World: Addressing Food Insecurity in Protracted Crises*. Rome: Food and Agriculture Organization.

——— (2011). *State of Food and Agriculture, 2010-11: Women in Agriculture – Closing the Gender Gap for Development*. Rome: Food and Agriculture Organization.

——— (2012). *The State of Food Insecurity in the World: Economic Growth is Necessary but Not Sufficient to Accelerate Reduction of Hunger and Malnutrition*. Rome: Food and Agriculture Organization.

——— (2013). *The State of Food and Agriculture: Food Systems for Better Nutrition*. Rome: Food and Agriculture Organization.

——— (2018). *The State of Food and Agriculture: Migration, Agriculture and Rural Development*. Rome: Food and Agriculture Organization.

——— (2019). *FAO Framework for the Urban Food Agenda*. Rome: Food and Agriculture Organization. https://www.urbanagendaplatform.org/sites/default/files/2021-03/urban-food-agenda.pdf. Accessed on 21 September 2021.

——— (2020). *World Food Situation: FAO Food Price Index*. http://www.fao.org/worldfoodsituation/foodpricesindex/en/. Accessed on 6 January 2020.

FAO, IFAD and WFP (2015). *The State of Food Insecurity in the World: Meeting the 2015 International Hunger Targets – Taking Stock of Uneven Progress*. Rome: Food and Agriculture Organization.

FAO, IFAD, UNICEF, WFP and WHO (2017). *The State of Food Security and Nutrition in the World: Building Resilience for Peace and Food Security*. Rome: Food and Agriculture Organization.

——— (2018). *The State of Food Security and Nutrition in the World: Building Climate Resilience for Food Security and Nutrition*. Rome: Food and Agriculture Organization.

——— (2019). *The State of Food Security and Nutrition in the World: Safeguarding against Economic Slowdowns and Downturns*. Rome: Food and Agriculture Organization.

————— (2020). *The State of Food and Agriculture: Transforming Food Systems for Affordable Healthy Diets*. Rome: Food and Agriculture Organization.

Fleury, A. (2016). 'Understanding Women and Migration: A Literature Review'. KNOMAD Working Paper 8, World Bank, Washington, DC. http://www.atina.org.rs/sites/default/files/KNOMAD%20Understaning%20Women%20and%20Migration.pdf. Accessed on 8 March 2021.

Foster, A. D., and M. R. Rosenzweig (2004). 'Agricultural Productivity Growth, Rural Economic Diversity, and Economic Reforms: India, 1970–2000'. *Economic Development and Cultural Change* 52(3): 509–42.

Gangopadhyay, S., R. Lensink and B. Yadav (2012). 'Cash or Food Security through the Public Distribution System? Evidence from a Randomized Control Trial in Delhi, India'. Unpublished paper. https://papers.ssrn.com/sol3/papers.cfm?abstract_id=2186408. Accessed on 16 May 2014.

Gardner, K. (1993). 'Desh-Bidesh: Sylheti Images of Home and Away'. *Man* 28(1): 1–15.

Ganguly, S., and N. S. Negi (2010). 'The Extent of Association between Husbands' Out-Migration and Decision Making Power among Left Behind Wives in Rural India'. Asia Research Institute Working Paper No. 147, Asia Research Institute, National University of Singapore. https://papers.ssrn.com/sol3/papers.cfm?abstract_id=1743932. Accessed on 12 May 2021.

Gartaula, H. N., A. Niehof and L. Visser (2010). 'Feminisation of Agriculture as an Effect of Male Out-Migration: Unexpected Outcomes from Jhapa District, Eastern Nepal'. *International Journal of Interdisciplinary Social Sciences* 5(2): 565–77.

Ghosh, S. (2006). 'Food Dole or Health, Nutrition and Development Programme?' *Economic and Political Weekly* 41(34): 3664–66.

Ghosh, M. (2012) 'Regional Economic Growth and Inequality in India during the Pre- and Post-Reform Periods'. *Oxford Development Studies* 40(2): 190–212.

Gillespie, S., and S. Kadiyala (2012). 'Exploring the Agriculture–Nutrition Disconnect in India'. In *Reshaping Agriculture for Nutrition and Health*, edited by S. Fan and R. Pandya-Lorch, pp. 173–81. Washington, DC: International Food Policy Research Institute.

Gillion, K. L. (1956). 'The Sources of Indian Emigration to Fiji'. *Population Studies* 10(2): 139–57.

Giuliano, P., and M. Ruiz-Arranz (2009). 'Remittances, Financial Development, and Growth'. *Journal of Development Economics* 90(1): 144–52.

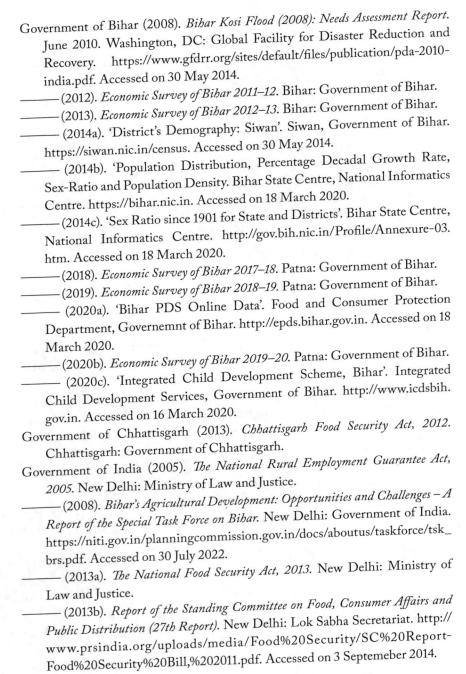

Government of Bihar (2008). *Bihar Kosi Flood (2008): Needs Assessment Report*. June 2010. Washington, DC: Global Facility for Disaster Reduction and Recovery. https://www.gfdrr.org/sites/default/files/publication/pda-2010-india.pdf. Accessed on 30 May 2014.

———(2012). *Economic Survey of Bihar 2011–12*. Bihar: Government of Bihar.

———(2013). *Economic Survey of Bihar 2012–13*. Bihar: Government of Bihar.

——— (2014a). 'District's Demography: Siwan'. Siwan, Government of Bihar. https://siwan.nic.in/census. Accessed on 30 May 2014.

——— (2014b). 'Population Distribution, Percentage Decadal Growth Rate, Sex-Ratio and Population Density. Bihar State Centre, National Informatics Centre. https://bihar.nic.in. Accessed on 18 March 2020.

———(2014c). 'Sex Ratio since 1901 for State and Districts'. Bihar State Centre, National Informatics Centre. http://gov.bih.nic.in/Profile/Annexure-03.htm. Accessed on 18 March 2020.

———(2018). *Economic Survey of Bihar 2017–18*. Patna: Government of Bihar.

———(2019). *Economic Survey of Bihar 2018–19*. Patna: Government of Bihar.

——— (2020a). 'Bihar PDS Online Data'. Food and Consumer Protection Department, Governemnt of Bihar. http://epds.bihar.gov.in. Accessed on 18 March 2020.

———(2020b). *Economic Survey of Bihar 2019–20*. Patna: Government of Bihar.

——— (2020c). 'Integrated Child Development Scheme, Bihar'. Integrated Child Development Services, Government of Bihar. http://www.icdsbih. gov.in. Accessed on 16 March 2020.

Government of Chhattisgarh (2013). *Chhattisgarh Food Security Act, 2012*. Chhattisgarh: Government of Chhattisgarh.

Government of India (2005). *The National Rural Employment Guarantee Act, 2005*. New Delhi: Ministry of Law and Justice.

——— (2008). *Bihar's Agricultural Development: Opportunities and Challenges – A Report of the Special Task Force on Bihar*. New Delhi: Government of India. https://niti.gov.in/planningcommission.gov.in/docs/aboutus/taskforce/tsk_brs.pdf. Accessed on 30 July 2022.

——— (2013a). *The National Food Security Act, 2013*. New Delhi: Ministry of Law and Justice.

——— (2013b). *Report of the Standing Committee on Food, Consumer Affairs and Public Distribution (27th Report)*. New Delhi: Lok Sabha Secretariat. http://www.prsindia.org/uploads/media/Food%20Security/SC%20Report-Food%20Security%20Bill,%202011.pdf. Accessed on 3 Septemeber 2014.

———— (2017). *Economic Survey 2016–17.* New Delhi: Department of Economic Affairs (Economic Division), Ministry of Finance.

Government of Rajasthan (2013). *State Agricultural Policy, 2013.* Jaipur: Department of Agriculture, Rajasthan.

Grantham-McGregor, S., Y. B. Cheung, S. Cueto, P. Glewwe, L. Richter, B. Strupp and International Child Development Group (2007). 'Development Potential in the First 5 Years for Children in Developing Countries'. *The Lancet* 369(9555): 60–70.

Greiner, C. (2012). 'Can Households Be Multilocal? Conceptual and Methodological Considerations Based on a Namibian Case'. *Die Erde* 143(3): 195–212.

Griffiths, P., Z. Matthews and A. Hinde (2002). 'Gender, Family, and the Nutritional Status of Children in Three Culturally Contrasting States of India'. *Social Science and Medicine* 55(5): 775–90.

Guha-Khasnobis, B., and K. S. James (2010). 'Urbanization and the South Asian Enigma: A Case Study of India'. UNU-WIDER Working Paper No. 2010/37, World Institute for Development Economics Research, United Nations University, Helsinki. https://www.wider.unu.edu/sites/default/files/wp2010-37.pdf. Accessed on 30 July 2022.

Gulati, A., and S. Saini (2015). 'Leakages from Public Distribution System (PDS) and the Way Forward'. Working Paper 294, Indian Council For Research On International Economic Relations, New Delhi.

Gulati, L. (1987). 'Coping with Male Migration'. *Economic and Political Weekly* 22(44): 41–46.

————. (1993). *In the Absence of Their Men: The Impact of Male Migration on Women.* New Delhi: SAGE Publications.

Gupta, P. N. (1923). *Final Report on the Survey and Settlement Operations in the District of Saran, 1915–1921.* Patna: Superintendent, Government Printing, Bihar and Orissa.

Gupta, S., N. Sunder and P. L. Pingali (2020). 'Are Women in Rural India Really Consuming a Less Diverse Diet?' *Food and Nutrition Bulletin* 41(3): 318–31.

Guruswamy, M., R. A. Baitha and J. P. Mohanty (2013). 'Centrally Planned Inequality: The Tale of Two States – Punjab and Bihar'. Centre for Policy Alternatives, New Delhi. http://www.scribd.com/doc/7007966/Centrally-Planned-Inequality-Punjab-Bihar. Accessed on 30 July 2022.

Guyer, J. I. (1980). 'Household Budget and Women's Income'. Working Paper 28/1980, African Studies Center, Boston University, Boston, MA.

Haddad, L., H. Alderman, S. Appleton, L. Song and Y. Yohannes (2003). 'Reducing Child Malnutrition: How Far Does Income Growth Take Us?' *World Bank Economic Review* 17(1): 107–31.

Hadi, A. (2001). 'International Migration and the Change of Women's Position among the Left-Behind in Rural Bangladesh'. *International Journal of Population Geography* 7(1): 53–61.

Hagen, J. R., and A. A. Yang (1976). 'Local Sources for the Study of Rural India: The "Village Notes" of Bihar'. *Indian Economic and Social History Review* 13(1): 75–84.

Harris, J. R., and M. P. Todaro (1970). 'Migration, Unemployment and Development: A Two-Sector Analysis'. *American Economic Review* 60(1): 126–42.

Hebinck, P. (2018). 'De-/Re-Agrarianisation: Global Perspectives'. *Journal of Rural Studies* 61: 227–35. https://doi.org/10.1016/j.jrurstud.2018.04.010. Accessed in August 2022.

Headey, D. (2011). 'Turning Economic Growth into Nutrition-Sensitive Growth'. In *Reshaping Agriculture for Nutrition and Health*, edited by S. Fan and R. Pandya-Lorch, pp. 39–46. Washington, DC: International Food Policy Research Institute.

Headey, D., A. Chiu and S. Kadiyala (2011). 'Agriculture's Role in the Indian Enigma: Help or Hindrance to the Undernutrition Crisis'. IFPRI Discussion Paper 1085. International Food Policy Research Institute, Washington, DC. https://ebrary.ifpri.org/utils/getfile/collection/p15738coll2/id/124911/filename/124912.pdf. Accessed on 30 July 2022.

Hewage, P., C. Kumara and J. Rigg (2011). 'Connecting and Disconnecting People and Places: Migrants, Migration, and the Household in Sri Lanka'. *Annals of the Association of American Geographers* 101(1): 202–19.

Hirschman, A. O. (1981). *Essays in Tresspassing: Economics to Politics and Beyond*. Cambridge, MA: Cambridge University Press.

Himanshu (2011). 'Employment Trends in India: A Reexamination'. *Economic and Political Weekly* 46(37): 43–59.

Hirway, I. (2003). 'Identification of BPL Households for Poverty Alleviation Programmes'. *Economic and Political Weekly* 38(45): 4803–08.

HLPE (2012). *Social Protection for Food Security: A Report by the High Level Panel of Experts on Food Security and Nutrition of the Committee on World Food Security*. Rome: Food and Agriculture Organization. http://www.fao.org/3/a-me422e.pdf. Accessed on 4 May 2020.

Hochschild, A., and A. Machung (2012). *The Second Shift: Working Families and the Revolution at Home.* New York: Penguin Books.

International Food Policy Research Institute (IFPRI) (2017). *Global Food Policy Report.* Washington, DC: International Food Policy Research Institute.

International Institute for Population Sciences (IIPS) (1995). *National Family Health Survey, 1992–93: India Report.* Mumbai: International Institute for Population Sciences.

IIPS and ICF International (2017a). *National Family Health Survey 2015–16: Bihar.* Mumbai: International Institute for Population Sciences.

IIPS and ICF International (2017b). *National Family Health Survey, 2015–16: India.* Mumbai: International Institute for Population Sciences.

IIPS and ICF International (2020). *National Family Health Survey 2019–20: Facts Sheets (22 States/UTs from Phase I), India.* Mumbai: International Institute for Population Sciences. http://rchiips.org/NFHS/NFHS-5_FCTS/NFHS -5%20State%20Factsheet%20Compendium_Phase-I.pdf. Accessed on 12 November 2021.

Institute of Human Development (2010). *Poverty in Bihar: Pattern, Dimensions and Eradication Strategies: A Report.* Patna: Institute of Human Development.

IOM (2013). 'IOM Position Paper for 2013 United Nations General Assembly High Level Dialogue on International Migration and Development'. Geneva: International Organization for Migration. https://www.iom. int/files/live/sites/iom/files/What-We-Do/docs/IOM-Position-Paper- HLD-en.pdf. Accessed on 30 July 2022.

——— (2015). 'Inclusion of Migration in UN Sustainable Development Goals, a Milestone'. *International Organization for Migration News*, 25 September. https://www.iom.int/news/inclusion-migration-un-sustainable- development-goals-milestone. Accessed on 30 July 2022.

——— (2020). *IOM Institutional Strategy on Migration and Sustainable Development.* Geneva: International Organization for Migration.

IPCC (2014). *Climate Change 2014: Impacts, Adaptation, and Vulnerability.* Part A: Global and Sectoral Aspects. Contribution of Working Group II to the Fifth Assessment Report of the Intergovernmental Panel on Climate Change. New York: Cambridge University Press.

Jain, M. (2015). 'India's Struggle against Malnutrition: Is the ICDS Program the Answer?' *World Development* 67: 72–89. https://doi.org/10.1016/j. worlddev.2014.10.006. Accessed in August 2022.

Jandu, N. (2008). 'Employment Guarantee and Women's Empowerment in Rural India'. Unpublished manuscript. Right to Food India. http://www.righttofoodindia.org/data/navjyoti08_employment_guarantee_and_women's_empowerment.pdf. Accessed on 4 August 2014.

Jassal, S. T. (2012). *Unearthing Gender: Folksongs of North India*. Durham, NC, and London: Duke University Press.

Jetley, S. (1987). 'Impact of Male Migration on Rural Females'. *Economic and Political Weekly* 22(44): 47–53.

Jha, M. K. (2002). 'Hunger and Starvation Deaths: Call for Public Action'. *Economic and Political Weekly* 37(52): 5159–63.

Joshi, P. K., G. Tripathi and M. Gautam (2012). 'Transforming Bihar's Agriculture: Challenges and Opportunities'. Paper presented in Global Bihar Summit 2012 Patna, Bihar, 17–19 February 2012. http://www.globalbihar.net/wp-content/uploads/2012/02/papers/pk_joshi_agri.pdf. Accessed on 3 June 2014.

Jodhka, S. S. (2014). 'Emergent Ruralities: Revisiting Village Life and Agrarian Change in Haryana'. *Economic and Political Weekly* 49(26–27): 5, 7–17.

Jülich, S. (2011). 'Drought Triggered Temporary Migration in an East Indian Village'. *International Migration* 49: e189–e199. https://doi.org/10.1111/j.1468 -2435.2010.00655.x. Accessed in August 2022.

Kar, S., and S. Sakthivel (2007). 'Reforms and Regional Inequality in India'. *Economic and Political Weekly* 42(47): 69–77.

Karmali, N. (2021). 'India's 10 Richest Billionaires 2021'. *Forbes*, 6 April. https://www.forbes.com/sites/naazneenkarmali/2021/04/06/indias-10-richest-billionaires-2021/?sh=30b046e659b7. Accessed on 12 October 2021.

Karan, A. K. (2003). 'Changing Patterns of Migration from Bihar'. In *Migrant Labour and Human Rights in India*, edited by K. G. Iyer, pp. 102–39. New Delhi: Kanishka Publishers.

Kaur, B. (2019). 'AES in Bihar: Poor Anganwadi Centres Failed to Deliver'. *Down to Earth*, 25 June. https://www.downtoearth.org.in/news/health/aes-in-bihar-poor-anganwadi-centres-failed-to-deliver-65269. Accessed on 27 September 2021.

Keshri, K., and R. B. Bhagat (2012). 'Temporary and Seasonal Migration: Regional Pattern, Characterstics and Associated Factors'. *Economic and Political Weekly* 47(4): 81–88.

Khera, R. (2008). 'Access to the Targeted Public Distribution System: A Case Study in Rajasthan'. *Economic and Political Weekly* 43(44): 51–56.

———. (2011a). 'India's Public Distribution System: Utilisation and Impact'. *Journal of Development Studies* 47(7): 1038–60.

————. (2011b). 'Revival of the Public Distribution System: Evidence and Explanations'. *Economic and Political Weekly* 46(44–45): 36–50.

————. (ed.). (2011c). *The Battle for Employment Guarantee*. New Delhi: Oxford University Press.

————. (2012). 'Revival of the PDS and the Cash Alternative'. Unpublished Presentation at the Growth Week Conference, London School of Economics, London, 24–26 September. http://www.theigc.org/sites/default/files/sessions/Reetika%20Khera_IndiaCentral_GW2012.pdf. Accessed on 12 May 2014.

King, E., and A. Mason (2001). *Engendering Development: Through Gender Equality in Rights, Resources, and Voice*. Washington DC: World Bank. https://elibrary.worldbank.org/doi/abs/10.1596/0-1952-1596-6. Accessed on 29 Decmber 2021.

Kishor, S. (1993). '"May God Give Sons to All": Gender and Child Mortality in India'. *American Sociological Review* 58(2): 247–65.

Kotwal, A., B. Ramaswami and M. Murugkar (2011). 'PDS Forever?' *Economic and Political Weekly* 46(21): 72–76.

Kujur, R. (2008). 'Naxal Movement in India: A Profile'. IPCS Research Paper No. 15. Institute of Peace and Conflict Studies, New Delhi. http://www.ipcs.org/pdf_file/issue/848082154RP15-Kujur-Naxal.pdf. Accessed on 20 June 2014.

Kundu, A. (2003). 'Urbanisation and Urban Governance: Search for a Perspective beyond Neo-Liberalism'. *Economic and Political Weekly* 38(29): 3079–87.

————. (2009). 'Exclusionary Urbanisation in Asia: A Macro Overview'. *Economic and Political Weekly* 44(48): 48–58.

————. (2011). 'Method in Madness: Urban Data from 2011 Census'. *Economic and Political Weekly* 46(40): 13–16.

————. (2014). 'Exclusionary Growth, Poverty and India's Emerging Urban Structure'. *Social Change* 44(4): 541–66.

Kurian, N. J. (2000). 'Widening Regional Disparities in India: Some Indicators'. *Economic and Political Weekly* 35(7): 538–50.

Lastarria-Cornhiel, S. (2008). 'Feminization of Agriculture: Trends and Driving Forces'. Background Paper for the *World Development Report 2008*. Washington, DC: World Bank. https://openknowledge.worldbank.org/handle/10986/9104. Accessed on 16 August 2021.

Lei, L., and S. Desai (2021). 'Male Out-Migration and the Health of Left-Behind Wives in India: The Roles of Remittances, Household Responsibilities, and

Autonomy'. *Social Science and Medicine* 280: 113982. https://doi.org/10.1016/j. socscimed.2021.113982. Accessed in August 2022.

Lerner, A. M., and H. Eakin (2011). 'An Obsolete Dichotomy? Rethinking the Rural–Urban Interface in Terms of Food Security and Production in the Global South'. *Geographical Journal* 177(4): 311–20.

Ligon, E., and E. Sadoulet (2008). 'Estimating the Effects of Aggregate Agricultural Growth on the Distribution of Expenditures'. Background Paper for the *World Development Report 2008*. Washington, DC: World Bank. https://openknowledge.worldbank.org/handle/10986/9096. Accessed on 30 July 2022.

Lipton, M. (1975). 'Urban Bias and Food Policy in Poor Countries'. *Food Policy* 1(1): 41–52.

———. (1977). *Why Poor People Stay Poor: Urban Bias in World Development*. Cambridge, MA: Harvard University Press.

———. (1980). 'Migration from Rural Areas of Poor Countries: The Impact on Rural Productivity and Income Distribution'. *World Development* 8(1): 1–24.

Lipton, M., and R. Longhurst (1989). *New Seeds and Poor People*. Baltimore: Johns Hopkins University Press.

Losada, H., H. Martínez, J. Vieyra, R. Pealing, R. Zavala and J. Cortés (1998). 'Urban Agriculture in the Metropolitan Zone of Mexico City: Changes Over Time in Urban, Suburban and Peri-Urban Areas'. *Environment and Urbanization* 10(2): 37–54.

Lowder, S. K., J. Skoet and T. Raney (2016). 'The Number, Size, and Distribution of Farms, Smallholder Farms, and Family Farms Worldwide'. *World Development* 87: 16–29. https://doi.org/10.1016/j.worlddev.2015.10.041. Accessed in August 2022.

Mahapatro, S., A. Bailey, K. S. James and I. Hutter (2017). 'Remittances and Household Expenditure Patterns in India and Selected States'. *Migration and Development* 6(1): 83–101.

Mahaprashasta, A. A. (2013). 'Getting Away with Murder'. *Frontline Magazine*, 15 November. https://frontline.thehindu.com/social-issues/getting-away-with-murder/article23559228.ece. Accessed on 20 June 2014.

Maharatna, A. (2014). 'Food Scarcity and Migration: An Overview'. *Social Research* 81(2): 277–98.

Maharjan, A., S. Bauer and B. Knerr (2012). 'Do Rural Women Who Stay Behind Benefit from Male Out-Migration? A Case Study in the Hills of Nepal'. *Gender, Technology and Development* 16(1): 95–123.

Maharjan, A., R. S. de Campos, C. Singh, S. Das, A. Srinivas, M. R. A. Bhuiyan, S. Ishaq, M. W. Umar, T. Dilshad, K. Shreshtha, S. Bhadwal, T. Ghosh, N. Suckall and K. Vincent (2020). 'Migration and Household Adaptation in Climate-Sensitive Hotspots in South Asia'. *Current Climate Change Reports* 6(1): 1–16.

Maitra, P., and A. Rammohan (2011). 'The Link between Infant Mortality and Child Nutrition in India: Is There Any Evidence of a Gender Bias?' *Journal of the Asia Pacific Economy* 16(1): 81–110.

Malthus, T. R. (1798). *An Essay on the Principle of Population, as It Affects the Future Improvement of Society with Remarks on the Speculations of Mr. Godwin, M. Condorcet, and Other Writers*. London: Printed for J. Johnson, in St. Paul's Church-Yard.

Mander, H. (2012). *Ash in the Belly: India's Unfinished Battle against Hunger*. London: Penguin Books.

Manikandan, A. D. (2014). 'A Tragedy Unfolding: Tribal Children Dying in Attapady'. *Economic and Political Weekly* 49(2). https://www.epw.in/journal/2014/2/reports-states-web-exclusives/tragedy-unfolding.html?0=ip_login_no_cache%3Deafc03a8e29b1cc66bb5e416b64e038d. Accessed on 6 September 2021.

Martin, S. F. (2004). 'Women and Migration'. Working Paper 1 for Consultative Meeting on Migration and Mobility and How This Movement Affects Women, 2–4 December, Division for the Advancement of Women, United Nations, New York. http://www.un.org/womenwatch/daw/meetings/consult/CM-Dec03-WP1.pdf. Accessed on 30 July 2022.

Mazumdar, I., N. Neetha and I. Agnihotri (2013). 'Migration and Gender in India'. *Economic and Political Weekly* 48(10): 54–64.

Mcdowell, C., and A. de Haan (1997). 'Migration and Sustainable Livelihoods: A Critical Review of the Literature'. Working Paper 65, Institute of Development Studies, Sussex.

Mehrotra, S., A. Gandhi, P. Saha and B. K. Sahoo (2013). 'Turnaround in India's Employment Story: Silver Lining amidst Joblessness and Informalisation?' *Economic and Political Weekly* 48(35): 87–96.

Mehrotra, S., J. Parida, S. Sinha and A. Gandhi (2014). 'Explaining Employment Trends in the Indian Economy: 1993–94 to 2011–12'. *Economic and Political Weekly* 49(32): 49–57.

Mehrotra, S. (2019). 'Informal Employment Trends in the Indian Economy: Persistent Informality, but growing positive development'. Employment Working Paper 254, International Labour Organization, Geneva. Accessed

online from https://www.ilo.org/wcmsp5/groups/public/---ed_emp/---ifp_
skills/documents/publication/wcms_734503.pdf. Accessed on 30 July 2022.

Mendola, M. (2008). 'Migration and Technological Change in Rural
Households: Complements or Substitutes?' *Journal of Development Economics*
85(1–2): 150–75.

Meng, X. (2012). 'Labor Market Outcomes and Reforms in China'. *Journal of
Economic Perspectives* 26(4): 75–102.

Menon, P., A. Deolalikar and A. Bhaskar (2009). 'India State Hunger Index:
Comparison of Hunger across States'. Bon, Washington, DC, and Dublin:
International Food Policy Research Institute, Welthungerhilfe and Concern
Worldwide.

Miller, B. D. (1981). *The Endangerd Sex: Neglect of Female Children in Rural North
India*. Ithaca and London: Cornell University Press.

Ministry of Agriculture (2019). *Agriculture Census 2015–16: All-India Report on
Number and Area of Operational Holdings*. New Delhi: Government of India.

——— (2021). 'Agricultural Census Data Online (Various Years)'. Agriculture
Census, Department of Agriculture and Farmers Welfare. https://agcensus.
dacnet.nic.in/DatabaseHome.aspx. Accessed on 10 August 2021.

Ministry of Home Affairs (2020). 'Answer of the Minister of State in the
Ministry of Home Affairs to the Lok Sabha Unstarred Question Number
1179'. New Delhi: Government of India. https://www.mha.gov.in/MHA1/
Par2017/pdfs/par2020-pdfs/rs-21092020/1179.pdf. Accessed on 30 July 2022.

Ministry of Rural Development (2012). 'MGNREGA Sameeksha: An
Anthology of Research Studies on the Mahatma Gandhi National Rural
Employment Guarantee Act, 2005'. New Delhi: Orient Blackswan. https://
nrega.nic.in/Circular_Archive/archive/MGNREGA_SAMEEKSHA.
pdf. Accessed on 16 March 2020.

——— (2020). 'MGNREGA Public Data Portal'. The Mahatma Gandhi
National Rural Employment Guarantee Act 2005, Ministry Of Rural
Development, Government Of India. http://nrega.nic.in. Accessed on 18
March 2020.

Ministry of Statistics and Programme Implementation (2005). *Millennium
Development Goals: India Country Report 2005*. New Delhi: Government of
India.

——— (2009). *Millennium Development Goals: India Country Report 2009*. New
Delhi: Government of India.

——— (2016). *SDG National Indicator Framework Baseline Report 2015–16*. New
Delhi: Government of India.

———— (2017). *Millennium Development Goals: Final Country Report of India*. New Delhi: Government of India.

———— (2020). *Sustainable Development Goals: National Indicator Framework Progress Report 2020*. New Delhi: Government of India.

Ministry of Women and Child Development (2020). 'Integrated Child Development Scheme'. https://icds-wcd.nic.in. Accessed on 19 March 2020.

Minwalla, S. (2003). 'Sugar Sours School Careers of Workers' Children'. *Times of India*, 20 June. https://timesofindia.indiatimes.com/city/mumbai/sugar-sours-school-careers-of-workers-children/articleshow/31946.cms. Accessed on 30 July 2022.

Mishra, A. (2010). *Hunger and Famine in Kalahandi*. Delhi: Pearson Education (Longman).

Mohapatra, S., G. Joseph and D. Ratha (2012). 'Remittances and Natural Disasters: Ex-Post Response and Contribution to Ex-Ante Preparedness'. *Environment, Development and Sustainability* 14(3): 365–87.

Moniruzzaman, M. (2020). 'The Impact of Remittances on Household Food Security: Evidence from a Survey in Bangladesh'. *Migration and Development*, 1–20. DOI: 10.1080/21632324.2020.1787097.

Mosse, D., S. Gupta, M. Mehta, V. Shah, J. F. Rees and Kribp Project Team (2002). 'Brokered Livelihoods: Debt, Labour Migration and Development in Tribal Western India'. *Journal of Development Studies* 38(5): 59–88.

Motiram, S., and V. Vakulabharanam (2011). 'Poverty and Inequality in the Age of Economic Liberalization'. In *India Development Report 2011*, edited by D. M. Nachane, pp. 59–68. New Delhi: Oxford University Press.

Mougeot, L. J. A. (2000). 'The Hidden Significance of Urban Agriculture'. Brief 6 of 10. International Food Policy Research Center, Wahington, DC. https://www.ifpri.org. Accessed on 30 July 2022.

MSME Development Institute (2012). *District Industrial Potential Survey: Brief Profile of Siwan District*. Muzaffarpur: Ministry of Micro, Small and Medium Enterprises, Government of India. http://dcmsme.gov.in/old/dips/DIPS%20-SIWAN.pdf. Accessed on 30 July 2022.

Mukherjee, A. (2011). 'Regional Inequality in Foreign Direct Investment Flows to India: The Problem and the Prospects'. Reserve Bank of India Occasional Papers, vol. 32, no. 2. Reserve Bank of India, Mumbai.

Mukherji, A., and A. Mukherji (2012). 'Bihar: What Went Wrong? And What Changed?' Working Paper 107, National Institute of Public Finance and Policy, New Delhi. http://www.nipfp.org.in/media/medialibrary/2013/04/WP_2012_107.pdf. Accessed on 30 July 2022.

Munshi, K., and M. Rosenzweig (2016). 'Networks and Misallocation: Insurance, Migration, and the Rural–Urban Wage Gap'. *American Economic Review* 106(1): 46–98.

National Sample Survey (2005). *Situation Assessment Survey of Farmers: Some Aspects of Farming.* NSS 59th round, report no. 496(59/33/3). New Delhi: Ministry of Statistics and Programme Implementation, Government of India.

—— (2010). *Migration in India 2007–08.* NSS 64th round, report no. 533 (64/10.2/2). New Delhi: Ministry of Statistics and Programme Implementation, Government of India.

Nayar, L. (2014). 'A Diet of Apathy'. *Outlook*, 18 August. https://www.outlookindia.com/magazine/story/a-diet-of-apathy/291626. Accesed on 30 July 2022.

Nayyar, G., and K. Y. Kim (2018). 'India's Internal Labor Migration Paradox: The Statistical and the Real'. Policy Research Working Paper 8356, World Bank, Washington, DC. https://openknowledge.worldbank.org/handle/10986/29416. Accessed on 16 November 2021.

NCEUS (2007). *Report on the Conditions of Work and Promotion of Livelihoods in the Unorganised Sector.* New Delhi: National Commission for Enterprises in the Unorganised Sector, Government of India.

Neetha, N. (2004). 'Making of Female Breadwinners: Migration and Social Networking of Women Domestics in Delhi'. *Economic and Political Weekly* 39(17): 1681–88.

Nguyen, P. H., S. Scott, D. Headey, N. Singh, L. M. Tran, P. Menon and M. T. Ruel (2021). 'The Double Burden of Malnutrition in India: Trends and Inequalities (2006–2016)'. *PLoS ONE* 16(2): e0247856. https://doi.org/10.1371/journal.pone.0247856. Accessed in August 2022.

Nichols, C. E. (2016). 'Time Ni Hota Hai: Time Poverty and Food Security in the Kumaon Hills, India'. *Gender, Place and Culture* 23(10): 1404–19.

Nussbaum, M. C. (2011). *Creating Capabilities: The Human Development Approach.* Cambridge, MA: Harvard University Press.

Nyamongo, E. M., R. N. Misati, L. Kipyegon and L. Ndirangu (2012). 'Remittances, Financial Development and Economic Growth in Africa'. *Journal of Economics and Business* 64(3): 240–60.

Oberai, A. S., and H. K. M. Singh (1983). *Causes and Consequences of Internal Migration: A Study in the Indian Punjab.* Delhi: Oxford University Press.

Obi, C., F. Bartolini and M. D'Haese (2020). 'International Migration, Remittance and Food Security during Food Crises: The Case Study of Nigeria'. *Food Security* 12(1): 207–20.

O'Malley, L. S. S. (2007 [1930]). *Saran: Bihar and Orissa District Gazetteers*. New Delhi: Logos Press.

OECD and ICIER (2018). *Agricultural Policies in India: OECD Food and Agricultural Reviews*. Paris: OECD Publishing. https://doi.org/10.1787/9789264302334-en. Accessed on 30 July 2022.

Olayungbo, D. O., and A. Quadri (2019). 'Remittances, Financial Development and Economic Growth in Sub-Saharan African Countries: Evidence from a PMG-ARDL Approach'. *Financial Innovation* 5(1): 1–25.

Oxford Poverty and Human Development Initiative (2018). *Global Multidimensional Poverty Index 2018: The Most Detailed Picture to Date of the World's Poorest People*. Oxford: University of Oxford.

Paciorek, C. J., G. A. Stevens, M. M. Finucane and M. Ezzati (2013). 'Children's Height and Weight in Rural and Urban Populations in Low-Income and Middle-Income Countries: A Systematic Analysis of Population-Representative Data'. *Lancet Global Health* 1(5): e300–e309.

Pandey, P. (2011). 'Siwan post office "richest" in Bihar'. *Times of India*, 25 April. http://timesofindia.indiatimes.com/city/patna/Siwan-post-office-richest-in-Bihar/articleshow/8082358.cms. Accessed on 1 October 2014.

Pani, N. (ed.) (2022). *Dynamics of Difference: Inequality and Transformation in Rural India*. Oxon and New York: Routledge.

Parikh, K. S. (1994). 'Who Gets How Much from PDS: How Effectively Does It Reach the Poor'. *Sarvekshna* 17(3): 1–37.

Paris, T., A. Singh, J. Luis and M. Hossain (2005). 'Labour Outmigration, Livelihood of Rice Farming Households and Women Left Behind: A Case Study in Eastern Uttar Pradesh'. *Economic and Political Weekly* 40(25): 2522–29.

Parulkar, A. (2012). 'Starving in India: A Fight for Life in Bihar'. *Wall Street Journal*, 9 April. https://www.wsj.com/articles/BL-IRTB-15054. Accessed on 23 January 2014.

Patel, V. (2018). 'Starvation Deaths in 2018'. *Indian Express*, 26 July. https://indianexpress.com/article/opinion/columns/starvation-deaths-in-india-global-hunder-index-unicef-poverty-national-health-mission-5276194/. Accessed on 30 July 2022.

Pathak, P. K., and A. Singh (2011). 'Trends in Malnutrition among Children in India: Growing Inequalities across Different Economic Groups'. *Social Science and Medicine* 73(4): 576–85.

Patnaik, B., S. Reddy and G. Singh (2008). *Supreme Court Orders on the Right to Food: A Tool for Action*. New Delhi: Right to Food Campaign Secretariat.

Patnaik, P. (2005). 'On the Need for Providing Employment Guarantee'. *Economic and Political Weekly* 40(3): 203–07.

Patnaik, U. (2004). 'The Republic of Hunger'. *Social Scientist* 32(9–10): 9–35.

Pattnaik, I., K. Lahiri-Dutt, S. Lockie and B. Pritchard (2018). 'The Feminization of Agriculture or the Feminization of Agrarian Distress? Tracking the Trajectory of Women in Agriculture in India'. *Journal of the Asia Pacific Economy* 23(1): 138–55.

Pelletier, D. L. (1994). 'The Potentiating Effects of Malnutrition on Child Mortality: Epidemiologic Evidence and Policy Implications'. *Nutrition Reviews* 52(12): 409–15.

Peters, P. E., M. G. Herrera and T. F. Randolph (1989). *Cash Cropping, Food Security, and Nutrition: The Effects of Agriculture Commercialization among Smallholders in Malawi*. Report to the United States Agency for International Development. Cambridge, MA: Harvard Institute of International Development.

Planning Commission (1956). *Second Five-Year Plan, 1956–61*. New Delhi: Government of India Press.

—— (1979). *Report of the Task Force on Projections of Minimum Needs and Effective Consumption Demand*. New Delhi: Government of India.

—— (1993). *Report of the Expert Group on Estimation of Proportion and Number of Poor*. New Delhi: Government of India.

—— (1997). *A Background Note on Gadgil Formula for Distribution of Central Assistance for State Plans*. New Delhi: Government of India. http://pbplanning.gov.in/pdf/gadgil.pdf. Accessed on 23 June 2014.

—— (2005). *Performance Evaluation of Targeted Public Distribution System*. New Delhi: Government of India.

—— (2006). *Approach Paper to Eleventh Five-Year Plan, 2007–12*. New Delhi: Government of India.

—— (2011). *Mid-term Appraisal for Eleventh Five Year Plan 2007–2012*. New Delhi: Government of India.

—— (2012). *Press Note on Poverty Estimates, 2009–10*. New Delhi: Government of India. https://niti.gov.in/planningcommission.gov.in/docs/news/press_pov1903.pdf. Accessed on 30 July 2022.

—— (2013a). *Press Note on Poverty Estimates, 2011–12*. New Delhi: Press Information Bureau, Government of India. https://www.niti.gov.in/sites/default/files/2020-05/press-note-poverty-2011-12-23-08-16.pdf. Accessed on 30 July 2022.

——— (2013b). *Twelfth Five-Year Plan, 2012–2017: Social Sectors*, vol. 3. New Delhi: Government of India.

Polgreen, L. (2010). 'Turnaround of India State Could Serve as a Model'. *New York Times*, 10 April. https://www.nytimes.com/2010/04/11/world/asia/11bihar.html. Accessed on 30 July 2022.

Potts, D. (2010). *Circular Migration in Zimbabwe and Contemporary Sub-Saharan Africa*. Woodbridge, Suffolk: James Currey.

Pradhan, M., D. Roy and V. Sonkar (2019). 'What Is the Effective Delivery Mechanism of Food Support in India?' *Economic and Political Weekly* 54(42): 37–44.

Prasad, P. H. (1975). 'Agrarian Unrest and Economic Change in Rural Bihar: Three Case Studies'. *Economic and Political Weekly* 10(24): 931–37.

Pritchard, B. (2014). 'The Problem of Higher Food Prices for Impoverished People in the Rural Global South'. *Australian Geographer* 45(4): 419–27.

———. (2016). 'Food and Nutrition Security: Future Priorities for Research and Policy'. In *Routledge Handbook of Food and Nutrition Security*, edited by B. Pritchard, R. Ortiz and M. Shekar, pp. 1–24. Oxon: Routledge.

Pritchard, B., A. Rammohan, M. Sekher, S. Parasuraman and C. Choithani (2014). *Feeding India: Livelihoods, Entitlements and Capabilities*. Oxon: Earthscan (Routledge).

Pritchard, B., A. Rammohan and M. Vicol (2019). 'The Importance of Non-Farm Livelihoods for Household Food Security and Dietary Diversity in Rural Myanmar'. *Journal of Rural Studies* 67: 89–100. https://doi.org/10.1016/j.jrurstud.2019.02.017. Accessed in August 2022.

Pritchard, B., J. Dixon, E. Hull and C. Choithani (2016). '"Stepping Back and Moving In": The Role of the State in the Contemporary Food Regime'. *Journal of Peasant Studies* 43(3): 693–710.

Radboud University (2021). 'Global Data Lab: Subnational Human Development Index, India'. https://globaldatalab.org. Accessed on 14 June 2021.

Radhakrishna, R. (2005). 'Food and Nutrition Security of the Poor'. *Economic and Political Weekly* 50(18): 1817–21.

Radhakrishna, R., K. H. Rao, C. Ravi and B. S. Reddy (2004). 'Chronic Poverty and Malnutrition in 1990s'. *Economic and Political Weekly* 38(28): 3121–30.

Radhakrishna, R., K. Subbarao, S. Indrakant and C. Ravi (1997). 'India's Public Distribution System: A National and International Perspective'. Discussion Paper 380. World Bank, Washington, DC.

Rai, P. (2012). *The Great MNREGA Robbery: Bihar Robbed of Nearly Rs. 6000 Crore*. New Delhi: Center for Environment and Food Security. https://www.im4change.org/docs/668corruption-bihar-NREGA.pdf. Accessed on 7 August 2014.

Rajivan, A. K. (2006). 'Tamil Nadu: ICDS with a Difference'. *Economic and Political Weekly* 41(34): 3684–88.

Ram, F., S. K. Mohanty and U. Ram (2009). 'Understanding the Distribution of BPL Cards: All-India and Selected States'. *Economic and Political Weekly* 44(7): 66–71.

Ramalingaswami, V., U. Jonsson and J. Rohde (1996). *Commentary: The Asian Enigma*. New York: United Nations Children's Fund (UNICEF).

Ramnarain, S. (2015). 'Universalized Categories, Dissonant Realities: Gendering Postconflict Reconstruction in Nepal'. *Gender, Place and Culture* 22(9): 1305–22.

Ranaware, K., U. Das, A. Kulkarni and S. Narayanan (2015). 'MGNREGA Works and their Impacts: A Study of Maharashtra'. *Economic and Political Weekly* 50(13): 53–61.

Rao, K. H. (2000). 'Declining Demand for Foodgrains in Rural India'. *Economic and Political Weekly* 35(4): 201–06.

Rao, M. G., R. T. Shand and K. P. Kalirajan (1999). 'Convergence of Incomes across Indian States: A Divergent View'. *Economic and Political Weekly* 34(13): 769–78.

Ravallion, M., and G. Datt (1996). 'How Important to India's Poor Is the Sectoral Composition of Economic Growth?' *World Bank Economic Review* 10(1): 1–25.

Ravenstein, E. G. (1885). 'The Laws of Migration'. *Journal of the Statistical Society of London* 48(2): 167–235.

———. (1889). 'The Laws of Migration'. *Journal of the Royal Statistical Society* 52(2): 241–305.

Ravi, S., and M. Engler (2009). 'Workfare in Low Income Countries: An Effective Way to Fight Poverty? The Case of NREGS in India'. Unpublsihed manuscript. http://knowledge.nrega.net/869/1/ShamikaRavi.pdf. Accessed on 2 August 2014.

Rawal, V. (2008). 'Ownership Holdings of Land in Rural India: Putting the Record Straight'. *Economic and Political Weekly* 43(3): 43–47.

Reardon, T., J. Berdegué and G. Escobar (2001). 'Rural Nonfarm Employment and Incomes in Latin America: Overview and Policy Implications'. *World Development* 29(3): 395–409.

Reserve Bank of India (2020). *Handbook of Statistics on Indian States 2019–20*. Mumbai: Reserve Bank of India. https://rbidocs.rbi.org.in/rdocs/Publications/PDFs/HS13102020_F947063857A8E4515A045CC91EE92BFAB.PDF. Accessed on 6 June 2022.

Rigg, J. (2006). 'Land, Farming, Livelihoods, and Poverty: Rethinking the Links in the Rural South'. *World Development* 34(1): 180–202.

Rigg, J., A. Salamanca and M. Parnwell (2012). 'Joining the Dots of Agrarian Change in Asia: A 25-Year View from Thailand'. *World Development* 40(7): 1469–81.

Right to Food Campaign (2020). 'Supreme Court Orders on Right to Food'. http://www.righttofoodcampaign.in. Accessed on 30 July 2022.

Robeyns, I. (2005). 'The Capability Approach: A Theoretical Survey'. *Journal of Human Development* 6(1): 93–114.

Rodó-de-Zárate, M., and M. Baylina (2018). 'Intersectionality in Feminist Geographies'. *Gender, Place and Culture* 25(4): 547–53.

Rose, E. (1999). 'Consumption Smoothing and Excess Female Mortality in Rural India'. *Review of Economics and Statistics* 81(1): 41–49.

Rosenzweig, M. R., and T. P. Schultz (1982). 'Market Opportunities, Genertic Endowments, and Intrafamily Resource Distribution: Child Survival in Rural India'. *American Economic Review* 72(4): 803–15.

Ruel, M. T., J. L. Garrett and L. Haddad (2000). 'Rapid Urbanization and the Challenges of Obtaining Food and Nutrition Security'. In *Nutrition and Health in Developing Countries*, 2nd edition, edited by R. D. Semba and W. B. Martin, pp. 639–656. New York: Humana Press.

Sachs, J. D., N. Bajpai and A. Ramiah (2002). 'Understanding Regional Economic Growth in India'. *Asian Economic Paper* 1(3): 32–62.

Sahu, G. B., and M. Mahamallik (2011). 'Identification of the Poor: Errors of Exclusion and Inclusion'. *Economic and Political Weekly* 46(09): 71–77.

Sainath, P. (2011). 'Census Findings Point to Decade of Rural Distress'. *The Hindu*, 25 September. http://www.thehindu.com/opinion/columns/sainath/article2484996.ece?homepage=true. Accessed on 30 March 2014.

Santhi, K. (2006). 'Female Labour Migration in India: Insights from NSSO Data'. Working Paper 4/2006, Madras School of Economics, Chennai. https://www.mse.ac.in/wp-content/uploads/2021/05/santhi_wp.pdf. Accessed on 30 July 2022.

Sarkar, S. (2019). 'Investigation: Why Two-Thirds of Bihar's Children Are Deprived of Nutrition'. *Week Magazine*, 6 July. https://www.theweek.in/

theweek/statescan/2019/07/05/investigation-why-two-thirds-of-bihar-children-are-deprived-of-nutrition.html. Accessed on 30 July 2022.

Schmidt-Kallert, E. (2009). 'A New Paradigm of Urban Transition: Tracing the Livelihood Strategies of Multi-Locational Households'. *Die Erde* 140(3): 319–36.

Scoones, I. (1998). 'Sustainable Rural Livelihoods: A Framework for Analysis'. Working Paper 72, Overseas Development Institute, London.

Selod, H., and F. Shilpi (2021). 'Rural-Urban Migration in Developing Countries'. *Regional Science and Urban Economics* 91: 1–13. https://doi.org/10.1016/j.regsciurbeco.2021.103713. Accesed in August 2022.

Sen, A. (1977). 'Starvation and Exchange Entitlements: A General Approach and Its Application to the Great Bengal Famine'. *Cambridge Journal of Economics* 1: 33–59.

———. (1981a). 'Ingredients of Famine Analysis: Availability and Entitlements'. *Quarterly Journal of Economics* 96(3): 433–64.

———. (1981b). *Poverty and Famines: An Essay on Entitlement and Deprivation*. Oxford: Oxford University Press.

———. (1983). 'Development: Which Way Now?' *Economic Journal* 93(372): 745–62.

———. (1984a). 'The Living Standard'. *Oxford Economic Papers* 36: 74–90.

———. (1984b). 'Well-Being, Agency and Freedom'. *Journal of Philosophy* 82(4): 169–221.

———. (1985). *Commodities and Capabilities*. New York: Elsevier.

———. (1987). 'Gender and Cooperative Conflicts'. WIDER Working Paper 18, World Institute for Development Economics Research, Helsinki. https://www.wider.unu.edu/sites/default/files/WP18.pdf. Accessed on 30 July 2022.

———. (1990). 'More Than 100 Million Women Are Missing'. *New York Review*, 20 December. https://www.nybooks.com/articles/1990/12/20/more-than-100-million-women-are-missing. Accessed in August 2022.

———. (1992). 'Missing Women: Social Inequality Outweighs Women's Survival Advantage in Asia and North Africa'. *British Medical Journal* 304(6827): 587–88.

———. (1993). 'Markets and Freedoms: Achievements and Limitations of the Market Mechanism in Promoting Individual Freedoms'. *Oxford Economic Papers* 45(4): 519–41.

———. (1999). *Development as Freedom*. Oxford: Oxford University Press.

———. (2009). *The Idea of Justice*. Cambridge, MA: Harvard University Press.

————. (2013). 'Bihar: Past, Present and Future'. In *The New Bihar: Rekindling Governance and Development*, edited by N. K. Singh and N. Stern, pp. 3–7. Noida: HarperCollins Publishers India.

Sen, A., and S. Sengupta (1983). 'Malnutrition of Rural Children and the Sex Bias'. *Economic and Political Weekly* 28(19–21): 855–64.

Sen, P. (2005). 'Of Calories and Things'. *Economic and Political Weekly* 40(43): 4611–18.

Shariff, A., and P. Lanjouw (2004). 'Rural Nonfarm Employment in India: Access, Incomes and Poverty Impact'. *Economic and Political Weekly* 39(40): 4429–46.

Sharma, A. N. (1995). 'Political Economy of Poverty in Bihar'. *Economic and Political Weekly* 30(41–42): 2587–2602.

————. (1997). *People on the Move: Nature and Implications of Migration in a Backward Economy*. New Delhi: Vikas Publishing House.

————. (2005). 'Agrarian Relations and Socio-Economic Change in Bihar'. *Economic and Political Weekly* 40(10): 960–72.

————. (2013). 'Development in Bihar: An Unfinished Agenda'. In *The New Bihar: Rekindling Governance and Development*, edited by N. K. Singh and N. Stern, pp. 47–66. Noida: HarperCollins Publishers India.

Singh, M. (1995). *Uneven Development in Agriculture and Labour Migration: A Case of Bihar and Punjab*. Shimla: Indian Institute of Advanced Study.

————. (1997). 'Bonded Migrant Labour in Punjab Agriculture'. *Economic and Political Weekly* 32(11): 518–19.

Singh, N. K., and N. Stern (2013). 'Introduction'. In *The New Bihar: Rekindling Governance and Development*, edited by N. K. Singh and N. Stern pp. xvi–xxxix. Noida: HarperCollins Publishers India.

Singh, C., A. Rahman, A. Srinivas and A. Bazaz (2018). 'Risks and Responses in Rural India: Implications for Local Climate Change Adaptation Action'. *Climate Risk Management* 21: 52–68. https://doi.org/10.1016/j.crm.2018.06.001. Accessed in August 2022.

Sinha, A. (2011). *Nitish Kumar and the Rise of Bihar*. New Delhi: Penguin.

Sinha, K. (2014). 'Average Indian Male Consumes 33 Litres of Alcohol/Year: WHO'. *Times of India*, 15 May. http://timesofindia.indiatimes.com/india/Average-Indian-male-consumes-33-litres-of-alcohol-/year-WHO/articleshow/35139360.cms. Accessed on 30 July 2022.

Siwan Head Post Office (2012). 'Data on Domestic Money Orders Paid by Post Offices in Siwan (2002–03 to 2009–10)'. Data obtained through personal visit, Siwan Head Post Office, Bihar.

Smith, L. C., M. T. Ruel and A. Ndiaye (2005). 'Why Is Child Malnutrition Lower in Urban than in Rural Areas? Evidence from 36 Developing Countries'. *World Development* 33(8): 1285–1305.

Smith, L. S. (2015). 'The Great Indian Calorie Debate: Explaining Rising Undernourishment during India's Rapid Economic Growth'. *Food Policy* 50: 53–67. DOI: 10.1016/j.foodpol.2014.10.011.

Smith, R. T. (1959). 'Some Social Characteristics of Indian Immigrants to British Guiana'. *Population Studies* 13(1): 34–39.

Solesbury, W. (2003). 'Sustainable Livelihoods: A Case Study of the Evolution of DFID Policy'. Working Paper 217, Overseas Development Institute, London.

Srivastava, R., and S. K. Sasikumar (2003). 'An Overview of Migration in India, Its Impacts and Key Issues'. Paper presented at the conference 'Migration, Development and Pro-Poor Policy Choices in Asia', Dhaka, 22–24 June 2003. http://www.shram.org/uploadFiles/20131014063711.pdf. Accessed on 30 July 2022.

Srivastava, R. (2019). 'Emerging Dynamics of Labour Market Inequality in India: Migration, Informality, Segmentation and Social Discrimination'. *Indian Journal of Labour Economics* 62(2): 147–71.

Stark, O. (1978). 'Economic-Demographic Interactions in Agricultural Development: The Case of Rural–Urban Migration'. Rome: Food and Agriculture Organisation.

———. (1981). 'On the Optimal Choice of Capital Intensity in LDCs with Migration'. *Journal of Development Economics* 9(1): 31–41.

———. (1983). 'Towards a Theory of Remittances in LDCs'. Discussion paper number 971. Harvard Institute of Economic Research, Harvard University, Cambridge, MA.

———. (1991). *The Migration of Labor.* Oxford: Basil Blackwell.

Stone, I. (1984). *Canal Irrigation in British India: Perspectives on Technological Change in a Peasant Economy.* Cambridge: Cambridge University Press.

Strauss, J., and D. Thomas (1998). 'Health, Nutrition, and Economic Development'. *Journal of Economic Literature* 36(2): 766–817.

Subramanian, V. (1975). *Parched Earth: The Maharashtra Drought 1970–73.* Bombay: Orient Longman.

Supreme Court of India (2003). 'Interim Order of May 2, 2003 in the Case People's Union for Civil Liberties versus Union of India and Others'. https://www.globalhealthrights.org/wp-content/uploads/2013/10/Peoples-Union-India-2003-Interim-Order.pdf. Accessed on 30 July 2022.

Sushmita (2014). 'Politics of Massacres and Resistance'. *Economic and Political Weekly* 49(2): 41–45.

Svedberg, P. (2012). 'Reforming or Replacing the Public Distribution System with Cash Transfers?' *Economic and Political Weekly* 47(7): 53–62.

Swaminathan, M., and N. Misra (2001). 'Errors of Targeting: Public Distribution of Food in a Maharashtra Village, 1995–2000'. *Economic and Political Weekly* 36(26): 2447–54.

Tandon, B. N. (1989). 'Nutritional Interventions through Primary Health Care: Impact of the ICDS Projects in India'. *Bulletin of the World Health Organization* 67(1): 77–80.

Tawodzera, G. (2010). 'Vulnerability and Resilience in Crisis: Urban Household Food Insecurity in Harare, Zimbabwe'. PhD Thesis. Department of Environment and Geographical Science, University of Cape Town.

Taylor, J. E., and T. J. Wyatt (1996). 'The Shadow Value of Migrant Remittances, Income and Inequality in a Household-Farm Economy'. *Journal of Development Studies* 32(6): 899–912.

The Hungry Cities Partnership (2020). https://hungrycities.net. Accessed on 30 July 2022.

Thomas, D., and E. Frankenberg (2002). 'Health, Nutrition and Prosperity: A Microeconomic Perspective'. *Bulletin of the World Health Organization* 80(2): 106–13.

Thomas, J. J. (2012). 'India's Labour Market during the 2000s: Surveying the Changes'. *Economic and Political Weekly* 47(51): 39–51.

Timberg, T. A. (1982). 'Bihari Backwardness: Does Feudalism Frustrate?' *Asian Survey* 22(5): 470–80.

Timmer, C. P. (2007). 'A World without Agriculture: The Structural Transformation in Historical Perspective'. Wendt lecture delivered at the American Enterprise Institute, Washington, DC.

Todaro, M. P. (1969). 'A Model of Labor Migration and Urban Unemployment in Less Developed Countries'. *American Economic Review* 59(1): 138–48.

Tripathy, T. (2009). 'Changing Pattern of Rural Livelihood Opportunities and Constraints: A Case of Orissa, India'. *IUP Journal of Applied Economics* 8(3–4): 116–39.

Tumbe, C. (2011). 'Remittances in India: Facts and Issues'. Working Paper No. 331, Indian Institute of Management, Bangalore.

———. (2012). 'Migration Persistence across Twentieth Century India'. *Migration and Development* 1(1): 87–112.

————. (2015a). 'Missing Men, Migration and Labour Markets: Evidence from India'. *Indian Journal of Labour Economics* 2(58): 245–67.

————. (2015b). 'Towards Financial Inclusion: The Post Office of India as a Financial Institution, 1880–2010'. *Indian Economic and Social History Review* 52(4): 409–37.

————. (2018). *India Moving: A History of Migration*. Gurgaon: Penguin Random House India.

Udry, C. (1997). 'Recent Advances in Empirical Microeconomic Research in Poor Countries: An Annotated Bibliography'. *Journal of Economic Education* 28(1): 58–75.

UN-DESA (2013). 'Cross-national Comparisons of Internal Migration: An Update on Global Patterns and Trends'. Technical Paper No. 2013/1. New York: Department of Economic and Social Affairs, United Nations. https://www.un.org/en/development/desa/population/publications/pdf/technical/TP2013-1.pdf. Accessed on 30 July 2022.

———— (2020). 'International Migration 2020: Highlights (ST/ESA/SER.A/452)'. New York: Department of Economic and Social Affairs, United Nations. https://www.un.org/development/desa/pd/news/international-migration-2020. Accessed on 30 July 2022.

United Nations (2007). 'Gender, Remittances, Development: Feminization of Migration'. UN-INSTRAW Working Paper 1, United Nations International Research and Training Institute for the Advancement of Women, Santo Domingo, Dominican Republic. http://www.renate-europe.net/wp-content/uploads/2014/01/Feminization_of_Migration-INSTRAW2007.pdf. Accessed on 1 Dember 2014.

———— (2008). *The Millennium Development Goals Report 2008*. New York: United Nations. Accessed on 30 Jully 2022.

———— (2012). 'Zero Hunger Challenge'. United Nations. https://www.un.org/zerohunger. Accessed on 30 July 2022.

———— (2013). *The Millennium Development Goals Report 2013*. New York: United Nations.

———— (2015). *Transforming Our World: The 2030 Agenda for Sustainable Development*. Document A/RES/70/1. New York: Sustainable Development, Department of Economic and Social Affairs, United Nations. https://sustainabledevelopment.un.org/content/documents/21252030%20Agenda%20for%20Sustainable%20Development%20web.pdf. Accessed on 30 July 2022.

————(2016). 'Decade of Action on Nutrition'. United Nations Decade of Action on Nutrition. https://www.un.org/nutrition. Accessed on 30 July 2022.

———— (2017). *Women Migrant Workers' Contributions to Development.* UN-Women Policy Brief 2. New York: UN Women, United Nations. https://www.unwomen.org/en/digital-library/publications/2017/7/women-migrant-workers-contributions-to-development. Accessed on 30 July 2022.

————(2019). *World Population Prospects: The 2019 Revision*, vol. 1: *Comprehensive Tables*. New York: Population Division, Department of Economic and Social Affairs, United Nations.

United Nations Children's Fund (UNICEF) (2006). *The State of the World's Children 2007*. New York: United Nations Children's Fund.

————(2012). *Inequities in Early Childhood Development: What the Data Say*. New York: United Nations Children's Fund.

———— (2020). *The State of the World's Children, 2019*. New York: United Nations Children's Fund.

United Nations Development Programme (UNDP) (1990). *Human Development Report*. New York: United Nations Development Programme.

———— (2009). *Overcoming Barriers: Human Mobility and Development (Human Development Report 2009)*. New York: United Nations Development Programme.

————(2020). *The Next Frontier: Human Development and the Anthropocene*. New York: United Nations Development Programme.

United Nations Population Fund (UNFPA) (2007). *State of World Population 2007: Unleashing the Potential of Urban Growth*. New York: United Nations Population Fund.

Valentine, G. (2007). 'Theorizing and Researching Intersectionality: A Challenge for Feminist Geography'. *Professional Geographer* 59(1): 10–21.

van Duijne, R. J. (2019). 'Why India's Urbanization Is Hidden: Observations from "Rural" Bihar'. *World Development* 123(104610): 1–13

van Duijne, R. J., C. Choithani and K. Pfeffer (2020). 'New Urban Geographies of West Bengal, East India'. *Journal of Maps* 16(1): 172–83.

van Duijne, R. J., and J. Nijman (2019). 'India's Emergent Urban Formations'. *Annals of the American Association of Geographers* 109(6): 1978–98.

Vijay, R. (2012). 'Structural Retrogression and Rise of "New Landlords" in Indian Agriculture: An Empirical Exercise'. *Economic and Political Weekly* 47(5): 37–45.

von Grebmer, K., J. Bernstein, M. Wiemers, K. Acheampong, A. Hanano, B. Higgins, ... and H. Fritschel (2020). *Global Hunger Index: One Decade to Zero Hunger – Linking Health and Sustainable Food Systems*. Dublin and Bonn: Concern Worldwide and Welthungerhilfe.

Wiesmann, D., H. Biesalski, K. von Grebmer and J. Bernstein (2015). 'Methodological Review and Revision of the Global Hunger Index'. ZEF Working Paper Series 139, Center for Development Research, University of Bonn. https://www.econstor.eu/bitstream/10419/121435/1/837161932.pdf. Accessed on 28 September 2021.

Wilson, K. (1999). 'Patterns of Accumulation and Struggles of Rural Labour: Some Aspects of Agrarian Change in Central Bihar'. *Journal of Peasant Studies* 26(2–3): 316–54.

Witsoe, J. (2012). 'Everyday Corruption and the Political Mediation of the Indian State: An Ethnographic Exploration of Brokers in Bihar'. *Economic and Political Weekly* 37(6): 47–54.

Wodon, Q., A. Liverani, G. Joseph and N. Bougnoux (eds.). (2014). *Climate Change and Migration: Evidence from the Middle East and North Africa.* Washington, DC: World Bank.

World Bank (1986). *Poverty and Hunger: Issues and Options for Food Security in Developing Countries.* Washington, DC: World Bank.

——— (2006). *Repositioning Nutrition as Central to Development: A Strategy for Large-Scale Action.* Washington, DC: World Bank.

——— (2007). *World Development Report 2008: Agriculture for Development.* Washington, DC: World Bank.

——— (2009). *World Development Report 2009: Reshaping Economic Geography.* Washington, DC: World Bank.

——— (2011a). *Migration and Remittances Factbook 2011*, 2nd edition. Washington, DC: World Bank.

——— (2011b). *Perspective on Poverty in India: Stylised Facts from Survey Data.* Washington, DC: World Bank.

——— (2018). *Groundswell: Preparing for Internal Climate Migration.* Washington, DC: World Bank.

——— (2019). 'Migration and Remittance: Recent Developments and Outlook, 2013–16'. *Migration and Development Brief* 31 (April). https://www.knomad.org/sites/default/files/2019-04/Migrationanddevelopmentbrief31.pdf. Accessed on 23 November 2021.

——— (2021a). 'Distribution of Gross Domestic Product (GDP) across Economic Sectors from 2009 to 2019, India'. World Bank's Online Data Repository. https://databank.worldbank.org/. Accessed on 23 November 2021.

——— (2021b). 'GDP Per Capita Growth (Annual %)'. World Bank's Online Data Repository. https://databank.worldbank.org/. Accessed on 23 November 2021.

———— (2021c). 'World Development Indicators: India Profile'. World Bank's Online Data Repository. https://databank.worldbank.org/. Accessed on 24 November 2021.

World Food Programme (WFP) and Institute for Human Development (IHD) (2008a). *Food Security Atlas of Rural Chattisgarh*. New Delhi: World Food Programme and Institute for Human Development.

———— (2008b). *Food Security Atlas of Rural Jharkhand*. New Delhi: World Food Programme and Institute for Human Development.

———— (2008c). *Food Security Atlas of Rural Madhya Pradesh*. New Delhi: World Food Programme and Institute for Human Development.

———— (2008d). *Food Security Atlas of Rural Orissa*. New Delhi: World Food Programme and Institute for Human Development.

———— (2009a). *Food Security Atlas of Rural Bihar*. New Delhi: World Food Programme and Institute for Human Development.

———— (2009b). *Food Security Atlas of Rural Rajasthan*. New Delhi: World Food Programme and Institute for Human Development.

———— (2010). *Food Security Atlas of Rural Uttar Pradesh*. New Delhi: World Food Programme and Institute for Human Development.

World Health Organization (WHO) (2010). 'Nutrition Landscape Information System Country Profile Indicators: Interpretation Guide'. Geneva: World Health Organization. https://apps.who.int/iris/handle/10665/44397. Accessed on 24 February 2015.

———— (2021). *The Global Health Observatory: Anaemia in Women and Children*. Geneva: World Health Organisation. https://www.who.int/data/gho/data/indicators. Accessed on 20 February 2015.

Yabiku, S. T., V. Agadjanian and A. Sevoyan (2010). 'Husbands' Labour Migration and Wives' Autonomy, Mozambique 2000–2006'. *Population Studies* 64(3): 293–306.

Yang, A. A. (1979). 'Peasants on the Move: A Study of Internal Migration in India'. *Journal of Interdisciplinary History* 10(1): 37–58.

————. (1989). *The Limited Raj: Agrarian Relations in Colonial India, Saran District, 1793-1920*. Berkerly: University of California Press.

————. (1998). *Bazaar India: Markets, Society, and the Colonial State in Gangetic Bihar*. Berkeley: University of California Press.

Yaro, J. A. (2006). 'Is Deagrarianisation Real? A Study of Livelihood Activities in Rural Northern Ghana'. *Journal of Modern African Studies* 44(1): 125–56.

Ye, J., H. Wu, J. Rao, B. Ding and K. Zhang (2016). 'Left-Behind Women: Gender Exclusion and Inequality in Rural–Urban Migration in China'. *Journal of Peasant Studies* 43(4): 910–41.

Zezza, A., C. Carletto, B. Davis and P. Winters (2011). 'Assessing the Impact of Migration on Food and Nutrition Security'. *Food Policy* 36(1): 1–6.

Ziegler, J. (2006). *Mission to India (20 August–2 September 2005): Report to the United Nations Economic and Social Council, Commission on Human Rights.* Sixty-second session, item 10, Document E/CN.4/2006/44/Add/2. New York: Economic and Social Council, United Nations. http://www.righttofood.org/wp-content/uploads/2012/09/ECN.4200644Add.2.pdf. Accessed on 12 February 2014.

INDEX